THE IRANIAN TRIANGLE

THE IRANIAN TRIANGLE

The Untold Story of Israel's Role in the Iran-Contra Affair

Samuel Segev

translated by
HAIM WATZMAN

THE FREE PRESS
A Division of Macmillan, Inc.
NEW YORK

The Free Press
A Division of Macmillan, Inc.
866 Third Avenue, New York, N.Y. 10022

Collier Macmillan Canada, Inc.

Printed in the United States of America

printing number
1 2 3 4 5 6 7 8 9 10

Library of Congress Cataloging-in-Publication Data

Segev, Samuel,
    The Iranian triangle : the untold story of Israel's role in
    the Iran-Contra affair / Samuel Segev : translated by Haim
    Watzman.
        p.   cm.
    Bibliography: p.
    Includes index.
    ISBN 0-02-928341-8
    1. Iran-Contra affair, 1985– 2. Military assistance,
    Israeli–Iran. 3. Israel—Foreign relations—Iran. 4. Iran
    —Foreign relations—Israel. I. Title.
    E876.S43   1988
    327.5694—dc 19   88-21247
                                                        CIP

To PHYLLIS, my beloved wife,
for her tolerance and encouragement,
with love

Contents

Preface

From a single story in a small Middle Eastern newspaper at the end of 1986, the Iran-Contra affair has emerged as an intricate international web of financial, political, and military dealings. Its exposure dealt a severe blow to the Reagan administration's foreign policy and undermined the administration's credibility both at home and abroad. The activities of American officials and private agents dealing with Iran have already been revealed by investigations of the Tower Commission and the congressional committees. But a critical leg of the triangle has yet to be fully illuminated: Israeli involvement both in direct dealings with Iran and as a middleman between Iran and the U.S.

The roots of this involvement extend back to the 1950s. American and Israeli participation in supplying arms to Iran was the result of an unofficial policy of cooperation that crystallized during the Eisenhower administration and reached its peak two decades later during the Nixon years. The relationship between Israel and Iran encompassed a wide range of activities, but the most important involved defense and oil. For more than 20 years, the U.S., Israel, and Iran worked together in the context of a regional strategy aimed at halting Soviet expansion in the Middle East and weakening the U.S.S.R.'s friends in the Arab world. During that time, almost all of Israel's leaders and senior army officers visited Tehran, and many met privately with the Shah. The accounts of these meetings are revealed in this book for the first time.

Although the Khomeini revolution led to the severance of all formal ties with Israel, it did not put an end to Israel's efforts to keep channels to Tehran open, nor—despite its public declarations—to Iran's receptivity to such efforts. As in the days of the Shah, Iran under Khomeini attempted to use secret channels to Israel as a means of influencing the U.S., seeking primarily to gain access to American arms. My account opens at a turning point between the two Iranian regimes and for Israeli and American involvement with them.

In researching this book, I interviewed most of the Israeli participants in the events described and I had access to government papers not yet declassified. Because of the need for confidentiality, I am unable to cite most of these primary sources or reveal the identities of persons interviewed. They know who they are—and they have my gratitude in their anonymity.

I am especially indebted to my wife Phyllis, who has been deprived of so many hours of companionship throughout the many months when I sat behind closed doors.

Haim Watzman, my skillful translator, made a special effort to meet time requirements without compromising accuracy and quality.

Deborah Harris of Domino Press, my publisher in Hebrew, also became my friend. She invested tremendous effort and a great show of faith in her determination to see the book published in English.

Laura Wolff, my senior editor at The Free Press, kept after me to bring this project to completion. Her talents are very much reflected in the English version.

Edith Lewis, the editing supervisor, was instrumental in ensuring the accuracy and clarity of the final book.

Finally, Irit Markan-Shenhav, who typed and retyped her way through a maze of unfamiliar people and places, has my profound appreciation for her devotion and patience.

Tel Aviv, Israel
May 1988

1

The Aborted Anti-Khomeini Coup

In March 1985 Israeli Prime Minister Shimon Peres heard, through an intricate web of connections running from Tehran to Saudi Arabia through Paris and London to Jerusalem, that Iran was interested in buying weapons from Israel. According to the reports that reached him, the Iranian leadership headed by Ayatollah Ruhollah Khomeini was not as monolithic as it seemed from the outside. There was, apparently, a faction of moderates opposed to the excesses of the fundamentalist Islamic regime, and its members hoped to win themselves prestige and influence by obtaining for their country's army the weapons and spare parts it badly needed in order to pursue its war with Iraq. They wanted American components, both because of their superior quality and because they had to obtain spare parts compatible with the U.S.-supplied equipment left over from the Shah's days. The U.S., boycotting all trade with Iran because Iranian-backed Shiite terrorist groups in Lebanon were holding six Americans hostage, would not sell. The Iranian government vociferously professed unending hostility to the Jewish state—but Israel had large supplies of American arms. There were those in the Iranian leadership, the story went, interested in knowing whether Israel would do business.

It was not at all clear whether the news was reliable, or

1

whether it was advisable for Israel to embroil itself in the morass of the Persian Gulf. In order to find out whether the intelligence was genuine and the proposal a realistic one, Peres needed the help of men who had long experience with Iran and its people. He had one such man on his staff—his science and technology adviser, Al Schwimmer. After hearing of the reports from Peres, Schwimmer consulted his friend and business partner Ya'acov Nimrodi. For the next nine months they would be the leading Israeli players in a series of secret contacts and arms sales between Jerusalem and Tehran.

Colonel (Res.) Ya'acov Nimrodi was the more experienced of the two. Twenty-five of this powerfully built, spectacled, and balding man's 62 years had been spent in Tehran, spread over three periods of his career. He had been a representative of the immigration department of the Jewish Agency, the Israeli army's first attaché in Tehran, and later a successful businessman there. This gave him firsthand knowledge of how Iranians lived and thought.

Nimrodi had been born in Iraq in 1926 and had come to Jerusalem when only ten days old. As one of 11 children, he was sent out to work early to help support the family. At the age of 16 he was drafted into the *Hagana*, the Jewish defense force in prestate days. Fluent in Arabic, Nimrodi was assigned to a unit of the elite Palmach forces that was sent on missions in neighboring Arab countries. His accomplishments there in the intelligence field are still classified information. After the establishment of the State of Israel, Nimrodi became an officer in the Israel Defense Force's intelligence service.

In the summer of 1955 Nimrodi and his wife, Rivka, went to Tehran as representatives of the Jewish Agency. They were to assist in the immigration of Iranian Jews to Israel. It was his first acquaintance with Iran and a turning point in his career.

Nimrodi returned to Israel in the summer of 1958, but not for long. It was during those days that the first links between Israel and Iran were being established. General Ali Kia, the chief of Iranian military intelligence, visited Israel, and Nimrodi was introduced to him. Kia, wanting to foster military links between the two countries, suggested that Israel send a liaison officer, later to become a military attaché, to Tehran. He thought Nimrodi's qualifications would enable him to fill the post successfully. Israel was willing to make the appointment, but the

Shah was not yet ready. Only after Kia's next visit to Israel, in 1959, was the foundation laid for military ties between Israel and Iran. After Kia met Ben-Gurion, General Chaim Herzog (now President of Israel), then Israel's chief of military intelligence, appointed Nimrodi to be the Israeli army's representative in Iran. Nimrodi left for Tehran in March 1960. Thanks to his efforts, nearly all Chiefs of Staff and top officers of the two armies met each other, and the Iranian market opened to the Israeli arms industry.

Upon returning to Israel in 1970, Nimrodi was to be appointed coordinator of Israeli activity in the West Bank. The minister of defense at the time, Moshe Dayan, approved the appointment, but for various reasons it did not go through. In protest, and against the advice of his family, Nimrodi resigned from the army and entered business. He joked that the State of Israel had decided to make him a millionaire. He was right.

Nimrodi soon returned to Tehran, for the third time. At the request of Major General (Res.) Zvi Tzur, assistant to the minister of defense. Nimrodi was sent to represent Israeli arms manufacturers in Tehran. With the help of his wide-ranging connections with the royal family—especially with Queen Farah Diba's uncle—and with other high officials, it was not long before he felt thoroughly at home with the Iranian business community. Among his accomplishments were supplying Iran with 50 water desalination plants, and by selling weapons to the Iranian army he contributed to the expansion of the Israeli arms industry and created steady employment for hundreds of Israeli workers. Nimrodi made most of his money, however, from commissions he received from Swiss and German firms. Despite reports to the contrary, he sold no military goods to the Khomeini regime before March 1985.

Born in the U.S. in 1917, Al (Adolf) Schwimmer founded Israel Aircraft Industries, initiated the development of advanced technologies, and was among the first businessmen to enter the Iranian arms market. With Nimrodi's help, Schwimmer won several contracts to repair airplanes belonging to the Iranian national airline, and afterward for the overhauling of Iranian F-86 fighter planes, of American make. Schwimmer visited Tehran numerous times in his capacity as president of Israel Aircraft Industries. He met with the Shah on several occasions and hosted Iranian ministers and senior officers in Israel. A true believer in the importance of the strategic link between the two countries, Schwimmer drafted an ambitious plan for the joint development of advanced technology. In September 1976 the plan was presented to the Shah by Shimon Peres, then minister of defense in Yitzhak Rabin's government. Within the framework of that program, code-named "Tzur," the two countries were to establish an integrated defense complex for the production of middle-range ground-to-ground missiles in Iran, with research and development costs to be split between them.[1] The agreement also included examining the possibility of joint production of a new fighter plane, an improved version of the French Mirage 5.

After Menachem Begin was elected Prime Minister in May 1977, Schwimmer left Israel Aircraft Industries and went into business on his own. This included some deals in partnership with Nimrodi. Schwimmer and Nimrodi, aided by the Saudi millionaire Adnan Khashoggi, helped set up various development projects throughout the Middle East.

The Iranian Revolution of February 1979 was a severe foreign policy setback for both the U.S. and Israel. Khomeini's Islamic theology labeled them as demon countries, at the root of all evil in the world, and the close ties that both countries had had with the Shah made it all the easier for the Ayatollah to inflame his countrymen against them. Hatred of Israel was, however, especially intense.

Khomeini ended Israel's low-level diplomatic contacts with Iran almost immediately after assuming power. His public statements about Israel were more bellicose than his threats against any other country. He spoke not about Israeli withdrawal from the territories it had captured in the Six Day War, but rather its "elimination" from the Middle East and the establishment of a Palestinian state on its ruins. Israel had every reason to work against the Khomeini regime.

Yet there were also reasons for trying to reach a modus vivendi with whoever Iran's rulers were, even if they were virulent Israel-haters. For Israel, Iran was strategically important like Ethiopia and Turkey, due to its location on the perimeter of the Arab world. Israel had long fostered economic and military cooperation with Iran, even though the two countries never exchanged ambassadors. As a result, Israel, like the U.S., never gave up hope of regaining a certain measure of influence in Iran, as it had had during the Shah's reign. Iran's strategic importance; its economic potential; and its traditional enmity with Iraq, Arab countries in general, and Russia all made it worthwhile for Israel and the Western powers to keep an eye on what was going on in Tehran and not abandon it to the U.S.S.R., Syria, and Libya.

Israel did not simply keep its eyes open. It managed to establish communication with senior army officers and various elements in revolutionary Iran.[1a] The information it gleaned from these sources enabled Israel to keep its finger on the Iranian pulse.

Israel has had a long tradition of using military aid to establish relations with countries that preferred not to maintain normal diplomatic ties with the Jewish state. Israel found this method successful with the Shah's Iran and with Haile Selassie's Ethiopia, and carried on from there throughout Africa, Asia, and Latin America.

It turned out to be applicable to Khomeini's Iran as well. At the beginning of 1980, a few months after Iranian "students" and Revolutionary Guards took over the American embassy compound in Tehran, Prime Minister Menachem Begin approved a shipment of tires for Phantom fighter planes, as well as small amounts of weapons for the Iranian army. This shipment was the subject of an angry exchange between President Carter and Begin.[2] Israel, Carter insisted, was not to ship military equipment to Iran until the hostages were released.

After the election of Ronald Reagan and the release of the American hostages on January 19, 1981, Israel and the countries of Western Europe considered themselves no longer bound by the sanctions imposed by the Carter administration. As a consequence, an Israeli arms dealer (not Nimrodi) closed a small contract with Iran in July 1981, through the agencies of a French firm. He met in Lisbon with Ahmed Khudari, a weapons merchant acting for the Iranian Chief of Staff and with the authorization of then Iranian minister of defense Jawwad Fakih. Khudari requested 250 tires for Phantom jets, communications equipment, 106mm recoilless artillery, mortars, and ammunition—for a total value of $200 million. The only condition the Iranians made was that it be kept under cover, and publicly denied if revealed.[3]

An Israeli plane with 100 106mm cannon on board took off for Lisbon that same month. In Lisbon the cargo was transferred to an Iran Air craft. But before the second shipment was made Khudari absconded with $56 million belonging to the Iranian government.

Despite this, the shipments continued. A British arms agent chartered a small Argentinian cargo plane that answered to the radio call Yankee Romeo 224. After making a night landing in Amsterdam, the plane arrived in Tel Aviv. On July 11 it took off for Tehran, making a refueling stop in Cyprus. While in Turkish airspace the pilot, Stuart Macafferty, told the Ankara air control tower that he was carrying a cargo of "fruit and vegetables" to Tehran. The plane completed its journey and then returned to Israel, taking off again three days later with an additional shipment to Tehran. On July 18 Macafferty took off for his third run. On his way back, however, he strayed from his route over Turkey and crashed over the border, in the U.S.S.R.[4]

The cause of the accident remains a mystery, but the result was the exposure of the arms link between Israel and Iran, even though both countries categorically denied it. The publicity, however, did not put an end to the trade. In May 1982, Israeli Minister of Defense Ariel Sharon informed the American secretaries of state and defense, Alexander Haig and Caspar Weinberger, that Israel had signed another arms deal with Iran.[5] Concluded with the help of a European country, the contract provided for the supply of 160mm mortars, 106mm artillery, and shells, for a total value of several tens of millions of dollars. The only reaction the U.S. made to the deal was to warn Israel not to supply Iran with American-made weaponry, or with weapons containing American components. This limitation was not a serious one for Israel (though it was for Iran)—the war in Lebanon had left Israel with huge quantities of Soviet arms taken from the PLO and other Palestinian guerrilla groups. Since the Israel Defense Forces are equipped for the most part with American arms, it was natural for Israel to try to sell what it could not use.

In September 1982, Ariel Sharon received another Iranian request for weapons—but this time it was not from the Khomeini regime. It came from a group of former Iranian military men, supporters of the pretender to the Peacock Throne—Reza, the fallen Shah's son.

Accompanied by Nimrodi, two former generals in the Iranian army came to Sharon's Tel Aviv office on a personal mission from the Shah-in-exile. They asked for Israel's help in overthrowing Khomeini. "We can raise $2 billion. We need arms, and later—maybe instructors as well. Are you willing to help us?" General Said Razvani asked Sharon. "The weapons will be transferred from Israel to Sudan. Sudanese President Gaafar Nimeiri is willing to give us a military base for storing the equipment and training the people who will take part in the revolution."[6]

General Razvani had once served as deputy to the Chief of Staff, General Feridoun Jam, and like many other officers who served in the past in the Shah's army, he had become part of the royal family's expatriate entourage and was looking for an opportunity to return to power. Razvani arrived in Israel in the wake of secret talks between Nimrodi, Schwimmer, and the claimant to the Iranian throne in the latter's residence in Morocco. In February, 1982 Nimrodi had appeared on a broadcast of the prestigious British television program, "Panorama," that dealt with the supply of arms to Iran. He spoke of Iran's strategic importance, praised the Shah's leadership and his efforts to improve his people's lot, and openly called for the overthrow of the Khomeini regime. The West should redouble its intelligence efforts, he argued, and begin training the forces that would eventually restore the monarchy. A few days later Reza telephoned him from Morocco to thank him for his expression of support.

Reza had crowned himself Shah in a modest ceremony performed in the Kubbeh Palace in Cairo on October 31, 1980, his twentieth birthday, two days after his father's death in his Egyptian exile. Among those attending were his mother, Queen Farah Diba, his aunt, Princess Ashraf, and several loyalists. Reza swore to topple Khomeini and reclaim the throne. Despite the fact that no country recognized his claim to the crown, he began gathering Iranian exiles around him. Most were military men who could help him in his crusade. He was determined to be more successful than a group of Iranian air force officers who had planned a revolt the previous July. They had intended to bomb Khomeini's house in Qom, but the conspiracy was uncovered and scores of officers and pilots were arrested and executed.

Reza worked out of Cairo at first. President Sadat put one of the Egyptian broadcasting service's studios at his disposal, so that he could beam his message to his people. A few months later, however, the young Shah and his retinue removed themselves to Rabat, where the Moroccan King gave them one of his palaces. The new location did not bring Reza any more luck. Iraq's invasion of Iran united the nation under Khomeini's leadership, while the exiled Iranian opposition was divided and lacked any real support in Tehran. Reza's chances of returning to the Peacock Throne looked bleak. Nimrodi's television appearance was a ray of light for the young Shah. He called Nimrodi at once and invited him to his residence.

Nimrodi left for Rabat in the summer of 1982 in the company of Al Schwimmer. The two of them were greeted at the Rabat airport by General Razvani and a representative of the Moroccan government. During their three days in Rabat Nimrodi and Schwimmer were received three times by Reza and his advisers.

The first conversation lasted six hours, and included an exchange of opinions on the situation in Iran and the great suffering of the Iranian people under Khomeini. The Shah-in-exile was surrounded by generals and advisers, including the former Chief of Staff, General Jam, who now lived in London. There was also Colonel Oveissi, once Iran's military attaché in Paris. He was the son of General Gholam Ali Oveissi, who had once served as commander of ground forces and who had in his time urged that the Shah deal harshly with Khomeini's supporters in Iran. General Oveissi had then been supported by the CIA, and he would later be murdered in Paris in the summer of 1984 by Khomeini's agents.

After their visit to Rabat, Nimrodi and Schwimmer told their Saudi friend, Adnan Khashoggi, about their conversation with the young Reza.

Khashoggi had once had dealings with the Shah—not long before the revolution he had inquired into buying Kish Island, which the Shah hoped to turn into a resort for wealthy Europeans and a gambling center for the princes of the Persian Gulf. But the deal never materialized. Khomeini's rise to power put an end to this transaction.

Khashoggi, son of the late King Ibn-Saud's private physician, had gone to the prestigious Queen Victoria School in Alexandria, where he had been a classmate of King Hussein of Jordan. He then enrolled at Stanford, but dropped out and went into business. Within a few short years he had reaped millions as a middleman in arms sales between American companies and the Saudi royal family.

Khashoggi was a man with contacts in high places. He had met, in turn, with Presidents Nixon, Ford, and Carter. He had known William Casey during Nixon's presidency, and had spoken to him several times in London before his appointment as CIA director. Never an official envoy of the Saudi government, that country's rulers had always been of two minds about him. Some saw him as a traitor because of his connections with Israel and the United States, and took exception to his ostentatious life-style. Others were impressed by his vision and the energy with which he accomplished his business. Khashoggi himself acknowledges that he was closer to King Fahd when he was Crown Prince; upon ascending the throne, the King became harder to approach.[7] In his conversations with Americans and Israelis he claimed that he enjoyed the trust of the King and the minister of defense, Prince Sultan. The Saudi ambassador in Washington, Prince Bandar Bin-Sultan, introduced Khashoggi to Robert McFarlane, Reagan's national security adviser, and Khashoggi made a practice of sending him occasional evaluations of the situation in the Middle East. King Hussein, Anwar Sadat, Husni Mubarak, and PLO Chairman Yassir Arafat were all personal acquaintances.

According to Khashoggi, he first became acquainted with the former director-general of the Israeli foreign ministry, David Kimche, in Paris, when the latter was the European representative of the Mossad, Israel's intelligence service. It was, however, through Al Schwimmer that he came to know figures in the Israeli government. He met Menachem Begin in New York immediately after the conclusion of the Camp David accords in September 1978. He met Shimon Peres twice—once as leader of the opposition and again as Prime Minister. In the summer of 1982, on his farm in Kenya, Khashoggi met with Israeli defense minister Ariel Sharon, then on his way to make an official visit to Zaire. Participating in the meeting were Schwimmer, and Nimrodi.

Khashoggi was a great believer in Israel's scientific and technological capabilities, and in his discussions with the Israelis, he said he hoped that Israel could influence American policy in the Persian Gulf. He developed close and varied relations with Schwimmer and Nimrodi. The latter two arranged, for example, for an Israeli doctor to examine Khashoggi in Europe, and Israeli experts installed a security system on his yacht, *Nabila*.

Schwimmer had made Khashoggi's acquaintance 12 years previously through a common friend—Hank Greenspan, a Jewish Las Vegas millionaire and owner of the *Las Vegas Sun* newspaper. Schwimmer, after retiring from Israel Aircraft Industries, introduced Khashoggi to Nimrodi. All three men were able to combine their personal business interests with the conduct of international relations. Such methods may not be normal practice in the West, but they are routine in the Middle East. Over the years Nimrodi and Schwimmer became rich enough to allow them to devote their energy and thoughts to more risky channels in which profit was not always guaranteed.

After he was contacted by Schwimmer and Nimrodi, Khashoggi went to work immediately on a plan to support Reza. He flew to Riyadh and obtained the tacit support of King Fahd. Saudi Arabia was willing to help finance the operation. This, together with the money promised by the Shah's family and by several Iranian exiles, came to about $2 billion. Nimeiri (who now lives in exile in Cairo) was willing to assist in the execution of the operation. In exchange for a sum of $100 million, he would give the conspirators the base they needed.

The conspirators thought that the plan could not succeed without Israel's help. General Razvani and his comrade had come to Israel in September 1982 to find out whether it was available. Had Israel agreed to lend a hand—even indirectly— Reza, President Nimeiri, and several former Iranian generals would have set out for Riyadh in Khashoggi's private jet in order to close the deal with King Fahd.

Sharon asked for several days to consider the proposal. Four months previously, on June 6, 1982, he had sent the Israeli army into its most controversial war. He was now the target of mounting attacks from the opposition. A few days before General Razvani's arrival, Lebanon's President-elect, Bashir Gemayel, had been assassinated by Syrian intelligence agents.

Gemayel's supporters responded with a massacre of Palestinians in the Sabra and Chatila refugee camps in Beirut, and Sharon was at the center of a new controversy. Although the slaughter had been carried out by the Christian militia, Israeli soldiers had been nearby but failed to stop them. Sharon was accused of not preventing the massacre. So, when the two Iranian generals came to petition for Israel's help in overthrowing Khomeini, Sharon had to be exceedingly careful.

The Iranians submitted their request in writing and said that the U.S. knew about their plans. CIA director William Casey had, they claimed, given them the go-ahead. When the two Iranian generals came to Israel, Sharon saw their request as an opportunity to rid himself of his excess Soviet weaponry and thereby reduce the price tag on the war in Lebanon. Sharon, it should be noted, did not believe that a royalist revolution could succeed in Iran in the absence of support from within the country. He saw no harm, however, in the conspirators' request to buy in Israel $800 million worth of Lebanese spoils and send it off to Sudan.

Despite American support, the planned counterrevolution never took place. Certain Israeli officials inalterably opposed getting involved. The report of the official commission of inquiry into the Sabra and Chatila massacres forced Sharon to resign from the defense ministry in February 1983. Menachem Begin soon also resigned, and was succeeded by Foreign Minister Yitzhak Shamir. Still caught up in the controversy of the war in Lebanon, Shamir and Sharon's successor, Moshe Arens, previously ambassador to Washington, were wary of getting involved in any new adventure in Iran. They displayed a distinct lack of enthusiasm toward the Shah-in-exile's plan and washed their hands of the matter.

This was the last time that Israel seriously considered a request for aid from the Iranian monarchists. From that point onward the Israeli government accepted the Islamic Revolution as an established fact and tried with determination to find a way into the hearts of those elements likely to be Khomeini's heirs.

In the fall of 1984 it looked as if Khomeini's revolution had burnt itself out. The time had come, it seemed, for Israel, the U.S., and the rest of the industrialized world to take a new look at Iran. The war with Iraq continued, but neither side could hope for victory in the foreseeable future. The Iranian army was at odds with the war-weary citizenry on the one hand and with the zealots of the Revolutionary Guards on the other; morale was low. Many people were short of food and heating oil. Tens of thousands of refugees from the countryside filled the streets of Tehran. While this did not affect Khomeini's personal standing, his health was tenuous and the struggle to succeed him had already started. Several prominent members of the religious and military establishment in Iran wished to break through their government's isolation. They were searching for ways to improve relations with the West in general, and with the U.S. in particular.

It was against this background that, in the fall of 1984, Adnan Khashoggi met the Iranian arms dealer Manucher Ghorbanifar in Hamburg. The Saudi had come there to buy Persian rugs that had once belonged to the Shah and the royal family. Ghorbanifar came to lunch at the invitation of a sometime business partner, an Iranian carpet dealer.

Ghorbanifar presented himself as "chief of Iranian intelligence in Europe," and devoted much of his conversation to the Iran-Iraq War. "The Beard," the code name Israeli agents gave him, spoke with evident sorrow about the "Moslem blood" flowing into the Persian Gulf, and about how the Iranian and Iraqi armies had been caught up in a deadly and pointless war. He argued that the United States had intentionally ignored Iranian provocations on the Iraqi border, knowing full well that Saddam Hussein, President of Iraq, would react swiftly and forcefully. Had Iraq continued its string of early victories, there would have been a military coup against Khomeini. But Iran had contained the Iraqi attack and, since May 1982, had reversed Iraq's victories. The two superpowers and countries in the Middle East had done all they could to perpetuate the war and so exhaust both countries. When the war broke out both sides had large financial reserves, but they now lacked hard currency and their economic infrastructures had been seriously damaged.

The war, Ghorbanifar argued, presented tremendous economic opportunities to the U.S. and other industrialized countries, since only they had the resources to reconstruct both nations. And, of course, Iran and Iraq would need huge quantities of weapons to reequip their armies. Ghorbanifar estimated that reconstruction would cost $200 billion. In his opinion, the U.S. should be as interested in resuming its friendship with Iran as Iran should be about getting American help. The U.S. should not miss this opportunity. And agents who succeeded in bringing the two countries together could expect to receive their fair share of the reconstruction contracts in the future.

Ghorbanifar claimed to represent the thinking of the Iranian leadership. According to him, Iran's leaders agreed that the war had very much strengthened the position of the U.S. in the Persian Gulf: the American bases in Oman were now larger than originally planned; the Gulf countries were more dependent on the U.S. and trusted it to come to their aid in the event of an Iranian attack; and Iraq had moderated its former vociferous opposition to the U.S. and had even reestablished the diplomatic relations severed 17 years previously. Soviet involvement in Afghanistan had, of course, given the Russians some strategic advantages, but had also weakened their economy. Iranian aid to the Afghan rebels—money, weapons, and training—had led to the enlistment of large numbers of guerrillas from among the 1.5 million Afghan refugees in Iran. Finally, the Islamic revival had battered the Iranian Communist party, the Tudeh, which Khomeini had suppressed with no less cruelty than the Shah had used in 1953.

During the course of the conversation Ghorbanifar revealed to Khashoggi that he had information about certain changes Iran planned for the coming *haj* season, the summer of 1985.[8] He related that Khomeini had decided to remove responsibility for the pilgrimage to Mecca from Hajjotelislam Mussavi Khoneikha, the Islamic Republic's general prosecutor, and transfer it to one of the Ayatollah's intimates, the deputy speaker of the Majlis, Ayatollah Mehdi Karoubi, who headed the national charitable fund that aided victims of the war. In the past Khoneikha had been suspected of having connections with Soviet intelligence, and had been among the organizers of the 1979 seizure of the American embassy, and the capture of 52 hostages in Tehran. In 1982, Saudi Arabia had expelled Khoneikha, along with 140 other Iranian pilgrims, after they had been suspected of planning a terrorist attack in Mecca. Ghorbanifar said that Mehdi Karoubi's brother, Hassan, was his personal friend. Through him, he claimed, he could ensure that the behavior of Iranian pilgrims during the coming holiday season would be less explosive.[9]

Of all the things that Ghorbanifar said over that lunch, this last revelation was the most important. Ever since Khomeini had come to power, his plans for exporting his Islamic Revolution had hung over the Gulf countries like the sword of Damocles. In addition to the fact that 200,000 Iranians lived in other Gulf countries and could form a potential fifth column, a large portion of the population of each Gulf country belonged to the Shiite Moslem sect. In Bahrain, for instance, 70 percent of the population is Shiite; 55 percent of the population of Iraq is Shiite. In Saudi Arabia, only 4 percent is Shiite, but they are concentrated in the eastern, oil-rich part of the country. The largest refinery and oil depot in the country, at Ras Tanura, are only a 15-minute flight from Iran.

Khomeini made his policy accordingly. In November 1979 Shiite fanatics took over the Great Mosque in Mecca. The Shiite underground group El-Da'awa, established in Iraq, was involved in subversive activity in Kuwait, and in December 1981 Iranian operatives attempted a coup in Bahrain. Most threateningly, Shiite pilgrims from Iran plotted against King Fahd and tried to incite the population against the Saudi royal house. The 1984 *haj* season was particularly tense and placed a heavy burden on the Saudi security forces. For this reason, information that Iran planned to revise its policy in anticipation of the coming pilgrimage season was of top-level operational importance.

Khashoggi took Ghorbanifar to Saudi Arabia in his private plane and arranged for a meeting with Saudi officials. Ghorbanifar told them about the planned changes and emphasized his acquaintance with the Karoubi family.[10] His story confirmed other evidence that Iran was trying to present a more conciliatory face to its neighbors. The Saudis had shot down two Iranian planes in June 1984; the Iranian response was subdued. This mild response paved the way for the Saudi foreign minister, Saud Al-Faisal, to visit Iran in early 1985. As a token of appreciation for the information he had delivered, and in order to strengthen the moderate Iranian forces Ghorbanifar had told them about, the Saudis agreed to fund a small arms deal carried out through Khashoggi and Ghorbanifar.

The Saudi decision led to the first contact between Ghorbanifar and Israel. Since he knew that the U.S. had imposed an embargo on weapons shipments to Iran, Khashoggi decided to see whether Jerusalem might sell. Israel sold Iran, under the Shah, locally produced weapons, and on occasion was also used to influence American policy. Khashoggi's first contact was through Ronald Furer, an Israeli businessman living in London. Furer was the man who brought the proposal to Peres.

After Furer's March 1985 visit to Jerusalem, Khashoggi (whose Israeli code name was "the Eagle") called Schwimmer and asked to meet him for an "important conversation" in London. Schwimmer received Peres's approval, but was authorized only to hear what Khashoggi had to say and not to make any obligations in the name of the State of Israel. Nimrodi was in London at the time, and the two of them went to visit Khashoggi in his hotel. Two Iranian arms merchants—Ghorbanifar and Cyrus Hashemi—were in the Eagle's room. An American businessman of Iranian extraction who lived in London, Hashemi had been involved in the negotiations leading up to the release of the 52 American hostages. Since the outbreak of the Iran-Iraq War, he had also sold weapons. Like other arms dealers, that special breed of businessmen that live in a world of huge profits, secret deals, political intrigues, and betrayals, Hashemi also saw the Iran-Iraq War as a goose laying golden eggs. He claimed family ties with the speaker of the Iranian parliament, Ali Akbar Hashimi Rafsanjani. In the arms business he became partner to Khashoggi in a company called the World Trade Group, headquartered in London. Although he commuted to and from his London office in a Rolls Royce, his business empire did not stand on a firm foundation. In addition to business debts, Hashemi lost money in a chain of British casinos owned by department store millionaire Tiny Rowlands.

In May 1984 Hashemi, along with his two brothers, Reza and Jemshid, was charged by a federal prosecutor with having violated American law in trying to export arms to Iran. His lawyers saved him from prison by reaching an agreement with the American customs authority that Hashemi would become a double agent and report to them on attempts by other arms dealers to sell American weapons to Iran.[10a]

As soon as they were presented to him, Schwimmer joked with Khashoggi and said: "What are the Iranians doing here? The Saudis are sure to kill you if they find out whom you're consorting with."

Khashoggi answered in utmost seriousness: "All I can tell you at this point is that King Fahd and Prince Sultan know about this meeting and gave me their blessing."[11]

Since the purpose was to get acquainted, the conversation was very general and noncommittal. Khashoggi recommended Ghorbanifar and related that he had introduced him to King Fahd. Khashoggi spoke of the aspirations of "moderate elements" in Iran to open channels of communication with the

U.S. Since, however, the Iranians did not know how President Reagan would react, Khashoggi asked that Israel sound out the Americans. Ghorbanifar spoke of Iran's desire to equip itself with food and arms, but that subject, he said, was of secondary importance. The main thing was to begin talking with the U.S.

The London meeting was held at the height of the Iranian spring offensive. On March 5, 1985, Iran shelled Basra as part of a wider effort to cut Iraq's second city off from Baghdad. In the meantime the "tanker war" recommenced, and the Iranian and Iraqi air forces bombed various cities in the two countries. These activities emphasized again and again the inferiority of the Iranian tank and air forces and their need for appropriate antitank and antiaircraft weapons. In light of the danger to oil supplies from the Persian Gulf, the UN secretary-general set out for Iran and Iraq on April 7 in a new attempt to put an end to the war. As could have been expected, Khomeini informed the secretary-general that the war would end only with the overthrow of President Saddam Hussein. The attempt at arbitration failed, as did the Iranian attack.

It was against this background that, in March 1985, Nimrodi met Ghorbanifar again, this time at the Noga Hilton Hotel in Geneva.[12] This conversation was more businesslike and lasted for a few hours. Nimrodi decided he was dealing with one of the most colorful and devious men he had ever met. "The Beard's" manners, wide horizons, and sense of humor were misleading, and inexperienced officials would be easy prey to his sharp tongue and his carefully crafted ambiguity.

After describing himself as "a greedy cheat," Ghorbanifar began relating the story of his life. He had been born in Isfahan in September 1945. One of nine children of an Iranian army colonel, the young Manucher first attended a religious high school, and later studied history and political science at Tehran University. As was customary in those days, Manucher followed in his father's footsteps, enlisted in the army, and was made an officer. He first served as adjutant on the staff of General Kamal, chief of military intelligence. After a little more than a year and a half, however, the then Chief of Staff, General Feridoun Jam, advised him to leave the army and enter politics. He did not take this advice, transferring instead to the Savak, the Iranian intelligence agency. Before long Manucher had attracted the attention of Savak chief General Ne'ematullah Nas-siri (who would later be executed by Khomeini's Revolutionary Guards).

Work in the Iranian secret service did not, however, live up to Ghorbanifar's expectations and did not satisfy his desire to get rich quickly. He left the Savak and went into business. At first he imported food, and later cranes and shipping equipment. He eventually became a licensed importer for the Iranian navy. The Yom Kippur War and the rise in oil prices that came with it gave a huge push to the import-export business and opened new financial possibilities to this clever and ambitious youth. In partnership with Dr. Yoram Almogi, the son of the former Israeli minister of labor Yosef Almogi, he set up the Black Star Shipping Company, in which the Iranian Prime Minister was a silent partner. This business connection with Israel led to suspicion that Ghorbanifar was an Israeli spy. He was not. Israeli intelligence did not trust him.

The fall of the Shah and the rise of Khomeini severed Ghorbanifar from his past. The new regime hunted down the Shah's loyalists, and whoever had served in the Savak was a target for the new lords of Tehran. After his property was confiscated and his shipping company dissolved, Ghorbanifar packed a few suitcases and took his wife, two sons, and daughter to Germany.

Hamburg had long had a small but wealthy Persian community of carpet importers. Ghorbanifar became a partner in one of these businesses. He succeeded in making friends with several of the Khomeini men scouring the arms markets of Europe during those days. Before long "the Beard" had become an arms salesman and this business naturally put him in contact with Adnan Khashoggi. There was, of course, a great difference between the scale of Khashoggi's business and that of Ghorbanifar. Their life-styles are also completely different. Ghorbanifar lives modestly relative to Khashoggi's glittering luxury. The Iranian merchant does not go around the world in a private plane, and does not have a luxury yacht with slender young women sunning themselves on its deck. He lives in a (relatively, again) small apartment in Nice, on the French Riviera, and has an additional apartment in Paris, partly as living quarters but mostly for business meetings. His English is good, but despite his French residence he does not speak the language fluently. His German is also halting. He travels on any of several passports he holds—Iranian, German, Irish, Greek, and Portuguese.

In his conversation with Nimrodi, Ghorbanifar boasted that he was in close contact with Iran's Prime Minister, Mir Hussein Mussavi, and with Mohsen Kengarlou, officially deputy prime minister but actually chief of Iranian intelligence operations abroad. He was also in touch with Dr. Shahbadi, who headed Iran's purchasing team in Europe. Khomeinism had passed its peak, he claimed. The people were tiring of the war and ready to return to the embrace of the West. The question was whether the United States would be willing to resume talking to Iran.

After this meeting, Schwimmer and Nimrodi met with Peres and reported that Ghorbanifar was interested in buying weapons and food from Israel in the amount of $2 billion. The Prime Minister had doubts about supplying arms and suggested selling only food. Although he was aware of the insufficient orders facing Israel's defense industries, he feared upsetting relations with the U.S. This reservation led him to appoint General (Res.) Shlomo Gazit, formerly chief of military intelligence, as coordinator for Iranian and other sensitive matters.

The two Israeli businessmen returned to Geneva and passed on Peres's decision to Ghorbanifar. They gave him the list of food items that Israel had in the past exported to Iran, and reminded him of the 50 water desalination plants as well.

Ghorbanifar was disappointed. He had been convinced that, in light of Khashoggi's endorsement—given, he said, with the knowledge of King Fahd—Israel would respond positively. He said that what Iran now needed was arms; food could be purchased at a later date. There were difficulties at the front and a severe shortage of spare parts and ammunition. He gave Nimrodi and Schwimmer a detailed list of weapons and ammunition he wished to purchase from Israel. It included 155mm artillery, 160mm mortars, shells, and air bombs. It came to a total of $33 million. Ghorbanifar claimed that King Fahd had given Khashoggi the go-ahead for the deal, even though the King did not know exactly where the weapons were coming from. The Iranian Prime Minister also knew about it. This being the case, he intended to enlist Khashoggi in finding a way into Peres's heart. "How can you behave this way?" Ghorbanifar complained to Nimrodi. "If the moderates take control, they will always remember that you turned your backs on them in their time of need."

At Schwimmer's suggestion, Peres allowed Manucher Ghorbanifar and Cyrus Hashemi to visit Israel, in order to assess them and test their reliability. The two arrived on April 9, 1985, and stayed at Nimrodi's house in the wealthy Tel Aviv suburb of Savion. During their three days in the country they met the director-general of the ministry of defense, General (Res.) Menachem (Mendi) Meron, Gazit, and several other government officials and army officers.[13] After taking all the necessary security precautions, and after their hosts were briefed on what to say and especially what not to say, the two arms merchants visited several defense industry plants. Ghorbanifar devoted much of his time to writing reports on the situation in Iran, and on its leaders and the relations between them. He also mentioned his contacts in Libya.

In order to prove his reliability, Ghorbanifar telephoned Mohsen Kengarlou, the Iranian deputy prime minister, from Nimrodi's home. Ghorbanifar told Kengarlou that he was speaking from "the land of citrus fruit" and was "working hard"[14] on the subjects they had agreed upon. Those who listened to the conversation received the impression that Ghorbanifar was lying in part. There was no doubt, however, that Ghorbanifar was speaking to the Prime Minister's office in Tehran, and that his contacts were aware of the kind of connections he had in Israel.

Ghorbanifar having proved himself, the Israelis began going over the shopping list he had submitted. Hoping to encourage a positive response, Ghorbanifar made a tempting offer. In exchange for the weapons, he said, Iran would be willing to give Israel a Soviet T-72 tank (a "tractor," in Israeli military parlance). The Iranian army had captured three such tanks from Iraq. Israel had in the past been of great service to the U.S. by allowing American air force officers to study a Mig-21 fighter plane that a deserting Iraqi pilot had flown to Israel. The plane had been used in the training of Israeli pilots, training that was of tremendous help in the Six Day War. Israel did not, however, know much about the T-72 tank that the U.S.S.R. had supplied in large numbers to the Syrian and Iraqi armies. During the war in Lebanon Israel had made great efforts to

capture such a tank, but without success. For this reason Ghorbanifar's offer was very attractive. Nevertheless, he did not receive an immediate response—that, he was told, would come
a few days later.

Peres had in the meantime received a detailed report on
the visit of the two Iranian arms dealers to Israel. Hashemi
had made a very negative impression. It was said that he had
a bad reputation in Europe, and that he offered his services
to the highest bidder. Peres was advised to break off any contact
with him. Opinions of Ghorbanifar's personality, flamboyance,
and inconstancy were also not particularly complimentary. Since
fleeing Iran in 1979 he had tried to sell his services to various
European governments. American officials had met him as early
as January 1980, and he was serving as an American intelligence
informer as late as September 1981. Although that tie had
been broken, Ghorbanifar continued to look for ways to reestablish it. On January 25, 1984, for instance, he told an American
intelligence officer in West Germany about an Iranian terror
network that had been established in Europe. In the middle
of March 1984 he told a CIA agent in Frankfurt that Kengarlou,
the Iranian deputy prime minister who oversaw Iranian spying
overseas, had been behind the kidnapping of William Buckley,
the CIA chief in Beirut. A lie detector test indicated that he
was not telling the truth. In June 1984 Ghorbanifar offered to
arrange a meeting between a CIA representative and Ayatollah
Hassan Karoubi—one of Khomeini's supporters. Ghorbanifar
underwent another test and was again shown to be lying. The
CIA described him as "a talented fabricator" and as a man
who mixed imagination with reality. It also said that he boasted
of doing things he had not done in order to make a profit.
On July 25, 1984, the CIA notified its stations all over the world
not to have anything to do with Ghorbanifar, and to consider
him "an intelligence fabricator and a nuisance."[15]

Another cloud hung over Ghorbanifar's personal trustworthiness. At the beginning of 1980, after he had escaped to Europe
and moved from Hamburg to Paris, he established ties with
the Iranian royalists and joined the faction led by Shahpour
Bakhtiar, the Shah's last Prime Minister. Bakhtiar organized
an operation code-named "Nojeh" that set up a military force
in Iraq to topple Khomeini. He appointed Ghorbanifar "ord-
nance chief" of the conspiracy. As a former head of the Khalij

(Gulf) Company of Abu Dhabi—a fictitious firm once set up by the Savak as a cover for Iranian intelligence operations in the Persian Gulf region, Ghorbanifar knew the Gulf area well and was able to choose hiding places for weapons and ammunition.

Then Ghorbanifar delivered the whole conspiracy into the hands of the Khomeini regime. He turned over the names of dozens of army officers and pilots who were to take part in the attempted revolt, as well as revealing the point on the Shatt al-Arab where the arms and equipment were to be hidden. The weapons were confiscated and more than 30 officers were executed. This most serious attempt to overthrow Khomeini was suppressed on July 9, 1980. In exchange for his "loyalty," Khomeini pardoned Ghorbanifar's sins from the Shah's days and his membership in the Savak, and Iranian intelligence began to liaise with him in Europe. This allowed him to make frequent visits to Tehran and establish contact with the country's new leaders.

Given the weighty evidence of Ghorbanifar's untrustworthiness, the natural tendency of the Israeli intelligence community and the Ministry of Defense was not to maintain contact with him. On the other hand, it was argued that, since Ghorbanifar was aware that the Israelis knew what kind of man he was, he would, fearing retribution, be very careful not to mislead them.

Peres took several days to ponder whether and how to react to the Iranian approach, coming as it had through a private agent. Beyond its purely business elements, there were a number of key factors in the Iran-Iraq conflict that directly affected Israel's national security. From Israel's point of view there was little difference between Khomeini's regime in Iran and Saddam Hussein's regime in Iraq. They were both extreme and hostile governments. The best result in Israel's eyes, therefore, was a stalemate that would seriously weaken both countries for a long time. If one side were to win, however, the Israeli defense establishment preferred that it be Iran.[16]

Over the course of the war the Iraqi army had grown dramatically. It now had some 40 divisions—more than the combined strength of Syria, Jordan, and Egypt. It had also gained experience and expertise in the creation, operation, and maintenance of large forces. Even if but a third of its armed strength was armored or mechanized, Iraq could organize an expeditionary force of 12 divisions—the number of standing armies in Syria and Jordan combined. In other words, Israel would face an eastern front that had doubled in strength. Adding the experience Iraq now had in sending expeditionary forces to Jordan and Syria in all of their wars with Israel, it was easy to reach the conclusion that an Iraqi victory would be a real threat to Israel's existence.

This was not the case with Iran. Khomeini had numerical superiority, and he certainly intended to take part in the destruction of Israel, but he lacked experience and the means to achieve that goal. In order to get to Israel, Iran's forces would have to cross rivers and travel a distance of more than 600 miles over desert—with no air cover and no way of concealing themselves. Even if they did so, there was no guarantee that Syria and Jordan would allow an Iranian expeditionary force to pass through their territory. For the foreseeable future, at least, Iran's ability to participate in a war against Israel would not increase significantly, even if it defeated Iraq.

From a diplomatic point of view also an Iranian victory was preferable. Since the fall of the Iraqi monarchy in July 1958, Iraq had experienced numerous military coups, but all its rulers displayed deep hostility to Israel. In several instances during the war with Iran, Iraq had made use of poison gas bombs, in direct violation of international law. Even if Iraq were to hesitate to use chemical weapons against Israel, for fear of an even worse retaliation, Israel could not rely on the reasonableness of the current rulers in Baghdad.

There was no reason to expect a revolution against Khomeini in the immediate future, and every ayatollah had the same extreme views and designs against Israel that Khomeini had. Over the previous two years, however, Israel had received information that, even among those close to Khomeini, there were some pragmatic men who were looking for a way to establish ties with the West. For this reason, as far back as May 1982, when Ariel Sharon was in Washington, he advised the secretaries of state and defense to make an opening to Iran and even supply it with a limited amount of weapons and military equipment, in order to strengthen the hand of those who might accede to Khomeini's place in the future. But, because of the anger and humiliation Americans felt after the capture of the hostages in the American embassy in Tehran, and because of Iran's support for international terror, the Reagan administration rejected the idea. Iran was seen by Washington as lost to the West for the forseeable future.[17]

It was these factors that Peres, Rabin, and Shamir considered while deciding how to respond to the approach from Iran via Hashemi and Ghorbanifar. The latter two had, in the meantime, returned to Europe. During the period that followed Ghorbanifar telephoned Israel daily, asking for an answer. In the second half of April, he returned to Israel, hoping that his presence would constitute pressure for a positive response. During his conversations with Nimrodi and Schwimmer he claimed that the opportunity should not be missed, and that aid to the "moderates" in Iran would serve everyone's interests.

The Prime Minister approved continuing the contacts with Ghorbanifar, but demanded that they be managed personally by Ya'acov Nimrodi. This was a crucial decision since it shut Israel's professional intelligence community out of the picture. Peres never publicly announced this decision, but he chose a private merchant so that he could deny any connection with the matter should there be a snafu or early revelation.

But before any final decision was made, it was necessary to check whether Ghorbanifar had the financial means to purchase the weapons from Israel. Nimrodi went to Geneva and found evidence that Ghorbanifar had access to a bank account belonging to the National Iranian Oil Company, and that $100 million had recently been deposited in the account. Ghorbanifar's access to the account was authorized by Iran's Prime Minister and oil minister.

Nimrodi returned to Israel to make the necessary preparations for the deal, which was code-named "Operation Cosmos." Ghorbanifar went to Tehran to make arrangements for the reception of the weapons from Israel. The deal involved only Israeli weapons—150mm artillery, 160mm mortars, shells, and air bombs, at a cost of $33 million. By prior arrangement, the weapons were to be transferred by ship from Eilat to the Iranian port Bandar Abbas. The ship would then return with the T-72 tank. The ship was to be ready to sail on April 23, 1985. Payment was to be deposited in Nimrodi's personal bank account at the Credit Suisse bank in Geneva, one day prior to the sailing. Iran was to pay for the ship's insurance and fittings, and an authorized Iranian agent would accompany the cargo to Bandar Abbas. The Israeli ministry of defense demanded and received Nimrodi's signature on a document setting out his irrevocable and full responsibility for every item in the shipment, including any possible damage to them. Nimrodi also paid for shipment overland to Eilat and port taxes, and took upon himself to compensate the shipowners, in the event that Operation Cosmos was canceled. Above all, when the ship was chartered, Nimrodi promised to pay its owners $50 million should it be confiscated by Iranian authorities. Nimrodi took care of all these arrangements in order to give the Israeli government the capacity to deny its involvement.

All the equipment was in Eilat on April 22, ready for loading. Men from the Ministry of Defense erased all Israeli identification marks from the merchandise. An Iranian army colonel came to Israel to examine the equipment before it was loaded and to accompany the ship on its journey. A few hours before sailing time, however, something went wrong. Ghorbanifar called urgently from Geneva and asked that the shipment be delayed. He explained to Nimrodi that "internal difficulties" had surfaced in Iran, and he asked permission to come to Israel to explain.

This mishap caused Nimrodi much agony and great financial loss. In addition to the ship's rental fees, the cost of painting the ship, and the overland shipment, the Ministry of Defense had obligated him to pay the cost of eliminating the Israeli identification markings. That, however, was not the essential point. What was important was to know whether Ghorbanifar was an international embezzler who could not be trusted, or whether the sudden difficulty was real and whether it could be overcome.

Ghorbanifar arrived for his third visit at the end of April and again stayed at Nimrodi's house. In a meeting with Schwimmer and Nimrodi, he apologized for the mishap, and asked that the shipment be delayed by a month or two. In the meantime, so he claimed, Iranian Prime Minister Mir Hussein Mussavi wished to purchase American-made TOW antitank missiles from Israel. Nimrodi exploded, accusing Ghorbanifar of causing him unnecessary financial losses, and called him a liar. Ghorbanifar swore by all that was dear to him that he was telling the truth and that he was acting on the authority of the Iranian Prime Minister. The great superiority of the Iraqi armored units made it urgent for Iran to purchase TOW missiles and delay for the meantime the Israeli-made equipment. Ghorbanifar knew, of course, that Israel was not allowed to sell American weaponry to a third country, and that such a sale would require Washington's approval. For this reason Ghorbanifar threw in a bonus for the U.S. He would try to obtain the release of William Buckley, the head of the CIA station in Lebanon, who had been kidnapped in Beirut on March 16, 1984. This was the first time that an Iranian source—even if it was an arms salesman—acknowledged to Israel that there was a direct connection between Iran and the extremist Shiite terrorist organizations in Lebanon. After the mishap with the Israeli shipment, however, Nimrodi had doubts about Ghorbanifar's ability to free Buckley. The Iranian replied that he should wait and see.

For a moment it seemed as if the Israeli arms deal with Iran had come to an end. In early May 1985, however, a special American envoy arrived in Jerusalem for a discussion about Iran with Prime Minister Peres. The seeds for what was to become "Irangate" were sown.

2

Constructing the Iranian Triangle

The news that Israel was supplying American weapons to Iran stunned the Arab countries. True, there had been rumors of shipments of Israeli weapons to Iran almost as soon as Khomeini had seized power, but the public exposure of the Iran-Contra affair and the official confirmation the Arab countries now received, eye-opening in and of itself, left many questions unanswered.

The Arab astonishment was the inevitable result of the contradiction between the public statements of President Reagan and Ayatollah Khomeini and their actual pursuit of policy. Of all the Moslem countries, Iran and Libya had displayed the most extreme hostility to the U.S. and Israel. While the Shah had enthusiastically supported the Camp David agreements of 1978, Khomeini had damned the peace treaty between Israel and Egypt, had derided the Reagan peace plan of September 1, 1982, had rejected the Fahd plan and the Fez plan that followed, had attacked the renewal of diplomatic relations between Egypt and Jordan, and had made known his violent opposition to the February 1985 agreement between Jordan and the PLO, which spoke of a Jordanian-Palestinian confederation. Khomeini called the U.S. "the Great Satan," and Israel "the Great Satan's bastard." In his public statements he would constantly ask, "Who in the world did not know that the Shah's relations with Israel were among the greatest differences between us? Who in the world did not listen to our lessons and sermons, for 20 years in exile, in which we compared Israel to the American Satan?"

The Khomeini revolution gave immediate expression to its anti-American and anti-Israeli views. Iran cut off all its links with Israel and began actively supporting the Palestinian terrorist organizations. In the summer of 1982 it commenced active involvement itself in terrorist actions against Israel and the U.S. in Lebanon.

Yet here, in complete opposition to the declared policies of the three countries, cynically ignoring their own public statements, Iran worked to obtain American weapons through the active mediation of Israel. The pro-Western Arab regimes wondered to what extent this had affected the course of the war between Iran and Iraq. Even when the U.S. hurried to reassure them that the small quantity of weapons supplied could not have upset the balance of power or decided the war, America's credibility was now stained, and this had serious consequences.

Jordan's King Hussein was the first to express his anger at what he considered an American betrayal. On Saturday, November 22, 1986, Hussein flew to Cairo and met three times with President Husni Mubarak during the course of the day. At a joint press conference the President and the King condemned the behavior of the U.S. and expressed their concern that the American arms that Iran had received would endanger Iraq's existence. Saudi Arabia and the Persian Gulf principalities reacted similarly.

The storm subsided a few weeks later, however, and the Arab states' continuing need for generous American aid overcame their anger and frustration. The escalation of the Gulf War, and the Iranian threat to the Persian Gulf shipping lanes, increased the dependence of Saudi Arabia and the Gulf states on American military strength—forcing them to keep their responses restrained.

It was Egypt, in particular, that adopted a more balanced position. When, for example, Iraq sent a delegation to Cairo to plan joint diplomatic action against the U.S., President Mubarak's enthusiasm cooled immediately. He asked why Iraq was so surprised that Israel was helping Iran? The Iraqi army had proliferated and now had 40 divisions. Israel was afraid of that strength. If Iraq were to declare that it had abandoned its 'war option' against Israel and take part in the peace process in the region, Israel would not feel it necessary to help Iran against Iraq, he told the members of the delegation. Mubarak advised President Saddam Hussein not to panic, and to see events in their proper perspective.

American and Israeli involvement in supplying arms to Iran was the result of a policy of cooperation that began during the Eisenhower administration in the 1950s, reaching its peak two decades later during the Nixon administration. For more than 25 years, the U.S., Israel, and Iran worked together in a strategic unofficial alliance aimed at halting the Soviet Union's expansion in the Middle East and weakening its friends in the Arab world. At first the U.S. tried to fit Egypt into this framework, supporting the Colonels' rebellion against King Farouk in July 1952. After Secretary of State John Foster Dulles's visit to the area in 1953, however, it was clear that Egypt did not want to be part of the pro-Western bloc, and that it preferred pursuing a nonaligned foreign policy and advancing its cause among the Arab leaders by encouraging the two superpowers to vie for its favors.

This Egyptian policy alarmed Washington, the pro-Western Arab states, and Tehran, and increased their worries about the stability of the Persian Gulf region. The U.S. and Britain persuaded the Shah to overcome his traditional enmity with Iraq and, on February 24, 1955, Iran joined the Baghdad Pact, together with Britain, Turkey, Iraq, and Pakistan. Through arms supplies and intelligence cooperation, this pro-Western alliance was aimed to contain Soviet expansion and Communist subversion in the Arab world. In order to keep the door open to Egypt, the U.S. did not officially join the pact, satisfying itself with the status of "observer." Nasser, however, immediately began sending out feelers to Syria and Saudi Arabia for the establishment of a counteralliance. His prestige at its height after his participation in the Bandung conference of April 1955, Nasser in October signed his first arms deal with the Soviet bloc. The Soviet Union thus "jumped" the Baghdad Pact and, from its new outpost in Egypt, began staking out a place for itself in Syria, at the backs of Turkey, Iraq, and Iran. Nasser managed to keep Jordan out of the Baghdad Pact, too. In the summer of 1956, Syria and the Soviet Union signed their first arms deal, and a joint Syrian-Egyptian-Saudi Arabian command was established.

All these developments spurred the Shah to widen, gradually, his cooperation with Israel. His attitude toward the Jewish state had been complex and ambiguous from the start. Despite its great worries about the growing strength of some Arab countries, especially Egypt and Iraq, Iran voted in the UN against the establishment of the State of Israel and supported the Arab position calling for the establishment of a "Palestinian Confederation" in which a "Jewish entity" would have wide autonomous administrative powers. Israel's victory against seven Arab armies in its War of Independence, however, made the Shah rethink his position. He now saw the Jewish state as a wedge between Egypt and the Arab countries on the Asian continent. He hoped that Israel, with its military strength, would help erode the Arab power ranged against him. By confining Egypt to its borders, Israel prevented it from trying to undermine the pro-Western Arab countries, including the Persian Gulf principalities.

After Turkey, in March 1949, became the first Moslem country to recognize Israel de facto, the Shah decided to follow suit. On March 11, 1950, the Iranian government headed by Mohammed Saed decided to grant de facto recognition to Israel. Iran established a consulate general in Jerusalem and turned a blind eye to the mass flight of Iraqi Jewry to Israel through its territory. With the active encouragement of the U.S., and conscious of the influence of the American Jewish community, the Shah improved the conditions of the Jews of his country and began selling oil to Israel.

For several years relations between the two countries were limited to trade. Israel's lightning victory in the Sinai campaign of October 1956, however, changed this. Countries fearful of Nasser's designs on them suddenly saw Israel as the one hope of defeating him. This was the first opportunity for Israel to enter into strategic cooperation not only with Turkey and Iran, but with Ethiopia as well. Contrary to Nasser's vision of an Arab Middle East, Israel conceived of a multinational Middle East where the Arabs were a majority but not the only party. This conception evolved gradually and formed an official Israeli policy that would eventually be called "the peripheral alliance."

This policy was based on the assumption that Israel, Turkey, Iran, and Ethiopia were all united in their opposition to Soviet penetration and each was worried about Nasser's interference in other countries.

The cooperation between the four countries, which began in the summer of 1957, was conducted simultaneously on several levels, although it never became a formal alliance between them. It developed on the basis of mutual self-interest and in the absence of any joint institutions. In retrospect it seems that all four countries preferred this loose framework over one that would restrict their room for diplomatic maneuver. Turkey was a member of NATO, and with Iran belonged to the Baghdad Pact. Israel and Ethiopia, on the other hand, were not members of any regional alliance and had no defense treaties with the U.S. or other Western powers. While Israel's relations with France were close during that period, they were never formalized, either.

The strategic relations between Israel and Iran began to develop in the summer of 1957, after the U.S. declared the "Eisenhower Doctrine," in which the President called for an active American policy in the Middle East aimed at blocking Soviet expansion. The U.S., along with Britain, also assisted in the reorganization of the Iranian intelligence service, and in the spring of 1957 the "National Intelligence and Security Agency" (*Sazman Kashvar Va'amniyat Ettela'at*, or "Savak") was established. The first chief of the new agency was General Taimour Bakhtiar, the cousin of the former queen, Soraya. He had previously served as commander of an armored division and as the military governor of Tehran. On the Shah's orders, the Savak chief received the title of deputy prime minister. While technically responsible to the Prime Minister, he in fact reported directly to the Shah.

The U.S. encouraged the countries of the region to cooperate in the field of intelligence. Right after declaring its independence, Israel set up one of the best intelligence services in the Middle East, both in gathering information on its Arab enemies and in frustrating espionage and sabotage at home. The U.S. wished, therefore, to integrate Israel into the regional intelligence effort.

In September 1957, Bakhtiar arrived in Paris and asked to meet with Israel's ambassador in France, Ya'akov Zur. He made the request through the first secretary of Iran's embassy, Dr.

Mohammed Sadrieh, who would later become his country's diplomatic representative in Israel. The meeting took place in the home of the political counselor of the Israeli embassy, Ya'akov Caroz, later head of Israel's diplomatic mission in Athens and now a columnist for Israel's largest newspaper, *Yediot Aharonot*.[1] Bakhtiar praised the Israel Defense Forces and expressed his concern about Nasser's attempts to destabilize the region. He offered, in the Shah's name, cooperation with Israel and the exchange of views on various developments in the Middle East.

Israel welcomed Iran's proposals, understanding well their significance and potential. Prime Minister David Ben-Gurion saw the opening to Iran as an overture to a wider diplomatic initiative in Asia. The feeling in Israel was that cooperation with Iran and Turkey could counter the hostility of an India which had sacrificed its relations with Jerusalem on the altar of its friendship with Cairo.

In the wake of the Paris meeting the two countries decided on an additional meeting in Rome at a more senior level. This took place in October. Iran was represented once again by General Bakhtiar, while Israel sent a special envoy, former Mossad chief Isser Harel.[2] The two of them reached full agreement with regard to the danger Nasser presented to the countries of the region, as well as with regard to the Soviet threat. On the basis of their agreements Caroz was sent in December on his first visit to Tehran, where he laid the practical foundations for the strategic cooperation between the two countries and prepared the ground for mutual visits in the future. At this delicate stage, however, Israel and Iran decided to keep their contacts secret.

The Rome meeting was, of course, an important foundation of Israel's new strategy. The union between Egypt and Syria in February 1958 and the military coup in Iraq the following July helped solidify the "peripheral alliance." In response to the former, Jordan and Iraq established a federal union between them, with the support and encouragement of Turkey and Iran. Israel expressed its concern about the Egypt-Syria union in personal letters that Ben-Gurion sent to the Shah and to the Emperor Haile Selassie of Ethiopia. The letter to the Shah was sent by special envoy and handed to the Iranian monarch by Deputy Prime Minister Bakhtiar.[3] In it, the Israeli Prime

Minister surveyed the new balance of power in the region and noted the danger to Jordan and other pro-Western countries. He praised the developing cooperation between Israel and Iran and suggested widening its scope. The Shah's enlightened treatment of the Jews of his country, Ben-Gurion declared, was in the tradition of Cyrus the Great, who had allowed the exiled Jews to return to Jerusalem from their Babylonian captivity.

In his response, the Shah agreed completely with Ben-Gurion's evaluation, and he ordered his aides to widen the framework of the exchange of information with Israel, especially in uncovering anything that would help frustrate attempts to undermine the Jordanian king. As for the Jews, he wrote to Ben-Gurion, the example of Cyrus the Great was dear to him too, and he promised to continue to follow that ancient precedent.

A series of attempts to tighten the economic links between the two countries followed. Israel had begun buying Iranian oil in 1954, but there were practically no other commercial ties. In January 1958, Dr. Zvi Doriel was sent to Tehran to open an office of the Israeli Chamber of Commerce. An educated and cultured man, Doriel had been an outstanding member of the Israeli reparations delegation in Germany. When he came home in the summer of 1957, Minister of Finance Levi Eshkol decided to send him to Tehran in order to lay the basis for economic and trade relations between the two countries. Doriel quickly found his niche in the diplomatic community of Tehran and began acquainting himself with the business and intellectual circles there.

This, however, was not sufficient. Creating a comfortable atmosphere for Israel also meant establishing contact with the Iranian press and with the universities. At the suggestion of Ben-Gurion and Foreign Minister Golda Meir, Meir Ezri was sent to perform this task. Ezri had been born in Iran in 1924, moving to Israel in 1950. As a former activist in the Zionist Hehalutz youth movement he had helped Iraqi and Iranian Jews leave their countries for Israel. He became the director of the Persian-speaking department of the ruling Mapai party and chairman of the Association of Persian Immigrants in Israel. He was to be a Mapai candidate for the Knesset when he was lent to the Foreign Ministry for "a few months." In the end he abandoned his political ambitions for a diplomatic career.

Ezri was not sent with official diplomatic credentials. He presented himself as an Israeli-Iranian who had decided to return to the country of his birth. Having completed two years of law school in Iran, he knew personally many men at the pinnacle of the political and economic establishment. Several former classmates were government ministers, including those of the interior, labor, and communications. His fluency in the Persian language and his acquaintance with Persian mores won him the trust of the Shah and his government. During Ezri's 15 years in Tehran, first as minister and then as ambassador, Israel's activity in Tehran gained impressive momentum.

His activity inevitably caught the attention of the Iranian security services. In August 1958 he was summoned to the offices of the Savak, where an officer in civilian dress, Colonel Shaheen, wanted to find out why he had returned to Tehran, and who his contacts were.[4] Knowing that Ezri had edited the Persian-language monthly magazine *Kochav HaMizrach* ("The Eastern Star") in Israel, Shaheen offered him money to return to Israel and turn the newspaper into a daily. Ezri turned him down politely, claiming that there were no people in Israel capable of putting out a daily newspaper in Persian. He was later offered the post of minister of labor in the cabinet of Assadullah Alam, but turned this down as well.

Not long after arriving in Tehran, Ezri paid a courtesy call on an old family friend, General Ali Kia. Kia was then chief of military intelligence and chairman of the committee of intelligence service chiefs that oversaw the Savak, the Vijeh (the court intelligence service headed by General Fardoust), the police, and the gendarmerie. Kia had previously been head of the Shah's military bureau and commander of the Royal Guard. During the Second World War, Kia had been military attaché in Berlin. Upon returning to Tehran he had been appointed commander of the border guard and developed particularly good relations with the Jewish community and with Moshe Tov, chairman of the Zionist Organization of Iran.

The "peripheral alliance" crystallized into its final form in mid-1958. In May of that year a civil war broke out in Lebanon, fanned by incitement from Cairo and Damascus. The events in Lebanon led to unrest in Jordan as well. The kinship of the ruling families in Jordan and Iraq and the conditions of the

federal union between the two countries led King Faisal of
Iraq to send a mechanized brigade to the aid of King Hussein
on July 14. The brigade was commanded by Colonel Abdul
Karim Qassem; he equipped it with arms and ammunition,
but instead of marching to Amman, he attacked the royal palace
in Baghdad, deposed Faisal, and declared a republic.
The Iraqi coup seriously upset the balance of power in the
Middle East. Colonel Qassem immediately led his country out
of the Baghdad Pact and asked Nasser for assistance. For a
short while it looked as if, with Syria as bridge, an Arab empire
stretching from the Nile to the Euphrates was about to be
established. In a message to President Eisenhower, Ben-Gurion
urged the United States to put down the revolt in Baghdad
by force. Eisenhower rejected such a move, but in order to
prevent the collapse of American influence in the Middle East,
he sent the Marines into Beirut. Britain sent paratroopers into
Amman in order to shore up Hussein's regime; Israel allowed
them to fly through its air space.
These unsettling events led, however, to a gain for Israel.
At the Shah's instigation, Turkey overcame all its reservations
to close cooperation with Israel. On July 19, Turkish Foreign
Minister Fatin Zorlü summoned Eliahu Sassoon, Israel's first
ambassador to Ankara (now ambassador to Rome), to an urgent
meeting. Ben-Gurion wrote in his diary that day: "We are in
historic times, and this opportunity for action will not repeat
itself. Elias has notified me of Turkey's agreement in principle
to a meeting of the two Prime Ministers. If the Arabs find out
about this, the whole thing will explode and then the Americans
will interfere as well."[5]
On July 20, Golda Meir held a discussion in her house, with
Ben-Gurion's participation, in order to discuss ways of enlisting
America's support for the "peripheral alliance." Ben-Gurion
believed that if the U.S. told Iran, Turkey, and Ethiopia that it
supported this idea, the alliance could accomplish more than
originally conceived. On July 24, Ben-Gurion sent a personal
letter to President Eisenhower in which he analyzed the situation in the Middle East in the wake of the Iraqi coup. Presented
to Secretary of State John Foster Dulles by then Israeli ambassador to the United States, Abba Eban, the letter expressed Ben-
Gurion's concern about the future of Jordan, Lebanon, and
Saudi Arabia, and warned that if Nasser were to take control

of the entire Arab world, the Libyan monarchy would also fall, the danger of a Communist revolution in Iran would increase, and Egypt would try to overrun Sudan, endangering Ethiopia. He also wrote that,

> with the purpose of erecting a high dam against the Nasserist-Soviet tidal wave, we have begun tightening our links with several states on the outside perimeter of the Middle East— Iran, Turkey, and Ethiopia. We have made contact with and have developed relations of mutual trust and friendship with the Iranian Shah and with the Ethiopian Emperor. Our relations with Turkey have tightened lately, and go beyond routine diplomatic contacts. Our goal is to organize a group of countries, not necessarily an official alliance, that will be able to stand strong against Soviet expansion by proxy through Nasser, and which might save Lebanon's freedom and, maybe in time, Syria's.[6]

Eisenhower agreed with Ben-Gurion's analysis and ordered Dulles to inform Turkey, Ethiopia, and Iran that the U.S. accepted the idea of a peripheral alliance.[7]

The results were quick to come. On August 28, 1958, Ben-Gurion left on a secret trip to Ankara to meet Turkish Prime Minister Adnan Menderes and Foreign Minister Zorlü. Accompanying him were his foreign minister, Golda Meir, Chief of Staff Chaim Laskov, and Ambassador Sassoon. By prior arrangement with Turkey, Ben-Gurion was to leave on a special El Al plane that would land in Istanbul "because of engine problems." From there the Israeli party would continue on a Turkish plane to Ankara.

The Istanbul air control tower, however, took the announcement of engine trouble seriously and summoned a fleet of fire engines and ambulances to the airport. It was clear that, with so many eyes on him, Ben-Gurion could not switch planes. The Turkish security forces had to work quickly to get the first aid vehicles out of the airport and allow the Israelis to continue on to the capital.

Ben-Gurion and Menderes reached wide-ranging understandings about several joint activities aimed at blocking Nasser's influence in the Middle East. These understandings remained in force for several years, but gradually faded in the mid-1960s, victims of Ankara's revision of its Middle East policy.[8]

Ezri and Kia met only a few weeks after the Iraqi coup of July 1958 that led to that country's break with its Baghdad Pact allies. This was a cause of great concern in Tehran, and the Shah added the new ruler of Iraq, General Abdul Karim Qassem, to his list of enemies.

Kia admired Israel and advocated full diplomatic relations with the Jewish state. He told Ezri that the Iranians were not Arabs, and since Israel was also not Arab and was anti-Communist, Israel and Iran had a common interest in blocking Communist subversion and Egyptian expansionism. Kia concluded the conversation by telling Ezri, "I am the key to the palace. Take the key and use it to open any door you wish."[9]

With Kia's help, Ezri met Prime Minister Manucher Eqbal, Foreign Minister Abbas Aram, Chief of Staff General Hedayet, and the Chief of Police, General Alavi Mokaddam. Golda Meir encouraged Ezri, and with the approval of Ben-Gurion and Israel's Chief of Staff, Chaim Laskov, he invited General Kia to Israel. Kia accepted immediately, but asked to have the invitation in writing in order to receive the Shah's approval. This was provided by Ambassador Doriel that same day. Kia suggested coming to Israel on his way back from an already scheduled trip to London and Paris that October.

Kia arrived in Israel with his wife and daughter and stayed for a week as the guest of the chief of military intelligence, General Yehoshafat Harkabi. Ezri came to Israel to prepare the visit and, at his recommendation, Kia was received with full military honors. He met with Chief of Staff Laskov and his deputy, General Yitzhak Rabin, as well as with Ben-Gurion, Golda Meir, and Defense Ministry Director-General Shimon Peres.

It was during this visit that Kia met Nimrodi for the first time and hinted that he should be appointed Israel's military attaché in Tehran.

Kia invited Harkabi to give a series of lectures to the Iranian leadership, and the Israeli general left for Tehran in December 1958. During his visit there he met with the Shah and top army commanders. His talks with Kia laid the basis for the future cooperation between the two countries.

To keep his presence secret, Harkabi's lectures were scheduled for the early morning, before the workday began. Harkabi presented his analysis of events in neighboring countries and their effect on the Middle East as a whole. He attended five such meetings, summaries of which were presented to the Shah. At the end of his visit, Kia notified Harkabi that the Shah wished to see him. Since it was the first meeting between the Shah and an Israeli army officer, Harkabi asked for instructions from Israel. The Chief of Staff and Deputy Minister of Defense Peres approved the meeting and told Harkabi what points to emphasize.[10]

The audience took place in the Shah's office. Gifts presented to the Shahs of Persia in previous centuries were prominently displayed around the room. Harkabi had been told to address the Shah as "Your Imperial Majesty," a title he practiced in advance. The Israeli general opened with a short speech noting the historical link between the two nations dating back to Cyrus the Great. He also recalled the battle of Nahavand in A.D. 642, when Persia was conquered by the Arabs, a national tragedy in Persian historical memory. Harkabi then briefly summarized his talks with Iran's military leadership.

The Shah accepted Harkabi's estimation that the Iraqi coup did not put Iran in danger, but he immediately went on to what he intended to be the major subject of the conversation— an invective against the U.S. which, the Shah maintained, did not understand the Middle East. He added that, because of Israel's strong position in Washington and the great influence of American Jewry, Israel must explain events in the region to the Americans. The Shah spoke heatedly. He argued that the U.S. did not understand Iran's need for weapons and for financial aid. The Shah, it seemed, wanted Israel to lobby with President Eisenhower for Iran's aid requests.[11] The Shah would return to this request at every meeting he held with Israeli leaders. Israeli President Chaim Herzog later said that he saw every Israeli as a link to Washington.

Harkabi's visit to Tehran was a great success and his meeting with the Shah strengthened the feeling in Israel that the links between the two countries would in the future become much stronger.[11a] This was reinforced in December 1958, when the Shah approved the opening of an Iranian diplomatic mission in Israel—even if this was kept secret by having it run out of the Swiss embassy in Tel Aviv.

General Chaim Herzog (now Israel's President) took over military intelligence from Harkabi on April 1, 1959, and that summer he and his wife arrived in Tehran as General Kia's guests. Herzog was also received by the Shah. In his talks with General Kia and his staff, Herzog renewed the suggestion that the two countries exchange military attachés; the Shah remained unwilling.

Nevertheless, cooperation with the Iranian government and armed forces continued to broaden. In February 1960, General Kia arrived for his second visit to Israel. In his conversations with Ben-Gurion, Chief of Staff Laskov, and Military Intelligence Chief Herzog, he and his interlocutors analyzed the situation in the Middle East and exchanged ideas about increasing military cooperation between the two countries. Herzog again suggested an exchange of military attachés, to allow the two countries to become better acquainted with each other's armed forces, and in order to identify those areas in which there was potential for cooperation. Kia revealed that the Shah now agreed to the appointment of an Israeli Military attaché in Tehran. In his concluding conversation with the Prime Minister, Kia asked Ben-Gurion to appoint Nimrodi to the post.[12] Nimrodi and his family returned to Iran the following month.

Nimrodi succeeded, more than any of those who came after him, in leaving his mark on the varied range of military cooperation that developed between Israel and Iran. Nimrodi knew the country, its language, and its customs well from his days as Jewish Agency representative there. One of his forbears had died in the Persian city of Yazd 200 years previously and, according to a family legend, the dead man miraculously returned to life during his funeral. The stunned crowd of mourners had called out "na mord!"—"not dead!"—hence the name Nimrodi. Nimrodi told the legend to several top Iranian officers, and it soon found its way to the Shah.

While the links between the two countries covered a wide range of activities, the most important of them were defense and oil.

Iran began supplying oil to the Jewish state when it was still very young. Israel had begun buying small quantities as early as 1954, through private dealers. The nationalization of Iran's oil riches by Mossadegh changed the legal status of the oil concessions. With American help, the National Iranian Oil Company was established in 1954, along with two subsidiaries—one for drilling and the other for refining. An international oil consortium, including American companies, was established, but it left the National Iranian Oil with a certain quantity for Iran's own needs and for direct export. Israel was a natural customer.

The first arrangements for a regular supply of Iranian oil to Israel were made in London in the fall of 1954. Mordechai Gazit, later director-general of the Prime Minister's Office under Golda Meir and Israeli ambassador to France, was then first secretary of the Israeli embassy in London. Shortly after the establishment of the National Iranian Oil Company, he was called by Sultan Hossein Sanandaji, a young Iranian Kurd who served in a junior position in the Iranian embassy in London. Sanandaji, later one of the three directors-general of the Iranian Foreign Ministry, offered his government's cooperation with Israel. Given the low rank of the emissary, Gazit doubted the seriousness of the offer. He nevertheless asked Sanandaji whether Iran would sell oil to Israel. The young man answered in the affirmative, without any hesitation. Gazit immediately cabled Jerusalem.[13]

Abba Eban was scheduled to dine with the Iranian ambassador to Washington soon thereafter. The Foreign Ministry in Jerusalem passed on the contents of Gazit's message to Eban, but the Iranian ambassador knew nothing about the oil offer to Israel.

Gazit met Sanandaji again two weeks later at a reception held by Queen Elizabeth in Buckingham Palace. The Iranian diplomat revealed to his Israeli colleague that the deputy director of the National Iranian Oil Company was to arrive in London soon, and that if Israel were still interested in buying oil, this was an opportunity for a preliminary discussion. Israel's finance minister, Levi Eshkol, sent Yisrael Kozlov, head of Israel's oil authority, to London. The Iranian representative gave Kozlov and Gazit his agreement in principle to the transaction, but the details were worked out in a secret visit by Kozlov to Tehran.[14]

The temporary closing of the Suez Canal in 1956 brought about increased Israel-Iran cooperation in oil. Seventy-three percent of Iran's imports and 76 percent of its oil exports went through the canal. Iran thus had to find new shipping routes, and quickly. In parallel, the Soviet Union broke off relations with Jerusalem in October 1956, immediately after the Sinai campaign, and halted its supply of oil to the Jewish state. Iran was the obvious alternative.

In the summer of 1957 a representative of the National Iranian Oil Company arrived in Israel for talks with Levi Eshkol and Israel's minister of trade and industry, Pinhas Sapir. To preserve secrecy, the "Persian," as he was called, was lodged in a private home in the Tel Aviv suburb of Ramat Gan and only a handful of officials met with him. At the end of several days of negotiations, a contract was signed. The oil was to be sold to Israel for $1.30 a barrel.[15]

Prime Minister Ben-Gurion saw this as a diplomatic as well as a commercial achievement. The contract would not have been signed without the Shah's blessing. Israel decided to lay an 8-inch pipeline to carry the oil from Eilat to Beersheba, from where it would be taken by truck to the oil refineries in Haifa. The pipe was laid in a record-breaking 100 days, and began to operate in December 1957.

A year later it was already clear that Israel needed larger supplies of oil. Israel's massive immigration and economic development raised consumption and necessitated a continuous supply of oil based on a long-term contract. So, in the fall of 1958, Ben-Gurion sent Levi Eshkol to Tehran to raise the subject with the Shah.

The minister of finance set out with Kozlov and the ministry's controller of foreign currency, Dr. Zevi Dinstein.[16] The visit was arranged through special channels and not even Doriel, the representative of the Israeli Chamber of Commerce in Iran, was told about it. Eshkol's party was received at the airport by Deputy Prime Minister Bakhtiar, and they were lodged at the official guest residence in the northern part of the city. After several preparatory sessions, Eshkol went for a personal audience with the Shah. It was the first meeting between an Israeli cabinet minister and the Shah, and its very occurrence proved the desire of both countries to raise the level of contacts between them. Eshkol gave the Shah Ben-Gurion's greetings, and in an hour-long conversation in English, in a most comfortable atmosphere, the two agreed on increasing Iran's supply of oil to Israel.

Such a regular supply of oil from Iran required Israel to lay a new, 16-inch pipeline at a cost of $18 million. It was completed at the end of 1960, and Iran doubled the quantity of oil it supplied Israel.

In the summer of 1965 it became clear that a 32-inch pipeline was now needed. Eshkol, by now Prime Minister, wanted to convince Iran to approve the new pipeline and assigned Foreign Minister Golda Meir to go to Tehran. This was Meir's first visit to Tehran, although she had met the Shah once before, in 1961, while he was on a ski trip to Norway. The Shah was well aware, of course, of Meir's great prestige in Israel and the U.S., and he carefully followed her efforts to build Israel's relations with the new countries of black Africa. He was most interested in the Israeli proposal, but did not believe that a larger pipeline would be profitable. The president of the National Iranian Oil Company, Manucher Eqbal, opposed the idea, while the foreign minister, Ardeshir Zahedi, ruled it out for political reasons. Meir returned to Israel empty-handed, and the 16-inch pipeline remained Israel's major oil artery until the Six Day War.[17]

Before returning to Jerusalem, Meir met with the staff of the Israeli mission in Tehran. Some of the lower-ranking diplomats argued that the time had come to take a more aggressive line with the Shah. They proposed posting a sign on their building that would clearly identify the place as Israel's diplomatic representation in Tehran. Meir ruled out any such action.[18] She accepted instead Meir Ezri's position. Ezri told her that the Shah's views were not stable and that he often changed them in an extreme way. Even if he were to declare his intention to recognize Israel de jure three years from now, this should not be taken as a commitment. Everything depended on his mood of the moment. Two years ago, after all, he had promised establishing relations with Israel "in another year," and nothing had happened. Ezri recommended not bringing the subject up again with the Shah and, instead, to press the U.S., France, Britain, Germany, and Canada—all of them countries that the Shah listened to—and to ask them to explain to the Shah how much Iran was losing by not having full relations with Israel. These countries did press the Shah on Israel's behalf, but to no avail.

Military cooperation began in the summer of 1957, after the Israeli envoy met Bakhtiar in Rome, and it gained momentum with Nimrodi's appointment as military attaché in Tehran. The Shah himself acknowledged the existence of the cooperation in an interview with the Arabic-language Paris weekly El-Mustaq-bal, in October 1975. He said that it had resulted from Nasser's hostility to Iran. Western newspapers began uncovering links between Iran's Savak, Israel's Mossad, and the CIA. Sadek Qot-bzadeh, one of the first Foreign Ministers of revolutionary Iran, would later reveal that the Shah had sent several of his intelligence and army officers for courses in Israel.[19] He said that the cooperation between the intelligence services included exchanging evaluations of events in Arab countries, and the exchange of information about Palestinian terrorist activities and the training of young Iranians at PLO bases in Lebanon.

Two senior Savak officers, General Manucher Vajdi and General Reza Parvaresh, revealed many details about the extent of intelligence cooperation between Iran and Israel. In their appearance before a Revolutionary Court in Tehran in May 1979, the two related that the U.S., Britain, Germany, and Israel had helped organize the Iranian army and intelligence services. They admitted taking part in meetings with Israeli intelligence officers, and that in the exchange of information about Palestinians they had "revealed many of the outposts of the Palestinian organizations in Lebanon." General Rahmatullah Razmara, a prosecution witness at the same trial, told of visits exchanged between officers of the Savak and the Mossad.[20] For their part in this cooperation with Israel, General Vajdi, once chief of Iranian counterintelligence, was sentenced to 15 years in prison, while General Parvaresh was sentenced to 12 years.

In addition to cooperation in intelligence matters, Israel helped train some 400 Iranian pilots, paratroopers, and artillery-men,[21] and supplied the Shah with arms and military equipment. From the beginning of 1961 all of the Israeli army's Chiefs of Staff visited Tehran (the only exception was Major General Chaim Bar-Lev, who was preoccupied with the War of Attrition along the Suez Canal; he visited Tehran, however, as Chief of Operations). Air force and navy commanders, as well as most of the heads of the various branches of the general staff also made such visits. Several Iranian army Chiefs of Staff, and almost all its general staff branch chiefs and service chiefs visited Israel.[22]

In his appearance before a Revolutionary Court in Iran in

April 1979, Amir Hossein Rabi'i, formerly commander of the Iranian air force, related that most Iranian officers of the rank of major and upward visited Israel, some of them as many as seven times. He said that the vice minister of war for armament, General Hassan Toufanian, had visited Israel "perhaps a hundred times," and that he himself had made two such visits, the first immediately after the Six Day War in 1967, and the second in February 1978, as commander of the air force.

Knowing General Kia from his two visits to Israel, Nimrodi quickly found his way into Iran's military establishment. His first real achievement came at the end of 1960 with Israeli army intelligence chief Chaim Herzog's ten-day visit to Tehran. After talks with the Shah in the marble palace and a working session with Chief of Staff Hedayet, Herzog discussed with his counterparts a wide-ranging plan for cooperation between the two countries. Its purpose was to set the wheels in motion for eventual diplomatic recognition between the two countries. In addition to cooperation between the various military branches, it also envisaged ties between the military industries of the two countries.

Herzog arrived in Tehran during an especially stormy period in the Middle East. In the wake of a visit to Tehran by Reuven Shiloah, adviser to the Israeli foreign minister, in the spring of 1960, and in opposition to the recommendation of his Prime Minister, Manucher Eqbal, the Shah decided to establish full diplomatic relations with Israel. Golda Meir recommended appointing Moshe Sassoon, a senior Israeli diplomat who now serves as ambassador to Egypt, as Israel's first ambassador to Iran. His name was passed on to the Iranian Foreign Ministry, as protocol requires, and the assumption was that the appointment would be approved within the framework of Iran's announcement of its decision to recognize Israel de jure. Iran, however, decided first to sound out the reactions of the Arab countries. The Shah, answering reporters' questions on July 23, 1960, confirmed that his country "had recognized Israel ten years previously and that it continued to do so."[23] Nasser responded furiously by cutting off relations with Iran. The Arab world, however, was split, and no other country followed in Nasser's footsteps. Nasser and Qassem launched into a vehement verbal attack on the Shah and encouraged their followers to eliminate the Kings of Jordan, Saudi Arabia, and Libya. The denunciations of King Hussein were accompanied by vigorous subversive activity planned in Damascus against his regime, Jordan's Prime Minister, Hazza el-Majali, fought back and—thanks to hints passed on to him by Israel via the Shah and the American government—was able to foil two attempted military coups in Amman. In August 1960, however, Nasser's long arm found him. Syrian agents from Damascus came to Amman where they hid a powerful bomb in a drawer of el-Majali's desk. The tremendous explosion killed the Prime Minister and nine other cabinet members; 50 other officials were injured.[24]

It was a harsh blow to King Hussein's prestige, and he considered taking revenge on Syria. To do so, however, he needed his Israeli flank protected. At the beginning of September 1960, the Jordanian liaison officer on the Israeli-Jordanian armistice committee notified Israel that King Hussein wished to have "a meeting at the most senior level" with Israel. One of the Israeli Prime Minister's aides suggested conducting the meeting between Hussein and Ben-Gurion at the Shah's palace in Tehran, but Ben-Gurion first wanted to find out what was behind Hussein's request. General Herzog met with Hussein's bureau chief at the Mandelbaum Gate in Jerusalem and heard of the King's intentions of invading Syria.[25] The idea did not arouse enthusiasm in Jerusalem. At Ben-Gurion's request, the U.S., Britain, and Iran persuaded Hussein to abandon his plans, and not to entangle himself in a move that might have unexpected consequences.

The Shah was very pleased with Israel's positive contribution to protecting Hussein's throne, and he expressed his appreciation by extending his cooperation with Israel in many areas. While full diplomatic relations were not established, on the practical level ties grew even tighter.

Yet the internal situation in Iran and the growing opposition to the Shah was also of concern to Israel, and aroused fears about the stability of relations between the two countries. Iran held parliamentary elections at the end of 1960; all the Shah's loyalists won. The religious and left opposition groups accused the government of falsifying the election results. After a series of clashes between demonstrators and the police, and after accusations that various senior officials had been corrupt, the Shah fired the chief of police, General Alavi Mokaddam, and the chief of military intelligence, Ali Kia.

In March 1961, the Shah was forced to fire the head of the Savak, General Taimour Bakhtiar, as well.[26] The CIA had revealed to the Shah that Bakhtiar had, during a visit to the U.S. embassy, said that "the Shah is not in control of the situation," and had asked the U.S. for help in overthrowing the monarch and assuming the presidency of an Iranian Republic. Bakhtiar was called into the Shah's chambers on March 15, 1961. He knew what awaited him from the moment he entered the palace. The Royal Guard disarmed him, and his successor as head of the Savak, General Hassan Pakravan, stood at the Shah's side. The Shah told Bakhtiar he was being fired for corruption— the Savak chief had built a luxurous mansion not far from the royal palace at a cost of some $1 million.[27] Bakhtiar went into exile in Europe, but since he continued to conspire against the Shah (and even tried to link up with Khomeini), he was murdered by Savak agents in Baghdad on August 22, 1980.[28]

Bakhtiar's dismissal did not end the disturbances. On May 5, 1961, Prime Minister Sherif Emami submitted his resignation after only six months in office. The Shah replaced him with Dr. Ali Amini, an economist of high reputation who had studied in France. Amini had been minister of finance when the government had signed its agreement with the international oil consortium in early 1954, and he also served as Iran's ambassador to Washington. The Israeli representative in Tehran, Meir Ezri, was among the first to inform Amini that the Shah intended to appoint him to the high office. When the news turned out to be true, Amini was convinced that Israel had advised the Shah to make the appointment.

The dismissal of Kia and Bakhtiar gave rise to understandable concern in Israel about the future of military and security cooperation with Iran. Israeli leaders knew, of course, that the Shah was well aware of the importance of his relations with Israel, both for their intrinsic value and as a means of winning American favor. But in order to avoid putting weapons in the hands of the mullahs, who had used the ties with Israel to incite the populace against the government, the Shah ordered that all relations with Israel be kept as low-key as possible. The Shah was no doubt fearful that open cooperation with Israel would deter Saudi Arabia, Jordan, and the Gulf principalities from allying themselves with his country. In this he had the support of Prime Minister Amini, Foreign Minister Abbas Aram, Savak chief Pakravan, and to a certain extent also of the new chief of military intelligence, General Azizulla Kamal. Yet, even during as tense a time as this, it seems that the Shah did not intend to cut off his ties to Israel, and that he believed that Israel would prevail upon the U.S. to help him out of his troubles— in fact, he made use of Israeli leaders to pass aid requests to the American government. Ben-Gurion, who was about to travel to the U.S. to meet President Kennedy, sent the director of the Middle East division of the Foreign Ministry, Shmuel (Ziama) Divon, to meet the Iranian Prime Minister. Amini handed Divon a request for American economic and military aid and asked that Ben-Gurion raise the subject with the President. He promised Divon that, despite the need to keep the relations between their two countries quiet, Iran would not surrender to Arab pressures and would not loosen its ties with Israel.[29]

In parallel with this diplomatic attempt to sound out Iran's intentions, Military Attaché Nimrodi was told to meet with General Kamal and ask about the Shah's intentions. Kamal reassured Nimrodi and said that Kia's dismissal was an internal matter and that it would not affect policy toward Israel. At Herzog's invitation, Kamal paid a short visit to Israel in April 1961. He met with the Chief of Staff and other top officers, and discussed with them future cooperation between the two countries. As an expression of reciprocity, and in order to identify possible areas of cooperation, Herzog again proposed that Kamal send an Iranian military attaché to Israel. The Shah, however, was still not ready.

On July 4, 1961, Herzog arrived in Iran for another visit. In his seven days in the Iranian capital, he met with the Shah, the Prime Minister and his deputy, the Chief of Staff, and, of course, with General Kamal.

Herzog's audience with the Shah took place on July 9 at Saadabad Palace. The Shah opened with thanks to Herzog for the widening cooperation between the two countries, and expressed his appreciation of Ben-Gurion's attention to Iran's interests in his talks with President Kennedy. He complained, however, that the American Jewish community was not helping him lobby for American aid, and asked that Israel ask the Jewish lobby in Washington to work for greater American aid to Iran.

The Shah severely criticized President Kennedy and his government. He asked Herzog whether he could perhaps explain once and for all, what the Americans wanted of him. He said that they were really destroying him militarily. Iran was the central element of CENTO (the Central Treaty Organization), and while Iraq was then building its sixth division, Kennedy was refusing to supply him with arms, he complained.

Herzog expressed his opinion that Kennedy preferred to grant economic rather than military aid, and that this position should not be interpreted as anti-Iranian. The Shah was not satisfied with this explanation. In a philosophic voice the Shah noted that the truth was that he didn't know who was more right—Nehru and Nasser, who turned their backs on the Americans, or he, who remained loyal to them.

Herzog was impressed by the Shah, who gave him the impression of being an intelligent and cultivated man of great personal charm. Herzog nevertheless suspected that the Iranian monarch was indecisive and weak. He seemed to be oversensitive about the U.S., and saw every Israeli he met as a pipeline to President Kennedy.

Two weeks after his meeting with the Shah, Herzog returned to Tehran—this time in order to accompany Israel's Chief of Staff, Zvi Tzur, on his first visit to Tehran. This was the first visit to Iran by any commanding officer of the Israel Defense Forces, and it indicated the level of military cooperation between the two countries. Tzur met with the Shah and his Iranian counterpart, General Abd El-Hussein Hijazi, as well as with Prime Minister Amini and the service chiefs.

In his meeting with the Israeli Chief of Staff at the palace, on July 25, the Shah repeated his customary attack on the U.S., and it was obvious that he wanted Tzur to pass this message on to Washington. The Shah said that he still could not change the character of his relations with Israel. Iraq was unstable, Nasser continued his subversion, and the moderate Arab leaders did not want Iran to publicly acknowledge its diplomatic relations with Israel.

Tzur presented several proposals for wider cooperation between the two armies. But the Shah was reluctant. Tzur's impression was that the Shah feared that such wider cooperation could become a center of dissent within his army.

Tzur's visit to Tehran led to an increase in the flow of Iranian visitors to Israel and to an extension of the cooperation between the two countries. Since Tehran was, in the eyes of Israeli leaders, in the backyards of Syria and Iraq, they encouraged these visits without demanding any immediate compensation. Israel did not even insist on reciprocity; the Iranian visitors were a long-term investment, both politically and financially— air travel and lodging were all paid for by the Israeli government, and the Israeli military attaché's office in Tehran often paid even for passport fees and arranged the necessary permits from the palace. The Iranians continued to demand that all this be kept secret; relations were wide-ranging but most sensitive.

Nimrodi, however, did not stop at sending Iranian officers to Israel. He also took an interest in their families. Every Iranian officer who came was given a thorough medical examination at the Tel Hashomer Military Hospital; now they began bringing their wives along. Later on, the Shah's sister, Princess Ashraf, would also come for a checkup. The links between the two countries being secret, the medical help had to remain under cover also. This put heavy security demands on Israel. In one of his cables to Nimrodi, Herzog joked: "Give some thought to your commanding officer, and be more choosy about the Iranian women you send here for medical care. Despite the effort it demands, we do our best—we host them, look after them, pay for them, hospitalize them, nurse them, operate on them, and as custom demands we even give them presents. But please, a little more consideration."[30]

This cable says much about the contradictions between Iran's official policy and the personal behavior of its leaders. Despite the official desire to keep the relations with Israel under wraps, when it came to the health of the ruling class, even the Shah's family ignored his instructions and preferred advanced care in Israel over less up-to-date care in Iran.

In the fall of 1961 a series of developments in the Middle East demanded a meeting of the senior leaders of the two countries. On September 28, officers from the Syrian army organized the sixth coup in the country's history, dissolved the union with Egypt, and declared their country's independence. Jordan, Turkey, and Iran immediately recognized the reborn Syria, and the rest of the Arab countries followed suit. The coup ended the first attempt at voluntary union between sovereign Arab states and overturned the balance of power in the Arab world. Israel, Jordan, Iraq, Turkey, and Iran gained a weakened Syria on their borders in place of the strong UAR. Nasser lost his foothold in the Fertile Crescent, and Damascus became once again a theater of the battle for influence between Cairo and Baghdad.

These developments were the background to the short visit that Israeli Prime Minister David Ben-Gurion paid to Tehran on December 4, 1961.[31] This was the first visit by an Israeli head of government to Tehran, but not the last—Prime Ministers Levi Eshkol, Golda Meir, Yitzhak Rabin, and Menachem Begin would follow. Ben-Gurion was on his way to a state visit in Burma and, by prior arrangement it was announced that there had been a "malfunction" in his plane and that he had been "forced" to land in Tehran. He was received at the airport by Dr. Doriel, Meir Ezri, and Nimrodi, and was immediately whisked off to the airport's VIP lounge for a two-hour meeting with his Iranian counterpart, Ali Amini. Also present were Chief of Staff Hijazi and Savak chief Pakravan. Ben-Gurion was accompanied by his bureau chief, Yitzhak Navon.

Ben-Gurion and Amini surveyed Nasser's setback and his difficulties in the Arab world. Amini was obviously pleased with Nasser's troubles, and expressed his hope that Egypt would moderate its attempts to destabilize Iran. He reemphasized the great importance the Shah attached to good relations with Israel. Yet the religious community, he explained, headed by Ayatollah Ruhollah Khomeini, used these relations as a pretext for attacking the government, accusing it of having sold Iran to the U.S. and Israel. Amini emphasized that Ben-Gurion should be aware of these trends in Iran, and therefore of the Iranian government's need to keep its ties with Israel secret. The Shah expressed the belief there was no chance of reconciliation with Nasser, and that there was no point in even trying to reach any agreement with him.

Ben-Gurion was very pleased with his "forced landing" in Tehran. While he did not meet the Shah, he was convinced that Amini would not have met with him without the monarch's approval. On the other hand, Amini's report of the growing internal opposition to the Shah's rule was a matter of concern for the Israeli Prime Minister and led him to give more serious thought to the future of Israel's connections with Iran. These links had always been restricted to the Shah and his ministers and were thus dependent on the continuation of the current regime. Ben-Gurion was interested in examining whether Israel could broaden its base of support in Iran.

An attempt to do this was made in May 1962 by General Meir Amit, who had six months earlier succeeded Chaim Herzog as chief of military intelligence. Amit arrived in Tehran on April 28 and, during his ten-day visit there, met with the Prime Minister, the Chief of Staff, the chief of military intelligence, and other senior officers. He also held talks with the acting foreign minister and the minister of agriculture.

Amit's meeting with Amini came just before the Prime Minister set out on the pilgrimage to Mecca (the *haj*). Also present were Doriel, Ezri, and Nimrodi. At the beginning of the conversation Amini expressed his hope that Amit did not intend to bring up the subject of diplomatic relations between their countries. He related that the Saudi ambassador had pressed him to issue an anti-Israeli declaration before going to Mecca. He had rejected the suggestion, but certainly could not do the opposite and publicly encourage fostering relations with the Jewish state. When Amit noted that the relations between Israel and Iran were like those between a married man and his mistress, Amini joked, asking what was wrong with that, so long as both sides were happy? Ezri agreed, but rejoined, also in jest, that the drawback was there wouldn't be any children. Amini summed up the conversation by saying that it was best to concentrate on the quality of the relations and not on their formal structure. He asked that the Shah be given time to put his regime on a strong footing and prepare the public for full diplomatic relations between the two countries in the future.

Amit reported to Ben-Gurion and Golda Meir upon his return from Tehran on May 8, 1962. He recommended trying to establish contacts outside the narrow ruling circles. He mentioned that Israel was, by the nature of things, tied to various government institutions, but that these were not popular with the people. Israel needed to think about the future. Within a few years new forces would arise in Iran, forces with which Israel had had no contact. Amit advised trying to develop links with the universities and the press, and even with figures in the religious and liberal opposition. This would have to be done with care, of course, so as not to anger the Shah.

Amit's recommendations were the subject of a discussion among all the Israelis involved in its Iran policy. While there was broad agreement about the desirability of the policy he recommended, there were many difficulties in carrying it out. Israel's relations with Iran during the monarchy always remained limited to the Shah and his court.

After Amit's visit to Tehran in 1962, there were visits by Israel Aircraft Industries director Al Schwimmer and by the director of Military Industries, Zvi Dar. Schwimmer's visit was preceded by a huge effort to win a contract for overhauling Iran Air's piston engines. Thanks to his personal contacts, Nimrodi succeeded in obtaining from General Ali Khademi, director of Iran Air, permission for Israel to bid for the contract. Schwimmer submitted a low bid and won. Yet nothing happened. It took much lobbying with the minister of defense and the Chief of Staff to get them to approve the contract, which was finally signed on September 23, 1962.

Dar's visit was also successful, and laid the foundations for cooperation between the military industries of the two countries. The Iranians made it clear that they were interested not only in buying arms and military equipment, but also in actual industrial ties. Among other things, there was talk of manufacturing Uzi submachine guns in Iran, and it was agreed that an Israeli military industry delegation would visit Tehran in August 1962 to go over the details.

In preparation for this, Nimrodi met on July 30 with General Hijazi. The Iranian Chief of Staff was very old and was not well-acquainted with the complexities of the relations between Israel and its Arab neighbors. When Nimrodi once again suggested that Iran send a military attaché to Israel, Hijazi said that he intended to send an attaché to Damascus soon and that the same man could serve as attaché in Tel Aviv, too. Nimrodi, taken aback, delicately explained to the general that this was not a practical arrangement, since Israel was still at war with her Arab neighbors. Hijazi responded in disbelief: Hijazi replied that he knew, of course, that Israel had problems with Nasser. But after the dissolution of the UAR, he thought Israel could establish relations with Damascus. He asked about Israel's relations with Jordan and Lebanon. Hijazi was obviously disappointed when Nimrodi explained to him that Israel was still officially at war with all its Arab neighbors.

The conversation between Nimrodi and the Iranian Chief of Staff took place a short time after Prime Minister Amini's resignation and the appointment of Assadullah Alam to replace him. Alam, a Baluchi nobleman of great wealth and influence, had been a school friend of the Shah's. He was absolutely loyal to the Crown and was called to stand by the Shah whenever there was a crisis. His pleasant nature, his wide horizons, his cultured manners, his fluency in English and French, and especially his intimacy with the Shah were the source of his great popularity with the ruling elite. He was considered a friend of Israel, but like Amini opposed making the relations between the two countries public.

The Chief of Staff expressed his satisfaction at Amini's resignation. He claimed that Amini's approach to military and defense matters was determined by his education in economics; he had wanted to cut 15 percent off the army's budget. Like his sovereign, Hijazi was also critical of the U.S. He claimed that, were President Kennedy to enlarge the aid to Iran, there would be no need to cut the military budget. Since, however, the U.S. was stingy with its aid, what good came out of Iran's membership in CENTO and its declared friendship with America?[32]

A huge earthquake hit Iran in September 1962. Centered in the Qazvin region, it killed more than 14,000 people and completely destroyed 14 villages. Many countries, Israel among them, sent aid to the 20,000 families left homeless. Israeli Minister of Agriculture Moshe Dayan arrived on a quickly arranged official visit to Iran a few days later. Well-liked in Tehran for his victory over Nasser in 1956, Dayan was treated as a military hero and not a politician. In contrast with the visits of other ministers, Iran did not try to keep this one secret, and the Iranian press reported it at length. Accompanied by his Iranian counterpart, Arsanjani, Dayan set out in the royal train to the earthquake-damaged area—a privilege that no other Israeli personage had been granted. He promised his host that Israel would help reconstruct the Qazvin region.

Dayan's visit came a short time after a Yemenite military force commanded by Colonel Abdallah Sallal deposed the Yemenite monarch Imam El-Badr and declared a republic. Sallal immediately received military aid from Egypt. The Imam escaped to the mountains, gathered a fighting force and, with Saudi Arabia's help, tried to regain his throne. Nasser thought Yemen could replace his lost Syrian province, and he hoped to use it to rehabilitate his reputation. Iran saw the Yemenite coup as a clear threat to Saudi Arabia and the Gulf principalities and so Iran also sent aid to the deposed Imam. Israel was pleased to see Nasser caught up in Yemen, since it diverted him from making trouble in other Arab countries and reduced his efforts to subvert them. Dayan discussed this at length with the Shah, and they agreed that the events on the Arabian Penninsula required constant surveillance by Iran and Israel.

In December the Chiefs of Staff of the two countries met again in Tehran. Major General Tzur and Ministry of Defense Director-General Asher Ben-Natan toured the Far East and, on their way back from Rangoon to Israel, stopped off in Tehran for two days. Tzur and Ben-Natan met with Hijazi and the other members of the Iranian army's general staff, as well as with the commanders of the air force and navy and the heads of the military industry. Tzur complained to Hijazi that the military cooperation between the two countries was at a stand-still and that, despite Israel's efforts, there was only slow progress in other fields. While Iran's air force commander and the members of its general staff had all visited Israel, only the Israeli Chief of Staff and Chief of Military Intelligence had been allowed to visit Tehran. Israel was interested in immediate visits by its air force commander, Ezer Weizman, and its chief of operations, Chaim Bar-Lev. Tzur pointed out that Israel's military attaché in Ethiopia, Colonel Emmanuel Yardeni, had been given official recognition there, and he asked Hijazi why Nimrodi could not be given the same status in Iran.

As might have been expected, the Iranian Chief of Staff asked his Israeli guest to be patient. He explained the internal problems the regime faced, and the hostility of religious groups to both the Shah and to Israel. Under the circumstances, Iran could not move forward any more quickly.

Before returning to Israel, Tzur paid a courtesy visit to the Shah. The Iranian monarch asked the Israeli Chief of Staff to explain to Ben-Gurion how important it was that the American press stop its attacks on him and requested Israel's assistance in this matter.[33]

Then, at the beginning of 1963, a series of events demanded Israel's and Iran's attention. On February 8, a group of Iraqi army officers led by Colonel Abdul Salam Aref and supported by the Ba'ath party organized a coup in Baghdad. The Ministry of Defense, where Iraqi President Abdul El-Karim Qassem resided, was bombed from the air; Qassem himself was killed in this thirtieth attempt on his life. Colonel Nimrodi was the first to tell Iran's chief of military intelligence, General Kamal, of the coup and the end of Qassem's 55-month tyranny. A month later, on March 8, a Ba'athist group took over the Syrian government as well. The new regime in Damascus committed itself to cooperating with Aref and negotiations began over a triple federal union with Iraq and Egypt. The unification agreement was signed in Cairo on April 17 and roused great enthusiasm in the Arab world, along with much fear in Israel, Iran, and the pro-Western Arab states. The renewed recognition of Nasser's leadership put the remaining Arab kingdoms in danger. Riots again broke out in Jordan and the survival of the Jordanian monarchy was in danger. The concept of Arab unity, so seriously damaged by the dissolution of the United Arab Republic, now gathered new momentum, and gave ideological depth to the military strength accumulated on the banks of the Nile, the Tigris, and the Euphrates.

In the meantime, a public debate was raging inside Israel about the extent to which Nasser's intention to develop, with German help, his own medium-range ground-to-ground missiles endangered Israel. The dispute led Isser Harel, head of the Mossad, to submit his resignation on March 25, 1963. Ben-Gurion appointed General Meir Amit to replace him. Amit's deputy, General Aharon Yariv—who today heads the Jaffe Center for Strategic Studies at Tel Aviv University—was appointed chief of military intelligence and went to Tehran on April 5, 1963, to talk with senior Iranian officers about the significance of the recent developments in the Middle East. Nimrodi also proposed a meeting of foreign ministers, but the Shah rejected the idea.

At the height of Yariv's visit bloody riots broke out in Iran, presenting the Shah with a serious challenge to his regime. Religious leaders, who had been stung by the agrarian reform announced by the Shah the previous January, took advantage of Israel's involvement in the Qazvin region to stir up dissent. The Shah had confiscated much of the Muslim establishment's land properties, thus reducing its political influence. The antireform campaign was led by Ayatollah Khomeini, and it was accompanied by a wave of violence, incitement, and bitter clashes with the authorities. In a speech before thousands of demonstrators on April 11, Khomeini said: "The Shah attacks religion in accordance with Israel's instructions. The Shah announced his 'White Revolution' at Israel's instigation. But Israel will not save the Shah—only the Koran can save the country from the heretics. The Israelis are engaged in spying and sabotage in Iran. Why not say so out loud? All this leads us to ask whether the Shah himself is not Israeli, or even a Jew."[34]

During the following months Khomeini would take control of the religious establishment and turn it into a powerful tool in his struggle against the regime. In his speeches, Khomeini compared the Shah to Yazid Bin-Muawiya, the murderer of the Imam Hussein, the grandson of the prophet Mohammed and the founder of the Shiite sect.

In retrospect, it seems clear that the Shah did not properly appreciate the power of the religious establishment. In contrast with the clerics in Turkey and the Arab countries, the religious establishment in Iran never accepted the separation of church and state, and always searched for opportunities to restore the social status it had once enjoyed. Khomeini in particular called for a return to "clean and pure Islam." He preached rolling back the Westernization of Iranian society, called for a revocation of the "independence" of women, and vociferously opposed giving women the right to vote. As early as the beginning of the 1960s Khomeini called for the elimination of the monarchy and the establishment of an Islamic republic that would draw its authority from the Koran and from religious law. He sought the unification of the Moslem world, and claimed that the idea of the nation-state, as it was formulated in nineteenth-century Europe, was nothing more than an imperialist plot to divide the Islamic world.

The Shah decided to take strong measures against the religious establishment. Khomeini was arrested and sentenced to death. At the intervention of Savak chief Pakravan, however, the Shah was persuaded to commute the sentence and Khomeini was instead sent into exile. He first tried settling in Turkey, and then moved in 1964 to Najaf in Iraq. In October 1978 he left the Middle East for France, from where he returned to Tehran the following year.

Despite the dangers posed—to the Shah and to the region—by the Iranian religious forces hostile to Israel, Israel continued

to pressure the Iranian monarch to establish diplomatic relations between the two countries. Ben-Gurion, in the context
of the diplomatic initiative he undertook after the announcement of the triple union between Egypt, Syria, and Iraq, sent
personal letters to friendly leaders in Europe, Asia, Africa, and
the Americas.

In his letter to the Shah, delivered by special envoy on May
23, 1963, Ben-Gurion wrote that the geopolitical positions of
Israel and Iran had always forced them to cooperate diplomati-
cally and militarily against their enemies at home and abroad.
Ben-Gurion noted the cooperation that had developed between
Israel and Iran in the military, security, agriculture, and propaganda fields, and argued that the two countries could get more
out of this cooperation were it not for the Iranian leadership's
hesitancy and the opposition of the Iranian Foreign Ministry.
He emphasized that, so long as full relations did not exist
between the two countries, and so long as the cooperation
between them needed to remain shrouded in secrecy and
mystery, it would not be possible to enlist, either in Israel or
abroad, the people and institutions which would give this activity the momentum it needed.

Writing of the establishment of the union between Egypt,
Syria, and Iraq, Ben-Gurion wrote that the growth in Nasser's
prestige, daring, and power was liable to endanger vital interests
of Israel and Iran. He emphasized that the union was not an
additional threat, since Arab leaders had always been united
in their hatred of Israel. Nasser, however, was liable to be
tempted into adventures into less protected areas, such as
the Persian Gulf principalities, Kuwait, and the Khuzistan region
of Iran, just as he might be tempted to interfere with freedom
of navigation in the Suez Canal and the Shatt el-Arab, and so
to prevent the free passage of oil from Iran and Kuwait. Iran's
indecisive position with regard to Israel actually encouraged
the Egyptian dictator to continue his adventures. For this reason,
Ben-Gurion opined, only "active opposition" would force Nasser
to stay within his own borders and keep him from gaining
power and prestige throughout the Arab world.

Ben-Gurion noted in his letter to the Shah that Iran was
not the only country to which the Arab states had tried to
dictate policy regarding Israel. They had tried to do the same
with Ethiopia, Cyprus, and Greece, but all three of these coun-

tries had repelled this interference in their internal affairs. There was no reason why Iran could not take a similar position. The Israeli Prime Minister dismissed the argument that the opposition of religious leaders prevented establishing full diplomatic relations between the two countries. Ben-Gurion asked whether those same religious leaders opposed diplomatic relations between Iran and atheist communist states as well.

Finally, Ben-Gurion argued that cooperation between Israel and Iran would not only contain Nasser's expansionism, but would also encourage moderate Arab states to stand up to him.

The Shah read Ben-Gurion's letter with great interest, and told the Israeli envoy that he was ready to endorse every word in the letter. He claimed that if he himself had written the letter, he would not have worded it differently. The Shah called Nasser "an enemy" and noted that Nasser had adopted not only Soviet military doctrine, but also Soviet philosophy and propaganda techniques. A similar situation existed in Syria, and to a certain extent even in Iraq. For this reason, Iran feared active Soviet involvement in Egypt to protect Nasser's regime. The Shah meditated out loud whether it might not be logical for Turkey to act in Syria and Iran in Iraq in order to encourage those elements opposed to the Egyptian leader. The Shah asked Israel to use its influence in Washington to increase American military aid to Iran.

As for the question of diplomatic relations with Israel, the Shah said that he understood Ben-Gurion's approach, but that the religious opposition was real. The mullahs were exploiting his links with Israel in order to frustrate his development plans. In any case, since the triple union still needed to be confirmed in referendums to be held in September, the Shah suggested putting off any decision on the matter until then.

Ben-Gurion's letter to the Shah was his last as Prime Minister. An internal power struggle in his Mapai party led him to submit his resignation on June 16, 1963. Minister of Finance Levi Eshkol formed a new government in which Golda Meir continued to serve as foreign minister and Shimon Peres as deputy defense minister. While Eshkol tended to put all his trust in the U.S., rather than maintaining the balance between the U.S. and Europe that Ben-Gurion had maintained, the continuation of Meir and Peres in their posts ensured the continuity of policy toward Iran.

The best expression of this was the trip to Tehran of the members of Israel's National Defense College, led by General Uzi Narkiss, in May 1964. Summarizing the visit in a May 10 letter to Chief of Staff Yitzhak Rabin, Ambassador Doriel wrote: "This is not something to be taken for granted—an Israeli air force plane in the skies and airports of Iran; the appearance of Israeli officers in their uniforms; enthusiastic receptions at the General Staff Headquarters, military bases and camps, where the Israeli flag is raised; official ceremonies and enthusiastic speeches by senior officers in the Iranian army about the need to further relations in order to stand together against the enemy—Nasser; and most of all, the enthusiasm of the Jews of Isfahan and Shiraz when they saw an Israeli military plane and Israeli officers in uniform. The entire activity is the fruit of the labors of Colonel Ya'acov Nimrodi. The Iranian foreign ministry opposed the visit and tried to interfere with the ceremonies. Even King Hussein was enlisted to try to prevent the visit. But it happened nevertheless, and with great success. At the farewell dinner the Chief of Military Intelligence, General Kamal, declared in the presence of the Shah's adjutant that he intended to send an Iranian military attaché to Israel soon."[35]

The warming of relations was also influenced by the changes that occurred in Egypt's policies during the same period. Nikita Khrushchev visited Cairo in May, ending the period in which Nasser had tried to develop good relations with President Kennedy. Nasser believed Lyndon Johnson to be a "pro-Israeli president," so he returned to the embrace of the Soviet Union and helped it accomplish its goals in Africa and the Middle East. This Egyptian policy was even more evident after Leonid Brezhnev came to power on October 15, 1964. Brezhnev ordered increasing military aid to Egypt and soon Egypt's propaganda machine again turned against the U.S. and the pro-Western Arab states. As a part of this anti-Western policy, Egypt and Iraq announced on May 26 the establishment of a joint military command and the transfer of several Egyptian units to Baghdad. Even if this action was aimed principally at Syria, the Shah feared a joint Egyptian-Iraqi effort to detach the Arab-inhabited Khuzistan region from Iran. He also feared intensified Egyptian and Iraqi efforts to subvert the Saudi and Gulf regimes. Egypt also escalated its verbal attacks on Israel.

These developments were the focus of the Shah's visit to Washington on June 5, 1964. President Johnson praised his leadership and called him a "reformer" who was working to bring his country into the twentieth century. Johnson created a warm atmosphere for the Shah and gave him the feeling of being a loyal friend and desirable ally. This atmosphere was very different from the coolness that characterized the Shah's visit hosted by President Kennedy in 1962. People close to the Shah at the time told various Israeli officials that the Shah had truly hated Kennedy because of his stand on human rights and that he was not at all sorry when the President was assassinated.

The changes in the Middle East were the subject of a long letter that Prime Minister Eshkol sent the Shah on November 23, 1964. Eshkol expressed his opinion that a discussion of the problems of the region could not be separated from international developments. President Johnson's victory in the American elections, Labour's assumption of the reins of government in Britain, and the changes in the Soviet leadership all required most careful attention. Johnson's election, in particular, ensured continued American support for the independence and territorial integrity of the countries of the region. Eshkol added that, at his last meeting with President de Gaulle of France, he had heard similar support for the same principles. Britain also promised to act in pursuit of the same goals. Khrushchev's replacement with Brezhnev, however, would bring no immediate change in Soviet policy in the Middle East. The Israeli Prime Minister saw in these developments a rare opportunity to take concerted action and to conduct a joint policy that would strengthen peace and security in the region. He concluded his letter by saying that he had always believed that the security and welfare of Iran and Israel depend on the unity of their goals and actions, on a correct understanding of the problems they face, and on their willingness to consult and cooperate with each other in vital areas, to defend their joint interests.

After the Shah read the letter, he spoke with the Israeli envoy for 45 minutes. When the envoy noted Nasser's serious economic problems, and President Johnson's ability to use this to put pressure on Egypt, the Shah cut him off and commented that it was very strange that Iran evidenced a much harsher line against Nasser than Israel did. If it depended on the Israelis, they would have talked with Nasser already. The Iranians didn't think this was possible and argued that the man should be eliminated.

The Shah said that they should aspire to keep Nasser bogged down in Yemen. As for Iraq, it would be helpful if Aref were overthrown, but the question was who would replace him. Iran itself was not sitting with its arms crossed. He was about to set up an armored division equipped with Patton M-60 tanks, which had cost $200,000 each. Iran would also soon receive Hawk antiaircraft missiles. The armored division would be stationed in Khuzistan, where it could keep close watch on Iran's Arab minority.

The Shah rejected the envoy's hints that relations with Israel had cooled. He said that Iranian and Israeli interests were identical, and the Iranians were most appreciative of the cooperation with Israel and wished to continue it. But the Israelis had to take the Iranian situation into account. Furthermore, the Israelis had to convince their friends in the U.S. The Iranians had the impression that the Americans were not all that enthusiastic about the establishment of full diplomatic relations between Israel and Iran. Whenever Iran brought it up, the Americans answered that the time was still not ripe for it. If that was the opinion in Washington, why were the Israelis pressuring him?

At the end of 1964 a new factor was added to the cooperative worries of Israel and Iran. In the spirit of the decisions made at the first Arab summit conference in Cairo, the Palestine Liberation Organization was established in Jerusalem in May 1964 under the leadership of Ahmed Shukeiri. This expression of an independent Palestinian national identity renewed the unrest in Jordan and once again put King Hussein's regime in danger. The common concern was expressed in a conversation between Israel's deputy prime minister, Abba Eban, and the Iranian foreign minister, Abbas Aram. Eban came to Tehran on December 23, 1964. He argued that the developments in Jordan might lead to a new Middle East war. Aram agreed, and said that Iran opposed turning the Palestinian problem from one of refugees to one of national liberation. He shared Israeli worries about Jordan and proposed following the situation closely. Neither Eban nor Aram could then predict, however, the danger the PLO presented to Iran itself. It was not long before Iran began receiving information about cooperation between the Palestinian terrorist groups and the religious and left opposition in Tehran. Palestinian training camps were opened to the Shah's opponents, and this cooperation between the PLO and the Iranian opposition continued until the downfall of the monarchy and Khomeini's rise to power.

3

The Egyptian Connection

Khomeini's banishment had left the Iranian mullahs without a leader, but they nevertheless vigorously pursued their war against the Shah's agrarian reform and modernization campaign, threatening to murder anyone who took part in it. On January 21, 1965, religious extremists belonging to the Fedaiyan Islam terrorist group murdered the young Prime Minister, Hassan Ali Mansour, for his uncompromising support of the land reform.[1] The Shah accused the Savak of negligence in protecting Mansour's life. With discreet American encouragement, the Shah on January 30 dismissed General Pakravan as Savak chief and appointed him ambassador to Pakistan. The police chief of the previous ten years, Ne'ematullah Nassiri, was appointed to head the Savak, while one of the Shah's most faithful supporters, Amir Abbas Hoveida, was appointed Prime Minister.

Hoveida's government brought relative stability to the country, allowing the Shah to prepare for the power vacuum to be left by the evacuation of the British bases in Aden and the Gulf principalities. With support from the U.S., Iran and Saudi Arabia decided to fill the vacuum soon to be created. To help them do so, the U.S. supplied the Shah with 460 Patton M-60 tanks, to be used in setting up two new armored divisions. The U.S. also agreed to help out with a major expansion of the air force and navy.

In order to maintain U.S. support, the Shah decided to widen his cooperation with Israel beyond the areas of agricultural assistance and military training. In March 1965, over the objections of his foreign minister, the Shah allowed General Hassan Toufanian, vice minister of war for armament, to purchase a quantity of Uzi submachine guns for the police and Royal Guard. These were first seen in public in December of that year, when King Faisal of Saudi Arabia inspected an honor guard sporting the Israeli rifles at the beginning of a state visit to Iran.

On May 24, 1966, General Ezer Weizman came to Tehran, together with Captain Avihou Bin-Nun, now commander of Israel's air force. During his three-day visit to Iran, Weizman spoke with the Shah and the new Chief of Staff, General Bahram Ariana, as well as with the Iranian chief of operations and air force commander. He also flew to Isfahan in a Russian Iliyushin plane that Khrushchev had given to the Shah as a gift when the latter visited Moscow in 1965.

Weizman met with the Shah on May 25 for a 55-minute conversation. It centered on Iran's preparations for the British evacuation scheduled for 1968. The Shah expressed his fear that Nasser would move in after the British left and increase his attempts to overthrow the governments of the Persian Gulf region; he might even try to attack the oil fields. Hoping that Weizman would report on the conversation to Washington, the Shah hinted that, should the U.S. not be generous, he might buy Soviet weaponry—just as the Pakistani air force had bought Mig-19 planes manufactured in China. The Shah admitted that the Iranian air force would have trouble absorbing a Soviet aircraft, and he preferred American products, but that it all depended on how forthcoming the U.S. was with money. Weizman received the impression that this remark was one the Shah planted in their conversation in hopes of pressuring the U.S. to be more generous with his requests.[2]

Iran's interest in broadening its cooperation with Israel gained additional momentum from events in Syria and Iraq. On February 23, 1966, the "Young Turks" of the Syrian Ba'ath party had engineered a bloody coup in which they toppled President Amin El-Hafez; most of the elderly and moderate leaders of the party had been exiled or imprisoned. The new leadership, under Ba'ath Party Secretary General Salah Jedid, had cooperated with the Communists, turning Syria into the most pro-

Soviet state in the Middle East. The new regime in Damascus fiercely supported the Palestinian guerrilla groups, increasing the tension along the Israel-Syria border.

In Iraq, President Abdul Salam Aref had died in a plane crash on April 14 and his brother, Chief of Staff Abdul Rahman Aref, had succeeded him. The new President had turned out to be weak and lacking in authority and did not arouse much respect in Iran.

These events stood at the center of the talks between Israeli Prime Minister Levi Eshkol and his Iranian counterpart, Amir Abbas Hoveida, in Tehran on June 2, 1966.[3] Eshkol stopped off in Tehran on his way back from East Africa. The Shah was then in Morocco. Eshkol and two of his aides, Ya'akov Herzog (Chaim Herzog's brother) and Adi Jaffe, were taken by General Nassiri to a meeting with Hoveida in the VIP lounge of the Mehrabad Airport. It was the first meeting between the two Prime Ministers, and they spent two hours surveying the relations between their two countries and recent developments in the Middle East. Given Nasser's continued intervention in Yemen, and given Egypt's struggle against the pro-Western Arab monarchies, Eshkol and Hoveida decided to strengthen their ties in all fields. Hoveida, however, had a request: because of the unrest within Iran, the visit should be kept secret. The story nevertheless found its way into the Israeli and international press, angering the Shah and his men. In response they delayed several times the planned visit to Tehran of Foreign Minister Abba Eban. The visit finally took place toward the end of 1966, and only after special measures were taken to preserve its secrecy.

Eban left for Tehran in disguise. Israeli security men equipped him with a wig, a bushy moustache, and a thick coat of makeup. He was brought straight to the El Al plane without going through the normal checks, taking a first class seat without arousing any special interest. He thought the costume was a success. But immediately after takeoff, an American Jew approached him with great enthusiasm and said, "Mr. Ambassador, I enjoyed hearing your lecture in Tulsa, Oklahoma. It was really wonderful!" Israel thereafter decided not to endanger its relations with the Shah, and most later official visitors to Tehran traveled in special planes.[4]

The Shah's conversation with Eban lasted several hours. The

Iranian monarch expressed much satisfaction at Israel's and Iran's strong position in the region, and he did not hide his happiness at the defeat Kurdish rebels had recently inflicted on the Iraqi army. In an effort to create more problems for Nasser in Yemen, the Shah decided to help the royalist forces there by channeling aid through Saudi Arabia. The Shah also marveled at the defection of an Iraqi Mig-21 pilot, with his plane, to Israel. Finally, the Shah agreed that the foreign ministers of the two countries should meet at least once a year, and he also acceded to Eban's request to increase Iran's supply of oil to Israel.[5]

A short time afterward the Shah gave more concrete expression to his close relations with Israel. Despite heavy competition from Italy and Pakistan, on November 1, 1966, Nimrodi signed an agreement for overhauling 35 Iranian F-86 combat planes in Israel; the deal was valued at $3 million. Nimrodi also signed another $3 million contract, this one for supplying Iran with 120mm and 160mm heavy mortars made by Israel's Soltam company. The contracts were signed for the Iranians by General Toufanian, whose friendship with Israel was no longer a matter of doubt.[6]

Toufanian, today an exile in the U.S., was a unique personality; his biography is a microcosm of Iran's progress from its medieval traditions to the technological age. Born in a small village near Isfahan, the son of a large, religious family, the young Hassan was unsure after completing high school whether to enlist in the army or whether to become a teacher or merchant. He chose the military and became one of the first officers in the Iranian air force. At the height of World War II he was sent to a British flight school. Upon returning to Tehran, he became the Shah's personal flying instructor, paving his way to the pinnacle of power in his country. At the beginning of the 1960s, when Israel and Iran began cooperating in defense matters, Toufanian developed close personal ties with Ambassador Meir Ezri and with Ya'acov Nimrodi. Thanks to the sale to the Iranians of the Uzis, the mortars, and other arms—all through Toufanian's good agencies—Israel's military industries began to expand.

These transactions led to the first visit to Israel of the Iranian Chief of Staff, General Bahram Ariana, and of Toufanian himself. The two of them arrived in a special Iranian executive plane on November 20, 1966, and at Nimrodi's recommendation they were met with an impressive reception. Unlike his predecessor, who had been very close to King Hussein of Jordan, Ariana turned out to be a true friend of Israel who urged the Shah to increase cooperation with the Jewish state in a large number of areas. Unmarried and a graduate of France's Ecole de Guerre, he had a Ph.D. in Persian language and literature. His French was fluent and flowery and his English was reasonably good as well. His talks with Prime Minister Eshkol and Chief of Staff Rabin were most successful, and in their wake he persuaded the Shah to try to achieve peace between Israel and Jordan. To this end, in December 1966 the Shah sent a special envoy to Amman, who suggested a meeting in Tehran between Hussein and Eshkol. The envoy returned empty-handed. He said that the Jordanian King had been "astonished" by the Iranian offer to mediate, and claimed that "Israel cannot be believed; it has its eyes on the West Bank." Hussein also argued that, given the current situation in the Middle East, the time was not ripe for peace with Israel. It would be possible to discuss the matter afresh should that situation change.[7]

In his conversation with the Iranian Chief of Staff, Eshkol noted that Israel had good relations with the U.S., Britain, and France, but that "the friendship with Iran derives from the depths of the heart and is as such more valuable." Eshkol related that during his visit to Washington he had urged President Johnson to strengthen Iran militarily, and had been happy to hear that the U.S. afterward agreed to supply the Shah with 50 modern Phantom jets—while Israel's request for the same planes had not yet won a response. Eshkol thanked Iran for the mortar purchase, and promised to get them supplied as soon as possible.[8]

Nimrodi took Ariana and Toufanian on visits to military and aircraft industry plants, where they examined various types of weapons and asked about the possibility of producing Israeli 81mm mortars in Iran. They also observed the renovation and rearming of old Sherman tanks. At the end of the visit, Ariana invited Rabin to come to Tehran and expressed his hope that by then the Shan would grant Israel de jure recognition, so that Rabin could come in uniform.

Ariana's visit to Israel came at a time of growing tension between Israel and its Arab neighbors, and with Syria in particular. While Egypt was still embroiled in Yemen, exchanges of fire on the border with Syria became more frequent and serious. The large number of such incidents, and the fear of Israeli retaliation, led Egypt and Syria to sign a military alliance on November 4, 1966. With encouragement from the U.S.S.R., the two countries committed themselves to come to each other's aid, should there be a new war with Israel. In reaction, and on Rabin's recommendation, Israel lengthened mandatory military service from 24 to 30 months and reinforced its positions along its northern border. These precautions raised fears in Damascus and brought on Soviet accusations that Israel was deploying its army on the border in preparation for a new war. The tension reached its height when Syrian positions on the Golan Heights shelled Israeli fishing boats in the lake of Tiberias. In retaliation, the Israeli air force shot down six Syrian Mig-21 planes on April 7, 1967, following which the Israeli Mirages made a victory flight over Damascus.

The downing of the planes dealt a serious blow to Syria's military strength and to Nasser's prestige. It proved the absolute superiority of the Israeli air force. The pro-Western Arab states, and Jordan in particular, ridiculed the Egypt-Syria defense pact. The Middle East began moving toward a new war.

Amid this heightened tension, the Israeli Chief of Staff Yitzhak Rabin, paid an official visit to Tehran. Rabin, his wife, Leah, and his bureau chief, Colonel Rafael Efrat, left for Iran on a special plane on Friday afternoon, April 14. They were received at Mehrabad Airport by General Ariana and Ya'acov Nimrodi. During his six days in Iran, Rabin met the Shah, the Prime Minister, and the foreign minister and, in addition to his talks with Ariana, toured Persepolis, Shiraz, and Isfahan. Despite the friendly atmosphere, the Shah did not have the courage to give public expression to his intimacy with Israel.

This was especially evident in the reception Rabin received in Tehran. The Israeli Chief of Staff inspected an honor guard from a moving automobile; during his visits to Iranian army bases he wore civilian clothes. Rabin visited the splendid Tehran Mausoleum with its carpet-lined marble halls, and laid a wreath of white flowers on the tomb of Reza Shah, the current Shah's father. Rabin surprised his hosts by signing his name in Hebrew in the guest book, the only time any visiting Israeli had done so.

Rabin's audience with the Shah came on April 16 in his new marble palace. The Shah asked how the downing of the planes on April 7 had affected the governments of Syria and Egypt. He said he would like to see the Ba'athist regime in Syria replaced, and that this would certainly happen eventually without any outside help. Nasser, however, would not fall of his own accord, and the Shah considered Nasser his major enemy, a threat to the stability of the Arabian Peninsula and the Persian Gulf. The Iranian monarch acknowledged that he had been slow in understanding the danger Nasser presented. His great admiration of King Hussein of Jordan was evident. He said that he pitied Hussein and that he was in a difficult position. The Shah asked Israel not to harm the Jordanian king and revealed that Hussein had finally decided to throw down the gauntlet and fight back against the PLO and its chief, Ahmed Shukeiri, whom the Shah called a very dangerous man.

In his response, Rabin analyzed the situation on Israel's borders and explained the causes of the tension with Syria. He explained that the new military leadership in Damascus, including the minister of defense and air force commander, General Hafez Assad, and Chief of Staff General Ahmed Sweidany, had built fortifications on the Golan Heights and had concentrated large forces in that area. Rabin nevertheless did not believe that there would be war. Nasser was busy in Yemen, and it was doubtful whether Syria would dare attack Israel on its own. The Israeli Chief of Staff focused on the triangle of hostility made up of Egypt, Syria, and Iraq. He explained that if Iran and Israel could contain Nasser, the Syrian threat would be reduced and Iraq would also be forced to halt its subversive activities in the Arabian Peninsula.

A few weeks after Rabin returned to Israel, a string of events took place that ended in a complete revision of the balance of power in the region and diverted attention from the Persian Gulf. On May 15, after a series of clashes along the Israel-Syria armistice line, Egypt concentrated military forces along its border with Israel and ordered the UN emergency force in the Sinai to leave. On May 23, Nasser anounced that he was blockading the Tiran Straits, cutting off all shipping to Israel's southern port of Eilat. Fearing that Israel would see this as a casus belli (an occasion of war), Nasser evacuated his forces from Yemen and stationed some of them in the Sinai. At the end of May, King Hussein joined the joint Egypt-Syria military command, and Iraq also made preparations to join the war. Iraq's President, General Abdul Rahman Aref, on June 2 sent his deputy chief of staff to meet the leader of the Iraqi Kurdish rebels, Mulla Mustafa Barazani, and asked him to demonstrate his solidarity with the Arabs by sending a symbolic force to fight Israel. Barazani rejected the proposal, and advised Iraq to convince Nasser to take his forces out of Sinai and reopen the Tiran Straits. He warned the Iraqi officer that if Nasser did not do so, the Arabs would be soundly defeated by Israel.

The war broke out on June 5, 1967, and within six days the map of the Middle East had changed. The Israel Defense Forces' resounding victory over Egypt, Syria, Jordan, and Iraq amazed the world and put the Shah in a most difficult situation. The Shah was in Paris when the war broke out; the Tehran press was very hostile to Israel and members of the government refrained from voicing their opinions in public. In the army, however, the opposite was true. Chief of Staff Ariana sent Nimrodi an elaborate wreath of flowers with the dedication: "To the brave, strong, and invincible IDF" (Israeli Defense Forces). His deputy, General Feridoun Jam, sent a telegram congratulating Yitzhak Rabin on his great victory.[9]

On his way back from Paris the Shah stopped off in Ankara and spoke with Turkish leaders about the meaning of the Israeli victory. Answering reporters' questions, the Shah said that the time of conquest and annexation had passed, and that Israel had to withdraw immediately from all the territories it had captured, including Jerusalem. The Shah's position surprised Israel. Having destroyed Nasser's army, Israeli officials believed that the Shah would actually want to work more closely together with them and might even establish normal diplomatic relations. Just the opposite happened. The Shah froze his joint projects with Israel and his public statements became more hostile. What especially bothered the Shah was the defeat of Hussein and the reunification of Jerusalem, holy also to Moslems, under Israeli sovereignty.

The Shah met with Hussein in Tehran before his August trip to the U.S. Speaking in the name of all the Arab countries, Hussein asked the Shah to use his influence in Washington to get the U.S. to pressure Israel to retreat from the territories it had occupied. In his meetings with the Shah, President John-son categorically rejected the idea of pressures. He said that, unlike in the past, the U.S. now had no intention of putting pressure on Israel, and intended to link withdrawal from the territories with peace. The Shah was made aware during his visit of the great regard the American people had for Israel, and, in particular, of the American determination not to allow the Soviets to rob Israel of what it had gained in the war.

When he returned to Tehran the Shah told King Hussein that the time had come for the Arab countries to accept Israel's existence and to negotiate for peace directly. The Shah approved the purchase of another 6,000 Uzi submachine guns, signaling to his aides that cooperation with Israel should be renewed. This new position had practical repercussions for Iran's supply of oil to Israel. After the war Israel began exploiting the oil wells in the Sinai, thus reducing its dependence on outside sources and hence its vulnerability to pressures from its Arab neighbors. On the other hand, Israel had to consider the possibility of a withdrawal from the Sinai, so it had to ensure the continued supply of oil from Iran.

The Shah had similar considerations in mind. During the years before the war, Iran began marketing oil on its own—to Israel, Japan, Argentina, Romania, and Yugoslavia. As long as the Suez Canal was open, Iran had no special problems in this regard. The blockage of the canal made it almost impossible for Iran to get its oil out. This situation gave rise to an imaginative idea in Jerusalem—that Israel itself serve as an oil route instead of the Suez Canal. A new, 32-inch pipeline could make it possible to pump oil from Eilat to Ashkelon, from where it could be loaded on tankers for Europe. Golda Meir had already brought up such an idea in her 1965 conversation with the Shah, but the Iranian government had rejected it then. Now conditions were different. Prime Minister Levi Eshkol held a long consultation in his office. He believed that, since Iran now had its own economic reasons for adopting such a shipping route, there was a chance it would agree. Minister of finance, Pinhas Sapir, was assigned to clarify the Shah's position.

On September 12, Sapir, accompanied by Ambassador Meir Ezri, met the Shah in Tehran. Sapir explained that, in the space of ten years, the Suez Canal had been closed twice. All the signs were that the Suez Canal would now remain closed for a long time, and that a new way of transporting oil had to be found. Israel was offering its territory. A 32-inch pipeline, at a cost of $110 million, could pump oil from Eilat to Ashkelon, from where it could be shipped by tanker to Europe. The cash investment would not need to be more than $15 million, with the rest coming in the form of loans from foreign banks. The U.S. supported the idea, and the British Prime Minister had sent a special envoy to Israel to discuss the matter.

The Shah agreed with Sapir that construction of the new pipeline now made economic sense, and that the Israeli proposal was farsighted and imaginative. He himself supported the idea and, despite the opposition of the National Iranian Oil Company, he was willing to reconsider the matter. He asked for a few days to make a decision. He also had to take into account, he noted, the reaction of the Arab world and of the international oil companies. The Shah asked Sapir to meet with the chairman of the National Iranian Oil Company, Dr. Manucher Eqbal, to work out a detailed proposal. Sapir asked the Shah what he could tell Prime Minister Eshkol. The Shah answered that he should tell him the subject was very important, and that he personally supported it and would try to get him a positive answer.

The following days would make it clear that the Shah's foreign minister, Ardeshir Zahedi, and his interior minister, Jamshid Amouzegar, both had reservations about the pipeline, fearing the negative reactions of the Arab countries. On the other hand, the three most powerful men around the Shah supported the project—the lord chamberlain, Assadullah Alam; the Prime Minister, Amir Abbas Hoveida; and the chairman of the National Iranian Oil Company, Manucher Eqbal. The Shah gave a positive answer. To lay the pipeline the two countries created a Canadian-registered firm, the Trans-Asiatic Oil Company, with branches in Tel Aviv and Tehran. The company was headed by Dov Ben-Dror, formerly Israel's economic attaché in France, and it bought from the Rothschild Group its share in the existing Eilat-Beersheba pipeline. Work on the new pipeline began in June 1968, and was completed in December 1969.

Its completion came at the height of the War of Attrition along the Suez Canal, and it seemed as if there would be a delay in operating it. But in February 1970 Iran overcame its hesitation and sent 10 million tons through the pipeline that month. In July 1971 Israel announced its intention of gradually increasing the quantity of oil pumped through the pipeline to 45 million tons per year. The Iranian navy regularly protected the tankers in the Persian Gulf up to the Strait of Hormuz, while the Israeli navy, working out of its Sharm El-Sheikh base, could defend passage through the Tiran Straits.

The oil supply from Iran seemed fairly secure, and the Shah no longer feared the reactions of the Arab countries. In answer to a reporter's questions, the Shah said: "When the tankers leave Iranian ports, we are unaware of their final destination. Tankers change direction in mid-journey in accordance with orders from their owners. Who can swear that Arab oil does not reach Israel?"[10]

The unrest within Iran continued, while incitements by religious groups against Israel and against Iranian Jews increased. In September 1968, the slogans "Heil Hitler" and "Israel out" were painted on Nimrodi's car. The most severe anti-Israel outburst came, however, during a soccer match in Tehran. Despite the opposition of the Iranian foreign minister, Israel took part in the Asian soccer tournament held that year in the Iranian capital. The contest turned into an ugly anti-Israel demonstration. Balloons blazoned with swastikas were released over the stadium, and the crowd raised an effigy of Moshe Dayan, spitting on and beating it. The Shah was stunned by the intensity of the anti-Israel sentiments, and looked for ways to restore calm.

A series of Iranian national interests and considerations nevertheless forced the Shah, in the spring of 1969, to embark on a more aggressive policy in the Persian Gulf region and increase his cooperation with Israel. In accordance with an old treaty that Iraq had inherited from the Ottoman Empire, President Aref forced Iran into accepting Iraqi control of the entire Shatt al-Arab waterway, not only half, as international law stipulated. As a result, Iranian ships that sailed down the river to the refineries at Abadan and Khorramshahr had to raise the Iraqi flag, allow Iraqi navigators on board, and pay Iraq a passage fee. The Shah decided to put an end to this, and in April 1969 he tried to assert his rights by force, but the Iraqis quelled the attempt.

It was a severe blow to the Shah's prestige. On May 3 he

fired his elderly Chief of Staff, General Bahram Ariana, appointing in his place his deputy, General Feridoun Jam—one of the best-liked officers in the army and the idol of the middle- and lower-ranking officers. Jam, born in 1913, was the son of a former Prime Minister, and a graduate of Oxford and of France's staff and command academy. In 1937 he married the Shah's elder sister, Princess Shams, but they divorced four years later. Normally, the royal divorce would have ended his military career. But his excellence, and his popularity in the U.S. and Western Europe, led him to the pinnacle of the Iranian army nevertheless. Jam visited Israel in October 1965, the guest of Israel's chief of operations. General Chaim Bar-Lev. Now both of them had acceded to the post of Chief of Staff, and Bar-Lev was among the first to congratulate him on his new appointment.

The new Iranian army chief repeated his predecessor's attempt to assert Iran's rights in the Shatt al-Arab, but with much more success. Accompanied by warships and protected by fighter planes, Iranian vessels passed down the river with neither Iraqi flags nor navigators. Iraq reacted furiously. Radio Baghdad characterized Jam as a Zionist, and accused the Shah of appointing his new Chief of Staff at the instigation of Israel. Iraq also accused Jam of hating Arabs and being anti-Islam. Yet despite these verbal attacks, Iraq was not able to change the new facts that Iran had created along their border.

Encouraged by their success, the Shah and the Chief of Staff decided to expand military cooperation with Israel and teach their officers the lessons Israel had learned in its wars. This involved, among other things, sending Iranian pilots, paratroopers, and artillerymen for training in Israel.[11]

This change of atmosphere was also expressed in public statements of the Iranian government. In a June 3, 1969, interview with the *Financial Times*, for instance, the Shah said that he recognized Israel's right to exist, and that his relations with the Jewish state were improving in many areas. The British newspaper termed the wide range of links between the two countries an "alliance" and the "Tehran-Jerusalem axis." In another interview with the *Washington Post*, on June 8, 1969, the Shah declared that "Iran opposes in principle the annexation of territories by force. But Israel is an established fact, and the Arab countries must recognize it and grant it secure borders." The Shah also argued that human society would soon be based on science and technology, "and Israel is strong in both those fields."

In October 1969, however, the Shah met an Egyptian leader he liked. In the wake of an arson attempt on Jerusalem's al-Aksa Mosque, a summit of Moslem nations was held in Rabat, and the Shah attended. Nasser suffered a heart attack on the eve of the summit, so his vice president, Anwar Sadat, represented Egypt.

During the course of the summit meeting, Sadat found a way to open the door to improved Iranian-Egyptian relations. The gathered heads of state called on Iran to cut off its relations with Israel, and accused the Jewish "heretic state" of desecrating the Islamic holy places in Jerusalem. The Shah rejected these resolutions and called on the Arab countries to make "realistic decisions," and not to delude themselves into thinking they could defeat Israel. King Hassan of Morocco, who as host also presided over the conference, gave the floor to Anwar Sadat. The Egyptian vice president called the Shah's words "lukewarm," and called on the summit to address the incident of the burning of the mosque with more seriousness. But, in speaking directly to the Shah, Sadat took a conciliatory line. He recited a poem by a noted Iranian poet preaching brotherhood among men and nations. The Shah marveled at Sadat's excellent Persian accent, and applauded him enthusiastically. This gesture considerably improved the atmosphere between these two men, and it would in the future be seen as the beginning of the thaw in Egypt-Iran relations, leading in the end to full reconciliation.[12]

It was against the background of the conflict with Israel that this reconciliation began, and which was completed after Egypt's turnabout in its relations with the two great powers. During a sudden visit to Moscow in the summer of 1970, Nasser realized that the Soviet Union was not willing to involve itself more deeply in the War of Attrition that Egypt was conducting with Israel along the Suez Canal. Therefore, Nasser accepted a U.S. proposal "to stop shooting and start talking," and on August 7 he agreed to a cease-fire with Israel. A senior Iranian diplomat, Amir Mahmoud Ispendiari, arrived in Egypt on August 23. After meeting the Egyptian foreign minister, Mahmoud Riad, Egypt and Iran announced that they were reestablishing diplomatic relations. Nasser's death on September 30 and Anwar Sadat's accession to the presidency injected more momentum into the efforts of Saudi Arabia and Jordan to bring about a significant improvement in Cairo-Tehran relations.

In Jerusalem, of course, worries grew that the Shah's new friendliness with Egypt would lead him to weaken his ties with Israel. Israel's defense minister, Moshe Dayan, had at that time proposed a partial Israeli withdrawal along the Suez Canal front. The Shah and Sadat responded favorably. Sadat believed that the industrial powers' continued dependence on Middle Eastern oil created mutual dependence between Egypt on the one hand and Iran and the Persian Gulf principalities on the other. Iran needed the Suez Canal, to ship its oil. Egypt, as the country which controlled the two ends of the Suez Canal, was the cheapest and shortest oil route. By reopening the canal to free navigation, it could regain its strategic importance and weaken the Israel-Iran alliance. In addition to the possibility of reopening the international waterway, Sadat hoped to receive Iranian funding for an oil pipeline from Suez to Alexandria that would serve as a sort of "reinforcement" of the passage of oil tankers through the canal, and that might render the Eilat-Ashkelon pipeline redundant. Fearing such a possibility, Prime Minister Golda Meir's government in the end rejected Dayan's proposal.

Not many days passed and the U.S. and Israel realized that the reversal in Egypt's position was much more significant: Sadat was about to repudiate his alliance with the Soviet Union, and with the help of Iran and Saudi Arabia began getting closer to Washington.

In October 1971, the slow revolution in Egypt's position began revealing itself in the relations between Iran and Israel. In an effort to discover the depth of Soviet commitment to Egypt's security, President Sadat on October 11 set out for talks with Kremlin leaders in Moscow. The visit was a deep disappointment for Sadat. On his way back to Cairo Sadat stopped off in Tehran airport for a three-hour conversation with the Shah. This was the first visit of an Egyptian President in Iran since relations had been reestablished, and it laid the first foundations of a new Middle East axis based on Iran, Egypt, and Saudi Arabia— replacing the Shah's alliance with Israel.

Since, however, matters were still at an initial stage, the Shah and Sadat were careful not to reveal their intentions publicly. In April 1972, a month before the planned Nixon-Brezhnev superpower summit. Sadat went for his fourth and last presidential visit to Moscow. Brezhnev refused to supply Egypt with Mig-23 planes and Scud middle-range ground-to-ground missiles, and Sadat cut his visit short by a day. Brezhnev did not even come to the airport to bid him farewell. In contrast to this humiliation of the Egyptian leader, Syria and Iraq were winning preferential treatment from the Soviets. That same month the Soviet deputy defense minister and the Chief of Staff went to Syria for talks with President Hafez Assad and promised him that, despite détente, Soviet aid to his country would continue. Alexei Kosygin went to Baghdad and signed a "treaty of friendship and cooperation" with Iraq, a treaty that made clear Soviet ambitions in the Persian Gulf and Indian Ocean regions. The U.S., Saudi Arabia, and Iran saw in the treaty a threat to their oil resources and shipping lanes, and they now redoubled their efforts to enlist Egypt in blocking Soviet expansion toward the Persian Gulf.

These developments were at the center of the talks between Golda Meir and the Shah in May 1972, during Meir's first visit to Tehran as Prime Minister. She arrived in a special plane, accompanied by her adviser Simcha Dinitz and her administrative assistant Eli Mizrahi. In accordance with now-routine practice, Meir's plane landed late at night on an out-of-the-way runway at Mehrabad Airport.

In a conversation lasting several hours in the Niavaran Palace, the Shah reported at length to the Israeli Prime Minister on his contacts with Sadat, and urged her to take a more moderate stance with Egypt. He explained that, despite the détente between the superpowers, the U.S. and the Soviet Union continued to compete in the Persian Gulf region, with each of them trying to prevent the other from gaining any strategic advantage. For this reason, now that the Soviets had made a gain in Iraq, it was important to try to detach Sadat from the Soviet camp and bring him over to the Americans. The Shah believed Sadat's assertion that he wanted to find a political solution to the conflict with Israel, and he complained that Israel did not understand the changes taking place in the Middle East nor Iran's priorities. At no point, however, did the Shah threaten to take, or even hint at taking, any measures against Israel should it not moderate its position on Egypt. "After renewing relations with Egypt, the Shah is no longer what he was," Meir told her aides at the end of the meeting.[13]

The Nixon-Brezhnev summit in Moscow in May 1972 was a grave disappointment to Sadat, and strengthened his resolve to end his alliance with the Soviet Union and join the pro-Western bloc in the Middle East. As part of their new détente, Nixon and Brezhnev decided to freeze all existing conflicts and refrain from intervening in regional disputes liable to erupt into new wars. This was a death blow to the Egyptian President's hopes that the superpowers would try to impose a solution in the Middle East. Two months later, in July 1972, Sadat expelled all the Soviet technical advisers from his country.

The reversal in Egypt's policy prodded the Shah to create a new "Iranian Triangle," uniting Iran with Egypt and Saudi Arabia, and with the backing of Jordan, Morocco, and Sudan. In time, Israel could also become part of this regional alliance. But this new alliance also subjected the Shah to greater pressures from Arab countries with regard to Israel. Egypt, Saudi Arabia, and Jordan applied varying amounts of pressure on the Shah to induce him to stop supplying oil to Israel, and to use his influence in Washington to force Israel to moderate its stance against the Arab world. The Shah was still not willing to use oil as a means of pressuring Israel, but since the success of his new triangle depended on a solution of the Israel-Arab dispute, he tried to persuade the U.S. to pressure Israel. This was apparent during a visit the Shah made to Washington in July 1973. In a conversation at the White House with President Nixon on July 25, the Shah argued that the continued conflict in the Middle East was liable to threaten the peace and stability of the Persian Gulf region. The Shah asked Nixon and his national security advisor, Dr. Henry Kissinger, to conduct a "more evenhanded policy" between Israel and its Arab neighbors.[14] In talks with various American officials, the Shah argued that a balanced Middle East policy would pave the way for a new regional framework that would include the largest Arab state, Egypt; the wealthiest Moslem states, Saudi Arabia and Iraq; and the most militarily daring state, Israel. Such a combination could work wonders in the Middle East.

The Nixon administration agreed with the Shah's analysis, but asked to delay any American activity until after the elections to the Israeli Knesset in November 1973. The administration believed that, for internal political considerations, Golda Meir could not make significant concessions to Egypt before the elections.[15]

After returning to Tehran, the Shah reported to Israel and Egypt on his talks in Washington. Sadat's attention, however, had been diverted for the time being from new regional alliances. Egypt and Syria had already begun their countdown toward the Yom Kippur War of October 1973.

The Shah at the Center

The Arab successes of the Yom Kippur War, in particular Egypt's success in crossing the Suez Canal, astonished the Tehran regime and set off waves of pro-Egyptian enthusiasm among the Iranian populace. The surprise attack, and the fact that the Israelis did not succeed in pushing the Egyptian army back over the canal, damaged Israel's reputation and seriously eroded its position in the Middle East. Hostility to Israel previously repressed now suddenly burst out, and the local media were full of descriptions of the Arab "victory." There were spontaneous demonstrations in several cities, encouraged by the religious leadership. This reaction of the Iranian people put huge pressure on the Shah, and he had to tread carefully and keep his distance from a country that his subjects obviously considered an enemy.

While the battles were still in progress the Shah tried to maintain some balance in his relations with the belligerents. He rejected demands to close the Israeli mission in Tehran, and despite the Arab embargo on oil shipments to Europe and the U.S., Iran continued to supply oil to Israel. On the other hand, the Shah also brushed off American inquiries about whether he could send Phantom planes to Israel to replace those lost during the first days of the war. The suddenness

81

with which the war broke out left Israel worried about its store of weapons and equipment. After the failure of the Israeli counterattack along the Suez Canal on October 8, it was clear that this war would last longer than its predecessor had. In light of this, the Shah acceded to an Israeli request to return a quantity of artillery shells and electronic equipment Iran had purchased. This, however, did not meet all of Israel's needs. It was Senator Henry Jackson who suggested to Secretary of Defense James Schlesinger that he look into the possibility of sending Israel American tanks from Turkey and Phantom jets from Iran. But, fearing that it would destroy its efforts to improve relations with the Arab world, the Iranian government rejected the proposal.

Moreover, in contrast to his neutrality in the Six Day War, the Shah now took several steps that helped the Arabs claim that Iran was on their side. Oil still went to Israel, but 600,000 tons to Egypt as well—at a time that Libya was refusing to sell to its neighbor. Iranian transport planes brought a Saudi infantry battalion and military equipment to the Golan Heights, and took wounded Syrian soldiers to be treated in Tehran. The Shah also allowed the Soviet airlift to fly through Iranian airspace on its way to Syria and Iraq, while refusing the same concession to Jewish volunteers on their way from Australia to Israel.

This policy produced some immediate gains for the Shah. While he had reestablished diplomatic relations with Egypt and Syria before the war, he was now able to do the same with Iraq and Sudan. His major interest, however, was in Egypt. The separation of forces agreement compelled the Israeli army to withdraw from the western bank of the Suez Canal, while the Egyptian army continued to hold the bridgehead it had established on the east bank. This allowed President Sadat to begin dredging the waterway and preparing it for international shipping. At the end of a visit to Tehran by Egyptian Prime Minister Abdul Aziz Hijazi in May 1974, Iran granted Egypt a billion-dollar loan to widen the canal, rebuild the city of Port Said, and lay a pipeline from Suez to Alexandria. The cleaning of the canal and the laying of the new pipeline immediately reduced the importance of the Eilat-Ashkelon pipeline. The National Iranian Oil Company no longer needed the Israeli route to export its oil to Europe, and began looking for ways to limit its use of the Israeli pipeline. The late Levi Eshkol's fears of such a turn of events were now shown to be justified, and it was necessary to put much pressure on the Shah in order to convince him to continue the existing arrangements.

The change in the strategic positions of Israel and Egypt, which had begun even before the war, forced Israel to reexamine its assumptions and relations with Iran in light of the new situation. As part of this reevaluation, Golda Meir approved the recommendation of her foreign minister, Abba Eban, and appointed Ambassador Uri Lubrani to head the Israeli mission in Iran in place of Meir Ezri, who had served 12 years in the job.

Lubrani, who had been Prime Minister David Ben-Gurion's adviser on Arab affairs and Levi Eshkol's bureau chief, had visited Iran before and had served as ambassador to Uganda and to Ethiopia. He made his second visit to Tehran in the summer of 1972, when he looked into ways of increasing Israeli exports to Iran.

The Israeli government tried to take advantage of the change in ambassadors to make changes in protocol as well, changes that would advance Israel's diplomatic position in Iran. Since Iran did not recognize Israel de jure, the Israeli representatives had not in the past presented their credentials to the Shah. Lubrani, however, was supplied with a regular letter of credentials signed by the President of Israel, and addressed to the Shah. He was also given a personal letter from Eban to his Iranian counterpart, Abbas Ali Khalatbari. The minute, however, that Lubrani landed in Mehrabad Airport, he knew that Jerusalem's hopes had been exaggerated. No one from the Iranian Foreign Ministry had come to greet him, as custom demanded. His first meeting with the Iranian protocol chief was uncomfortable and he began to fear that there would be regular problems. He was quickly proven correct.

A few days after coming to Tehran, Lubrani went to meet the Iranian foreign minister, to whom he presented Eban's letter.[1] Khalatbari was a veteran and experienced diplomat with a liberal French education and European manners. In contrast with his predecessor, Ardeshir Zahedi, who had been hostile to Israel, Khalatbari possessed the kind of delicacy that made it clear that, even as he expressed his adherence to the Shah's policies, he himself had feelings of friendship for Israel. Lubrani asked Khalatbari to arrange a meeting with the Shah, so that he could "bring him greetings from the government of Israel." Here the new ambassador encountered a phenomenon he would face during all of his five years of service in Tehran—Persians never say no. Khalatbari told him that he saw no reason why he should not see the Shah and promised to arrange the audience "as soon as possible." Lubrani left pleased and hopeful that diplomatic relations would soon be normalized. Two weeks later, when the Iranian reply had still not come, Lubrani reminded Khalatbari of his promise. He was told that there was still no answer. When three weeks had passed he raised the subject again, but Khalatbari responded that he was "working hard" on the matter and that the Israeli representative had to be patient. When a few more days passed and there was still no answer, it was clear that, for the time being at least, the Shah was not interested in meeting an Israeli representative and that his credentials would remain filed away in the embassy as silent testimony to the complexity of Israel-Iran relations.

In June 1974, Israel and Syria signed an agreement to separate their forces on the Golan Heights. According to its terms, the two countries returned to the previous cease-fire lines, ending the first stage of Henry Kissinger's efforts to find a peaceful solution to the Israel-Arab conflict. The agreement signed, Golda Meir resigned and her government was reconstituted by Yitzhak Rabin, with Yigal Allon as deputy prime minister and foreign minister and Shimon Peres as defense minister.

The new Israeli government adopted a strategy of trying to win incremental concessions from Egypt and Syria in exchange for incremental withdrawals from the territories it occupied, an approach it called "a piece of land for a piece of peace." Rabin explained the concept to President Gerald Ford and Secretary of State Kissinger in Washington in September 1974. In November, as part of the effort to maintain good relations with Iran, Rabin presented it to the Shah in Tehran. His trip was a secret one; in Israel, only the foreign and defense ministers knew of it in advance. In order to disguise his absence from the country, Rabin left in a special plane on Friday afternoon, after business hours, and returned on Saturday close to midnight. His military secretary, Brigadier General Ephraim Poran, and his bureau chief, Eli Mizrahi, accompanied him. Their plane landed in Tehran at the height of a blizzard during which the roof of the airport terminal had caved in. Lubrani and Savak chief Ne'ematullah Nassiri were there to greet them.[2]

On Saturday at 11:00 A.M., the Shah and Rabin met for two hours and exchanged analyses of the international situation, developments in the Middle East, and the positions of Israel and Iran in the region. Rabin reported to the Shah on his visit to the U.S. and spoke about the possibilities of achieving an additional interim agreement in the Sinai. He was more pessimistic about the possibilities for progress with Jordan and Syria. The Shah urged Rabin to display more flexibility to Sadat and Hussein, and said that he believed these two leaders did indeed want peace with Israel.

The Israeli Prime Minister's visit to Tehran also dealt with bilateral matters. Rabin asked the Shah for a billion-dollar loan, like the one he had given Egypt, in order to finance several development projects in Israel. The Shah refused, but the two leaders exchanged gifts. Rabin gave the Iranian monarch an ancient urn from the Persian period in Israel, while the Shah gave Rabin a Persian carpet.

As expected, Rabin's visit to Tehran did not halt the rapprochement between Egypt and Iran. On the contrary, as the result of the twin developments of the growth in Arab power and the crystallization of a moderate anti-Soviet Arab camp, the Shah continued to work for Egypt's integration into the pro-Western bloc. In December 1974 the Iranian Chief of Staff, General Gholam Reza Azhari, visited Cairo and looked into the possibilities for cooperation between the two countries. Egypt asked Iran for modern radar systems like those supplied to Iran by the U.S., in order to close a hole in its air defenses. Egyptian pilots went to Iran and examined Phantom jets, in preparation for the integration of those planes into the Egyptian air force.

The Iranian Chief of Staff's visit to Cairo set the stage for the Shah's visit a month later. It was the first visit by an Iranian monarch to Cairo in 23 years, and the sumptuous reception the Shah received there testified to the turnabout Sadat had achieved in relations between the two countries. The Shah reported to Sadat on his conversations with Rabin in Tehran, and heard from him details of the preparations for the coming negotiations with Israel for an interim agreement, due to begin soon under U.S. auspices. Knowing the depth of the ties between

Israel and Iran, Sadat asked the Shah to use his influence to convince the Rabin government to moderate its positions in future talks. Sadat also asked the Shah to stop using the Eilat-Ashkelon pipeline, and obtained Iran's support for reconvening the Geneva Peace Conference with PLO participation. In doing so the Shah endorsed the decisions of the Arab summit conference at Rabat in November 1974, which had removed the Palestinian issue from Jordan's care and given it to the PLO. This major change in Iran's position alarmed Jerusalem, but the Israeli government was powerless to do anything about it. It devoted all its strength to preserving its foothold in Iran.

Then, at the beginning of 1975, Iran again told Israel that it wished to stop using the Eilat-Ashkelon pipeline. Sadat had announced his intention of demanding an Israeli withdrawal to the Gidi and Mitla passes in the Sinai and evacuation of the Abu-Rudeis oil fields. Since the Sinai oil supplied an important part of Israel's annual consumption, Israel's ability to agree to Sadat's demands depended on how secure the continued supply of Iranian oil was. The Shah thus became an influential party to Israel's decision.

In February, Israeli Foreign Minister Yigal Allon went to Tehran to discuss the pipeline with the Shah. Accompanied by his aide, Chaim Baron, he flew on a regular El Al flight, wearing a wig and thick sunglasses. The conversation with the Shah was short and to the point; the Shah then ordered Dr. Eqbal, the chairman of the National Iranian Oil Company, to continue to cooperate with the Trans-Asiatic Oil Company, which owned the pipeline. In order to improve its profitability, Allon agreed to raise the transfer fees on oil meant for use in Israel, while Iran lowered the price of this same oil and lengthened the credit period to four months.

The spring months were nevertheless difficult ones for Israel-Iran relations. Negotiations with Egypt for an interim agreement reached a dead end. Israel had demanded that Egypt officially end the state of war in return for a partial withdrawal. Sadat rejected the demand. The halt in the talks led Kissinger to recommend to President Ford that he "reassess" U.S. policy toward Israel. At Sadat's request, the Shah put pressure on Israel. On April 24 the Egyptian President arrived in Tehran to report to the Shah on the failure of the talks. In a conversation with reporters in Tehran, Sadat said that the time was ripe for a solution to the Israel-Arab problem, and that the thing delaying this agreement was Israel's refusal to withdraw from the territories it had occupied in the Six Day War. The Shah declared at the same opportunity that he fully supported President Sadat's policy. He said that the Egyptian position was based on justice and logic, while Israel's policy was rigid and unwise.

In mid-May 1975, Iranian pressure on Israel was exerted in Washington, too. On May 15 the Shah met with President Ford and Kissinger in the White House. The Shah supported Sadat, and argued that Israel was displaying a lack of flexibility and did not understand Egypt's position. He demanded that Ford and Kissinger increase their pressure on Israel.

The Israeli government was now worried that Iran might sever all its ties with Israel. While the oil was still flowing, the Shah had frozen military cooperation and had stopped buying arms from Israel. For several weeks it was difficult even to maintain a minimum level of communication. Top Iranian officials did not hestitate to tell Lubrani that, as long as the talks with Egypt were deadlocked, Israeli relations with Iran would be frozen.

In the summer of 1975 this pressure on Israel began to show results. After a meeting in June between Presidents Ford and Sadat in Salzburg, Kissinger renewed his attempt at mediation. The negotiating framework was now more realistic. Egypt continued in its refusal to repeal the state of war, but in exchange for a partial Israeli withdrawal and the evacuation of the Abu-Rudeis oil fields Sadat was willing to commit himself to a three-year cease-fire. In order to calm Israeli fears about its oil supply, Kissinger succeeded in getting an express promise from the Shah not to cut off oil to Israel. Rabin was not satisfied with this, and demanded an even clearer promise. So, on Friday, August 16, about two weeks before the agreement was to be signed, Rabin paid another visit to Tehran. His conversation with the Shah was held in the summer palace at Nushahr on the coast of the Caspian Sea. Despite the care taken by the security services of both countries, Rabin could not remain anonymous. He set out for Nushahr after spending the night in Tehran, traveling in the personal plane of the Iranian deputy prime minister, General Nassiri, and checking into the Ramsar Hotel. Several Iranian Jews and Israeli technicians who worked on various development projects in Iran happened to be spending the weekend at the same hotel. They immediately recognized the Israeli Prime Minister and waved to him. The news of his presence quickly spread through the Israeli community in Tehran, and among the local Jews. The Iranian authorities prevented the news from being published in the local press, but they could not prevent it leaking out of the country and appearing in the international media.[3] While the details of the talks were not officially published, the behavior of the two governments in the days that followed made it clear that the Shah had indeed succeeded in reassuring Rabin about his oil supply.

There was an immediate thaw in Israel-Iran relations after the interim agreement was signed in September. Lubrani thought it an appropriate opportunity to renew the military cooperation between the two countries. Without having received instructions from Jerusalem, Lubrani arranged a meeting with Lord Chamberlain Assadullan Alam and invited him, in the name of Prime Minister Rabin, to visit Israel and tour its military industry plants. Alam spoke to the Shah. Since the subject of the visit was well-defined, the Shah decided to assign it to the vice minister of war, General Hassan Toufanian, who was responsible for acquisitions and military production.

The Shah's decision to send Toufanian raised Lubrani's expectations for the visit. Since being assigned to Tehran, Lubrani had fostered and deepened his friendship with the deputy defense minister. Thanks to large oil profits and to the Shah's decision to develop his country's industrial and technological infrastructure, Toufanian had reached the peak of his power. Many countries did their best to be in his good graces, trying to win a slice of the Iranian bounty. In a report to the American Congress, Toufanian's name was listed among those who had received generous "service payments" from the Lockheed Corporation. Toufanian also had the title of "technical adviser" to joint American-Iranian manufacturing concerns, and was a secret partner in an aircraft trading company set up by General Muhammed Khatemi, the Shah's brother-in-law and formerly commander of the Iranian air force. These revelations were not, however, published in Tehran, and did not affect Toufanian's position.

The Shah's willingness to deepen his cooperation with Israel came as a surprise. Since the Yom Kippur War, when oil prices had quadrupled, Iran had no longer needed Israeli credit to buy arms and military equipment, and the international arms market opened wide before it. The Shah's ambitions, however, went even further. With the help of the large sums available to him, and with the full encouragement of the U.S., he aimed at widening his military infrastructure in order to achieve independence in the manufacture of sophisticated weapons and the development of advanced technologies. The U.S. and Iran signed an agreement for the assembly in Iran of TOW antitank missiles and Bell combat helicopters. An agreement with Britain provided for the manufacture of Rapier missiles in Iran, as well. This situation gave rise to fears in Jerusalem that Iran would stop buying weapons from Israel, either because the U.S. would supply all the Shah's needs, or because the Iranians would become self-sufficient in certain types of weapons and ammunition. Taking into account the improvement of Iran's position in the Arab world and the lessening importance of the Eilat-Ashkelon pipeline as well, the affects of these developments on Israel's strategic position were liable to be extremely painful. Israel hoped to blunt them by integrating itself into Iranian acquisition plans.

Immediately upon becoming minister of defense, Shimon Peres initiated a series of detailed discussions of recent developments in the Middle East, and ways of preserving Israel's position in Iran. He voiced the opinion that, despite the opening of the Suez Canal to international shipping, and despite the reduced importance of Israel's pipeline, it was possible to strengthen Iran's interest in cooperation with Israel by laying a basis for technological cooperation between the two countries. In contrast to the political level, where the Shah was limited by internal and regional factors, scientific and technical cooperation could be of benefit to both sides. Iran had the financial resources to fund the research and development of new technologies, while Israel had the necessary human resources. The marriage of Israeli knowledge with Iranian capital could offset Israel's reduced political importance to Iran.

One of the people who pushed for cooperation with Iran in this sphere was Al Schwimmer, director-general of Israel Aircraft Industries. His company had for several years overhauled Iranian commercial aircraft, and had also won a contract to do the same for Iranian air force F-86 planes. After an American company set up a plant in Isfahan for assembling Bell helicopters, Schwimmer had pushed for the establishment of a joint Israeli-Iranian airplane maintenance plant. In 1970, however, the U.S.'s Northrop had succeeded, along with Iranian entrepreneurs, in setting up such an operation—which Northrop also hoped, in the future, would serve Saudi Arabia and Kuwait. Schwimmer was furious at the American preemption of his idea, but he did not give up. Given the success of the Israeli Kfir jet in the Yom Kippur War, Israel Aircraft began developing a more advanced plane, the Arieh. Schwimmer hoped to interest the Shah in developing this plane and, at his recommendation, the Israeli Ministry of Defense included this project in its proposal.

Rabin did not believe that the Shah would be willing to participate in such an ambitious scheme, partly for political considerations and partly because Iran did not have the necessary technical infrastructure. He nevertheless presented the proposal to the Shah and enumerated its advantages. The Shah, in 1974, had not been interested. Now in 1976, however, conditions had changed and it was worth checking to see whether this approach to increasing cooperation with Iran might be fruitful.

In anticipation of Toufanian's arrival Israeli leaders conducted detailed discussions of how to present Israel's technological abilities to the guest, without damaging Israel's security. Iran was a Moslem country and its relations with the Arab world were on the upswing. Israel had to take care that technological secrets did not find their way to hostile Arab countries. Nevertheless, given the great efforts the U.S., Britain, France, and West Germany were making in the same field in Iran, it was decided to show Toufanian all those projects that the professional journals in the West had already reported. It was also decided to emphasize those projects that would be important to Iran's security, thus increasing the Shah's interest in developing them. Rabin, Peres, and Allon were aware that the very fact that the deputy defense minister was visiting was an expression of a thaw in Israel-Iran relations, and sought to ensure that the opportunity did not fall through their fingers.

Toufanian arrived in January 1976 for a four-day visit. He was accompanied, in a Mystère-20 executive jet, by Lubrani and two of Toufanian's aides. Toufanian met with Rabin and

Peres together, and then with Peres and Chief of Staff Mordechai Gur. While the Iranians were not allowed to see any secret technologies, what they did see was certainly impressive. On a tour of Israel Aircraft Industries, the guests observed the Kfir assembly line, and heard details about the next plane and about the problems of getting engines from the U.S. They also visited several military industry factories and toured the Golan Heights.

Toufanian gave the Shah a very positive report on his visit to Israel, but the monarch was worried about the political repercussions of working more closely with Israel. He feared not only the reactions of the moderate Arab states, but also that of the Iranian general staff. He explained to Toufanian that Israel was talking about the development of weapons that the general staff had still not evaluated. It was especially difficult to decide about the development and manufacture of a new plane without the air force commander being party to the decision. The Shah asked for time to consider the matter.

The political climate of the time was actually comfortable. Since the conclusion of the interim agreement with Egypt in September 1975, there had been an easing of the Israel-Arab dispute. The Middle East's attention was now turned to the civil war in Lebanon and Syria's involvement in it. This calm atmosphere formed an appropriate background to Yitzhak Rabin's third and last visit to Iran as Prime Minister. It was during the Noruz holiday, the Iranian New Year, and the Shah was in his vacation palace on the Caspian Sea. Rabin ate lunch with the Shah and they exchanged evaluations of the Middle East situation. In contrast to previous visits, no problematic matters were discussed. The goal of the visit was simply to create a political dialogue with the leader of Iran in more pleasant surroundings as a counterweight to Arab influence.

In the summer of 1976, however, Iran once more expressed its desire to divert its oil from the Eilat-Ashkelon pipeline to other routes. Because of his success in dealing with this subject in the past, Rabin assigned Yigal Allon to go to Tehran in August and speak to the Shah. As on his previous visit, Allon flew to Tehran on an El Al commercial flight. When he landed in Tehran, apparently no one recognized him. He wore a wig and wore thick, funny glasses, and sported a Tyrolean hat with a feather.

Allon's audience with the Shah was conducted in the Niavaran Palace, the Shah's new residence in the north of the city. Here he lived for most of the year and kept his office. The conversation lasted for about two hours and dealt mostly with oil. Allon explained to the Shah that supply arrangements that had been convenient for Iran in the past could not now be canceled at the wave of a hand. He added that relations with Israel might today be a burden for Iran, but that the pendulum might swing back tomorrow. It was thus preferable that the relations between the two countries be placed on firm foundations. The Shah was convinced and told Allon that the supply of oil to Israel would continue.[4]

Inquiries about renewing military cooperation were being made simultaneously with Allon's work on the oil issue. An Israeli delegation, including representatives of the aircraft and military industries, was invited to Tehran and met with members of the Iranian defense establishment. The delegation screened a short film on Israel's scientific and technological achievements, and explained their ideas for future cooperation.

This preliminary discussion was good preparation for Minister of Defense Shimon Peres's visit to Tehran. The Iranians were aware, of course, of Peres's strong position in his party, and were interested in meeting a man who had such an important place in Israel's political life. The Shah also knew that Peres was considered Ben-Gurion's most prodigious student, and he wanted to see whether there were any similarities between teacher and pupil.

Peres set out for Tehran in September 1976, having done his homework well. He read the books the Shah had written and everything he could find that had been written about him, as well as inquiring about the Iranian monarch's character and personal traits.

The Israeli defense minister set out in an Israel Aircraft Westwind plane, together with his military secretary, Brigadier General Arieh Baron, Ministry of Defense assistant director-general Avraham Ben-Yosef, and Al Schwimmer. In contrast to the visits of Rabin and Allon, when the official host was Savak chief Ne'ematullah Nassiri, Peres and his party were received at the airport by Iran's deputy minister of defense, Hassan Toufanian. Peres, like his cabinet colleagues, was housed at the official guest residence.

Peres met with the Shah the next day at the Niavaran Palace.[5] This was preceded by a short preparatory conversation with Toufanian about what was likely to come up with the Shah, and in particular about what the Shah expected to get out of the conversation. The Shah began, as was his custom at meetings such as this, with a long monologue in which he presented his credo on various international matters. He spoke with surprising frankness, grading various world statesmen and more than once making serious criticisms of the United States, which he believed did not understand the changes taking place in the Middle East. He described the danger that the Soviet Union presented to his country, noting that, while relations were calm now, Moscow's historic ambitions were insurance that the calm was transitory. Soviet assistance to Iraq, he argued, was aimed at turning the Fertile Crescent into a Red Crescent, increasing the threat to the Persian Gulf and endangering vital Western interests. Soviet domination of Baluchistan, he warned, would make Communist rule of Afghanistan to Iran an established fact. The Shah also spoke of the instability in India, and of Indira Gandhi's leanings toward Moscow. He cast doubt on Western Europe's willingness to prevent such a development, meaning that Iran had to be strong enough to protect itself. Yet the Jewish lobby in the U.S. did not understand this and did not prevent attacks on him and his country in the American press. Iran for this reason had problems in the American Congress, with every new request for arms and military equipment passing only slowly through the foreign affairs committees of the Senate and House of Representatives. "Each time I gaze into Fate's sad face I get the feeling that he, too, had to endure the pains of Congressional committees," the Shah said with a bitter laugh. He asked Peres: "I don't know what they want of me in Congress. To surrender to terror? We recently captured a hundred terrorists, and I have no intention of giving in to blackmail. The Palestinians poison the atmosphere and do their best to subvert all the pro-Western governments in the region. Iran still covets Kuwait, and the Soviet Union is fanning the flames of the rebellion in Oman; Iran has no choice but to trust to itself."[6]

The Shah spoke very favorably of Sadat, and it was evident that he had been deeply impressed by the Egyptian President's personality and by his determination to integrate his country into the pro-Western camp in the area. Even if the Shah did not say so explicitly, it appeared that he was trying to give Peres the message that Israel must look after Sadat and be flexible with him.

The Shah asked to hear Israel's evaluation of the situation. Peres expressed his opinion that the Soviet Union was uncomfortable with Syria's involvement in Lebanon against the Palestinians and had not yet decided whether to support that country or the PLO. He expressed his satisfaction at the way the interim agreement with Egypt was being carried out, and he agreed with the Shah's estimation of the danger of Soviet expansion in the Persian Gulf region. He argued that in Saudi Arabia the fear of the Soviets was even greater than the fear of Israel. The Shah claimed that, after King Faisal's death, he had found common ground with King Khaled and Prince Fahd. He argued that Faisal always spoke of praying in Jerusalem, but Khaled and Fahd were more pragmatic.

The American election campaign was at its height and Peres devoted much time to this also, exchanging with the Shah impressions of Jimmy Carter's personality. The two of them wondered what the Democratic candidate's Middle East policy would be. In his campaign, Carter had attacked the "unlimited supply of weapons" to the Persian Gulf states, and had committed himself to give weight to human rights considerations in his foreign policy. Peres told the Shah that, despite the distractions of the campaign, the U.S. could be depended on. Iran and Israel had to realize, however, that the U.S. would not fight for them and that both countries, therefore, had to be strong. He assured the Shah that the Jewish lobby understood the importance of Israeli-Iranian cooperation to the protection of Western interests in the Persian Gulf, and that the Jewish establishment in the U.S. was aware that the Shah did not use his oil as a political weapon against Israel.

The Shah remarked that he had received a very positive report from Toufanian, and that he was also convinced that the two countries could gain much by working more closely together. He feared, however, complicating his relations with the U.S. and the Arab countries, and he also had to consider the reaction of his internal opposition.

Peres beamed as he emerged from the audience. Although the Shah had been noncommittal, Peres was left with the feeling that the discussion had been productive. A few hours later came confirmation that his impressions were correct. Toufanian told Peres that the Shah had been extremely satisfied with the conversation, and that he himself now felt that it was possible to expedite the negotiations for a "framework agreement" between the two countries.

A short time after the visit, the nuts-and-bolts negotiations over the agreement reached between Peres and the Shah began. Schwimmer returned to Tehran at the head of a delegation representing all Israel's military industries, and they reached an agreement in principle to begin six joint projects from among the 25 they examined. The most important of these was the development of a ground-to-ground missile with a 300-mile range and carrying a conventional warhead of 350 pounds. According to the agreement, Israel was to complete the development of its missile, while the tests and production would be done in Iran. Another project was the improvement of the American Harpoon antiship missile, code-named "Flower," with the aim of increasing its range to 125 miles, and another missile with a short range of 17.5 miles. The Israeli company Soltam was to establish in Iran a plant for the production of 155mm artillery and 120mm mortars at the cost of $370 million. To preserve secrecy, the discussions between the two delegations were held at Lubrani's house. The total deal was valued at $1.2 billion. Upon signing the treaty, Iran was to give Israel a down payment in oil at a value of $250 million. The general character of the agreement would be one of barter—"arms for oil." For this reason Iran demanded the establishment of a joint company, registered in Switzerland, with Iran paying for its share in oil, through the Trans-Asiatic Oil Company.

The two countries began exchanging delegations of experts. Israeli and Iranian engineers went out into the field and settled on a site in the Sirjan region in central Iran. The firing range was to be in Rafsandjan, from where the middle-range missiles were to be fired northward into the desert and southward in the direction of the Gulf of Oman. Until the agreement was signed, Israel and Iran agreed to keep the matter secret and not reveal anything to the U.S. They feared that the Carter administration would press both countries to cancel it.

By April 1977 all the contracts were ready to be signed. Minister of Defense Peres returned to Tehran and, after talking with the Shah, he and Toufanian signed the agreement on technological cooperation between the two countries.[7]

Lubrani, who had overseen the negotiations for Israel, was about to return to Israel. The agreement in any case demanded daily contact with Israel's defense complex, so it was now assigned to the military attaché. Peres, upon returning to Israel, appointed Brigadier General Yitzhak Segev to be the new military attaché in Iran. Segev had in the past served as commander of the Sinai and had later worked in the general staff's planning branch. He was originally meant to be appointed military commander of the West Bank, but Chief of Staff Mordechai Gur opposed the appointment and Peres decided to send him to Iran. Segev was introduced to Iranian Foreign Minister Abbas Ali Khalatbari when the latter visited Israel in March 1977; on June 15 he set out for Tehran and, after a short transition period with his predecessor, Brigadier General Rami Luntz, he assumed his new position on July 7.

In the meantime a political revolution had occurred in Israel. In elections on May 17, the Labor party under Peres and Rabin was defeated by the nationalist Likud faction. The results shook Tehran and gave rise to fears about the chances for peace in the Middle East and the future of relations between the two countries. Lubrani was questioned daily by top Iranian officials who wanted to know what the election results meant, what Prime Minister-designate Menachem Begin's views were, and what his policies were likely to be. At the beginning of June, before Begin's government was sworn in, Lubrani was summoned to an audience with the Shah. It was his first meeting with the Iranian monarch in his four years in Tehran, during which his contact with the palace had been limited to the lord chamberlain. Now, at the end of his term of service, he was suddenly called in to explain the political developments in Jerusalem. Lubrani reassured the Shah that Begin was not the fanatic terrorist the media made him out to be, and he said he was sure that Begin would also see Iran as the key to stability in the Persian Gulf region.

Begin and his government were sworn in on June 20. Moshe Dayan was foreign minister and Ezer Weizman minister of defense. There were changes in the Iranian government, too. Lord Chamberlain Assadullah Alam died and was replaced by Prime Minister Amir Abbas Hoveida. Economist and oilman Jamshid

Amouzegar was appointed Prime Minister; Khalatbari remained foreign minister.

Lubrani flew home the day after the new Israeli government assumed power, and Moshe Dayan asked him to remain in his post until an appropriate replacement could be found. After telling Dayan about his conversation with the Shah and about Iran's fears of the Begin government, Lubrani urged the new foreign minister to go to Tehran, both in order to renew his acquaintance with the Shah and to thaw the frozen military cooperation.

Dayan arrived in Tehran on July 7, 1977. He came in a special plane and was received by Savak chief Nassiri. He conferred with the Shah for three hours the next morning at Niavaran Palace. Dayan analyzed the goals of the Begin government and emphasized that it would continue the search for peace. This was, he said, the reason he, elected to the Knesset on the Labor list, had consented to join the cabinet. Begin had agreed that he would not annex the West Bank as long as there was a chance for peace, and that the legal status of the Gaza Strip would not be changed, either. Dayan said that the new Israeli government, like its predecessor, wanted to achieve peace through direct negotiations without prior conditions, a peace that would be free of "ifs and buts." If Israel could not achieve full peace, it would be willing to discuss partial arrangements. The Begin government was determined to exhaust all these possibilities. Dayan mentioned the difficulty of reconvening the Geneva Conference with Soviet participation, noting that, while Israel's position was that everything was open to negotiation, there were still two matters on which there could be no compromise: Israel opposed the establishment of an independent Palestinian state, and would not recognize the PLO or accept it as a party in peace negotiations. The Israeli foreign minister told the Shah of Begin's intention to go to Washington to talk with President Carter, and of Secretary of State Cyrus Vance's intention of visiting the Middle East. He proposed returning to Tehran to report on Begin's visit to Washington and on his talks with Vance.

Dayan's explanation came after his host's own survey of the world situation and of recent developments in the Middle East. The Shah pointed out that Pakistan was unstable, that Turkey was at the height of a government crisis, while Iraq was gradually turning into a "large storehouse" of Soviet weaponry in the Persian Gulf region, just as Libya had become in the central Mediterranean. There were only a few countries in the entire region that Iran could put its faith in, and Israel was one of them. Iran also considered Saudi Arabia, Jordan, and Egypt allies. Israel had to do all it could to protect Sadat and Hussein. The Shah said that it was important to Iran that Israel's image be that of a country seeking peace. For this reason, until the intentions of the Begin government became clear, he would freeze the joint technological program and delay the payment of the promised $250 million advance. The Shah said that he was most interested in this cooperation, and especially in the "Flower" project to improve the Harpoon missile, so that he could combat the Iraqi threat in the Gulf. After hearing Dayan's exposition of the Begin government's policies, the Shah said that he was willing to reconsider his decision, but until he did, the program would remain frozen.[8] It seemed, however, that Dayan's presentation impressed the Shah. Even before Israel had a chance to consider the meaning of the freeze, the Shah sent Deputy Defense Minister Toufanian and the joint project manager, Entezami to talk with Dayan and Ezer Weizman. The Iranians arrived on a special Mystère-20 plane on July 18, accompanied by Israeli military attaché Segev. During his visit, Toufanian was invited to see a test firing of the Israeli ground-to-ground missile. He was almost killed in the process—when the missile was fired, the Iranian deputy defense minister was flying over the Mediterranean and his plane was almost hit. Luckily the ground station was able to divert the missile's flight path and save the rattled guest. Toufanian himself later related the story to a New York Times correspondent, in an interview printed on April 1, 1986. "It was wonderful, really wonderful. The missile was completely developed, but there were still some technical problems that Israel had not yet succeeded in overcoming—for example, the navigation and guidance systems. The missile had an American system, but Israel wanted to develop its own."

During his conversation with Toufanian, Weizman tried to broaden the scope of the agreement Peres had reached with the Shah to include the development of the Arieh jet. Toufanian rejected the proposal. He said that the Arieh did not fit Iran's needs, but that if Israel were to develop a two-engine rather than a single-engine plane, Iran would consider joining the project.

Among the documents seized from the American embassy in Tehran by the Iranian students who overran it were transcripts of Toufanian's conversations in Israel with Weizman and Dayan. Since, at that time, Israel had not yet told the U.S. about the joint technological project, it was clear that the CIA had received the transcripts from Toufanian or from one of his aides. Following are some passages dealing with the project:

TOP SECRET

MEETING
Minister of Defense, Gen. E. Weizman, and Gen. Toufanian of Iran
Ministry of Defense, Tel Aviv
Monday, July 18, 1977, 3 P.M.
  Also present: Mr. Uri Lubrani
       Dr. Zusman, Director-General
       Mr. A. Ben-Yosef
       Col. Ilan Tehila

WEIZMAN: . . . You are familiar with our industry, probably in many respects now even more than I am. . . . We are building our own tank, which is a very good tank. We have built the Kfir, which is not one hundred percent ours. But it is a very interesting technology, a very good airplane.

And the big question now is, are we going to team together and do things or not. . . . I have gone over the six contracts in action now. I have also put my mind to those things that are not in contracts, for instance the future fighter. Are we going to or are we not going to develop a joint effort on a future plane. . . . For instance, in the program there are missiles, short ones . . . which are your requirement more than ours. Right or wrong?

ZUSMAN: It is ours, too. It is a joint requirement.

WEIZMAN: For 28 km?

. . .

TOUFANIAN: I don't think any of the subjects we discussed is an individual requirement, for us or for you. In all the subjects we discussed, you have had some development program or developed something. You had reached some stage, and then we agreed in principle to go on together. There are not individual things, where I said I want this or that. Except for the 120mm ammunition.

WEIZMAN: I will give you one example. I went over the program. And on the next stage of the Harpoon, what we call the Flower, I am having a discussion with our navy, and I am not sure that for our immediate future we need the 200 km missile.

. . .

TOUFANIAN: I agree to discuss the subject. Of course, we also think for the future. And no country has enough money for defense, no country whatsoever.

WEIZMAN: Not even Iran?

TOUFANIAN: Not even Iran, or the U.S. . . . And we don't want to waste our money. But in principle we think that we have to develop—you see this is our country (pointing to map), do you know from here the Russian units are here and it goes down and around to the Persian Gulf.

. . .

WEIZMAN: We started development when Abdul Nasser fired his Zapher ground-to-ground missile.

BEN-YOSEF: He didn't fire it. He demonstrated it but with no firing, in July 1962.

WEIZMAN: And we convened a meeting at 12 midnight. I was air force commander, Shimon [Peres] was deputy defense minister, and everyone got into a panic.

TOUFANIAN: I don't think those Egyptian missiles ever flew.

WEIZMAN: No, but this helped develop the missile you are going to see tomorrow. . . . You must have a ground-to-ground missile. A country like yours, with F-14s, with so many F-4s, with the problems surrounding you . . . we have been at it in Israel now, in the country itself, for about seven or eight years. I mean the present missile. . . . Twenty years ago we had a small missile we called Luz, and this is the forefather of the Gabriel. We started it as a ground-to-ground missile for 25 km, fired off a command car. We used to go

to the Negev to fire it. Once we took Ben-Gurion to see it
fire.

ZUSMAN: We spent over a billion dollars in developing our missile capacity.

WEIZMAN: Air-to-air, ground-to-ground. We never went into
ground to air.

The joint project also came up in Toufanian's talks with
Dayan. The foreign minister said that he personally knew Zablodovitz, director-general of Soltam, and valued his honesty, tal-
ent, and the technological abilities of his firm. Toufanian
answered that the Shah favored the establishment of a factory
to produce Salgad mortars. During Zablodovitz's last visit to
Tehran there had been progress in this matter. In accordance
with his proposal, an Iranian team would soon visit Israel,
Germany, and Sweden in order to examine plans for the production of 155mm guns. Toufanian said he preferred the Israeli
cannon, but that if the deal was signed, it would have to be
by Soltam's Finnish subsidiary. Dayan said he had no objections.
Finally, Dayan mentioned the American sensitivity to the development of missiles of the type included in the project. He
noted that a ground-to-ground missile with a 350-pound pay-
load could also carry a nuclear warhead. For this reason, he
felt, it was worth revealing the plans to the Americans. He
meant to raise this with the Shah during his next visit to Tehran.

At the end, Dayan raised the subject of credit for the oil
Israel bought from Iran. He noted that Israel received 120 days'
credit for 17 million tons of oil it bought through Trans-Asiatic,
and asked for better conditions. Toufanian suggested keeping
the existing arrangement, and promised that back in Tehran
he would look for ways to make the terms easier for Israel.

In mid-August, Dayan took off for a short "vacation." He
landed in Tehran, meeting with the Shah the next day in order
to update him on the peace process. Dayan's second visit had
a more routine character, and unlike the first one, it was prepared
with the participation of Iranian Foreign Minister Abbas Ali
Khalatbari. Despite Iranian efforts to preserve secrecy, however,
the news of the visit leaked into the international press. *Time*
and *Newsweek* reported on September 26 of Dayan's talk with
the Shah and of the secret meeting he had had with King
Hussein in London on August 22. Dayan reported to the Shah

on Begin's talks in Washington and on the Prime Minister's request that Carter help organize a meeting between him and the President of Egypt.

New developments in the Middle East diverted attention from the relations between Iran and Israel to President Sadat's peace initiative. The American and Soviet governments issued a joint communiqué on October 1 calling for the reconvening of the Geneva Peace Conference. Israel and Egypt, however, both wanted to avoid the inclusion of the Soviets in the peace process. At a secret mid-September meeting with an Egyptian envoy in Tangier, Dayan asked King Hassan of Morocco to help arrange a meeting between Begin and Sadat. Sadat went to Tehran just before the Shah was to visit the U.S. in order to enlist Iran's help in changing President Carter's stance and moderating Israel's positions. On November 9, Sadat astonished the world: in a public speech before the Egyptian parliament he announced that he intended to go to Jerusalem to negotiate peace with Begin.

Sadat's declaration shocked Tehran, but Iranian leaders soon recovered and told Lubrani and his staff: "We always told you that Sadat was serious about peace, and here is the proof."[9] The Shah took a similar line in his conversation with President Carter in the White House on November 16. The Shah urged the President to pressure Israel to change its stand on the Palestinian issue, so as to strengthen Sadat's position at home and in the Arab world.

On the eve of Sadat's arrival in Israel the Israeli army noticed suspicious movements of Egyptian forces on the western side of the Suez Canal. Fearing that Egypt was preparing a new surprise like the one of 1973, Chief of Staff Mordechai Gur publicly announced that Israel was aware of those movements and would not again be taken by surprise. His warning was published in the media on the day Begin was to officially notify the Knesset of his formal invitation to Sadat. Immediately after the publication of his warning, on November 13, Major General Gur set out on a special plane for Tehran. He was to meet the Shah on Kish Island just before the Iranian ruler was to leave for Washington. On the day he arrived he met Iran's top officers at a dinner party given in his honor by Iranian Chief of Staff Gholam Reza Azhari. The next day Gur and military attaché Segev set out for Isfahan and Kish. In the meantime

Israeli public opinion was seething over Gur's public warning to Egypt. Minister of Defense Weizman berated him and ordered him back to Israel immediately. Gur returned on November 16 without having met the Shah and without having concluded his talks with Iranian military leaders.

Sadat's visit to Jerusalem, beginning on November 19, 1977, was broadcast live by Iranian television, including large portions of Sadat's and Begin's speeches in the Knesset. Despite the great effort the Iranian government made to present the Egyptian initiative in a positive light, unrest among religious groups grew and there were demonstrations in different parts of Tehran against Sadat's visit. About 100 demonstrators attacked the El Al offices in Tehran, breaking windows and the door to the office, but they did not succeed in entering.

The optimism created by Sadat's move soon gave way, however, to growing pessimism. The day after Begin's visit to Ismailia on December 25, Dayan came to Tehran on a special plane, together with his administrative assistant, Elyakim Rubenstein. They had been invited by the Shah, whose mood was not at all good. Dayan advised Lubrani to take with a grain of salt the media reports on the Ismailia talks, and said that the gap between the positions of Sadat and Begin was very large.

The Shah and Dayan met alone; the monarch received him warmly and the conversation was relaxed and frank. Dayan explained the differences between the Israeli and Egyptian positions on the Palestinian issue, giving him details of the administrative autonomy plan for the West Bank and Gaza Strip. The Shah did not accept these explanations and gave his full support to Sadat. He told Dayan of the expected visits of President Carter and King Hussein to Tehran, and of his intention to visit Riyadh and Aswan thereafter.[10]

Carter arrived in Tehran with his wife on December 31, and received a colorful and impressive reception. The American President praised the Shah's leadership, seeing in it a strong support for the U.S. in the Persian Gulf area. Clearly ignoring his previous declarations about "human rights," Carter left no doubt among those who heard him that the Shah's regime had his full confidence, and that he believed that the Shah intended to continue the democratization and liberalization of his country.

In his talks in Tehran, the President expressed his opinion

that the results of the Ismailia summit reflected Sadat's inability to make a separate peace with Israel. He emphasized that strengthening Sadat strengthened the free world's position in the Middle East and East Africa, and that it was therefore necessary to preserve Egypt's leadership of the Arab world. America's diplomacy would therefore aim at restraining Arab attacks on Sadat and would encourage bringing Hussein into the negotiations. And indeed, before Carter's visit to Tehran, Hussein had asked the Shah to set up for him a meeting with the U.S. President in the Iranian capital. The Jordanian King and his wife, Alia, came and attended a New Year's party hosted by the Shah.

The next day, January 1, 1978, Carter and Hussein met for a short conversation in which they examined the possibility that Jordan would join the peace initiative. Hussein explained that he could not take part in talks on autonomy for the West Bank and Gaza Strip according to the Israeli plan. He argued that, if he did so, he would alienate Saudi Arabia, worsen his relations with Syria, and turn himself, should the talks fail, into an Arab scapegoat. The Shah gave Hussein his full support, and advised Carter to leave Jordan out of the peace talks for now, if only to keep Iran's lines open to Syria. The Shah in fact, at Carter's request, tried to get Syrian President Hafez Assad to come to Tehran as well, but Assad turned him down.

The impasse in the peace talks put new pressure on Israel-Iran relations. Sadat sent his vice president, Husni Mubarak, to Tehran on January 30, carrying a personal letter to the Shah. In it, Sadat explained to the Shah the factors that led him to cut off the negotiations in Jerusalem, and accused Israel of rigidity and unwillingness to solve the Palestinian problem. Israel sent its version of the negotiations to the Shah, as well, through normal diplomatic channels. The Shah continued to support Egypt. It was clear that, without a top-level meeting between Israel and Iran, there would be a crisis in their relations. The time seemed ripe for Prime Minister Begin to visit Tehran.

Begin left for Tehran in a Boeing 707 on Wednesday, February 22, and returned on Friday, February 24, at dawn. To ensure the secrecy of the meeting, only three cabinet members—Deputy Prime Minister Yigael Yadin, Moshe Dayan, and Ezer Weizman—knew of the trip; their colleagues learned of it only after it was over. Begin was accompanied by his administrative assistant, Yehiel Kadishai, and his military secretary, Brigadier General Efraim Poran. He met the Shah at the Niavaran Palace for talks lasting four hours, including lunch. In contrast to Yitzhak Rabin, who was always tense before his meetings with the Shah, Begin was at ease and in high spirits. He was very impressed with the Shah's personality and his wide horizons. Begin later told his aides that the Shah was an excellent monologist. Of the four hours of their meeting, the Shah had spoken for three hours and forty minutes. Begin said he was without a doubt a man of the world, and it was extremely interesting to listen to him.

The Shah spoke with authority about the competition between the superpowers, putting special emphasis on the situation in the Middle East and in the Persian Gulf region. He expressed his great concern about the pro-Soviet coup in Kabul, and revealed his doubts about the U.S.'s ability to halt Soviet expansion. The Shah sharply criticized the U.S. which, he said, did not understand what was going on. He said that the Americans had power, but they did not know how to use it. The Shah looked and sounded melancholy. He said that the Communists and religious groups had formed an alliance against him. He called the mullahs "reactionaries," and made clear his worries about their attempts to unseat him.

A large part of the conversation was devoted, of course, to the Middle East peace process. The Shah's survey of events was full of praise for Sadat and his leadership of the Arab world. The Shah believed that Egypt sincerely wanted peace, and urged Begin to display more flexibility toward Sadat, and not to let this opportunity for peace slip through his fingers.

Begin was party to the Shah's worries about Moscow's designs in the Middle East. He told the Shah about his experiences during the Second World War, his suffering in a Soviet prison camp, and his adventures in the Jewish underground prior to Israel's independence. As for the peace process, Begin had brought documents to prove to the Shah that the Israeli peace proposal was very generous. Israel was offering a full withdrawal from the Sinai and autonomy to the Palestinians. He said he was astonished that Sadat had cut off the negotiations in Jerusalem, and promised the Shah that Israel was ready to renew the talks without any preconditions. At the end of the conversation Begin presented the Shah with an ancient map of Jerusalem and an antique dagger. After a short rest Begin and his party left for Israel. This was the last time an Israeli leader would meet the Shah. The developments of the following months prevented any senior contacts between the two countries, and all the Shah's energies were devoted to preserving the Peacock Throne.

The coming weeks and months would see the internal unrest in Iran reach such proportions that few Iranian officials were willing to take upon themselves the danger involved in cooperation with Israel. As the opposition organized itself and united around Khomeini, the links with Israel became a burden to the Iranian establishment. Moreover, the support that the U.S., Egypt, and Israel gave to the Shah made all three countries unpopular in Iran, and officials feared associating themselves with them in public. Nevertheless, the ties between the Shah and Israel forced him to decide whether to continue to act for what seemed to him to be the good of his country, or to surrender to the religious and leftist opposition and cut off relations. The Shah came down in favor of the national interest.

The result was a week-long visit, beginning on May 26, by General Michael Barkay, commander of Israel's navy. In a conversation between him and his Iranian counterpart, Admiral Kemal Habibulla, the transcript of which was found among the papers of the American embassy in Tehran, the two men discussed various possibilities for cooperation between their fleets. General Barkay proposed accepting Iranian cadets into Israel's naval academy, and giving Iran Israeli information on faults in the operation of American-made 76mm guns. When Iran received its submarines the Israeli navy would be willing to send a small team to examine Iranian training programs. Barkay indicated that he was willing to allow Iran to look over the 30mm guns then under development by the Israeli navy, as well as to convert several Iranian combat jets into sea surveillance craft, according to a method developed by Israel Aircraft Industries. He enumerated a number of items developed in Israel that were now in the process of being installed on Israeli ships. Among them were a new radar system for boats and planes, digital equipment for the swift transmission of tactical information from planes to ships, and equipment to locate targets for Harpoon missiles. Finally, Barkay proposed joint development of an antimissile missile, the development of the "Flower" so that it could be launched from submarines as well, and the development of an acoustic submarine defense system which would confound enemy sonar devices and deflect their torpedoes.[11]

These ambitious programs were never realized. The coming months were to see the U.S., Israel, and Egypt involved in the problems of Middle East peace, barely giving thought to the internal tensions in Iran. That September President Carter hosted Sadat and Begin at Camp David, where for two weeks the three men and their aides conducted intensive negotiations. When the Camp David accords were signed at a festive ceremony at the White House on September 17, 1978, Tehran was already in turmoil and the reins of power were slowly being pulled from the Shah's grasp. At this juncture, Israel appointed Yosef Harmelin, a former head of the Shin Bet, Israel's security service, as its new envoy to Tehran, succeeding Uri Lubrani, who had completed five years as ambassadorship in Iran.

The sense that the twilight of the Iranian monarchy was at hand could be felt during the visit of Israel's air force commander, General David Ivry, to Tehran on October 27. Ivry would be the last senior Israeli officer to visit Iran before the Shah was deposed. The visit came at a time when the protest movement had become truly revolutionary. The strikes and demonstrations had spread all over the country; oil production dropped and was barely adequate for local consumption. The bureaucracy had ceased to function, the banks were closed, and there were serious shortages of basic food items. The Revolutionary Guards, trained in PLO camps in Lebanon and Libya, made their first appearance in the cities, sometimes with weapons. In the interests of secrecy and safety, Ivry and military attaché Segev were given their own helicopter, with which they hopped from place to place. Ivry met with, among others, Chief of Staff Gholam Reza Azhari, with his Iranian counterpart, General Rabi'i, and with Toufanian, but it was clear that Sherif Emami's government had lost control of the situation and that the Shah's days were numbered.

After the government displayed significant weakness in controlling the disturbances, the Shah gave into pressure from the army and dismissed the cabinet. The elderly Azhari formed a military government that used emergency powers to try to restore order. They were not successful. The country was in chaos; the foreign embassies, including the Israeli mission, began a gradual evacuation of their nationals. At the beginning of 1978 there were more than 1,500 Israeli families in Iran. The number shrank during the course of the year. On November 6 alone El Al planes evacuated 365 Israeli citizens, most of them women and children. Despite two attacks on the El Al office, with the active involvement of Palestinian terrorists, the Israeli airline continued its regular flights to and from Iran, in order to complete the evacuation and to get as many Iranian Jews out as possible.

The staff of the Israeli mission in Tehran displayed similar devotion. Despite the danger, they held their ground; the Israeli government refused to concede of its own accord its foothold in this important oil state. There were two reasons for holding on until the end:

• there was no guarantee that, should Israel voluntarily close its mission and recall Ambassador Yosef Harmelin and his staff to Jerusalem, they would be allowed to return once calm was restored; and

• a large Jewish community remained in Iran, and while many of its members had already left for Israel, Europe, and the U.S., close to 50,000 remained. The existence of the Israeli mission gave them a sense of security and reinforced their belief that Israel would not abandon them in times of trouble, and would make every effort to get them out of Iran.

At the beginning of 1979, however, the Shah's position further weakened. His inability to deal with the crisis led Iranian air force commander Rabi'i and Deputy Defense Minister Toufanian to suggest to Segev that either Moshe Dayan or Ezer Weizman come to Tehran to impress upon the Shah the serious nature of the situation and to suggest, perhaps, ways of dealing with it.

The Israeli government decided not to send a cabinet member; instead, former Ambassador Uri Lubrani, who had left Iran not long before and had good relations with several of the Shah's closest advisers, was dispatched to Tehran. He arrived on January 5, 1979, and immediately met with Toufanian and several people with access to Khomeini's circle. The report he gave upon returning to Jerusalem was not encouraging. He was convinced that the Shah's regime was at its end, and that the revolutionaries were not likely to be on good terms with Israel. The supply of Iranian oil, no longer flowing to Israel because of the general strike in Iran, would probably not be renewed. The same was true of the joint defense projects—all were frozen, and would certainly be canceled.

The Shah, on January 16, his last day in power, appointed as Prime Minister the number two man in the National Front party, Shahpour Bakhtiar. A few hours later it was already clear that Bakhtiar's government would be short-lived. Khomeini, from his exile in Paris, called on his followers to rise against Bakhtiar and overthrow his government. He claimed that, since the Shah had appointed him, Bakhtiar's government was illegal and illegitimate. The Ayatollah announced his intention of returning to Tehran forthwith, and he appointed one of his loyalists, Mehdi Bazargan, to form Iran's first Islamic government. For several days it was unclear who was ruling Iran. But on Saturday, February 10, Bakhtiar's government collapsed and Bazargan's position was uncontested. Bakhtiar fled to his home base in central Iran, and a few months later he succeeded in escaping the country, disguised as a steward on a European airline; he was granted political asylum in France.

In the midst of this chaos, the Israeli mission in Tehran was attacked and looted. A crowd of demonstrators, among them several dozen Palestinians, battered down the stone wall surrounding the building, climbed up to the roof, pulled down the Israeli flag, and burned it. Crying "Death to Israel, long live Arafat, Israel get out," they raised the Palestinian flag over the gate of the building. The Islamic republic, it was clear, would have nothing to do with the Jewish state.

Harmelin instructed Segev to contact the Iranian Chief of Staff and the deputy chief of military intelligence, General Reza Parvaresh, and ask them to arrange protection for the building and the few Israelis who remained in the city. The Iranian officers, however, could no longer help them. Segev asked the air force commander for a military cargo plane to enable the immediate evacuation of the Israelis. "The Revolutionary Guards control the airport and I cannot help you. But if you find a plane, please evacuate me as well," General Rabi'i responded.[12] Rabi'i would be among the hundreds of officers executed a few days later for their loyalty to the Shah.

On February 13, Bazargan's government dismissed Chief of

Staff Abbas Karabaghi and appointed General Karnay in his place. Karnay had been dismissed previously by the Shah and was returned to active service together with several dozen other officers who had made known their loyalty to Khomeini. Segev called the Chief of Staff's bureau chief and asked to meet the new appointee, in order to present him with his credentials as the Israeli military attaché in Tehran. There was a painful silence at the other end of the line. After a moment's silence, the Iranian officer recovered and asked incredulously, "Are you still here? Where are you?" Segev took a calculated risk and gave him the telephone number of his hideout. A half hour later the officer called back and advised Segev and the other Israelis to leave the country immediately. Since the Revolutionary Guards were at present hunting down Savak men and the Shah's loyalists, the Israelis still had a brief breathing space to plan their escape. He asked Segev to promise not to tell anyone about their conversation.[13]

There were at that time 33 Israelis remaining in Tehran. In addition to Harmelin and Segev, there was also former Knesset member Mordechai Ben-Porat, who had arrived in Tehran on February 4 to help save Iranian Jews; there were also representatives of the Jewish Agency, El Al employees, and several bodyguards. The Israelis lived in three separate apartments and were in constant telephone contact with each other and with Israel, Harmelin with the Foreign Ministry and Segev with Israeli Chief of Staff Mordechai Gur and Chief of Operations Yekutial Adam. Israeli leaders considered various options for rescuing their besieged countrymen. But they decided to concentrate on diplomatic activity. A special command center was set up under Foreign Ministry Director General Yosef Chechanover, which oversaw contacts with the U.S. and Western European governments concerning the evacuation from Tehran.

American Secretary of Defense Harold Brown was then touring the Middle East in order to evaluate the significance of the Shah's overthrow and Khomeini's victory. In a conversation with Moshe Dayan in Jerusalem, it was agreed that the Israelis would be evacuated together with American nationals on February 18.

The Israelis left the Hilton Hotel for the airport in a bus plastered with pictures of Khomeini. Two 16-year-olds, armed with Kalishnikov rifles and trained in Palestinian camps in Syria,

served as bodyguards. Other armed youngsters, wearing arm-
bands identifying them as members of "the Imam Khomeini's
Guards," subjected the Israeli passports to minute examination.
They arrested the El Al and Kour Corporation representatives
and one of the Israeli security men, charging that they were
not Israelis but Iranian Jews who were forbidden to leave the
country. Harmelin announced to the officer responsible for the
airport that he would not leave Tehran without the three men.
After five hours of nerve-racking negotiations, and at the personal intervention of Ayatollah Montazeri, a leading member
of the religious establishment, the three prisoners were freed
and allowed to leave Iran. The Israelis took off on a Pan American
flight to Frankfurt, arriving in Israel in a special El Al plane at
close to midnight, bringing to an end 25 years of Israeli cooperation with the Iranian monarch.

5

Khomeini Takes Charge

The Khomeini regime confronted the U.S. and Israel with new and painful realities. The new Iranian regime, in an effort to consolidate its base of power, embarked on a ruthless purge among the Shah's supporters. Cabinet ministers, thousands of senior army and police officers, and agents of the Savak were summarily executed. Thousands more were arrested because of their loyalty to the ancien regime or because of alleged corruption and other alleged crimes. A new reign of terror replaced its predecessor. No citizen was certain of his or her future.

This new reality was particularly damaging to the U.S. and Israel. Overnight, both countries were cut off from their sources of information as all their previous contacts had been executed or arrested. The intelligence services of the two countries, for all their reputation for excellence, had now little information on Iran, and what they had was insufficient and of poor quality. As a result, each country secretly hoped that the other knew more. Even the limited intelligence they did have was not regularly exchanged in due time, and so was not available to Israeli and American decision makers.

It took some time, for instance, for anyone to realize that terrorist actions sponsored by Iran were aimed at giving Khomeini's government leverage over American policy. The capture of the American embassy in Tehran, the bombing of American targets in Beirut, and the kidnapping of American nationals in Lebanon were not aimed at humiliating the U.S. or weakening American support of Israel, but at influencing America's Persian Gulf policy. Although information about Iranian assistance to Lebanese Shiite groups began coming in as early as July 1982, it was only in 1984 that the U.S. and Israel found clear Iranian (together with Syrian and Libyan) fingerprints on acts of international terrorism against American targets.

It is impossible to understand how the U.S. and Israel got themselves entangled in Iran in the Iran-Contra scandal without understanding the special relations that Khomeini established during the last years of the Shah's reign with the Palestinian guerrilla organizations, or the complete reversal of political realities in the Persian Gulf region and the special ties between Khomeini's Iran, Syria, and the Shiite militias in Lebanon.

The secret relations between Khomeini and the Palestinians were first revealed on February 18, 1979, during PLO chairman Yassir Arafat's visit to Tehran. Arafat came at the head of a 60-man entourage and was the first foreign leader to personally congratulate Khomeini on his victory. Arafat met with Khomeini immediately upon arriving, and thereafter told reporters: "When I entered Iranian air space, I felt as if I was about to pass through the gates of Jerusalem. Today the Islamic Revolution is victorious in Tehran; tomorrow we will be victorious in Palestine." At that same meeting, Arafat claimed that the PLO had trained more than 10,000 young Iranians in its military camps, and had equipped each of them with a Kalishnikov rifle. He also admitted that PLO fighters had taken an active part in the last stage of the Iranian Revolution, and expressed his hope that volunteers from Iran would take part in the struggle to liberate Palestine. Khomeini confirmed Arafat's words when he told reporters that "The Iranian Revolution will repay the Palestinians for the help they gave us in overthrowing the Shah, and Iranian volunteers will take part in the struggle to end the Zionist conquest and to liberate Jerusalem."[1]

Arafat received his first "repayment" even before his plane landed. In an official statement released on February 18, Prime Minister Mehdi Bazargan announced that all relations with Israel were being severed, including oil, mail, and air links between the two countries. An even more formal expression of Israel's new status in Tehran came soon afterward. In the presence of Bazargan, Foreign Minister Karim Sanjabi, and Revolutionary Council member Dr. Ibrahim Yazdi, Arafat raised the Palestinian flag over the Israeli mission building in Tehran. The street where it was located, Kakh Street, was renamed Palestine Street, and Hani El-Hassan, one of Arafat's closest advisers, was appointed the PLO's first representative in Iran.

El-Hassan soon became one of the most prominent figures in the Iranian capital. The local press regularly reported on his meetings with Khomeini; the Bazargan government also approved the establishment, in each city and at each university, of committees for the support of the Palestinian revolution. The newspaper *Ettela'at* reported in its May 7, 1979, issue that El-Hassan had been given all the Savak records dealing with Israel-Iran cooperation during the Shah's reign.

Arafat's appearance in Tehran was the climax of the partnership between Khomeini and the Palestinians, formed a decade previously to fight together against the Shah, the U.S., Israel, and Jordan. Since the PLO had been formed in Jerusalem in 1964 under the leadership of Ahmed Shukeiri, and especially after Arafat's el-Fatah organization had begun carrying out terrorist acts against Israel and undermining King Hussein in 1965, the Palestinians and the Shah had parted ways. They came together for a short period after the Six Day War, when the Palestinians were the only Arab force fighting Israel. This had made them popular among religious and nationalist groups in Iran, and this popularity increased when Shukeiri was replaced by Arafat in 1968. Khomeini saw in Arafat a fighter worthy of emulation, and he made contact with the PLO leader from his exile in Najaf, Iraq, through the PLO representative in Baghdad.

Hoping to abort this infant alliance, the then Iranian foreign minister, Ardeshir Zahedi, invited PLO representatives to visit Tehran. The Shah was not, however, willing to go beyond this gesture and extend active support to the Palestinian terrorist organizations.

The Shah met with Arafat for the first time in October 1969. The two were both participating in the summit conference of Moslem countries convened in Rabat, Morocco, after an arson attempt on the al-Aksa Mosque in Jerusalem. Arafat made a very bad impression on the Shah. He arrived at their meeting with a pistol in his belt, fabricating stories about nonexistent "victories." The Shah complained to the PLO leader about the developing cooperation between the Palestinian organizations and the opposition in Iran. Arafat claimed not to know anything about this, and avoided giving any definite answers. The Shah told his aides at the end of the meeting that "Arafat is no different from Shukeiri," and he refused to meet him again.[2]

Ties were soon to tighten between Arafat and Khomeini, and between the leftist Palestinian groups led by George Habash, Nayef Hawatmeh, and Ahmed Jibril and the leftist opposition in Iran. The Shah's opponents hoped that the PLO could help them gain support among left-wing groups in Western Europe and in the developing world, and saw the PLO as a channel of communications with the Kremlin. Khomeini saw the PLO as a means of influencing the large concentrations of Palestinians in Kuwait and the Persian Gulf principalities. In contrast to the Palestinians in Jordan, Syria, and Lebanon, who were under the constant scrutiny of the security services of each of those countries, the Palestinians in the Persian Gulf region had a strong economic position and relative political freedom; their national consciousness was high. Many of them had senior positions in the Gulf states, and some of them even served in the local police forces and armies. This made it easy for the terrorist groups to operate, giving them protection and a base from which to raise money for their struggle.

At the beginning of the 1970s, the PLO began admitting young Iranians into its training camps in Syria, Lebanon, Libya, and Iraq, making Arafat an active partner in the efforts to depose the Shah. Palestinian spokesmen echoed the propaganda of the Shiite mullahs, according to which the Shah was a Jew, distorting his family name of Pahlavi to "Papa Levy."

While Arafat's el-Fatah organization aided Khomeini and the Iranian Marxist-Islamic Mujahidin Khalk movement, George Habash's Popular Front for the Liberation of Palestine allied itself with the Marxist-Leninist Fedai'yin Khalk movement led by Hamid Ashraf. Habash tried to establish ties with the religious establishment as well, but his Marxist and atheistic ideology were clearly in conflict with Khomeini's religious fanaticism. Another leftist Palestinian faction, Hawatmen's Democratic Front, also supported leftist groups loyal to Moscow, while the Palestine Liberation Front headed by Abu El-Abbas lent support to the ethnic Arabs of the Khuzistan region; this group would later help Iraq try to incite a rebellion of these Persian Arabs against Khomeini in Iran's oil capital, Abadan.

The Palestinian-Iranian opposition alliance first become apparent in June 1971, in an attempt to attack oil tankers transporting Iranian oil to Israel. Since the Arab oil principalities along the Persian Gulf coast had an interest in free shipping, Iran had no special problem in sending tankers from its Kharg Island to Eilat. In June 1971, however, Palestinian guerrillas belonging to the Popular Front set out from Perim Island in a motorboat and shot a bazooka at a Liberian tanker, *The Coral Sea*, which had Israeli sailors on board. They missed, and the terrorists made a quick escape to South Yemen. The oil princedoms feared that the incident would disrupt navigation in the Gulf and, together with Saudi Arabia, prevailed upon the Palestinian groups to halt their attempts to attack the oil shipments to Israel. The Palestinians feared that continuing the campaign would bring an end to the financial support they received from the oil states, and to their ability to enlist men and buy weapons and equipment in these countries.

Additional proof of the strong ties between Habash and the Marxist opposition in Iran continued to fall into the Shah's hands. In July 1976, for instance, the Savak intercepted a letter from Habash to Hamid Ashraf dealing with joint operations of their two factions. On August 8 of that same year, a letter from Habash was read before gatherings of Iranian students in Chicago and Los Angeles, in which the Palestinian leader expressed his people's support for the struggle against the Shah.

When, at the beginning of 1978, the opposition opened its final struggle to unseat the Shah, it quickly became clear that the PLO was doing its best to take an active part in the revolution. During Israel's Operation Litani of March 1978, Israeli soldiers in southern Lebanon captured an Iranian who told them under interrogation of the training Iranian students were receiving in PLO camps in different Arab countries. Other Iranian prisoners related that they had been sent for training with the PLO in preparation for being infiltrated into the Iraqi Shiite community to incite rebellion against the Ba-athist secular regime there. The spiritual leader of the Shiites of south Lebanon, Imam Mussa Sadr, had in the past maintained close ties with the Savak, but after he was elected to head the Supreme Islamic Shiite Council, he resumed his ties with the religious establishment in Tehran, putting Khomeini in touch with Damascus. He disappeared mysteriously from Rome Airport at the end of 1978 after a short visit to Libya.

The disappearance created a vacuum in the Lebanese Shiite leadership. The Shah tried to fill it. The Lebanese Shiites had long suffered from the Palestinians who came to virtually rule their region, but they were also discriminated against by the country's Christian leadership. In Operation Litani the Israelis had expelled the Palestinian guerrillas from the Shiite villages, making life easier for the locals. The Lebanese Shiites did not, however, want to be detached from Lebanon, and saw the Israeli army as a foreign occupier. Yet they wanted to be able to protect themselves against the return of the Palestinians. Israel encouraged them, granting economic aid and community assistance, hoping to make the Shiites feel less victimized and less anti-Israel. The Shah shared this objective, not only in order to keep the Lebanese Shiites from supporting Khomeini, but also in order to expose those among them who were plotting against him. Iran's embassy in Beirut, however, strongly opposed any cooperation with Israel in this matter.

The PLO's involvement in the struggle against the Shah continued to grow. While many Iranians had contacts with the Palestinians, the most prominent of them was one of Khomeini's closest advisers, Mustafa Ali Chamran. Chamran, who had a Ph.D. in physics from the University of California at Berkeley, and would later become the Islamic republic's first minister of defense, had left Iran in 1957. After finishing his studies in the U.S., he had come to Lebanon and married a young Palestinian woman, leading him to identify with the PLO and its goals. Chamran was trained in PLO camps in southern Lebanon and, while working as the principal of a high school in Tyre, he looked after all the Iranians who came to the PLO bases in Lebanon. As revolutionary fervor swept through Iran, Chamran played an important part in smuggling arms and fighters into Tehran and in making the PLO's role in the revolution a prominent one.

On November 22, 1978, after Khomeini was expelled from Iraq and found asylum in France, he was visited by Farouk

Kaddoumi, head of the PLO political department, and a special Libyan envoy. The two of them offered the Ayatollah arms and money. The next day Radio Tripoli began broadcasting, in Persian, coded messages to Khomeini's supporters in Iran, while Palestinian guerrillas, supplied with false passports, were sent into Tehran. Under the circumstances, it is hardly surprising that Arafat, upon arriving in Tehran on February 18, 1979, called Tehran his second home, after Jerusalem.

Khomeini's revolution and the Iran-Iraq War that came not long afterward further polarized the Arab world, once again aligning the pro-Western states against the pro-Soviet ones. On September 22, 1980, the day after hostilities broke out, it was already clear that Egypt, Saudi Arabia, Jordan, and the Gulf principalities were unreservedly pro-Iraqi, while Syria and Libya stood behind Iran. This split the united front against Israel, weakened Iraq's position among the nonaligned nations, and embittered the propaganda war among the different Arab states. Arab diplomacy degenerated once again into catcalls and insults. Iraqi President Saddam Hussein called Khomeini "a maniac playing prophet, when in truth he is nothing but a heretic working in the service of the U.S. and Israel"; Khomeini called Saddam Hussein "a criminal and an enemy of Islam, whose hand pokes out of an American sleeve and grasps the hand of Israel."[3]

The Gulf War became the longest and bloodiest war the Middle East had ever seen, and its effects were felt far beyond the border between the two warring countries. It was not long before it had turned into a modern version of the religious struggles that had characterized the region from the beginning of the medieval period, when Shiite Islam became the refuge of the social and economic outcasts of the Sunni establishment. This religious tension was expressed in modern times by the unending struggle between Iraq and Iran over shipping rights, oil resources, and strategic position. Immediately after the signing on March 6, 1975, of the Algiers accords, under which Iran halted its support of the Kurdish rebels in northern Iraq in exchange for Iraqi recognition of Iranian rights in the Shatt al-Arab, it was clear that Iraq would not long live with this concession. The overthrow of the Shah, which provoked the fear of Saddam Hussein and his Arab neighbors that Khomeini would try to export his Shiite revolution to the other countries of the region, provided an opportunity. Saddam Hussein at first leaned toward working through the Iranian opposition led by Shahpour Bakhtiar and General Ali Oveissi. Contacts with these two men began in April 1980 and lasted through the summer. Bakhtiar and Oveissi visited Baghdad several times, infiltrated agents into Khuzistan and Kurdistan, and set up training bases for their loyalists. Bakhtiar planned to "liberate" part of Khuzistan in order to establish a new Iranian government headed by the late Shah's son, Reza. This government would win immediate recognition from Iraq, Egypt, Jordan, and the Gulf principalities. The revolution, code-named "Nojeh," was scheduled for July 10, 1980, but it was uncovered by the Iranian security services and crushed. Two hundred and fifty of Bakhtiar's supporters, including a number of army officers, were arrested, and 36 were executed.[4]

After this failure, Saddam Hussein decided to act directly. In May 1980, King Hussein and the Crown Prince of Kuwait visited Baghdad and promised their support in the war against Khomeini. On August 5, Saddam Hussein went to Riyadh for the first visit by an Iraqi President to the Saudi kingdom, and coordinated action against Iran. Upon his return he cut off diplomatic relations with Syria and began making careful preparations for the war. From Iraq's point of view, the timing was good—the U.S. was preoccupied with its election campaign and with the American hostages in Tehran; the Soviets were busy with the Polish crisis and with their war in Afghanistan; Syria was isolated in the Arab world, its alliance with Libya meaningless; Israel, despite its enmity toward the Baghdad regime, would certainly not exploit the opportunity to launch a surprise attack on Iraq, thus igniting the entire Persian Gulf.

However, despite the advantage of surprise and careful planning, the Iraqi army was unable to win a quick and decisive victory, and the war soon turned from a blitzkrieg into a long war of attrition with its end, and its results, still nowhere in sight. It has killed more than a million soldiers and damaged the oil production capacity of both countries, as well as destroyed a good part of their economies, and emptied their treasuries. In addition, the war has forced the U.S. into a more active role in the region.

The salient characteristic of the Persian Gulf region is the existence of a number of sparsely populated and militarily weak oil-rich states in strategically important geographic locations. Saudi Arabia, Kuwait, Oman, and the United Arab Emirates lack any significant ability to defend themselves, and each has a semitribal political system and undefined social structure. The independence of these countries has always depended on a regional balance of power, on generous technical and financial support of Arab countries weaker economically but stronger militarily than they are, and especially on American guarantees of help in time of need.

Since the 1970s, the U.S. had acted in accordance with the "Nixon Doctrine," founded on Iran's military might and Saudi Arabia's wealth. Iran became during that period the second most important oil-exporting state in the world, after Saudi Arabia, and Israel's major source of oil. Iran's strategic importance went, however, far beyond the narrow bounds of the oil market. As a country with a 1,550-mile border with the Soviet Union, Iran served as a formidable territorial barrier against Soviet expansion toward the Indian Ocean and the Persian Gulf. With the help of massive supplies of arms and military equipment, the U.S. turned the 350,000-man Iranian army into the police force of the Gulf, and set up seven early-warning and listening stations aimed at the U.S.S.R., two of them to monitor missile launches.

When Khomeini rose to power in February 1979, this pro-Western bulwark collapsed. The Shah's downfall meant the end of the American foothold in Iran and seriously weakened America's deterrent power against the Soviets in that region. The U.S. had port services in Bahrain, and it had a small anchorage at the island of Diego Garcia in the Indian Ocean, but it had no permanent bases in Saudia Arabia or the other Gulf states. Egypt, which controlled the oil route through the Suez Canal, could have helped defend the Red Sea region, but it was militarily weak and its internal stability uncertain. Of all the countries in the area, only Israel was militarily strong and politically stable. But since it was not at peace with Arab countries, the U.S. could not make use of it in defending the Gulf.

The day after the Israel-Egypt peace treaty was signed in Washington on March 26, 1979, the U.S. turned its attention to the implications of the events in Iran. After a trip to the Middle East in April 1979, the Foreign Relations Committee of the U.S. Senate recommended using bases in Egypt, Oman,

Kenya, and Somalia, but rejected the use of Israeli bases, out of fear that:

- it would be interpreted as support of Israel against the Arab countries, or as a direct American threat to the Persian Gulf nations and their oil wells;
- the establishment of a base in Israel would be seen as an abandonment of America's balanced policy in the Middle East, which would in turn damage President Carter's ability to bring peace to the region;
- in the case of a new Middle East war, regardless of which country began it, the American base would be a target of attack, and could thus draw the U.S. into direct involvement in the conflict;
- Arab states which had previously refused to give bases to the Soviets would be tempted to do so, simply to balance the American presence in Israel; and
- the U.S. would alienate Arab oil-producers by favoring Israel over pro-Western Arab countries.

Following policy reevaluation, the U.S. established the Rapid Deployment Force in 1980 and received the right to use the Kena air force base in Upper Egypt as a launching point for reconnaissance flights over the Red Sea and Persian Gulf regions.

The Soviet invasion of Afghanistan on December 25, 1979, changed the balance of power and increased the Communist threat in the Persian Gulf. The Soviets now had the ability to hit any target in the region and block the Straits of Hormuz by use of long-range bombers, intercontinental missiles, an airborne force stationed in the Caucasus, Afghan air bases, and ports in Aden and Eritrea. The U.S. was well aware of the danger. The election of Ronald Reagan as the fortieth president of the United States strengthened trends that had begun during the Carter administration with regard to the defense of the Gulf. Reagan pushed for an active American presence in the region not only as a display of force, but also as an expression of American willingness to use it. In the face of the threat to the countries of the region posed by the Khomeini regime, Reagan set three goals for his Persian Gulf policy:

- to guarantee free access to oil sources and prevent interference in the supply of oil to Japan and industrialized Europe;

- to deter Soviet aggression against pro-Western regimes that ran responsible oil policies with regard to price range and supply; and
- to preserve the territorial stability of the countries of the region by trying to bring the Iran-Iraq War to a conclusion in a way that would not lead to Iraq's defeat, but also leave the door open to renewing links with Khomeini's successors.

Within the framework of this policy, the anchorage in the horseshoe-shaped coral atoll of Diego Garcia was greatly expanded, so as to be able to serve a large task force. Over the previous six years, from 1972 to 1978, the U.S. had invested hundreds of millions of dollars on expanding its bases in Oman. Oman's ruler, Sultan Qaboos Bin-Said, allowed the U.S. to build a large airport in his country, as well as to deepen and widen the ports and build various facilities on Massira Island. Once every two years the U.S., together with Oman, engages in a military maneuver meant to test its ability to deploy, within a period of six weeks, a task force including 1,000 planes and several hundred thousand soldiers. Even Saudi Arabia, which like Egypt has refused to allow a permanent American military presence on its territory, bought a large quantity of ammunition and spare parts for the weapons in its possession. This emergency store could serve U.S. forces in an emergency. In addition, American-Egyptian military cooperation strengthened, and Reagan, unlike Carter, did not hesitate to establish the foundation for strategic cooperation with Israel.

Khomeini was fearsome enough for the U.S. initially to try its best to weaken and topple the fanatic Moslem regime. American intelligence officers met on a regular basis with the late Shah's son, Reza, in Morocco, as well as with General Gholam Ali Oveissi in the U.S., with former Chief of Staff Feridoun Jam in London, and with former air force commander Madani in Germany. The U.S. also maintained contact with the Islamic republic's first and now-exiled President, Abulhassan Bani-Sadr, and with two former Prime Ministers, Ali Amini and Shahpour Bakhtiar, who resided in Paris. None of this talk led, however, to any action.

The U.S. soon discovered that organizing a military coup in Iran was a very complicated matter.[5] The Iranian armed services had fallen apart and the Revolutionary Guards (the Pasdaran) had become the principal military force on which the regime depended for its own existence and for the war against Iraq. Khomeini did away with all the senior officers who had been loyal to the Shah and made sure that no man suspected of admiration for the West entered the government. There was, of course, a possibility that, given his advanced age, Khomeini might die suddenly or that an ambitious officer might seize power in Tehran, as Gamal Abd El-Nasser had in Cairo and Hafez El-Assad in Damascus. There did not, however, seem to be any Iranian Nasser on the horizon.

The Iran-Iraq War brought about a gradual loosening of the ties between Khomeini and the PLO and the establishment of a solid alliance between Syria and Iran that included direct Iranian involvement in Lebanon. Despite the ideological opposition of the Islamic Revolution and the secular, pan-Arab ideology of the Ba'ath regime, Syria and Iran found common ground for joint action in a number of areas.

Syria had been isolated in the Arab world during the last years of the Shah's rule by the formation of the Tehran-Riyadh-Cairo axis. This isolation grew when President Sadar signed his peace treaty with Israel. The new alliance with Iran gave Syria a needed way to counter its Ba'athist friend, rival Iraq, and strengthened Syrian influence among the large Shiite community in Lebanon. For Iran, now the enemy of all the Sunni Moslem Arab states, the alliance was important in disputing the claim that this war was another in the centuries-long history of Persian-Arab conflicts, and in giving Khomeini an opportunity to gain the loyalty of the Lebanese Shiites.

Nevertheless, cooperation between the two countries in Lebanon was at first limited and insignificant. In December 1979, for instance, a force of 300 Iranian volunteers set out for Damascus, on its way to southern Lebanon. Led by Mohammed Montazeri, it arrived in the Syrian capital without having made any prior arrangements, putting Assad in an awkward position. Lebanese President Elias Sarkis feared that this little army would intervene in his country's internal crisis under the pretense of fighting Israel, aiding the Shiites in their struggle against the Christians. Sarkis called Assad and asked him to prevent the Iranians from entering Lebanon. Assad, frightened that they would open up a second front for him with Israel, immediately agreed and sent the Iranians to an el-Fatah training camp near Damascus.[6]

Syria and Iran came to an agreement in March 1982 under which Syria would receive oil in exchange for closing its border with Iraq and shutting down the Iraqi oil pipeline that passed through its territory. In May, Syria concentrated forces on the Iraqi border, forcing Iraq to divert part of its military strength westward and northward. This aided the Iranian offensive that drove the Iraqis back from the border and brought the Iranian forces to the international border.

Israel's invasion of Lebanon in June 1982, which was aimed to destroy the PLO infrastructure and help elect the commander of the Lebanese (Christian) forces as the new President of that country, gave Khomeini his chance to prove his devotion to the struggle against "Zionist imperialism." Despite the strains of the Gulf War, Iran opened a "second front" against the U.S. and Israel in Lebanon, making use of the local Shiites in an attempt to bring the Islamic Revolution to that country.

Khomeini had never hidden his intention of exporting his revolution to other countries with large Shiite and Sunnite Moslem populations. A year before the war, on June 8, 1981, the Iranian Majlis approved legislation allowing "volunteers" to go and fight Israel in southern Lebanon. This decision was confirmed by the Supreme Security Council and the Revolutionary Guards command. Khomeini took another step in this direction in November when he established an Islamic Revolutionary Council assigned to coordinate Shiite subversive activities in Iraq, the Persian Gulf states, and Lebanon. Since Assad was not at all enthusiastic about the idea,[7] the activity in Lebanon was of a limited nature. In Iraq, despite—or perhaps because of—the war, the Shiite population tended to identify more with their own government than with Khomeini. The result was that most of Khomeini's efforts were directed toward the oil states of the Persian Gulf. Under the direction of Hajjotelislam Hadi Modaressi, Iran began to organize subversive activities in Bahrain, Qatar, and Kuwait, and supervised similar activity in Saudi Arabia during the pilgrimage season.

When Israel invaded Lebanon, Syria provided greater support to Khomeini's involvement there. The day after hostilities began, a high-level Iranian political-military delegation arrived in Damascus, headed by the commander of the ground forces, Colonel Sayyed Shirazi, as a show of solidarity with Syria and in order to plan the Jihad, or holy war, against Israel.[8] In an announcement to the Majlis on June 10, 1982, Iranian Prime Minister Mir Hussein Mussavi called for "war until victory in el-Quds"— the Moslem name for Jerusalem—and asked the parliament to budget funds for the war "until the liberation of Palestine," in his words "an inseparable part of the Moslem motherland."

In the wake of the Shirazi delegation's visit to Damascus, President Assad allowed 800 Iranian volunteers into Lebanon. Another 700 arrived later and were dispersed among different villages in the Bekaa Valley. Three hundred volunteers, all members of the Revolutionary Guards, set up a command post in Baalbek headed by Sheikh Emami. They worked together with the Islamic Amal organization headed by Hussein Mussawi, a high school teacher who had in May of that year resigned his position as commander of the military arm of the Shiite Amal movement headed by the lawyer Nabih Berry. Mussawi's brother, Sheikh Abbas Mussawi, together with Sheikh Subhi Tufayli, were among the leaders of the Shiite extremist Hezbollah group in the Baalbek region. One of Hezbollah's most prominent leaders in Beirut was Ibrahim el-Amin, the organization's spokesman and coordinator of the suicide unit headed by Imam Hussein Abdul Ilah Mussawi, also known as Mir Hashem. Members of this unit, sometimes called "Brigade 110," made up of fanatic volunteers from various Arab countries and Iran, would later carry out suicide attacks on American, French, and Israeli targets in Lebanon. Hezbollah found it convenient to operate under a variety of names—"El-Jihad el-Islami," "Amal el-Islami," "The Revolutionary Justice Organization," "The Oppressed of This World," and "The Islamic Jihad for the Liberation of Palestine," among others.

The arrival of the Revolutionary Guards and their cooperation with the Shiite militias changed the nature of Iranian involvement in Lebanon. Inspired by Khomeini, Sheikh Muhamad Hussein Fadhlallah, one of the most respected Shiite clerics in Beirut, agreed to head Hezbollah ("The Party of God"), which became a sort of umbrella organization for all the extremist Shiite groups in the country. Fadhlallah visited Tehran a number of times, meeting with Khomeini and members of the Iranian religious establishment. He organized his movement on the Iranian model, putting mullahs above political leaders and military commanders. Calling Lebanon part of the "world Moslem nation," Fadhlallah nevertheless recognized the complexity of

Lebanon's problems and did not see an immediate possibility for carrying out this program. In the meantime he hoped to ensure equality and social justice for the Shiite community. He realized that the Christians, Druze, and Sunni Moslems were determined to prevent Shiite rule of the country, and that Syria was also unwilling to see this. While President Assad belonged to the Alawite sect, an offshoot of Shiite Islam, most of Syria's population was Sunni and his support of a Shiite republic in Lebanon was liable to enrage most of his country-men. The activity of Hezbollah and other Lebanese pro-Iranian organizations was, therefore, dependent on the extent of the support it received from Damascus. When Assad came to under-stand Iran's real intentions, he gave his unreserved support to the more moderate Shiite faction, Amal, led by Nabih Berry.

Israel's intervention in Lebanon led Hezbollah to set for itself—with the active support of Syria and Iran—two major goals: getting Israel out and ending the influence of the "imperi-alist powers"—the U.S. and France—in Lebanon. It achieved both goals. Under pressure from Syria and Iran, President Je-mayyel repudiated the limited "normalization" agreement he had signed with Israel on May 17, 1983. The U.S. evacuated its Marines from Beirut in February 1984 following the October 1983 bombing of the Marine barracks, and in June 1985 the Israeli army withdrew from the Shouf Mountains and from Bei-rut, retreating to a security zone in south Lebanon without having made any real political gains.

Khomeini used the *Shahid*, or Martyrs' Fund, to funnel money to Sheikh Fadhlallah designated to be distributed among Shiite families in Beirut and southern Lebanon and to pay the mem-bers of the various militias. Iranian money also went to activists in the Shiite establishment, aimed at building a political, eco-nomic, and educational infrastructure that would serve as a base for the community's eventual takeover of Lebanon as a whole.[9] In contrast to Amal, Hezbollah did not set up an institu-tionalized, hierarchical organization, seeing itself as a mass organization without a bureaucracy, deriving authority from Khomeini and from Allah, based on a tight-knit core of fanatic fighters and on a wider militia. In a short time Hezbollah had metamorphosed from a marginal group into a large movement challenging Amal's influence.

Over time Iranian activity in Lebanon deepened and became

institutionalized; the large salaries it paid to Hezbollah men helped that movement gain on the larger Amal organization, despite the support it received from Syria. Iran's deputy foreign minister, Hossein Shekholislam Zadeh, was eventually made into a sort of Iranian "high commissioner" for Lebanon. He made (and still makes) frequent visits to Damascus, overseeing arms shipments to the Shiite militias in coordination with General Ghazi Kan'an, a Syrian intelligence officer in Beirut; he also funds the training of Hezbollah fighters in the Bekaa Valley. The Iranian ambassador in Damascus, Hajjotelislam Ali Akbar Moghtashemipur, the Iranian delegate in Beirut, Mahmoud Nurani, and Issa Tabatabai, appointed by the Revolutionary Guards to oversee the Palestinian refugee camps in the Tyre and Sidon regions, all work under Zadeh's direction. In April 1983 Syria allowed Iranian volunteers to enter Beirut as well.

Immediately afterward this Iranian involvement became evident. In two incidents in 1983, one on April 18 and the other on October 23, Shiite suicide fighters detonated car bombs next to the American embassy and the Marines headquarters in Beirut. The two attacks killed 258 American soldiers and civilians and 46 Lebanese. Another car bomb was used against the French military headquarters in Beirut, killing 58 paratroopers.[10] Investigations of the incidents revealed that Zadeh had been in Damascus at the time and had given the orders for the operations through an Iranian intelligence officer code-named "Abu Muslih." On November 4, 1983, a bomb was detonated in the Israeli army headquarters in Tyre, killing 29 soldiers. The investigation of this attack also revealed Iranian involvement. Israel retaliated by launching two air attacks on the Revolutionary Guard headquarters and on an Islamic Jihad camp in Baalbek, in which 23 Iranian volunteers were killed. On January 11, 1984, Professor Malcom Kerr, an American orientalist serving as president of the American University of Beirut, was murdered. In response to these incidents, on January 20, 1984, Secretary of State George Shultz declared Iran to be "a country abetting international terror."

These terrorist attacks came despite the fact that, at the beginning of 1983, it seemed that the U.S. had accepted Khomeini's revolution as an established fact and even, for a moment, seemed to have moderated its hostility toward the Islamic republic. Against the background of the opposition of both countries to the Soviet presence in Afghanistan, and the assistance lent by the U.S., Iran, and Saudi Arabia to the Afghan rebels, in early 1983 the U.S. made an important gesture toward Khomeini—it gave Iran detailed information about the dimensions of government and army infiltration by activists from the Tudeh, the Iranian Communist party.[11] It also turned over information about Soviet support for the left-wing Mujahidin Khalk movement. The U.S. hoped that this move would moderate Khomeini's attitude toward the Gulf states, and perhaps also prepare the ground for the end of the war with Iraq. On May 4, 1983, Khomeini made use of this information to liquidate 200 Tudeh activists, among them his naval commander, Bahram Afzali. The identity of the main Soviet contact in Iran was also uncovered—Abbas Zamani or "Abu Sharif," Iran's deputy director of intelligence and a former ambassador to Pakistan. Khomeini thus dealt a mortal blow to the pro-Soviet forces in Iran, although he did not destroy them completely. Yet Iran continued to attack American targets in Lebanon.

In fact, Iran increased its involvement in terrorism against Israel and the U.S. in Lebanon. A new era opened in Lebanon's long history of terrorism—the age of kidnapping. Between March 4, 1984, and June 9, 1985, seven Americans were kidnapped in Beirut and held hostage by the pro-Iranian Hezbollah organization and by the Islamic Jihad. The most prominent of the hostages was William Buckley, a 57-year-old bachelor and head of the CIA station in Lebanon. Tall, black-haired, with a deep voice and a broad smile, Buckley's external appearance was quite imposing. Behind his quiet facade hid a strong and adventurous personality. Buckley's cover as a CIA agent had been broken in a book about the CIA. Ignoring the risk, Casey posted him to Lebanon. As a result, when he was kidnapped, his pro-Iranian captors knew exactly who they had. They used cruel and horrendous tortures to wring every crumb of information about his actions and about American Middle East policy from him. His confession spread over 400 pages,[11a] and was sent to Tehran and Damascus—and by Syrian intelligence to the Soviet Union and its allies.

Concern about the fate of Buckley and other hostages was one of the main components of the complex drama in which American arms were secretly sent to Iran in direct opposition to the declared policy of the Reagan administration. The story had all the necessary elements of a spy thriller: envoys traveling on forged passports to enemy countries, clever and devious arms salesmen, huge sums passing from hand to hand and deposited in secret Swiss bank accounts. All these elements were woven into a fabric of intrigues and conspiracies in which the fate of innocent hostages became dependent on power struggles and wars of succession that lasted many months.

Reagan was particularly sensitive to the plight of the hostages. He owed his presidency in part to what American voters saw as President Carter's weakness in facing the hostage crisis involving the American embassy in Tehran. The long internment of the seven hostages in Beirut made Reagan's declarations about America's strength seem ridiculous. As time passed and the suffering of the hostages increased, the pressure on Reagan—and in CIA headquarters—grew.

There was little Casey could do to help, other than urge Reagan to tighten the siege on Iran and cut it off from its sources of arms. Within the framework of "Operation Staunch," coordinated by Secretary of State Shultz, the U.S. pressured its allies not to supply weapons to the Iranian war machine. Iran was, as a result, put in a strange position: its allies, Syria and Libya, were armed with Soviet weapons—but Iran needed American and European weapons.

Beginning in September 1984, however, several developments in the U.S. and Iran made it necessary for both countries to reevaluate their policies. As the Iranian Revolution institutionalized itself, it gave Khomeini and his supporters a sense of security, but did not ease the country's economic and social problems. The war caused discontent among important sectors of the population. Khomeini's waning health led to a power struggle to succeed him, with each faction looking for allies to help it overcome its opponents. The most important factor in the struggle for succession was weapons. It was clear that the faction that succeeded in breaking through the American embargo and supplying the army and the Revolutionary Guards with the weapons they needed to defeat Iraq would win power as well. The man who, more than any other, voiced the new tendency toward moderation was the Speaker of the Parliament, Hashimi Rafsanjani. At a press conference in July 1984, Rafsanjani praised the high quality of American arms and said they were better than Soviet or French equipment. He added that his country did not rule out the possibility of purchasing American arms, directly or indirectly. In November of that year Iranian arms agents invaded arms markets all over the world, offering information on what was going on in Iran, and captured Soviet weaponry, in exchange for American arms. Some salesmen even hinted vaguely that supplying arms would lead to the release of the American hostages in Beirut.[12]

A similar process of reevaluation was going on in the U.S. On August 31, 1984, National Security Adviser Robert McFarlane ordered the preparation of a detailed evaluation of what was likely to happen in Iran after Khomeini's death. McFarlane believed the reports of internal difficulties in Iran. Adding in the fall in world oil prices and its likely effect, it seemed worthwhile to examine if any political changes could be expected soon, and who had the best chance of succeeding Iran's aging leader.

On October 19, 1984, the State Department submitted its evaluation to McFarlane, expressing the views of the Defense Department and the American intelligence agencies as well. It analyzed at length the changes in Iran, both in its foreign relations and in its internal policies. The report also summed up the war situation and evaluated the chances of several key figures succeeding Khomeini. The conclusion was emphatic: the U.S. had no ability to influence events in Iran and, in the absence of additional information, it was recommended not to take any action.[13]

In October 1984 Shimon Peres visited Washington, his first visit as Prime Minister. Peres and Reagan discussed the subject of Iran and the hostages in general terms. They were both aware, of course, of the importance of the Persian Gulf and the role Iran could play in halting Soviet expansion. They agreed, however, that they were powerless to do anything for the hostages. Just as the U.S. was concerned about the fate of its hostages, Israel was concerned about four of its soldiers who had been lost in action in Lebanon, and about five Lebanese Jews who had been kidnapped in Beirut. Since neither country could rescue its hostages by force, Reagan could do no more than continue his "Operation Staunch" and keep pressuring his allies not to sell weapons to Iran.

Reagan's decision did not bind arms salesmen, of course. With this in mind, General Manucher Hashemi, former chief of counterintelligence in the Savak, and Manucher Ghorbanifar

met with Theodore Shackley, one of a group of American businessmen with intelligence backgrounds who were involved,
among other things, in smuggling arms to the Contras in Nicaragua. Since retiring from his position as deputy chief of operations of the CIA in 1978, Shackley had run a consultancy in
risk management, called Research Associates, Inc. It was through
this office that he had established contact with General Hashemi. They met at the Four Seasons Hotel in Hamburg, where
the Iranian exile introduced Shackley to Ayatollah Hassan Karoubi, Ghorbanifar, and Dr. Shahbadi, director of the Iranian
purchasing delegation in Germany and a personal friend of
Adnan Khashoggi. Hashemi presented Ghorbanifar as a man
who had "excellent connections" with Iranian government leaders. Ghorbanifar told Shackley that there was a danger that
Iran would become a Soviet client state within the next three
to five years. He claimed that he and General Hashemi wished
to return Iran to the West, but that they had not found anyone
in Washington willing to listen to them. Ghorbanifar said that
fate had placed the future of the Iranian people in the hands
of President Reagan, and he had to help the moderates in
Iran attain power after Khomeini's death.[14]

Aware of Shackley's past in the CIA, Ghorbanifar feared that
he knew that in 1980 the Americans had washed their hands
of him and decided that he was unreliable. As a result, he
tried to head off objections by telling Shackley in advance
that the CIA did not trust him and claimed that he was undisci-
plined and a fantasizer. He was especially angry at the Frankfurt
CIA station chief who treated him, he said, "like a piece of
Kleenex" that one wipes one's nose with and discards. So if
Shackley wanted to do business with him, the CIA would have
to stay out of the picture.

Ghorbanifar wished to purchase, through Shackley, TOW antitank missiles. In return, he said, he could supply captured
Soviet weaponry, including a T-72 tank. He also hinted that
he had information from his contacts in Tehran that all the
American hostages in Beirut, including Buckley, were still alive.
Shackley jumped at the offer. Despite his 28 years of intelligence
work, he was not able to evaluate accurately whether he was
being told the truth or led into a trap. He told Ghorbanifar
that if he had concrete suggestions about how to release the
hostages, he would be willing to convey Ghorbanifar's message

to "the right address." Three hours later Ghorbanifar repeated his offer to free the hostages in exchange for arms or cash ransom, but he made one explicit condition—that Iran's role in the matter should not be publicized. He asked for an answer by December 7.

On November 23 Shackley met in Washington with former deputy director of the CIA, now ambassador-at-large, General Vernon Walters and briefed him on the conversation with Ghorbanifar. Various other officials in the department studied his report, and on December 11, 1986, Shackley received an answer from Hugh Montgomery, the director of intelligence and research in the State Department: no thanks, we'll take care of it ourselves.[15] The fate of the hostages, important as it was to the President, still did not justify changing American policy by selling arms to Khomeini.

After his failure to influence the U.S. through American agents, Ghorbanifar decided to try going through Israel. In January 1985 he spoke with Adnan Khashoggi in Hamburg. They were brought together by Roy Furmark, who had in the past worked for the Saudis, and was also friendly with CIA chief Casey.[16] In the second half of March, Khashoggi and Ghorbanifar met for an additional "coordination talk" in Cologne, West Germany. Khashoggi brought Furmark, and Ghorbanifar brought Dr. Shahbadi and two other Iranians, Zaheri and Shojai. Zaheri was introduced as an American of Iranian extraction who lived in Houston, Texas. Zaheri had a falling out with Shojai over money and eventually gave up and returned to Houston.[17] The meeting occurred during a new wave of kidnappings of Americans and Europeans in Beirut. On January 8, 1985, Father Lawrence Martin Jenco, a Catholic missionary who headed the Lebanese office of the Catholic Aid Service was kidnapped; on March 16 the victim was Terry Anderson, Associated Press correspondent in Beirut; on March 22 it was Marcel Carton, 62, protocol chief at the French embassy in Beirut, along with Marcel Fontaine, 45, deputy consul at the same embassy. These kidnappings once again focused the world's attention on Beirut and once again underlined the helplessness of Western governments in fighting such terror.

At the same meeting in Cologne, Ghorbanifar reported to Khashoggi on the failure of his attempt to work through Shackley and his search for other channels of activity. Khashoggi consented to turn to Israel, but all participants agreed that Israel should not be told about the Ghorbanifar-Shackley conversation in Hamburg, nor about the CIA's reservations about Ghorbanifar. They concluded that Israel had close relations with the U.S. If the Americans decided to tell Israel about Ghorbanifar, they could not prevent it. But they must not volunteer to give Israel this information.

As they hoped, when Ghorbanifar reached Israel on April 9, no one in Jerusalem knew about his meeting with Shackley, even though the Israelis had very detailed information about the Iranian's personality and the CIA's suspicions about him. Moreover, despite Khashoggi's close relations with Schwimmer and Nimrodi, he refrained from telling them that his efforts were not restricted only to Israel, but involved in addition other countries in the region armed with American weapons. In fact, earlier in the spring of 1985 Khashoggi had asked for Egypt's help in supplying weapons to Iran. Khashoggi had known, of course, that Egypt supported Iraq against Iran. It had been sending Iraq its surplus Soviet weapons and supplying locally produced arms. Egypt also allowed those Egyptian nationals living in Baghdad to volunteer to help the Iraqi army. Khashoggi had also known, however, about Egypt's economic difficulties, and he had thought that President Mubarak would be tempted to supply Khomeini with arms and equipment—in return, of course, for a large amount of money. So, in the spring of 1985, he and Ghorbanifar had gone to Cairo.[18] Mubarak had not met them but over the course of several days Egyptian intelligence agents had interrogated the Iranian, asking him questions about his past, his motives, his contacts in Tehran, and his evaluation of the internal situation in Iran. They had discovered a large number of contradictions in his answers and turned him away. Apply directly to the U.S., they had advised him.

The Israeli channel was then the only one remaining for Khashoggi—and it succeeded better than he had expected. In an arrangement code-named "Operation Cosmos," Israel was to supply Iran with a small amount of locally produced arms and ammunition through Schwimmer and Nimrodi. But the failure of Operation Cosmos, because of Iran's desire to equip itself solely with American weapons, led Khashoggi to try to ready Washington for Iran's request through the Israeli channel.

On May 2 Khashoggi sent Robert McFarlane a memorandum

in which he urged the Reagan administration to open channels of communication with Iran. He argued that the succession struggle could begin in earnest even before Khomeini's death and that it was in America's interest to try to influence the choice of successor.

Khashoggi's May 2, 1985, letter to McFarlane was sent at a time when the U.S. was involved in a serious effort to gather information and improve its intelligence on Iran. The U,S. was aware of the existence of an internal struggle in Iran, but lacked information on the identity of the men taking part in it. One of the principal people seeking this information was Michael Ledeen, a researcher at the Center for Strategic Studies of Georgetown University in Washington, who served as a part-time adviser to the National Security Council. Dr. Ledeen, born in 1941, had developed an expertise in the political history of Italy during Mussolini's rule, and had written a number of books on the subject. He had a reputation as an excellent bridge player, and his sometime partner was the Egyptian actor Omar Sharif. In the years 1973–75, when he was studying at Rome University, he had been suddenly summoned to Israel to train its bridge team for its 1976 attempt at the world championship in Monte Carlo. One of his great successes during that period was revealing the links between Billy Carter, the President's brother, and Libyan leader Muammar Qadhafi. After the Khomeini revolution, he had come to Jerusalem to gather material for a book on the end of the Shah's rule. This book made him an "expert" on Iran, even though he had never visited the country. During the same period he also edited the prestigious journal, *Washington Quarterly*. He was associated with the group of intellectuals called the "New Right" that had gathered around Reagan. It did not take long for people to discover in him an interesting combination of academic ability and political ambition, together with pride and adventurousness. These characteristics made him admired in various circles, but intensely disliked in others.

After Reagan's election, Ledeen was appointed political adviser on Secretary of State Alexander Haig's staff, and he was assigned to maintaining contact with the Socialist parties in the West. As a result, he visited Israel and met Shimon Peres, who was then chairman of the opposition Labor party. After Haig's resignation Ledeen also resigned, and returned to his work at the Center for Strategic Studies. But when Robert McFarlane was named national security adviser on October 17, 1983, Dr. Ledeen was appointed to his part-time position as an NSC consultant and was assigned to Iran and the war against terror. In this capacity he had a loose working relationship with another NSC official, Colonel Oliver North, who was assigned to the Nicaraguan Contras and coordinated counterterrorism activities around the world.

Ledeen's work at the National Security Council was his golden period. During the invasion of Grenada, Ledeen revealed political and operational dexterity by proving, with the help of documents, that foreign elements intended to take over that small country. When Palestinian terrorists hijacked the *Achille Lauro* cruise ship in October 1985, North asked Ledeen to call Italian Prime Minister Bettino Craxi and ask for permission to bring the Egyptian plane carrying the terrorists, intercepted by American combat planes, to land at a NATO air base in Sicily. Ledeen knew Craxi from his days as a student in Rome, in 1965, and during the *Achille Lauro* crisis he spoke with the Socialist leader four times. In one of those conversations he served as interpreter for President Reagan, who called on Craxi not to give in to the terrorists' demands.

In the spring of 1985, Ledeen began to work on Iran in a more concentrated way. While visiting Europe in March of that year to prepare a comprehensive survey of Iran's role in international terror, he met a senior intelligence officer from a central European country who told him, among other things, about internal developments in Iran and the succession struggle there. The same man related that the situation in Iran was much more complex than it seemed at first sight, and advised him to consult Israel. Israel's intelligence on Iran was, in his opinion, much more detailed than that of the Western powers. Ledeen told McFarlane about the conversation when he returned to Washington at the beginning of April. He asked whether it might not be worthwhile making use of his acquaintance with Peres in order to find out what kind of information Israel had about Iran's connections with Arab and other international terror organizations and to explore potential U.S.–Israeli cooperation on Iran.[19] McFarlane approved, but demanded that the visit to Israel be kept secret and unofficial. Therefore, it was not coordinated by the U.S. embassy in Israel, but rather through

Israel's ambassador to the UN, Benyamin Netanyahu. Ledeen arrived in Israel on May 3, 1985, a few days after the failure of Operation Cosmos, and after Ghorbanifar's third visit to Tel Aviv. Peres had just rejected Ghorbanifar's request to purchase 500 American antitank TOW missiles.

In a private meeting with Peres on May 4, Ledeen explained the purpose of his trip, saying that the U.S. was interested in finding out about the possibility of talking with Iran, in the hope of improving its relations with Khomeini's possible successors. The U.S., however, did not have enough information about current developments in Iran, he said. Ledeen told Peres about his talks in Europe, and asked the Prime Minister whether Israel was willing to give the U.S. the information it had, and what Israel's long-range policy toward Iran was. He added that the U.S. was interested in bringing the Iran-Iraq War to an end in a way that would not upset the balance of power in the Gulf region.

Ledeen asked about Iran's role in Lebanon and its influence over the various terrorist groups there. The American hostages and the supply of weapons to Iran went beyond the scope of Ledeen's mission, but they did, understandably, come up during the conversation. Peres told the American representative that it was possible that Israeli information on Iran was better than the Americans', but it was still insufficient. It was necessary for both countries to make increased efforts to gather information. After more information was available there could be another discussion to examine to what extent it was possible to frame a new Iran policy. Peres told Ledeen that Iran wanted to purchase artillery shells and other weapons and military equipment from Israel, but that Israel was not prepared to do so without American consent. Peres asked Ledeen to sound out McFarlane about the Iranian request.

After his meeting with Peres, Ledeen spoke with retired General Shlomo Gazit, a former head of the intelligence branch of the Israeli general staff, who coordinated Iranian policy in the Prime Minister's Office.[20] Despite his interest in terrorism, Ledeen did not meet Amiram Nir, the Prime Minister's adviser on antiterror operations. He did, however, meet the director-general of the Ministry of Foreign Affairs, David Kimche, as well as Al Schwimmer and Ya'acov Nimrodi. The latter two told him of their conversations with "Iranian representatives" without mentioning Ghorbanifar by name. A few days later Ledeen returned to Washington convinced that, if the U.S. did not want the Soviet Union to reap all the benefits of the succession struggle in Tehran, it would have to take more interest in the changes now taking place in Iran.

McFarlane, as a result of Ledeen's report, asked the CIA to update the Special National intelligence Estimate (SNIE) of expected developments in Iran. On May 17, Graham Fuller, in charge of the Middle East desk at the CIA, submitted a five-page memorandum in which he recommended establishing contact with those Iranian elements willing to reestablish ties with the U.S. In his evaluation, the Soviet Union could have a preferred position with regard to the succession struggle. Even though it supplied arms to Iraq, it secretly pushed Poland and other Eastern European countries to supply Iran. Since the succession struggle could be drawn out, it was still too early to evalute the prospects of the Tudeh party or the Mujahidin Khalk organization—both of them helped by the Russians. The Soviets would improve their position in Iran if Khomeini were to stop supporting the rebels in Afghanistan. Fuller recommended arms sales through an ally as one option for pursuing an opening to Iran. The NSC staff contended that Israel should be that country.[21] The ideas contained in this evaluation, submitted to the State Department and the National Security Council on May 20, 1985, were similar to the conclusions found in Khashoggi's letter of May 2 to McFarlane. McFarlane was apparently persuaded by the letter, and his views held sway over opposing views within the administration.

Just as the administration was reconsidering its Iran policy, however, its attention was diverted to the subject of terrorism. Whether because he knew of Ledeen's visit to Israel and his conversation with Peres, or because he feared that the U.S. and Israel were exchanging information about Ghorbanifar, Khashoggi decided to work to make the Iranian arms dealer seem more reliable. On May 16 he had a long conversation with Ghorbanifar in London, during which the latter made a startling revelation: Ali Khamenei and Mir Hussein Mussavi, Iran's President and Prime Minister, had decided to assassinate Sheikh Jaber Ahmed As-Sabah, Emir of Kuwait. Iran accused the Emir of persecuting the Shiite population of his country and of refusing to free 17 Shiite terrorists of the pro-Iranian

El-Da'awa organization who had been given long sentences for having attacked the American and French embassies in Kuwait. Ghorbanifar cited not only the date of the planned assassination, but also the method: a booby-trapped automobile was to collide head-on with Sheikh Jaber's car. Immediately after the murder, pro-Iranian Kuwaiti officers were to take control of the principality. On the day Khashoggi and Ghorbanifar arrived, May 25, an attempted assassination similar to the one Ghorbanifar had warned of took place in Kuwait. Sheikh Jaber was saved, but several of his bodyguards were killed.

That Ghorbanifar had delivered precise information about an important event could help reform his reputation, and Khashoggi quickly related the story to his Israeli friends, hoping it would convince them to use Ghorbanifar as a channel to Iran. But no one in Jerusalem was willing to act without express permission from the U.S.; such permission was not given—yet. Ledeen's visit to Jerusalem was meant to be secret, but Israel's communications channels were not watertight. On May 30, Samuel Lewis, the American ambassador in Tel Aviv, inquired of Peres's and Rabin's offices what the purpose of Ledeen's visit to Israel had been. The Ministry of Defense told him that it was a "hot subject" and that during Rabin's coming visit to Washington he would make a personal report to the Secretary of State. Shultz and Rabin met at the State Department on June 1, 1985, but the latter did not mention—even in passing—Ledeen's visit to Jerusalem. Shultz later protested to McFarlane about Ledeen's mission and the fact that it took place without the knowledge of the State Department and behind the back of the American embassy in Israel. McFarlane replied that Ledeen had made the visit to Israel "on his own hook," but briefed Shultz on the talks in Jerusalem. In a telegram from Lisbon dated June 5, 1985, Shultz warned McFarlane that Israel's interests in Iran were not consistent with those of the United States, and that it would be a mistake to depend on Israeli intelligence in formulating American policy. Shultz added: "We are interested, of course, in knowing Israel's views on the Iranian situation, but we must also be aware that Israel has its own bias in this matter."[22]

Shultz's opposition caused much confusion in Israel, but the White House and the director of the CIA continued to search for ways to open up channels of communication with

Iran and bring about the liberation of the hostages. While the suffering of the hostages was the major factor motivating the President, the possibility of influencing developments in Tehran was what created enthusiasm among his advisers and among the few Israelis involved in the episode. While neither of these factors alone would perhaps have been enough to convince the U.S. and Israel to have secret contacts with the Khomeini regime, the combination of the two pushed the two countries into an adventure that was to become a scandal.

Despite Shultz's opposition to American-Israeli cooperation on Iran, the American and Israeli evaluations of Iran were identical on some points, although different on others. One basic conflict of interest existed between the U.S. and Israel. The former wanted the war to end, but in a way that would not topple the Baghdad regime or destabilize the Arab oil sheikhdoms. Israel, on the other hand, preferred that the war continue to erode the ability of both Iran and Iraq to take part in any further military adventures beyond their mutual border. It was for this reason that Israel saw no contradiction between giving Iran limited aid, so long as it did not change the balance of power with Iraq, and trying to make contact with Khomeini's possible successors. A selective supply of arms to Iran through Israel, Turkey, Pakistan, the People's Republic of China, and Japan could only help the West in its efforts to contain Soviet ambitions in the region. But Israel was not interested in pursuing such a policy without the explicit agreement of the U.S.[23]

Basing themselves on these evaluations, and noting the memorandum prepared by the CIA, two National Security Council staff members, Howard Teicher and Donald Fortier, prepared on June 11, 1985, a draft presidential decision (a National Security Decision Directive or NSDD) on changing American policy toward Iran. The document set out the immediate and long-term goals of the U.S. in Iran and recommended a series of steps to achieve them. It described the internal situation in Iran as unstable and liable to threaten American interests in the Persian Gulf. The major recommendation was to support opposition to Khomeini within Iran and to encourage some allies and friends to supply Iran with selective amounts of arms and military equipment. This was to strengthen Western and reduce Soviet influence within the country.

On June 17 McFarlane sent the document to Caspar Weinberger, George Shultz, and William Casey, and asked for their comments. Casey received it while engaged in another attempt to make contact with Iran.

After Khashoggi decided, for reasons of his own, to no longer include his partner, Cyrus Hashemi, in his future business with Israel, the latter tried again to offer Ghorbanifar's services to the U.S. The offer was made through John Shaheen, an Arab-American and a close friend of William Casey. In mid-June Shaheen passed on to Casey an offer from Hashemi to arrange a meeting with a "senior Iranian official" for the purpose of discussing Iran's willingness to aid in the freeing of the American hostages in Lebanon in exchange for American TOW missiles.[24] Casey had in the past rejected similar approaches from Hashemi, but this time he ordered one of his assistants to examine the offer. Casey reported his willingness to discuss the idea of meeting a senior Iranian official to Undersecretary of State Michael Armacost, but said nothing about supplying arms to Iran in exchange for the hostages. On June 22, the assistant secretary of state for Middle East affairs, Richard Murphy, recommended the approval of Casey's initiative. Armacost gave his OK two days later.

At the beginning of July, Hashemi told the CIA that his contacts in Iran were deputy prime minister Mohsen Kengarlou and the "senior intelligence officer," Manucher Ghorbanifar. The CIA expressed its willingness to meet Kengarlou, but wanted no business with Ghorbanifar.[25] In the end the meeting with Kengarlou did not come off, but in return for dropping charges against him, for having violated U.S. laws in May 1984 in trying to export arms to Iran, Hashemi continued to work as a "double agent" for the American Customs authority. His name would surface again on April 22, 1986, when he turned in several arms dealers, including retired Israeli Brigadier General Avraham Baram. They were arrested in the U.S. and accused of secretly trying to sell $2.5 billion worth of arms to Iran. Hashemi died in London in July 1986 under mysterious circumstances. His death certificate recorded a natural death, but according to various sources Hashemi was murdered by Iranian intelligence agents on charges of treason.

Future relations with Iran did not, however, have top priority in Washington at that time. The greatest concern was the fate of a new set of American hostages. A TWA jet, flight 847 from

Athens to Rome, was hijacked on June 14 by Shiite terrorists of the pro-Iranian Lebanese Islamic Jihad organization. The four hijackers were led by Imad Mughaniyeh, a Lebanese Shiite of Palestinian extraction. A seemingly quiet family man in his thirties, Mughaniyeh had also been behind the bombings of the American embassy and Marine headquarters in Beirut in 1983. The leader of Hezbollah's "action group," Mughaniyeh became personally involved in terror attacks after the arrest of his brother-in-law together with 16 other El-Daa'wa terrorists in Kuwait. He is also believed to have been involved in the kidnappings of Terry Waite and the American hostages Terry Anderson and Thomas Sutherland. Another member of the team that hijacked TWA flight 847 was Hassan Iz El-Din, who was also involved in the hijack of Kuwaiti Airways flight 422 on April 5, 1988.[26] Another hijacker of the TWA plane, Muhammed Ali Hamadeh, was later arrested in Frankfurt, on January 15, 1987, while traveling with a forged passport and a bomb. The U.S. asked for his extradition on charges of hijacking the TWA plane and murdering one of its passengers, but Bonn has insisted on trying him in Germany. The hijackers belonged to a unit called Alwiyat Al-Sadr (the Sadr Brigades), after Imam Musa Sadr, the Lebanese Shiite leader who had been kidnapped in Rome in August 1978 after a visit to Libya. The unit's commander was Akel Hamieh, whose code name was "Hamza."

After two stops in Algeria, and after the Iranian government announced that it would not allow the plane to land on its territory, it landed in Beirut. It contained 153 passengers and crew members, among them 139 Americans. The hijackers demanded freedom for 776 Shiites imprisoned in Israel. In order to prove that their threats were real, they murdered one American passenger, navy diver Robert Stetham, and threw his body out onto the runway. On June 18 the hijackers released most of the passengers so as to make it easier for them to control the plane. Thirty-six passengers and three crew members remained hostages. Israel refused the hijackers' demands; the U.S. did not encourage it to do otherwise. Israel made use of its contacts with Ghorbanifar and asked him to use his contacts in Iran to help free the hostages.

The hijacking put to the test President Reagan's declarations on the war against terrorism. During the previous several months Reagan and Shultz had declared several times that the U.S.

would pursue an active policy of "deterrence, prevention, and retaliation" against Iran. Speaking at the Park Avenue Synagogue in Manhattan on October 25, 1984, Shultz called for "swift and sure measures" against terrorists, both to prevent attacks and to retaliate for them: "We cannot allow ourselves to become the Hamlet of nations, worrying endlessly over how to respond.[27] And NSC adviser Robert McFarlane stated publicly, "It is my purpose to remind terrorists that no act of violence against Americans will go without a response."[28] The time had come to act on those words. In constant contact with Amiram Nir, the Israeli Prime Minister's adviser on the war against terror, Colonel Oliver North planned a military operation to rescue the passengers. America's Delta Force, a unit trained in counter-terrorism, was sent to Europe, and the *Nimitz* aircraft carrier was stationed off the Lebanese coast. Fearing American military action, 1,000 supporters of Hezbollah, including several hundred women, marched through the streets of Beirut, fists aloft, cursing the U.S. The hostages were dispersed among private houses in West Beirut and its suburbs, frustrating any military action. It was clear to all, however, that if the hostages were harmed the U.S. would react forcefully.

The hijacking threatened Iran's efforts to obtain American arms, directly or through Israel. To some of the Iranian leaders it became clear that kidnapping American, French, and British nationals, and increasing terrorism against the Israeli army in southern Lebanon, were no replacement for diplomacy and could not bring any long-term political and strategic gains. Moreover, the long war against Iraq was not ending, nor was Iran's involvement in Lebanon proving successful. This situation increased the feeling in Tehran that the Islamic Revolution had gone as far as it could and that it had already peaked. Several leaders decided that the time had come to improve Iran's image and try to change its reputation as a country supporting international terror. So, at the height of the crisis, on June 24, Hashimi Rafsanjani arrived in Damascus. At a press conference in the Syrian capital, the Speaker of the Iranian Majlis denied that his country was involved in the hijacking, and said: "had we known who the hijackers were, we would have frustrated their plans." Rafsanjani met the leaders of various terrorist groups and negotiated for the release of the passengers and crew members.

On June 25 President Assad made the proposal that led to the solution of the crisis. He gave his personal guarantee to the pro-Iranian terrorists that Israel would release an unspecified number of Shiite prisoners from its Atlit Prison. To prevent it appearing as capitulation to terrorist demands, the prisoners would not be released at the same time the hostages were, but some time later. Assad asked the U.S. if it accepted the plan. The U.S. asked Israel. The Israeli government replied that it had been planning to release some of the Shiite prisoners in any event, so that it had no objections to helping the U.S. in this matter. Iran also accepted the compromise, and ordered Hezbollah to accept it as well. On June 29 the hostages were sent by bus to Damascus and flown from there to Europe in a special plane. On July 3 Israel released 300 Shiite prisoners, fulfilling its obligation to the U.S.

Iran's quiet efforts to end the crisis aroused much interest in Washington and Jerusalem. Those who believed that terrorist acts in Lebanon and Europe were perpetrated by Lebanese Shiites with links high in the Iranian government found support for their contention. What needed to be determined now was whether there really was a "moderate" faction in Tehran interested in returning its country to a pro-Western orientation, and whether the faction had the power to realize this goal and end Iran's involvement in international terror. Joint activity by the U.S. and Israel in the following weeks was directed at answering these questions.

An Ayatollah in Hamburg

All Tehran Fridays are alike. Fathers who have lost their sons in the war against Iraq crowd into the cemeteries and read verses from the Koran, pounding their chests with mounting emotion until they collapse, insensible, to the ground. Not far away, black-clothed mothers and widows sprawl on the graves of their loved ones and lament their deaths in battle. Each headstone is wrapped in an Iranian flag, and next to the picture of the fallen hero (called a *shahid*, or martyr, in Moslem tradition) lie wreaths of flowers and baskets of fruit. Death howls from every corner, in the cries of the mourners.

Outside the graveyard, in the thousands of mosques scattered throughout the country, millions of Iranians gather for the Friday prayer service and to hear the weekly sermon of the local imam. Some of them, inspired by the preacher, leave the mosque shouting for the continuation of the *jihad*, the holy war. Others disperse quietly to their homes, silently praying that the war not demand a sacrifice of them.

The prayer service held at the Great Mosque at Tehran University in mid-June 1985 was not noticeably different from others of the previous seven years. Majlis Speaker Hajjotelislam Ali Akbar Hashimi Rafsanjani—one of the most fluent and popular preachers in Iran—had just finished his sermon and was about

145

to go home when a special messenger came to summon him to Ayatollah Khomeini's residence. Upon arriving at Khomeini's residence in the Djamaran neighborhood of north Tehran, he found that he had been preceded by many of the country's senior leaders—bearded, black-robed, black- and white-turbaned clerics, government ministers, and high-ranking army officers. All of them were crowded into their leader's yard, speculating about the reason for the sudden urgent meeting. Ahmed Khomeini, the elderly Ayatollah's son, ushered them into a large room with floor and walls lined with intricately patterned Persian carpets. In the center of the room, on a small platform, Khomeini sat with his legs crossed, leaning on a brightly colored pillow.[1]

The Ayatollah began to speak, slowly and deliberately. He was most troubled by the state of the country, he said. The war had not yet been won, the loss of life had been great, the economy was a shambles and the cities were under bombardment by the Iraqi air force. The army desperately needed arms and spare parts. The U.S. had isolated Iran, while the Soviet Union and Western Europe—primarily France—were continuously supplying Iraq with modern weapons and sophisticated military equipment. Iran could not even use what it had. Three hundred planes—80 percent of the air force—were grounded for lack of spare parts, he noted. Khomeini called for immediate steps to supply the cities with defensive antiaircraft weapons and for the immediate purchase of antitank weapons in order to throw back the Iraqi forces at the front. Speaking about conditions to end the war, while Khomeini did not say so outright, his audience understood him to mean that if Iraqi President Saddam Hussein were deposed or if he resigned, Iran would see in this the achievement of its war aims and would be willing to cooperate with whatever regime took power in Baghdad, even a secular government. Khomeini thus hinted that he was abandoning, for the present at least, his dream of exporting the Islamic Revolution to Iraq, Saudi Arabia, and the Gulf states.

Only two men responded to the Ayatollah's words: Rafsanjani and the Prime Minister, Mir Hussein Mussavi. They supported Khomeini's position in every respect, but also wondered whether the time had not come to pursue a more active peace policy in an effort to break Iran out of its isolation. Rafsanjani argued that the hijacking of a TWA plane by Lebanese Shiites had once again raised accusations that Iran aided terrorism, damaging its chances of receiving American and European weapons. Iran must, therefore, pressure its loyalists in Lebanon not to take any more American hostages for the time being and to free the hijacked plane and its passengers. This could raise Iran's standing in international opinion and make it easier to obtain American arms, either directly or through a third country.

Mussavi supported the same approach. He said that the capture of the American embassy in Tehran had taught both the advantages and the limitations of hostage taking as a method of achieving the country's objectives. Iran had encouraged its supporters in Lebanon to take hostages as a means of pressuring the U.S. to free the Shah's frozen American assets and cancel the embargo on arms shipments to Iran, but it had also encouraged Western retaliation. Neither had the kidnapping of French hostages in order to force President Mitterrand to halt arms shipments to Iraq and pay his country's debts to Iran brought about the desired results. Mussavi proposed, therefore, that Rafsanjani go to Syria and Lebanon to help free the TWA plane, and thereby lay the basis of a new policy that would lead to the eventual release of the hostages in Lebanon in exchange for arms shipments from the West.

With Khomeini's tacit agreement, a five-man committee was set up to coordinate matters dealing with the hostages. Rafsanjani headed the committee, which also included Prime Minister Mussavi; the minister responsible for the Revolutionary Guards, Mohsen Rafik-Doust; the commander of the Revolutionary Guards, Mohsen Rezai; and Ahmed Khomeini, who was to serve as a liaison between his father and the Iranian government. Mohsen Kengarlou, chief of Iranian intelligence operations and deputy prime minister, was later added to the committee. He would later emerge as the major link between the Iranian arms merchant Manucher Ghorbanifar and Prime Minister Mussavi. In mid-March 1984, in a meeting with a CIA officer, Ghorbanifar described Kengarlou as the man responsible for the kidnapping of William Buckley, CIA chief of station in Beirut.[2]

After the Iran-Contra initiative and its failure to obtain the release of the hostages was made public, there were those who argued that the Iranians had always intended to cheat the Americans. Khomeini had never intended to give up such important bargaining chips, so useful for humiliating and black-mailing the U.S., they reasoned. However, little hard evidence supports this contention. On the contrary, information now available indicates that Iran was in serious trouble during the summer of 1985, and this pushed some of its leaders into trying to reestablish contacts with the U.S. Obviously, no one in Israel or the U.S. could guess at the time what Khomeini's intentions were. But given the limited intelligence available about Iran, neither Israel nor the U.S. was ready to pass up an opportunity to regain influence in such an important country.

This was clearly expressed in a meeting between the director-general of the Israeli Ministry of Foreign Affairs, David Kimche, and Robert ("Bud") McFarlane in Washington, on July 3, 1985. Kimche, British-born, was one of the brightest intellects among Israel's officials. After fighting and being wounded in Israel's War of Independence, he began a career as a writer. He worked for a short time as news editor of the *Jerusalem Post* and, together with his brother John Kimche, a well-known British newspaper-man, he wrote the book *From Both Sides of the Hill*, which described the War of Independence from the Israeli and Arab points of view. Together with Dan Bavli, Kimche wrote *The Sandstorm*, one of the best books about the Six Day War of 1967. His search for a challenge led him to the Mossad, Israel's intelli-gence service, where he quickly advanced to the post of deputy director. While his many accomplishments there remain secret, the knowledge and experience he gained are evident in his doctoral dissertation in international affairs, on the subject of national liberation movements in Asia and Africa. During his 30 years in the Mossad, Kimche excelled at exploiting Israel's military and economic know-how in fostering political and mili-tary links with countries of the Third World.

Until his July 3 meeting with McFarlane, Kimche was not directly involved in the effort to open up lines of communication with Iran. From the time he was appointed director-general of the Ministry by Yitzhak Shamir, most of his efforts had been devoted to improving Israel's position in Europe and to renew-ing diplomatic relations with African countries. Furthermore, when Schwimmer and Nimrodi first established contact with Ghorbanifar, Prime Minister Peres had made the former chief of military intelligence, retired general Shlomo Gazit, responsi-ble for opening up Israel-Iran communications, leaving no reason for Kimche to devote attention to Iran. By the summer of 1985, however, it seemed that this effort had reached a dead end. Since Michael Ledeen's visit to Jerusalem at the beginning of May, Israel had been waiting for the American administration's reply to Iran's request to receive American weapons from Israel. The answer had not yet come. Peres decided to take advantage of Kimche's visit to Washington to inquire of McFarlane whether the U.S. had changed its position regarding Iran.

Kimche had developed a relationship of close friendship and trust with McFarlane, begun while McFarlane was an adviser to Secretary of State Alexander Haig. The two continued to cooperate with each other when Reagan made McFarlane responsible for Lebanon, replacing Ambassador Phillip Habib. The friendship became even closer when McFarlane was appointed national security adviser. "Bud" was impressed with "Dave" 's personality and his rich experience in developing countries, and he hoped to take advantage of that experience to increase Israeli-American cooperation in Central America and the Caribbean.

Israel had a tradition of cooperation with several Latin American countries dating back to the 1970s. Israeli experts helped develop agriculture and water resources, and supplied a limited amount of arms, airplanes, and electronic equipment there. The U.S. tried at first to prevent Israeli penetration of the Latin American arms market, but the Sandinista revolution in Nicaragua softened this opposition somewhat and Israel signed small contracts with Guatemala, Honduras, El Salvador, Colombia, and Costa Rica. The transactions included both Israeli-produced arms and Soviet weaponry captured in Lebanon. These minor sales to Nicaragua's neighbors gave rise to articles in the world press claiming that Israel was also supplying weapons to the Contras, the anti-Sandinista rebels. Israel consistently denied the allegations; but the Sandinistas consistently displayed Israeli-made arms captured from the Contras. An investigation by Israel revealed that the arms Israel had sold to Guatemala had been given to the Contras. Israel asked Guatemala to put an end to the practice for fear that it would damage Israel's relations with members of the American Congress.[3]

At the beginning of 1984, however, when congressional opposition to military aid to the Contras began growing, the Reagan administration began to engineer a plan to aid the rebels through contributions from other countries and from individual Americans. King Fahd of Saudi Arabia began donating large sums of money to the rebels in May 1984. The Sultan of Brunei contributed $10 million. At about that same time Kimche rejected McFarlane's request that Israel, too, aid the Contras. On April 17 Kimche arrived in Washington to ask for financial assistance for Israeli development projects in the Caribbean. McFarlane, in his testimony to the congressional committee investigating the Iran-Contra affair, said: "We were aware that, after Congress rejected any new allocation to the rebels, they [the rebels] would in May 1984 find themselves without funds. For this reason we asked for the help of country number one [Israel]. This country excels at agricultural development and the exploitation of water sources. It also excels at police activities and at training forces for internal security. I asked my interlocutor [David Kimche] if his country would be willing to help the Contras with arms and training. He promised to find out. Not long afterwards he notified me that his country could not fulfill that request."[4]

McFarlane told Howard Teicher, one of his aides, that he was "disappointed in the outcome but we will not raise it further . . . [we] will not press them on the question of assistance to the Contras."[5]

McFarlane's request to Israel was leaked to Ambassador Samuel Lewis in Tel Aviv, who immediately cabled the State Department. Shultz was incensed when he heard that Teicher had sent a message to Kimche, behind the State Department's back. He was angry at the way the contacts had been made, but he was furious at the attempt to entangle Israel with the Contras. He conveyed his opposition to McFarlane.

But this was not the end of the matter. William Casey was worried that the Sandinistas were a danger to the stability of other Central American countries and he urged McFarlane to request that Israel change its decision. In a note to the national security adviser, Casey suggested telling Israel that, if the Contras succeeded in toppling the Sandinista regime, the new government would establish normal diplomatic ties with Israel and end Nicaraguan support of the PLO.[6]

McFarlane instructed Teicher, on May 9, to contact Kimche once again and explain to him how important aid to the Contras was to the U.S. He suggested that Israel supply the rebels

In 1982, Israeli arms sale negotiator Colonel Ya'acov Nimrodi (far left) and his business partner Al Schwimmer (above left), science and technology adviser to Israeli Prime Minister Peres, met in Morocco with Cyrus Reza, the exiled pretender to the Iranian throne, and former Iranian army general Razvani (above right) to hear the Iranians' request for Israeli help in overthrowing Khomeini. Israel agreed to supply arms but not to participate in the planned coup attempt, which never took place.

Israel was again approached for military support for anti-Khomeini forces in 1985, this time by Saudi arms merchant Adnan Khashoggi (left), shown here in his Spanish villa with Nimrodi. The request prepared the ground for Operation Cosmos, the first plan to sell Israeli weapons to Iran.

The roots of Iranian-Israeli cooperation reach back to the late 1950s. Chief of Military Intelligence Chaim Herzog, shown here in a Tehran restaurant between Nimrodi and Ambassador Meir Ezri, met with the Shah three times beginning in 1960 and proposed the exchange of military attachés, all part of the Eisenhower Doctrine in which the U.S. encouraged regional alliances and intelligence gathering to thwart Soviet expansion.

As it would again in the 1980s, Iran also attempted to use the Israeli connection to exert influence on the U.S. In his meetings with Herzog and Israeli Chief of Staff Zvi Tzur (shown here between two Iranian soldiers on the Iranian-Soviet border in 1961), the Shah complained about American unwillingness to supply military aid to Iran.

Over the years, Israeli instructors (shown here in 1962 with their Iranian students in Isfahan) trained more than 400 Iranian pilots, paratroopers, and army officers.

Cooperation extended to nonmilitary areas too, as Israel joined other countries sending aid for the 20,000 Iranians left homeless by the September 1962 earthquake, and Minister of Agriculture Moshe Dayan (center) toured the earthquake-devastated region in a royal train. Admired in Tehran for his 1956 victory over Nasser, Dayan was treated as a military hero and his visit—unlike those of other Israelis—received wide press coverage.

In May 1966, Deputy Chief of Staff Ezer Weizman (holding helmet), shown here with the Iranian Air Force Commander (second from the left) and wearing an Iranian pilot suit, visited Tehran. Again using Israel as a go-between, the Shah conveyed to Weizman his need for more arms and threatened to turn to the Soviets if the U.S. would not be more generous.

Iranian involvement with Israel extended beyond bilateral matters to regional diplomacy. After talking with Prime Minister Levi Eshkol in 1966, Iranian Chief of Staff General Ariana (shown leaving the Prime Minister's Tel Aviv office) urged the Shah to mediate peace talks between Israel and Jordan, but King Hussein refused the offer.

In 1965, Iranian Deputy Defense Minister General Toufanian (right), shown here with Al Schwimmer (left) and Moshe Kashti, director general of the Israel Defense Ministry, first opened the Iranian market to Israeli arms. Almost 20 years later, the failure of Operation Cosmos to provide Israeli weapons to Iran, and Iran's desire for U.S. weapons, led arms merchant Khashoggi to write Robert McFarlane urging the Reagan administration to open channels of communication with Iran.

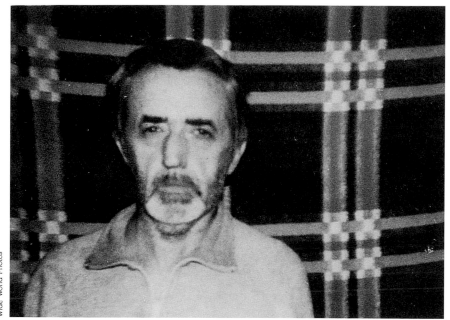

Concern about the fate of William Buckley (above), head of the CIA station in Lebanon, and the other Americans held hostage in Beirut by pro-Iranian groups was a key factor in the decision to supply American arms to Iran.

The first arms shipments from Israel to Iran—code-named "Operation Cappuccino"— were approved by the U.S. government and delivered to Iran on August 20 and September 14, 1985. On September 15, Benjamin Weir (right), held since May 1984 by the Islamic Jihad, was on his way to freedom.

In December 1985, Lt. Colonel Oliver North, who since mid-1984 had organized secret American efforts to aid the Nicaraguan Contras, was assigned to coordinate the Iran initiative for the U.S., and Amiram Nir (below), Prime Minister Peres's adviser on terrorism affairs, was appointed to represent Israel.

North enlisted Richard Secord (left), who was assisting him in providing covert aid to the Contras, to help with the Iran operation as well. North allowed Secord and business partner Albert Hakim to manage the finances of the Iran arms sales and the Contra aid through the same Swiss bank accounts. Despite previous CIA warnings and his failure of the polygraph tests, both Israel and the U.S. continued to rely on Manucher Ghorbanifar (right) in their efforts to build bridges to the Khomeini regime.

Wide World Photos

In January 1986, National Security Adviser John Poindexter proposed that the President authorize the CIA to purchase weapons from the Department of Defense and deliver them to Iran without notifying Congress. The assenting presidential finding reduced Israel's role by making the U.S. a direct supplier of arms to Iran.

Bettmann Newsphotos

Following the direct American shipment of TOW missiles to Iran, former National Security Adviser Robert McFarlane journeyed in May 1986 to meet with Iranian officials, expecting to improve relations and obtain the release of all American hostages. The talks proved fruitless; no hostages were released; and news of the visit leaked to the press in November, leading to the exposure of the whole Iran-Contra affair.

with arms and military advisers, and emphasized that, should Israel again reject the request, it would cause the President great disappointment. Kimche's reply was negative again. Shultz learned of this approach also, and when he again protested, McFarlane told him: "Teicher was operating on his own hook."[7]

Kimche's visit to Washington in July 1985 was not, however, connected with the Contras. It was devoted to a number of subjects, one of which was clarifying Iranian policy. At this meeting with Peres before his trip, Kimche related that McFarlane was angry at Israel for not keeping Ledeen's trip to Jerusalem a secret. The leak had caused friction between McFarlane and Shultz because the National Security Council was once more gaining the image of trying to form foreign policy independent of the State Department. Peres asked Kimche to assure McFarlane that the leak had not been from the Prime Minister's Office.

The conversation between McFarlane and Kimche at the White House on July 3, 1985, was frank and thorough. It took place on the day that Israel released 300 Shiite terrorists who had been held prisoner in southern Lebanon. This was part of the understanding reached with the hijackers of the TWA jet, through the mediation of Syria. McFarlane and Kimche felt, of course, much relief now that the hijacking was over, but both no doubt knew that this would not be the last act of terrorism against their countries.

The major part of the conversation, however, was devoted to the situation in Iran and the Persian Gulf region. Kimche told McFarlane that Roy Furmark and Ghorbanifar had visited Israel on June 19, and that at their meeting with Schwimmer and Nimrodi, Ghorbanifar had asked to purchase 100 TOW missiles and had expressed his willingness to arrange a meeting between an Israeli representative and a "senior Iranian official." As for the Gulf War, Kimche acknowledged openly that the interests of Israel and the U.S. were not complementary. While the U.S. was interested in bringing the war to an end, Israel wanted it to continue so as to exhaust even further Iraq's military capability. Kimche told McFarlane that Israel had identified several Iranian figures interested in improving relations with the U.S. This group was close to the Iranian leadership, was ready to guarantee the free passage of oil through the Persian Gulf, and was not inclined to export the Islamic Revolution to Saudi Arabia and the oil sheikhdoms. Kimche told McFarlane that these people had already made contact with Israel, from whom they were interested in purchasing American arms. Israel, however, was not willing to accede to the request before clarifying the American administration's position. "Bud," Kimche said, "I'm presenting you the information for your consideration. If the administration is ready to pen a dialogue with this group, fine. If not, that's also fine. Israel will understand."

McFarlane would later relate his own version of this conversation: "It was neither an Israeli nor an American initiative. What happened was that Israel received certain information, passed it on to us, and asked our opinion. Israel did not pressure us, only said that if we wanted to open a dialogue with these people in Iran, she would be willing to help. That is all you can ask of a loyal ally."[8]

During the course of the meeting, McFarlane told Kimche about the different opinions about Iranian policy circulating within the administration. He said that Shultz, for instance, disputed the argument that the Soviet Union was more favored than the U.S. in Iran. Shultz believed that Iran had entrenched fears of Soviet expansion and that the U.S. must foster this without regard for changing circumstances. The secretary of state was not impressed by reports of improving relations between Iran and the U.S.S.R. He argued that the Shah had also tried to improve relations with Moscow, but in the end his fear had overcome his rational attempt to achieve peaceful relations with a neighboring country. The situation today was no different. He thought that Khomeini had initiated a tactical move in the Soviet direction in order to prevent or restrict the Soviet supply of weapons to Iraq. For this reason there was no reason to get worked up about it and there should be no change in policy. In short, according to Shultz, the "moderate faction" was out to swindle America in order to prove itself to its rivals at home and, through trading with the U.S., lay the groundwork for arms deals with Europe as well.

Secretary of Defense Caspar Weinberger also opposed supplying arms to Iran. According to McFarlane, the Pentagon agreed that it was necessary to gather information and establish ties with moderate elements in Iran. But, in the Defense Department version, the real moderates had been liquidated and those remaining were crazy. Weinberger proposed discussing a change in policy only after Khomeini's death or overthrow. McFarlane quoted Weinberger as saying that talking with Khomeini was like inviting Qadhafi to Washington for a cozy chat.[9]

Among the top administration officials in Washington, only Casey was in favor of a new approach to Iran. Among the CIA's great achievements in the 1950s had been the deposal of Iranian Prime Minister Mohammed Mossadegh and the reinstatement of the Shah to the throne in Tehran. Casey wanted to repeat that success, not by getting rid of Khomeini but by making contact with possible successors. Thus, Casey now added to his zeal to free Buckley a strategic reason for talking to the Iranians. Casey's position was without a doubt the product of a wider view of the importance of Iran's geopolitical position in the Gulf region. The aid Iran gave to the Afghan rebels, its relatively good relations with two American allies, Turkey and Pakistan, and its strategic importance all made Iran an effective buffer between the Soviet Union and the Arab oil states. Defeat at Iraq's hands, economic troubles, a long war of succession, and widespread terrorist activities were liable to dangerously weaken the authority of the central government in Tehran. This would put the country in danger of a Soviet takeover, not by military invasion, but by deep penetration of government institutions. This could tip the scales in the Persian Gulf against the West, waken ethnic divisions in Turkey and Pakistan, and end aid to the Afghan rebels.

Kimche's visit to the White House came only two days after Adnan Khashoggi had sent McFarlane a detailed report on Iran. Copies of this document were sent to the Kings of Saudi Arabia and Jordan, to the President of Egypt, and via Schwimmer and Nimrodi, to Prime Minister Peres. In this 47-page analysis, dated July 1, 1985, Khashoggi discussed the situation in the Persian Gulf at length and noted the changes beginning to take place in Iran. He claimed that three factions were fighting to succeed Khomeini. All three were blindly loyal to their elderly leader, and were also united in their support of three basic principles: that the Islamic Revolution was irreversible and must continue; that Islam was the source of the government's authority; that there could be no separation of religion and state in the Islamic republic.

On all other matters there was a quiet struggle between the three factions. Each tried to place its loyalists in key positions in the government, army, and religious establishments. This was also at the root of the continuing power struggle between the army and the Revolutionary Guards. Khomeini was aware of the infighting and unhappy about it, but it continued nevertheless.

Khashoggi went on to analyze the differences between the three factions. The extremists were headed by President Ali Khamenei, Prime Minister Mir Hussein Mussavi, the Minister for Intelligence Affairs Hajjotelislam Mohammed Reishari, and Mohsen Kengarlou, chief of Iranian intelligence operations. This faction had 53 members in the Majlis. They supported uncompromising internal and external policies, agrarian reform and nationalization of the economy, and opposed releasing expropriated property. They also favored exporting the revolution and were willing to assign men and resources to undermine Arab Gulf states and to carry out terrorism in Lebanon.

The moderate faction's key leader was Ayatollah Hassan Karoubi, Khomeini's adviser of the last 15 years. The faction had the support of 63 members of the Majlis, the most prominent of whom was Ayatollah Mohammed Reza Kani, a former Prime Minister. The army's commander of ground forces, the commanders of the police and the gendarmerie, and the deputy commander of the Revolutionary Guards were among its other supporters. They also had the support of commercial interests. They wished to improve relations with neighboring countries, opposed exporting the revolution, and called for preservation of civil liberties in the framework of Islamic law. They supported free enterprise and property rights, fiercely opposed the Soviet Union and communism, and were willing to consider a cautious reorientation toward the West.

The largest faction was the one occupying the space between the extremists and the moderates. It had a solid majority in the Majlis and the Supreme Court, and controlled several well-endowed trust funds. It was headed by the Speaker of the Majlis, Ali Akbar Hashimi Rafsanjani; Khomeini's heir-apparent, Ayatollah Ali Montazeri; Hassan Karoubi's brother, Deputy Speaker Ayatollah Mehdi Karoubi, who, as chairman of the Martyrs' Fund, was responsible for large amounts of money; and Colonel Mohsen Rezai, commander of the Revolutionary Guards. The foreign and oil ministers also supported this faction. Some members of this group, such as Montazeri, favored exporting the Islamic Revolution, but the group generally decided each case on the merits.

Khashoggi explained to McFarlane that factional loyalties were not absolute and that some people could belong to more than one faction at the same time. For example, an official might support harsh internal policies and a moderate foreign policy, or the opposite. A wise and flexible American policy could, therefore, tip the balance in favor of one line or another.

Although he already had Khashoggi's memorandum in hand, McFarlane refrained from committing himself to Kimche, and asked to study the matter in detail. Kimche left Washington empty-handed. While in Paris, however, on his way back to Jerusalem, he received a telegram from the Prime Minister's Office ordering him to go to Geneva immediately to continue his work on Iran.

On July 7, Kimche met Nimrodi and Schwimmer at the Noga Hilton Hotel in Geneva. They updated him on recent developments in Iran, and Kimche told them about his talks with McFarlane. A few hours later the three met Adnan Khashoggi and Manucher Ghorbanifar. Khashoggi began by explaining the situation in Iran. He argued that the succession struggle was liable to break out while Khomeini was still alive, and that the faction that established its hold on Tehran could influence future developments. He said that Prime Minister Mussavi, his deputy, Kengarlou, and several clerics were interested in renewing the dialogue with the U.S. One of them, Ayatollah Hassan Karoubi, was to arrive in Hamburg the next day in order to dedicate a Moslem study house there. Khashoggi proposed a meeting with him. Ghorbanifar described Karoubi as Khomeini's "right-hand man," who had stood by him during his years of exile in Iraq and France. Since their return to Iran, Karoubi had lived with Khomeini in Qom, Iran's religious capital, and he delivered the weekly sermon in Khomeini's private mosque in Tehran. Ahmed Khomeini, the son of the leader of the revolution, was Karoubi's personal friend. Since Ahmed Khomeini was gaining influence, a connection to him was like a connection with the government itself. Ghorbanifar argued that the sale of 100 TOW missiles would give Ghorbanifar more influence and pave the way for the release of the American hostages.

The next day, July 8, they all set out to meet Karoubi in Hamburg. Khashoggi also brought along his son and his brother-in-law, Naim Ahmed, a Lebanese Shiite who had shown skill in his international business dealings. This delegation set out from Geneva on Khashoggi's private plane, a renovated DC-8 equipped with all the luxuries needed to make long flights pleasant. The plane had three tastefully furnished bedrooms, a large living room, a well-stocked kitchen, and a sophisticated communications system linking the plane with the rest of the world.

The meeting with Hassan Karoubi was held in the Four Seasons Hotel and lasted about four hours. Nimrodi, Kimche, and Schwimmer were introduced as Israelis. When he shook their hands, Karoubi remarked: "Meeting with Israelis is dangerous, but I am convinced that in doing so I am serving my country's best interests."

Karoubi was about 45 years old, thin, and short, with a clipped black beard and glasses. He was wrapped in the black robe of a Moslem cleric. His speech was quiet and considered. Although he knew Arabic fluently, he preferred to speak in Persian, with Ghorbanifar translating into English. After a few words of introduction from Khashoggi, the conversation became a dialogue between Kimche and Karoubi. Nimrodi occasionally interrupted, asking Karoubi some clarifying questions in Arabic. The entire conversation was recorded.[10]

The Ayatollah presented a lengthy exposition of the different factions in Tehran. He related that the one he represented believed it necessary to return Iran to the West, and warned of the dangers that the Soviet Union presented to his country. He claimed that the U.S. had made a grave error in positioning itself in opposition to the Khomeini regime. The image of the U.S. in Iran now was one of a country opposed to religion. Karoubi argued that the Islamic Revolution was the necessary outcome of the corruption of the Shah's regime. Khomeini had also made many mistakes, Karoubi acknowledged, and his rule was no less tyrannical than that which had preceded it. The endless war with Iraq had brought disaster on Iran, and it was necessary to find an "honorable solution" that would bring it to an end. In the meantime, however, Iran desperately needed antitank missiles, in order to defend itself against Iraqi tanks. He also mentioned the American hostages and the kidnapped Jews in Lebanon, and promised to act for their release. He promised to prepare a written survey of the factions struggling for power in Iran, which would also spell out the assistance that his faction required. Karoubi requested, finally, that he be given money and a way be established for coordinating future steps and meetings.

The importance of this conversation to the development of U.S.-Iranian-Israeli dealings warrants quoting it almost in full.

KAROUBI: My reason for coming here is to save Iran. We want an independent, free, and strong Iran that maintains good relations with its neighbors and the superpowers, especially with the U.S. We have common interests with the West. We want to cooperate with the West, and the U.S. can help us with this. We believe that, because of the Soviet Union's geographical location and its common border with us, Iran is even more important to the West than oil. If this is the case, one might ask, what is the most desirable regime for Iran from a Western point of view? Monarchy or nationalist-liberal? It is important to clarify this point. It is also important to find out what difficulties and dangers you expect and what solutions you propose. We must set a common goal and frame appropriate methods of action. We have information, influence, and a certain amount of power to put at the service of this common interest. But we must first decide what that goal is—are we to act for the moderation of the present religious regime, or work to overthrow it and establish a more liberal system in its place?

KIMCHE: Yes, there is need for cooperation and mutual assistance. We would also like to see a moderate government in power in Iran, one that lives in peace with its neighbors and maintains friendly relations with all the countries in the region. I admit that we have made some serious mistakes, but we have come to try to repair those errors and solve the problem.

KAROUBI: If that is really your approach, you must tell us how we can cooperate and what we must do.

KIMCHE: We would like to serve as a bridge for correcting the mistakes between you and the West. We want to achieve peace between Iran and its neighbors, so that there will be good relations in the region, so that all its countries can enjoy security and fruitful economic and commercial relations. We came here in order to find out what we can do together, and how to do it. We are prepared, together with Mr. Khashoggi, to cooperate and prepare joint action with you. We are ready to help you with preparations and with action.

KAROUBI: In a program of joint action, we must establish the role and contribution of each side. There are in Iran today movements that lack self-confidence. They do not know if they have support abroad, and if so, what they must do and what is asked of them. All these groups need coordination. So, in order to arrive at the final goal, we must coordinate. No outside element has the right to dictate the Iranian people's fate. But we will act together in order to return their freedoms and rights to the Iranian people.

NIMRODI: As you must certainly know, we have always worked to strengthen Iran. Our actions are not to strengthen any particular regime. Our goal is a strong, free, and developed Iran. You border on the Soviet Union, and there has been hostility between you and some Arab countries that are friendly with the Soviet Union. For this reason we always cooperated with you and we are willing to do so today, also. We want an Iran friendly with the West, not inimical to it. So we are willing to help those who have similar aspirations and who believe in freedom and human rights, who have moderate leanings and who oppose Communists and the Soviet Union. We would like to hear from you what to do and how to help you. What do you need?

KAROUBI: After World War II the U.S. had a positive image in Iran. It contributed to Iran's independence and defended it from the Soviet Union. It is necessary to return to that same situation. But the cooperation between us has to be well-defined. We can't speak in generalities. We must set out joint lines of action and go into detail. We are ready to put our power at your service, and suggest to you how to return Iran to the West. We are ready for a detailed and practical discussion of this subject.

SCHWIMMER: We are also ready. The best proof of the sincerity of our intentions is that we brought Khashoggi from the other side of the world.

KAROUBI: In short, if we reach an understanding, I will put my information about Iran and my experience at your service in order to return my country to the West. I am prepared to submit a detailed proposal in writing that can serve as a basis for discussion between us.

KIMCHE: May Allah bless you.

KAROUBI: I want it to be clear that we are not talking about annexation by or alliance with the West, but rather mutually beneficial cooperation.

SCHWIMMER: Of course. The West's strength is in its belief in the freedom of peoples. We believe in the Iranian people's freedom, and its sovereignty over its country.

KAROUBI: Our region, and yours, can expect a physical threat from the Soviet Union. We fear the Soviets and the Left in our country. The Left is strong and dangerous. The Reds and the Left have invested a lot of work in the field, and they today have much influence over the masses.

NIMRODI: If so, what you urgently need from us now is information on the activities of the Left and of the Soviets in Iran, so as to frustrate their plans.

KAROUBI: Yes, that is most important.

KIMCHE: Fine, that's one subject. Now let's talk about the Iran-Iraq War, because we think that the Left in Iran is not very strong, and has perhaps already been eliminated.

KAROUBI: No, that is not accurate. The Left is still in the government, although not officially. The Left also has influence. Here, for instance, the leaders of the Tudeh once appeared on television, confessed their transgressions, and recanted their errors. But that was a show. The government was interested in proving to the people that it was acting forcefully against the Left and its links to the Soviet Union. Or, for instance, the hostage crisis that damaged American prestige and served as a means of propaganda against it. I can reveal to you here that what happened at the American embassy in Tehran and the suicide attacks against the Marine headquarters and the American embassy in Beirut were all part of a single policy. That was not done by the Left, but by the Iranian government itself. I think that, on this subject, the government in Tehran is trying to play both sides. On the one hand it claims to be acting against the Soviet Union and the Left, but at the same time it also acts against the U.S. Sometimes I wonder—what is the real color of the Ira-

nian government? What is its identity? Are we really opposed to the Soviet Union and the Left, or do we in effect
stage shows against the U.S. and the West? If the Iranian
government is really anti-Soviet, why does it never take
Russian hostages?

NIMRODI: Because it's afraid of them.

KAROUBI: I think that undercover Soviet agents are working hard
in Iran. If you don't work carefully and energetically, the
West might lose Iran forever. You must act seriously and
swiftly.

KIMCHE: What is Khomeini's personal position on this?

KAROUBI: Isn't that clear to you?

KIMCHE: No, and I'll explain why. I think that Khomeini is two-
faced. Deep inside he knows that he's broken, but sometimes
he takes one line and sometimes another. So we really don't
know what he thinks.

KAROUBI: Khomeini pursues a clear anti-Soviet and anti-Western
line. He unalterably opposes the West. He thinks that the
West is working against him and against the Islamic Revolution he brought about. Khomeini was the first to spout anti-
American slogans and he was the one who approved capturing
the American hostages in Tehran.

The three Israelis were very favorably impressed by their
conversation with Karoubi. Yet they were also careful not to
jump to conclusions. It was necessary to confirm the Ayatollah's
veracity and find out who he really had behind him. They discovered, for instance, that Karoubi had been among the leaders
of the students who occupied the American embassy in Tehran
in November 1979. His brother, Mehdi, had been appointed
by Khomeini to organize the pilgrimage to Mecca, and was
for this reason of great interest to Saudi security officials. In
his report to the Israeli Prime Minister, Kimche described Karoubi as "a very intelligent man who, despite his religious
fanaticism, believes in the need to change the situation in
Iran." Kimche noted that he was not in a position to establish
definitely whether Karoubi was speaking truthfully or not. The
subject, however, was of too much importance to neglect. He
therefore recommended continuing the contacts with Karoubi
and his fellows.[11]

Peres reported to Rabin, while Kimche reported to Shamir. At one of the regular meetings of these three leaders (known as the "Prime Ministers' Forum," since all three had served in that post) it was decided to continue the effort to establish ties with Iran. "It was important to maintain these contacts," Shamir would later declare after the scandal exploded, "because it is important that the West have a foothold in Iran after it turns around."

In keeping with this decision, and because of the desire to help the U.S. and the need to check the reliability of Karoubi and his colleagues, the Israeli Prime Minister decided to tell the Americans about the results of the meeting in Hamburg. On July 11, 1985, Schwimmer went to Washington and met Michael Ledeen at the White House. It was at this meeting that Schwimmer first mentioned Ghorbanifar's name; he also handed over a transcript of the conversations with Karoubi. Schwimmer emphasized that Karoubi had given a detailed picture of the internal situation in Iran and the power struggles at the top of the government. Karoubi had also acknowledged— the first time any Iranian official had done so—the direct link between the Iranian government and the terrorist organizations in Lebanon. Schwimmer suggested that Ledeen meet Ghorbanifar in Europe or in Israel in order to form an impression of his personality and test his credibility.

Ledeen immediately reported to McFarlane.[12] He said that, since he had in any case planned to take his wife and children for a vacation to Israel, he would take advantage of his stay there to meet with Ghorbanifar. McFarlane agreed, but checked out the Iranian arms dealer's credentials before Ledeen left. Secretary of State George Shultz would later reveal that on July 16, 1985, he had read a CIA report of August 1984 describing Ghorbanifar as a "talented fabricator."[13] McFarlane was, of course, aware of this evaluation but decided on July 18 to submit the matter for a presidential decision. Reagan was then in hospital. In a decision conveyed orally to McFarlane, Reagan decided that, on principle, Israel could supply Iran with the TOW missiles it had requested.[14]

While Schwimmer was in Washington, Nimrodi continued to pursue the matter on the other side of the Atlantic. On July 16, in Geneva, he received from Ghorbanifar the memorandum promised by Karoubi. The document made it clear that

Karoubi was asking for help in assuming power after Khomeini's death. He refrained from making any promises about the hostages, but asked for money to pay to potential supporters, so that when the time came he would be in a position of power that would allow him to take over. A full translation of the memorandum follows:

TOP SECRET—DESTROY AFTER READING

27 Shawal Al-Mukaram
Year 1405 of the Hejira
16 July 1985

In the name of Allah the All-Merciful.
In continuation of our previous conversation.

I believe that if our friends in the West do not display dexterity, do not see that the forces supporting them are organized, and do not answer our requests positively—and we have goals, missions, desires, and interests in common— then, after Khomeini's death, and in light of his full support of the extremists and Left, support that even religious fanatics unwittingly become party to, and in light of the fact that Iran has a long border with Communist Russia, which does not hide its ancient designs on our land, our country faces two options:

- to become a second Lebanon, but on a much larger and more dangerous scale;
- or, within a few months, no longer than two years, Iran will become a Communist puppet state. This is particularly likely given that, during the last seven years, an atmosphere inimical to the West has been created in Iran.

For this reason, without delay, and while taking maximum care, we must immediately begin to bring together the moderate and patriotic forces of pro-Western sympathies who oppose the extremists and the anti-Western Left. These forces, who work within the existing regime, are: the Islamic Research Center of Qom and its faculty; the imams who preach on Fridays in the mosques; members of the Majlis, commercial interests, senior officers in the ground forces, police, and gendarmarie; commanders in the Pasdaran and the Basij organization [of youth volunteers for the war].

Since this is an especially sensitive subject, I mean to return to Tehran next week and hold several meetings with some of my friends and colleagues, in order to report to them on our talks. I will send you the final plans for operation and details of the things we need within one month at the latest.

In order for you to evaluate our ability and reliability, and so that we may also test your sincerity and seriousness, I ask that, before my return to Tehran, some financial aid be made available to me. In this way it will be possible to properly entertain—before the formation of the final plans—some of the people who support the extreme line. I believe that, at such a sensitive time, and with elections approaching [to the Iranian presidency, and supplementary elections to the Majlis] the appropriation of a few rials for activity among the clergy in Qom, the merchants in the bazaar, and in south Tehran, under camouflage of contributions to the *Buniad Shahid* [the Martyrs' Fund] could be very productive. Attached to this is a list of people who support our line. In order to protect these people and ensure the success of our common goal, please destroy the list after examining it.

I pray to the almighty Allah that he may give you health and happiness, and that our good prayer may accompany you always.

In thanks,
Your humble servant,
H. K.
(*Hassan Karoubi*)

The contents of the letter and the list of names attached to it were immediately passed on to Ledeen in Washington.

Ledeen and his family arrived in Israel for their vacation during the second half of July 1985, as guests of the Jerusalem Fund. They stayed at Mishkenot Sha'ananim, facing Mt. Zion and the walls of the Old City. A few days later Ghorbanifar also arrived in Israel and, as during his previous visits, he stayed at Nimrodi's house in Savion.

Ghorbanifar arrived just two days after Adnan Khashoggi had celebrated his fiftieth birthday with a sumptuous party at his estate at Marbella on the Spanish Riviera. The celebrations continued for a week, and among the 500 invited guests were a prince from Monaco, film stars Brooke Shields and Sean Connery, U.S. Ambassador to Italy Maxwell Raab, Saudi sheikhs, German industrialists, and more. They were all brought from the airport in sparkling limousines and taken directly to the luxury hotels reserved in advance. Khashoggi received his guests on the green lawn around his swimming pool, which was lit by colored lights. The guests were tempted with smoked salmon from Scotland, avocados stuffed with shrimp, different varieties of meat, fresh fruit, and large quantities of exquisite Swiss chocolate.

On the last day of the celebration British actors appeared on horseback, one of them dressed as King Henry VIII. At the prearranged time, "King Henry" announced his abdication, and Khashoggi ascended the throne in his place. During this grand coronation ceremony "King Adnan" received a small piece of paper from one of his aides that caused him to smile. His contacts in the U.S. were informing him that the negotiations between Israel and Ghorbanifar were progressing well, and that only a few technical details remained to be worked out. Khashoggi seemed to glow with pride at having had a part in cooking up an official arms deal between the U.S. and Iran. For Khashoggi, President Reagan's blessing for the secret deal was much more important than his accession to the throne.

At a meeting with Ledeen, Kimche, Schwimmer, and Nimrodi on July 26, Ghorbanifar made the link between supplying the weapons and freeing the hostages explicit, and for the first time mentioned the possibility that Iran would also ask for spare parts for Hawk missiles.[15] He said that, because of the lengthy lack of contact between the U.S. and Iran, the two sides must first repair their trust of each other. He emphasized that, in exchange for 500 TOW antitank missiles, the Iranian Western-oriented faction would see that Buckley was released by his Lebanese captors. He noted that the supply of missiles would do much to strengthen Karoubi's status in Iran. All those present made it clear to Ghorbanifar that Israel and the U.S. objected in principle to "arms for hostages" deals, and that the American Congress would frustrate any such procedure. Ghorbanifar, however, argued that this was not a ransom, but a demonstration of goodwill. "It is a necessary test to prove the sincerity of both sides," he insisted. Kimche explained to Ghorbanifar that Israel would be ready to supply the missiles only if secrecy could be guaranteed and the hostages freed.

The Iranian arms dealer called Mohsen Kengarlou from Nimrodi's house. Kengarlou did not want to pay for the missiles. He thought that the release of "the big one" (Buckley) was a fair payment. Ghorbanifar conveyed Kengarlou's position to his hosts. It immediately became clear, however, that supplying the missiles in exchange for Buckley's release was out of the question, and that Iran would have to pay for the arms it received. Ghorbanifar called Kengarlou back, and the deputy prime minister of Iran announced that, given Israel's stubborness, his country would be willing to pay for the TOWs.

Ghorbanifar did not know at this point, and Kengarlou did not tell him, that Buckley was no longer alive. It was months later, when Reverend Weir was released, that it was learned that Buckley had died on June 3, 1985, after being cruelly tortured.

Ghorbanifar warned that Iran might keep some hostages as a bargaining card, but that the others would be released within "two or three weeks."[16] "He makes a wonderful impression," Ledeen said of Ghorbanifar as he left the meeting in Savion. Nimrodi and Schwimmer told him not to get too enthusiastic. Ghorbanifar was without a doubt an enchanting conversationalist and he had access to the top Iranian leadership. But his major test was still before him. What especially impressed the Israelis was the feeling of "openness" that Ghorbanifar gave his listeners. During supper at a fish restaurant in Jaffa, for instance, with a glass of whiskey in his hands, Ghorbanifar would joke that in Tehran he would not dare to look at a drink, had to be careful to wear common clothes, and had to go to the mosque to pray with appropriate reverence. He spoke slightingly of Islam, but also said that he had twice fulfilled the religious obligation of pilgrimage to Mecca (the *haj*). Ghorbanifar said that he would like to bring his two sons to Israel "so that they could see what a kibbutz is and see a different way of life. You know, I make them work during their summer vacations as waiters, or in some other job, so they can see how hard it is to make money."

It was now necessary to obtain the approval of the Israeli and American governments. Ghorbanifar, in the meantime, returned to France on July 27, while Ledeen continued his vacation in Jerusalem.

Shimon Peres, his deputy prime minister and foreign minister Yitzhak Shamir, and Defense Minister Yitzhak Rabin consulted and agreed to continue trying to clarify the situation with Washington. Rabin said that, in principle, he did not oppose an arms-for-hostages deal, because Israel had made such deals since 1968, when it was clear that there was no military option to free its prisoners. But Rabin was not satisfied with the central role Michael Ledeen was playing in this matter. He recalled that, during Ledeen's previous visit to Jerusalem in May 1985, he had refused to meet him. Rabin said that, from his experience as an ambassador in Washington, he knew that it was best to negotiate with the decision-makers and not with their occasional messengers. Rabin insisted on a more unequivocal U.S. authorization.

With the knowledge and approval of Shamir and Rabin, Peres told Kimche to clarify several points with Washington before deciding what answer to give the Iranians. Kimche was first to ask McFarlane if the U.S. also saw the arms sale as a strategic move designed to establish contacts with Khomeini's successors, and not just as a tactic to free Buckley and his fellow captives. Freeing the hostages, no matter how much Reagan was concerned about them, had to be a secondary goal and serve as no more than a test of the Iranian mediators' ability to keep their promises. Kimche must also confirm that the American response had been given with the knowledge and agreement of the President and his cabinet. Finally, the Foreign Ministry director-general was asked to obtain a promise from McFarlane, in the President's name, that the U.S. would supply Israel with new and modern antitank TOW missiles to replace those supplied to Iran. This last request was meant to appease Israeli Chief of Staff Moshe Levy, who opposed removing the TOW missiles from Israeli army stores. He said that the army could not allow itself to run down its inventory of antitank weapons.

These problems were not insuperable. The technical obstacles could be overcome and an arms deal between Israel and Iran, with American acquiescence, was on the way.

Operation Cappuccino

The customary serenity of the east Tel Aviv suburb of Savion was interrupted for an evening of celebration. Ya'acov Nimrodi, a key figure in the intelligence and international arms businesses, was marrying his son Ofer—a former army officer and now a young attorney completing his education in the U.S.—to his chosen bride, Tali. Prime Minister Shimon Peres and most of his ministers, as well as large numbers of senior army officers and top men from the Israeli intelligence community, had come to celebrate with their friend.

In such a happy atmosphere, few of those present took notice of the discreet consultations between Peres and Kimche, and between Kimche, Schwimmer, and Nimrodi. During the course of the evening, Kimche left hurriedly but quietly and made his way directly to Ben Gurion Airport. The next day, on August 2, 1985, he was sitting with McFarlane at the White House.

Kimche had come to the U.S. with a concrete proposal—to begin by supplying 100 TOW missiles to Iran on a trial basis, in exchange for the release of four hostages. The supply of 400 additional missiles would depend on Khomeini's behavior. Kimche felt even before the conversation began that Washington was close to a decision. McFarlane leaned toward allowing Israel to supply Iran with a small amount of arms, hoping it would bring about the release of the four hostages, and he agreed to present the issue to the President.[1]

He would later publicly explain his position. In his testimony before the congressional investigatory committees, in May 1987, McFarlane said angrily: "It's very strange to me that we are unable to fight terrorism effectively. Some countries are good at it. Take Israel. Terrorists know that if they act against Israel— something, somehow, somewhere is going to happen. It won't always be a preemptive attack, or weapons. It might be negotiations, or bribery, or anything else. But, hell, you can be goddam sure that if an Israeli is taken hostage his government will be after the kidnappers until he's released."[2]

Kimche submitted a copy of Karoubi's memorandum to McFarlane, as well as the list of some 60 clerics, government ministers, and army officers with whom contact could be made in Iran. Kimche said that President Khamenei, Prime Minister Mussavi, and Speaker Rafsanjani had until recently been preoccupied with the presidential and Majlis elections scheduled for August 17, but were now confident of their victory and were once again free to attend to matters of state. He told McFarlane that Karoubi and his supporters were encountering more difficulty than they had originally expected in imposing their will on Hezbollah. They also felt more vulnerable. In order for the moderate faction to persist, it would have to widen its base of support in the army and the Revolutionary Guards. This could only be done by supplying weapons. They therefore wished to know whether the U.S. would be willing to make an immediate gesture of the sincerity of its intentions. This would help them prove to the other Iranian factions that their contacts with the U.S. were producing results. Kimche explained that the quantity of arms under discussion, only 100 missiles, could not affect the balance of power in the war, but could certainly strengthen the standing of the U.S. in Iran and in the Middle East as a whole. "If the standing of the U.S. improves, that helps Israel," Kimche emphasized.

In accordance with the guidelines given him in Jerusalem, Kimche asked McFarlane whether, if it should be decided that Israel would supply the 100 TOWs to Iran, the U.S. could supply Israel, within 30 days, with a similar amount to replace them. McFarlane answered: "Dave, you know that that's no problem. Israel has always bought arms here, and it will continue to buy arms in the future. But from the point of view of the U.S., this is a question of principle. I do not think it would be wise, or possible, for the U.S. to supply the weapons to Iran directly. But even if it comes from Israel, there is still a need to establish whether it is consistent with American policy and its goals."[3]

Kimche answered that, since what was under discussion at this point was only a demonstration of good faith, it was necessary to prevent any direct connection between the supply of the missiles and the release of the hostages. Neither Israel nor the U.S. would concede, of course, the demand for the release of Buckley and the other prisoners, but the goal must be a larger one—to begin a significant dialogue with Iran or, more accurately, with Khomeini's possible successors.

McFarlane refrained from giving Kimche a firm commitment, but the general impression was that the U.S. would reply favorably to the Iranian request. Israel knew, for instance, that President Reagan had responded with enthusiasm after hearing from McFarlane about his first conversation with Kimche at the beginning of July: "That's wonderful. It sounds good." Israel also knew that Casey enthusiastically supported renewing the dialogue with Iran, and that he had the support of Vice President Bush and White House Chief of Staff Donald Regan. The CIA seemed excited by the quality of the information Karoubi had given, and by the personal composition of his faction. The American reaction to the information Israel had passed on was, "Wonderful. It's the deepest penetration we've made into Iran since Khomeini came to power. We feel as if we were sitting at the heart of the regime." For this reason, the general impression was that the President would overrule the objections of Weinberger and Shultz and allow Israel to serve as a communications channel between the U.S. and Iran.

On August 6, 1985, McFarlane notified Kimche that the President had summoned the vice president, the secretaries of state and defense, and the White House Chief of Staff to a consultation at the White House. McFarlane told the gathering that Iran wanted a dialogue with the U.S. and 100 TOWs from Israel in return for the four American hostages. Secretary Shultz again opposed the idea. He told the President that despite the talk of better relations with Iran, the U.S. "is just falling into the arms-for-hostages business and we shouldn't do it." Shultz also opposed the idea that by Israel's serving as a "vehicle," the U.S. would be able to deny any connection to the sale.[4]

Secretary Weinberger also opposed the sale. He argued that such an initiative would contradict U.S. policy of attempting to persuade other countries not to sell arms to Iran.[5] No decision had been made. But the next day the President told McFarlane that he would agree to Israel supplying a modest quantity of TOW missiles, on condition that this not upset the balance of power in the Gulf War and that it not permit Iran to increase its terrorist activities. The President also agreed that the TOWs supplied by Israel would be replenished by the U.S.[6]

This was one of the most decisive moments in the Reagan presidency. His administration had listed Iran among those countries accused of abetting terror, and he had signed an executive order forbidding arms shipments to Khomeini. Several existing statutes (passed by Congress and signed into law by the President) also prohibited the sale of arms to Iran, and the State Department was pressing the Western alliance not to supply weapons to Iran, either. Khomeini, in the eyes of many Americans, was the incarnation of evil. Reagan seemed prepared to violate the policy of his own government.

Israel, for its part, saw the decision as a great achievement, since it was a concrete expression of the regional strategic understanding that had begun to develop between it and the U.S. Kimche's position as Israel's coordinator for Iran was now firm, Shlomo Gazit having been appointed to run the Jewish Agency. Because of his position as director-general of the Foreign Ministry, his deep friendship with McFarlane, and his vast experience from the Mossad, Kimche took charge of contacts with the U.S. Nimrodi, also an old intelligence operative, took care of the actual execution of the arms shipments and maintained the connection with Iran, while Schwimmer exploited his innumerable contacts throughout the world in order to make the logistic arrangements for the shipments.

In many ways, the "troika"—Kimche, Nimrodi, and Schwimmer—was the best team Israel could assign to this operation. They acted in accordance with the decisions of the White House, but because the U.S. was being careful not to burn its fingers at this early stage, the entire operation had to be carried out through Israel without leaving any traces of direct American involvement. Since the President's decision had been made under pressure from William Casey, despite the opposition of the State Department and the Pentagon,[7] the CIA preferred to operate through the National Security Council in the White House, remaining in the background but extending assistance to McFarlane and his staff.

Similarly, in order to keep the details of the operation from leaking to the press (in a country in which almost everything leaks), Peres, Rabin, and Shamir preferred to operate through the "troika" instead of through Israel's normal foreign policy channels. This gave Israel the possibility of denying the operation should it be revealed, while Kimche's experience in the Mossad and Nimrodi's in Iran made up for the inconvenience of not being able to use official channels. Nimrodi and Schwimmer also had the necessary sensitivity to what was permitted and what forbidden in Iran. This was important because it was already clear that Ghorbanifar was a man of great intelligence and even greater falsehoods. He tended to fantasize and elaborate in describing past events—including some which had never occurred. One member of the troika said of Ghorbanifar that he had so many identities that he didn't know who he was. Kimche, Nimrodi, and Schwimmer impressed Israel's leaders as knowing how to deal with Ghorbanifar, and how to distinguish reality from imagination.

In one respect only was there a basic difference between the U.S. and Israel. When President Reagan considered his policy toward Iran, he summoned his secretary of state and secretary of defense for an orderly discussion of the matter with the director of the CIA and the national security adviser. When the President decided to open a channel of communication to Iran, he did so after hearing differing opinions and being made aware of Shultz's and Weinberger's reservations.

Not so in Israel. While the Prime Minister, Shimon Peres, had the support of his foreign and defense ministers, he never brought the matter before the cabinet, nor did the "Prime Ministers' Forum" have position papers from the country's intelligence services in front of them. Other options were not discussed and experts were not asked to give their analyses of the significance of links with unofficial elements in Iran, especially with regard to the possible results of the contacts on Israel's future relations with Egypt and Jordan, two of Iraq's allies.

After receiving the President's approval, the representatives of Israel and the U.S. began organizing the first shipment of 100 TOW missiles to Iran. This was a covert operation in every respect—including a plethora of code names. The operation itself was called "Cappuccino"; Israel was "Perth"; Iran, "Norfolk"; McFarlane, "Henry"; North, "Michael"; Kimche, "Paul"; Nimrodi, "Peter"; Schwimmer, "the Accountant"; Ghorbanifar, "Nick"; and Khashoggi, "the Eagle."

There were indications from the start that the two sides did not completely trust each other. The Israelis insisted that their army would not take as much as a screw out of its armories without having full payment in hand. Ghorbanifar announced that Iran would not pay a cent until it received the merchandise.[8] He claimed that Iran had been burned several times already in such deals. The country had once paid in advance for a large shipment of canned foods—but when the shipment arrived in Tehran the cartons were found to be filled with gravel.

Ghorbanifar went to meet Khashoggi in Marbella, Spain, where he proposed that the Saudi tycoon "bridge" this gap by lending him the money for the first 100 missiles until Iran paid. Khashoggi agreed, and on August 7, 1985, he deposited $1 million in Nimrodi's private account (number 745–866–02–2) at Crédit Suisse in Geneva. Ghorbanifar signed a postdated check for the same sum, which Khashoggi was to cash as soon as the missiles arrived in Tehran and payment was made.

The price was set only after lengthy bargaining between the parties concerned. The Israeli Ministry of Defense asked for $12,000 per missile, the price of the new TOW missiles it was to buy from the U.S. as replacements. Iran paid this price to Ghorbanifar, but he was not willing to pay the Israelis more than $10,000 per missile. Nimrodi and Schwimmer, who had already absorbed the costs of the canceled Operation Cosmos earlier that year—and who had to cover the shipment costs for the new deal—were not willing to pay the Ministry of Defense more than $6,000 per missile. The matter was not settled until March 1986, when Nimrodi paid the Ministry $3 million for the 504 missiles supplied to Iran—his price.

Schwimmer saw to the logistics of the first shipment. He went to Miami, where there is a large concentration of mercenary pilots who have won their wings on secret arms supply flights to Central America. Schwimmer chartered a DC-8 cargo plane from a Florida company owned by Richard R. Wellman. But in order to avoid complications in Tehran, this American-registered plane was bought by International Air Tours of Nigeria Ltd, based in Brussels.[9] The pilot, Herman Duran, and the flight engineer were Americans of Colombian origin, while the copilot was a Portuguese-American. The three arrived in Israel with the plane on August 18 and stayed at Nimrodi's house in Savion. The Ministry of Defense had the symbols and Israeli army insignia removed from the missiles. Ghorbanifar arrived on August 19 in order to accompany the shipment to Iran. In a conversation with Kimche and Schwimmer, Ghorbanifar claimed that he had just come from Tehran, where he had bribed, he said, several important people. He still did not know, however, how many hostages would be released. He had the impression that the Iranians knew exactly what Buckley was worth, and would therefore release him last.

While waiting for all the arrangements to be completed, Ghorbanifar toured the country with Nimrodi's daughter, Semadar, and had long conversations with Yehuda Alboher, the assistant of the Israeli arms salesman. He related that he made a practice of changing passports every few months. He had come to Israel on his Greek passport, under the name Nicholas Keralis. Next time, he would come on his Portuguese papers. He claimed to have several brand new Irish passports, but said he did not know when, if at all, he would use them.

Ghorbanifar frequently focused on his financial needs. He said that when the operation was accomplished he would have enough money to buy a private plane or at least rent one for his personal use. His wife, two sons, and daughter were spending the summer vacation at Cannes, but he was very worried about his parents in Tehran. He sent them $1,000 each month, but their health was not good and he was looking for a way to smuggle them out of the country and bring them to Israel for treatment. "Here there is the best medical treatment in the world," he said.

On August 20, 1985, at close to midnight, Operation Cappuccino got under way. The DC-8 took off from Ben-Gurion Airport carrying 96 TOW missiles on 8 pallets. Ghorbanifar went along. The flight route caused Schwimmer quite a few headaches. In order to prevent the plane's being discovered by the various radar systems along the way, the Colombian-American pilot,

Herman Duran, flew westward at a very low altitude and, at a predetermined point over the Mediterranean, made a 180-degree turn, returning eastward and getting on the flight path to Cyprus. The pilot called the control tower in Nicosia, identified himself, and asked for right-of-way over Cyprus, "in order to carry a cargo of medical equipment to Tehran." Fifteen minutes before landing at its destination, however, the craft encountered two Iraqi fighter planes circling over Tehran. The pilot performed an escape maneuver and was about to leave Iranian airspace when two Iranian F-5 jets appeared and led him to Tabriz. Iran's two deputy prime ministers, Agha Zadeh and Mohsen Kengarlou, were waiting for them there. After eating breakfast at the airport, the two government ministers and Ghorbanifar flew to Tehran in Mussavi's private plane, with the DC-8 trailing behind them. When the planes landed in Tehran, the deputy commander of the Revolutionary Guards, Sham Khani, came to the airport and demanded that the missiles be given to his forces. Kengarlou called Mussavi and asked for instructions. The Prime Minister ordered the missiles be handed over to the Revolutionary Guards (Pasdaran), which needed them at the front.

While the chartered plane was on its way to Tehran, Nimrodi waited in Geneva for Ghorbanifar's signal that the shipment had arrived safely. In the meantime Kimche had set out for London for a meeting with Michael Ledeen. The American representative said that McFarlane was seriously interested in the subject of "moderates" in Iran, and believed that Karoubi should be supported. Kimche gave Ledeen several documents he had received from Ghorbanifar during his last visit to Israel, but also warned against unreasonable expectations. "From experience I can say that Iran has never kept all its promises. They always omit something. And then a new round of bargaining begins, with the Iranians trying to get more than what was originally agreed to," Kimche warned.

Events proved Kimche correct. The Iranians received the missiles but did not free any hostages. Nimrodi called Ghorbanifar in Tehran a number of times. He stressed that the release of the hostages was a test of Iranian good faith and was a condition for the continued supply of missiles. Ghorbanifar claimed that, since the missiles had been taken by the Revolutionary Guards, the army officials who had been meant to receive the weapons considered themselves no longer obligated to make an effort to free the hostages. Ghorbanifar nevertheless claimed to be certain that the promise would be kept after the remaining 400 missiles were supplied. The two agreed to meet during the next few days in France.

They met on August 27 at the Regency Hotel in Nice. Ghorbanifar related that on August 22, the day after the plane had arrived in Tehran, he had met with Mussavi and Kengarlou. The Prime Minister had been enthusiastic about the success of the operation and asked Ghorbanifar who in the U.S. was behind it. Ghorbanifar had told him that it was Vice President Bush. When he saw Nimrodi's skepticism, Ghorbanifar hurriedly explained: "They really hate President Reagan in Iran. If I had said that Reagan was behind the operation they would have cut off my head."

He also related that, on August 23, he had met with Rafsanjani. The Speaker asked what interests the U.S. and Israel had in helping Iran. Ghorbanifar told him that, with the Reagan-Gorbachev summit being planned for Geneva in November, the U.S. was interested in demonstrating that Iran leaned toward the West and not toward the Soviet bloc. The U.S., he explained, was very much aware of Iran's strategic position and saw it as an effective barrier to the spread of communism in the Persian Gulf area. The U.S. also appreciated the role Iran's government played in aiding the Afghan rebels and, most important, it could not afford to ignore Iran's oil, natural gas, and phosphate riches. Ghorbanifar said that he went on to explain to the Speaker that the Soviet Union would not let Iraq lose the war, so as to protect the reputation of Soviet arms and Soviet strategy. Finally, Ghorbanifar told Nimrodi that he had revealed a "hidden secret" to Rafsanjani. He told him that the Emir of Kuwait had asked Vice President Bush to sell Iraq weapons and planes that would allow it to destroy the Kharg Island oil storage and transfer facilities. Bush had rejected the idea, he said. When Nimrodi asked where his information came from, Ghorbanifar said, without blinking an eye: "I made it up as I went along."

As for the hostages, Ghorbanifar claimed that Khomeini had ordered Mussavi and Rafsanjani to act immediately to free them. Ahmed Khomeini, he said, had told him that his father was now convinced that the U.S. really was interested in turning over a new leaf in its relations with Iran, and that Khomeini was now willing to help free the captives.

These stories made the doubts about Ghorbanifar's reliability even stronger, but no one was willing to cut off contact with him at this point. On the contrary, after Israel had supplied the 96 TOW missiles, it was ready to supply the remaining 404—so long as some or all of the hostages were freed. North in particular argued that everything should be done to free Buckley from his Lebanese captors.

It was decided, however, that Ghorbanifar should once more be made aware of the importance of the hostages before going ahead with the second part of the transaction. So, on September 4, Ghorbanifar was summoned to a meeting with Kimche, Ledeen, Schwimmer, and Nimrodi at the George V Hotel in Paris. It was a hard, no-nonsense conversation. Israel and the U.S., it was emphasized, had demonstrated the seriousness of their intentions, and it was now Iran's turn to prove its sincerity. Ghorbanifar was given to understand that there were now serious doubts as to whether he really had contacts among the powerful men in Tehran. "The Beard" (as Ghorbanifar was known in Israel) asked to call the Prime Minister's office in Tehran on the spot, in order to remove any doubts as to his reliability. Out of fear, however, that the room in which they sat was bugged, Ghorbanifar said he would call Tehran from a pay phone at the nearby Le Fourquet Café, and proposed that Nimrodi accompany him to hear for himself. The White House, which knew the Iranian arms dealer's habits well—including his frequent use of the café's telephone—had requested that the National Security Agency intercept the entire conversation. In an era of microwave and satellite transmission of international telephone calls, the NSA has an extraordinary ability to intercept phone conversations and other communications by using computers to sort through information picked out of the airwaves.[10] Ghorbanifar really did speak with Kengarlou in Tehran. The deputy prime minister said that there was no possibility of releasing all the captives. Only one could be freed. When Ghorbanifar asked for "the big one," Kengarlou responded that Buckley was "very ill" and could not be moved. He promised to see to the release of one hostage. In another conversation, also intercepted, Kengarlou and Ghorbanifar agreed that a prearranged signal would prove to the U.S. that the contacts between Ghorbanifar and the Iranian government were genuine. In public statements during the coming days, Mussavi and Rafsanjani would refrain from attacking the U.S. and would instead criticize the Soviet Union. This in fact happened.

The practical arrangements for the shipment of the remaining 404 TOW missiles were identical to those of the first shipment. Israeli Prime Minister Peres and Defense Minister Rabin gave their approval on September 9. Schwimmer chartered the same DC-8 and the same three crew members. Nimrodi went to Geneva with Khashoggi to arrange the interim payment of $4 million. On depositing the sum in Nimrodi's private Swiss account on September 10, Khashoggi told him that "President Reagan, Shimon Peres, and King Fahd should congratulate themselves on the success of the operation and on the coming release of Buckley."

On September 11 Kimche notified McFarlane that Israel had encountered certain difficulties in its relations with Ghorbanifar, but that it now seemed that the obstacles had been cleared away. An Iranian delegation had gone to Beirut to arrange the release of one hostage, but it was now clear that it would not be Buckley. Kimche asked McFarlane if he had any preference. McFarlane answered in the negative.

On the night of September 14 the chartered plane took off from Israel, carrying 408 missiles on 34 pallets. (The total number of TOW missiles supplied was actually 504, not 500.) This time Ghorbanifar's personal aide, Mehdi Shahisteh, accompanied the shipment, and five hours later it landed in Tabriz. After unloading the cargo the plane left for Spain. But over Turkey there was a malfunction and the plane "disappeared." The pilot, Captain Duran, had much experience of such covert flights, and had performed a quick escape maneuver. On the morning of September 15 he landed in Israel. It was the eve of Rosh Hashana, the Jewish New Year, so it was not possible to repair the plane that day. After much maneuvering, Yehuda Alboher, Nimrodi's assistant, managed to obtain passage for Ghorbanifar's aide on a Lufthansa flight that departed for Frankfurt before the holiday began at sundown. The cargo plane and its crew, however, remained in Israel for the two-day vacation. The plane was repaired on September 18 and it took off for its next assignment.

The plane's "disappearance" over Turkey and its arrival in

Israel were widely reported in the world media,[11] but Israel made no official comment. There were momentary fears that the whole operation would be exposed, but the fact that government offices were closed for two days helped cool down the story and get it out of the headlines. Even Israeli cabinet ministers were unable to discover what had happened. Minister Without Portfolio Moshe Arens, for instance, asked the leader of his party, Yitzhak Shamir, what was going on. "It's a secret," Shamir apologized. "I can't talk to you about it."[12]

On the morning of September 15 Kimche notified McFarlane that "the minister will be freed today." Schwimmer also telephoned Ledeen. And in fact, three hours later the Reverend Benjamin Weir, kidnapped in West Beirut by the Islamic Jihad on May 8, 1984, was on his way to freedom. A short time later President Reagan called Prime Minister Peres and thanked him for Israel's contribution to the release of the hostage. "That's the nicest New Year's greetings I've ever gotten." Peres later told Schwimmer and Nimrodi, thanking them for their role in the operation.

With the completion of the TOW deal, Colonel North was told to make preparations for the release of the other American hostages. While North had had a short conversation with Schwimmer at the White House in July, this was the first time that he had been actively involved in Iranian affairs. Supplied with a passport issued by the State Department on August 30, in the name of William P. Goode, and with a personal letter from President Reagan to Benjamin Weir in hand, North set out for Wiesbaden, West Germany, in order to question the former hostage.

In his letter, Reagan congratulated Weir on his release and asked him to assist North, to the extent that he was able, in his effort to win the release of the rest of the hostages. The intention was to learn as much as possible about the kidnappers and the place where the other hostages were being held. This was not successful, however. It turned out that the kidnappers were aware of this possibility, and transferred their captives from one location to another in order to frustrate any military attempt to free them.

With the completion of the TOW missile shipments, the financial side of the deal was also wrapped up. On September 18, Iran transferred $5 million to Ghorbanifar's account at Crédit

Suisse in Geneva. Ghorbanifar had two accounts at the bank—
one, number 283–838–92–1, in his own name, and another,
370–113–12–1, under the name of Abdallah Khak. Ghorbanifar
refunded Khashoggi's $4 million advance and deposited
$250,000 in Nimrodi's account to cover the costs of shipment,
the price of the additional four missiles, and other payments
involved in the deal.

On September 21, 1985, a week after Benjamin Weir's release,
Ghorbanifar arrived in Israel after a one-day stopover in Damascus. He hoped to persuade the Israeli government to prevent
the Voice of Israel from broadcasting any more news about
the plane that had brought arms to Iran and made a forced
landing in Israel. Ghorbanifar claimed that many Iranians listened to Israel's Persian-language broadcasts, and that the
news about the plane was making things difficult for Kengarlou
and Karoubi's people and could endanger the operation. He
suggested putting out instead an item that would link Weir's
release with the attempt to free the 17 El-Da'awa Shiite prisoners
in Kuwait.

The most sensational information Ghorbanifar brought, however, was about the attempts supposedly made to unseat Iran's
Prime Minister, Mir Hussein Mussavi. Ghorbanifar claimed that,
together with Karoubi, Mussavi was plotting a coup that would
"return Iran to the West." Ghorbanifar called himself the "AIDS"
of the Iranian republic. Like the disease, he succeeded in pene-
trating all parts of the Moslem establishment's body. He claimed
that Karoubi's group—with Ahmed Khomeini's support—had
proposed to the elderly leader of the revolution that Mussavi
be deposed and that Jalal El-Din Faresi be appointed in his
place. Faresi was an Iranian who served as a colonel in the
Palestinian el-Fatah organization, and he was now both anti-
Arafat and fervently anti-Communist. Khomeini at first reacted
positively, but changed his mind after the TOW missiles arrived
from Israel. This shipment was credited to Mussavi and he
remained, therefore, in his post. Had the change been made,
Ghorbanifar claimed, the conspirators would have done away
with Kengarlou, as well as with General Prosecutor Khoneikha
and the minister for intelligence affairs, Reishari. Even though
Mussavi remained in power, Ghorbanifar proposed that the
Voice of Israel broadcast news items aimed at increasing the
internal turbulence in Iran and creating the proper atmosphere

for a coup. As examples of such news, Ghorbanifar suggested spreading rumors that the Saudis and Kuwaitis were planning to lower their oil prices to $15 a barrel—a signal to the Iranian masses that their country could not continue financing its war against Iraq. Knowing Ghorbanifar's productive imagination, no one in Israel took seriously his news of an impending coup and of the efforts to depose Mussavi, and the Voice of Israel also refrained from publicizing his fantasies.

The following days and weeks saw a certain slowdown in activity aimed at renewing the dialogue with Iran. The General Assembly of the United Nations met in a special session, attended by many heads of state, to mark the fortieth anniversary of the birth of the international organization. President Reagan spoke before the General Assembly, and afterward met 12 leaders, including Egypt's President Mubarak, Jordan's King Hussein, and Shimon Peres. The Soviet foreign minister, Edward Shevardnadze, met George Shultz to complete preparations for a summit meeting between Reagan and Gorbachev in Geneva. Together with this intensive diplomatic activity came a new wave of terror and retaliation that grabbed the world's attention and left little time for opening up a dialogue with Iran.

On September 25 Palestinian terrorists murdered three Israeli vacationers on the deck of their yacht in Larnaca, Cyprus. In retaliation, the Israeli air force destroyed the PLO headquarters in Tunis. The Islamic Jihad organization in Beirut took advantage of the occasion to announce on October 3 that William Buckley had been executed. The U.S. paid little attention to the announcement, because it already had information from independent sources that Buckley had died of his tortures four months previously.

But the terrorist act that made the biggest impression at that time was the hijacking of the Italian cruise ship, the *Achille Lauro*, on October 7, 1985. Four Palestinian terrorists, members of the Palestine Liberation Front, a splinter group headed by Mahmoud Abbas ("Abu El-Abbas"), seized the boat and its 400 passengers soon after it sailed from Alexandria, Egypt, on its way to Ashdod in Israel. The terrorists planned to sail the boat into the Israeli port, murder as many Israelis as possible, and afterward use the passengers on the ship as hostages—both to allow them to escape safely and to force the release of comrades imprisoned in Israel.[13]

Their plans went awry when they were discovered by a crew-man while preparing their weapons. Afraid that he would turn them in, they attacked immediately. They forced the ship to sail to the Syrian port of Tartous, but President Assad, acting upon a specific request from the U.S., refused to allow them to enter the harbor. The terrorists murdered one of the passengers—Leon Klinghoffer, an American Jew, confined to a wheelchair—and threw his body into the sea. In the face of the international outcry that resulted, the *Achille Lauro* returned to Port Said. Under pressure from President Mubarak, Abu El-Abbas ordered the ship and its passengers freed on October 9 in exchange for an Egyptian promise to give the hijackers a plane that would take them to Tunis. This promise was made on the assumption that the terrorists had not harmed any of the passengers. When, after the *Achille Lauro* anchored, it was learned that Klinghoffer had been killed (his body would be recovered by Syrian authorities a few days later), the U.S. government decided that it could not pass over the crime in silence.

Colonel North coordinated the American response to the hijacking. Acting himself on information supplied continually by the American Sixth Fleet in the Mediterranean, and thanks to "real, direct, and immediate"[14] information supplied to him by Israel, North received, through Robert McFarlane, President Reagan's authorization to free the boat and its passengers. After the *Archille Lauro* put down anchor in Port Said, the U.S. was determined to capture the terrorists. It was at this juncture that the Egyptians let Reagan down. In response to questions from journalists, President Mubarak said that the terrorists had left Egypt, and that he did not know where they were. This was not true. The Israeli chief of military intelligence, General Ehud Barak, and the Israeli Prime Minister's adviser on the war against terrorism, Amiram Nir, informed North that, despite Mubarak's public statements, the four hijackers were still in Egypt. A short time later Barak gave North the number of the Egypt Air plane in which the hijackers would fly, and the route it would take to Tunisia.

Reagan immediately ordered the plane captured. North remained in constant contact with the commander of the Sixth Fleet, and with the commander of the *Saratoga* aircraft carrier, whose planes were to carry out the mission. While preparations were being made for the operation, Nir informed North that the Egyptian plane would carry not only the four terrorists, but their leader as well—Abu El-Abbas. This was the first chance the U.S. had ever had to capture the leader of a Palestinian terrorist organization, especially one who, like Abu El-Abbas, had been the perpetrator of many murders. Reagan was determined that the opportunity not slip through his fingers.

A short while after the Egyptian plane took off, the planes of the Sixth Fleet located it in the dark skies over the Mediterranean and forced it to land in Sicily. Here, however, Reagan encountered the unexpected resistance of Italy. Its government, for its own reasons, reached a secret agreement with the terrorists before the country's courts had time to rule on the American extradition request. The hijackers are jailed in Italy but their leader, Abu El-Abbas, was allowed to make his way to Yugoslavia, and from there he took a regular commercial flight to Libya.

Despite the disappointment at Italy's behavior, North's personal star had never been brighter in Washington. There had never been such close coordination between the U.S. and Israel in the battle against terrorism. North confirmed this publicly. In his congressional testimony North praised Nir for his cooperation, and of the decisive role played by General Ehud Barak, the head of Israeli military intelligence, he said: "We could not have done *Achille Lauro* without the personal relationship between a National Security Council man [North himself] and the senior Israeli intelligence official."[15]

The capture of the plane caused Egypt much discomfort and brought down the Italian government. Fearing that he would be accused of conniving with Israel to betray the Palestinians, Mubarak quickly condemned America's "piracy." The diversion of the plane came only a few days after Reagan had met Mubarak and Hussein in Washington to talk about the peace process, which now ground to a temporary halt.

In the midst of all this uproar, Schwimmer, Nimrodi, and Ghorbanifar arrived in Washington for a short visit to discuss the continuation of the Iran initiative with North. After the release of the Reverend Benjamin Weir, North began playing a more active role in the efforts to free the remaining hostages and began gradually to assume the functions previously filled by Michael Ledeen. Schwimmer had therefore met with both North and Ledeen in Washington on September 26, and on October 7 he returned with Nimrodi and Ghorbanifar to introduce them to North. (Ghorbanifar had come to Washington on a Greek passport issued in the name of "Nicholas Keralis.") In expectation of the meeting North had, on the previous day, ordered the FBI to follow the movements of the two arms dealers and to listen to their phone calls. On October 8 the three of them met briefly with North but, because of the *Achille Lauro* crisis, he had little time to devote to Iran. They all agreed to continue their talk with Michael Ledeen.

On October 27, Ledeen, Kimche, Nimrodi, and Schwimmer met with the Ayatollah Hassan Karoubi and Manucher Ghorbanifar at the Noga Hilton Hotel in Geneva. It was Ledeen's first meeting with Karoubi, and he voiced America's interest in gradually establishing connections with Iran, in parallel with Israel or even without Israel's participation.

The Israelis who attended this meeting called it "very important." Karoubi claimed that he and his men were now in key positions, and that they could influence their country's policy and bring about the release of the five remaining American hostages—without Khomeini's knowledge. He said that he and his fellows were ready to commit themselves to halting terrorist actions against the U.S., and could also put pressure on the Hezbollah faction in Lebanon to refrain from further kidnappings once the current hostages were released. This meeting did not touch on the missing Israeli soldiers or the five Lebanese Jews who were also being held captive.

Karoubi explained to Ledeen that, while the faction he headed was faithful to its religion, it was guided more by its nationalist than by its religious feelings. He described himself as a pragmatist who understood the necessity of compromising in light of reality. For example, Moslem Iran was cooperating with secular Syria. Iran fought the Ba'ath party in Iraq and demanded President Saddam Hussein's overthrow, but at the same time supported President Hafez El-Assad, the leader of the Syrian faction of the Ba'ath party. In exchange for the release of the American hostages in Lebanon, Karoubi demanded 150 Hawk missiles for the defense of the holy city of Qom and for shooting down high-flying Soviet intelligence planes entering Iranian airspace. He also asked for 200 Sidewinder missiles and 30–50 Phoenix missiles. As with the TOWs, Karoubi did not want to pay for the Hawks and argued that the release of the hostages was payment enough.

Ledeen answered that he was not authorized to give Karoubi

an immediate answer, and that he would have to present the matter to his superiors in Washington. He made it clear, however, that if the U.S. decided to supply Iran with the Hawk antiaircraft missiles and the other arms, Iran would have to pay for them. Ghorbanifar persuaded Karoubi to agree. Ledeen also insisted that Iran free all the hostages at the same time, and not one by one. After their release the U.S. would be willing to enter a new era of relations with Iran, supply it with arms and intelligence, and send it technicians and advisers in various fields.

In a separate conversation with Ledeen, Kimche raised the question of the replenishment of 504 TOW missiles to replace those which Israel had sent to Iran. He said that Minister of Defense Yitzhak Rabin was very upset about the U.S. failure to live up to its commitment. "I have to tell you in all honesty that I doubt whether Rabin will agree to sending more arms to Iran until arrangements are made for supplying replacements for the TOWs," Kimche said. Ledeen promised to bring the subject of replenishment to the attention of McFarlane and North. On September 19, he had already sent a message to McFarlane stating: "The people who sold the soap for us want to replenish their supply."[16]

The next day, October 28, Ghorbanifar set out from Geneva to the Gulf sheikhdom of Dubai on a Malaysian plane, in order to meet with Kengarlou. At Geneva airport Ghorbanifar bought gold watches and expensive gifts for the wives of the two deputy prime ministers, Agha Zadeh and Kengarlou. The latter had come to the Sheraton Hotel in Dubai in order to close on a purchase of missiles from Austria through an Iranian intermediary, Muhammad Kiarashi. Kengarlou wanted to use the same occasion to send the U.S. "an important message" through Ghorbanifar. Kengarlou related that, on October 25, he had had a three-hour conversation with Ahmed Khomeini and with Rafsanjani, which concluded with the drafting of a statement to the U.S.

> From this moment onwards, Iran pledges not to engage in any hostile acts against the U.S.—neither bombings, nor kidnappings, nor attacks on American interests in the Middle East. Iran likewise pledges to aid the Afghan rebels in their struggle against the Soviet army of occupation, and to transfer

to them any equipment made available to them by the U.S. The aid will be delivered to whichever group the U.S. names. As for the hostages, Iran is prepared to guarantee the release of only five of them. Iran has no authority or involvement regarding other hostages. Four hostages will be released in advance, and the fifth when the promised arms are received.

According to Ghorbanifar, Kengarlou set two conditions for the release of the hostages:

• that each shipment include 35 "improved" Hawk antiaircraft missiles, 50 Sidewinders, and 15 Phoenixes; and
• that, because of the instability in Lebanon, the deal had to follow the following schedule:

1. The first plane had to land at Bandar Abbas on November 12, 1985, at 4:00 A.M. At 8:00 A.M. the Reverend Martin Jenco would be released and handed over to the American embassy in Beirut.

2. On November 15, at 5:00 P.M., Thomas Sutherland would be released and handed over to the American embassy in Beirut. At midnight, the second plane would land at Bandar Abbas.

3. On November 18, at 5:00 P.M., Peter Kilburn would be released, and at midnight the third plane would land at Bandar Abbas.

4. On November 21 David Jacobsen would be released, and at midnight the fourth shipment would arrive.

5. Finally, on November 25, Terry Anderson would be released, and at midnight the fifth and last arms shipment would arrive.

In a letter dated October 31 and delivered to Nimrodi, Ghorbanifar emphasized that, since this deal had the approval of Rafsanjani and Ahmed Khomeini, Kengarlou expected that, should it be exposed, the U.S. would deny it publicly and forcefully. After the release of the hostages, the U.S. was not to say anything about Iran's complicity in the matter. Immediately thereafter, Iran would be willing to host a visit by senior Americans, accompanied by Ghorbanifar.

This was Kengarlou's message. Ghorbanifar added comments of his own. He argued, for instance, that he thought Kengarlou's offer was "fair and serious." In his opinion, Iran had brought up the idea for fear that Reagan and Gorbachev would reach agreements between them in Geneva "at the expense of Iranian interests." He added that Iran-Soviet relations were at a nadir, and that no one in Tehran now expected the Soviets to halt their arms shipments to Iraq, and no one thought that the Russians were interested in reaching an honorable settlement with Iran. Furthermore, the power struggle in Iran had reached a critical stage, and Karoubi's faction hoped to take advantage of the arms shipments from the U.S. to tip the scales in its favor. Ghorbanifar concluded his letter to Nimrodi as follows: "The Moslem regime is on its knees and is trying to crawl towards the U.S. Even if I believe that this time they will keep their promises, no one should count on those criminals. They should be punished for their deeds. I hope that the U.S. is never involved with this criminal regime." As was his custom in such cases, Ghorbanifar also sent Nimrodi a few crumbs of intelligence. In an additional letter, also dated October 31, he wrote that Kengarlou sounded dissatisfied about his relations with the religious establishment.[17] He said that its leaders lived in luxurious mansions, while he continued to live in a small apartment of only 82 square meters in Khorassan Square in South Tehran, together with his wife, six children, and his parents. Kengarlou told Ghorbanifar:

> It's likely that my power derives from my modest life-style. Before the revolution, religious leaders were afraid to greet me, fearing they would get into trouble. Now they flaunt their riches as they did in the Shah's day. Despite my great influence and my high status in the Prime Minister's office, and despite the fact that I control a budget of millions, I prefer to continue to live modestly. No one can accuse me of taking advantage of my position. But it's becoming difficult and intolerable. My wife is in a depression, and in order to save myself from the crisis, I need a loan of 8 million tomans [approximately $1 million], but I do not want to act like the others.

Ghorbanifar offered to give him the "loan," and told Kengarlou that he could return the money when he was able. Kengarlou answered that Ghorbanifar was the only man he could trust. They agreed that Ghorbanifar would leave $1 million in a sealed envelope with his mother in Tehran, and Kengarlou would come and get it.

Kengarlou also brought up a more personal matter. He claimed that, while in Iran, he could not allow himself to engage in extramarital relations. Now that he was traveling abroad, he hoped that Ghorbanifar would find him "a nice Moslem girl" in Europe.

Ghorbanifar also reported that:

- Kengarlou had assumed some of the authority previously exercised by the other deputy prime minister, Agha Zadeh.
- Kengarlou's relations with Ahmed Khomeini and Rafsanjani were very good, and he could see them whenever he wished.
- Kengarlou was close to Montazeri, and he believed that this man would succeed Khomeini. Kengarlou asked for Ghorbanifar's help in being named Montazeri's first Prime Minister.
- In the new Iranian government, sworn in on October 13, Mussavi had been forced to accept five ministers who represented the right and commercial interests.
- "Very important documents"[18] had been found in the luggage of an American passenger on an Air France jet that had been hijacked in Tehran.
- Iran was planning a new offensive against Iraq.
- The most important element for Iran was the expatriates. Iran needed them. There were some three million Iranian exiles in Europe and the U.S., and Kengarlou had been appointed to take care of their problems.

Ghorbanifar concluded his letter by mentioning that he had suggested to Kengarlou that he meet with senior American officials, but Kengarlou asked that it be postponed for the time being. Ghorbanifar had been with Kengarlou in Dubai for 36 hours, and left for Europe on October 30.

The full content of both letters was passed on to the U.S., and while the reaction to the intelligence was positive, McFarlane had reservations about the continued supply of weapons. In a conversation with David Kimche in Washington on November 8, 1985, McFarlane expressed doubt about the existence of moderate elements in Iran, and about their ability to gain power. He emphasized that he had ordered North and Ledeen not to send Iran "even one single item" until "live Americans" were released.[19] Kimche explained that the two sides had already proven their trustworthiness, and that it was now possible to achieve a more significant dialogue. Despite his doubts, McFarlane agreed with Kimche that the presidential authorization for the supply of the 504 TOW missiles could also cover another arms shipment, on condition that the shipment not change the balance of power in the Iran-Iraq War. McFarlane in any case expressed disappointment at the release of only one hostage so far. He saw this as a breach of good faith on Iran's part, and asked himself whether it would not be best to end the matter then and there.

Prior to his conversation with McFarlane, Kimche had eaten lunch with North and Ledeen. The two Americans told him that their boss was planning to resign and, knowing McFarlane's great esteem for Kimche, they asked him to convince the national security adviser not to leave the White House and to continue the Iranian initiative. Ledeen believed that the arms deals, the hostage problem, and the wider effort to establish links with Iran should all be kept separate, and emphasized the need to concentrate on developing diplomatic connections between the two countries. While he was aware of the President's great concern for the fate of the hostages, Ledeen told Schwimmer and Nimrodi: "If we don't unlink the supply of weapons from the release of the hostages, we ourselves will become hostages of the hostages."

Ledeen proposed opening a Swiss bank account for money to support the Iranian moderates. Schwimmer accepted the idea enthusiastically and opened the account at Crédit Suisse in Geneva, giving the number to Ledeen. Ledeen, a part-time employee at NSC, gave the number to North, although the latter had no access to this particular account. At this point, Israel and the U.S. were in agreement that, despite their doubts, they must continue the Iran initiative for now.

According to McFarlane's instructions, Oliver North became more involved in the Iran initiative. He helped McFarlane overcome his doubts, and with the determination of a Marine officer and the ambition to succeed where others had failed, North relegated Michael Ledeen to a background role, and would shortly become the leading man in the Iranian drama.

Operation Espresso

The showstopper of the second half of November 1985 was the Reagan-Gorbachev team, and it pushed all other diplomatic activity into the wings. On Tuesday, November 19, at 10:05 A.M. Geneva time, the two leaders inaugurated the first summit conference between the two superpowers in six years. Secretary of State George Shultz and National Security Adviser Robert McFarlane had already been in Moscow for a week, making preparations.

McFarlane's preoccupation with the summit left the Iranian initiative in the hands of one of his closest and most ambitious staff members, Colonel Oliver North. Having been actively involved in the efforts to free the hostages in Lebanon, North knew something about the opening to Iran. He had already met with the principal actors—Kimche, Nimrodi, Schwimmer, and Ghorbanifar—and had discussed with them how the contacts with Iran might be continued.

At this point, the Israelis thought North's involvement was temporary, for the duration of the summit. They cooperated with him and accepted his directives because they understood that he, as McFarlane's aide, was acting on the authority of the President. It soon became clear, however, that North's involvement in the initiative would continue. McFarlane was to resign from his post on November 30, 1985; he would be replaced by his deputy, Admiral John Poindexter.

Poindexter, 51, tall and balding, had a wife and five children. He had graduated from the Naval Academy *cum laude*, received a doctorate in Nuclear Physics, and filled important positions in the American navy. Israelis who met him thought he was comfortable, honest, quick on the uptake, and blessed with an exceptional memory. He was considered conservative in his ideas on religion and government. He had expressed his positive feelings about Israel on a number of occasions.

McFarlane's resignation was the result of infighting within the administration and bore no relation to the Iranian affair. William Casey's influence in the White House had grown since Reagan's reelection in 1984. At the CIA chief's instigation, one of his loyalists, Donald Regan, was named White House Chief of Staff to replace James Baker.[1] Regan interfered with McFarlane's system of working and tried to block his free access to the Oval Office. More than once he barged in on the national security adviser's briefings of the President. McFarlane felt that the situation was becoming intolerable and decided to resign. Peres, Rabin, and the senior officials of the Israeli Foreign Ministry knew McFarlane well and admired his personal integrity and his view of the world. Poindexter was still an unknown. The only connection with him had been through Amiram Nir, the Prime Minister's adviser on the war against terrorism, and through Oliver North. North himself suddenly became more important when Poindexter named him to coordinate the Iran initiative.

This was the second time in his variegated career that North found himself involved with Iran. The first time had been in 1980, during the botched military attempt to rescue the hostages at the American embassy in Tehran. North had then been an officer in the backup Marine force in Turkey, meant to reinforce the rescuers should they need help. That, however, had been a passive role. His new assignment meant being actively involved in decision making—a role for which he had not been trained. It seems that, in the wake of his success in the *Achille Lauro* episode, no one in the White House or the CIA bothered to check his qualifications for dealing with Iran. Perhaps swept away by the image of this Marine officer who seemed able to solve any problem, they did not stop to consider how complex the new contacts with Iran were.

North, 43, with a wife and four children, had fought and been wounded in Vietnam, and had been decorated twice for heroism in battle. The range of his activities was staggering. Since mid-1984 he had headed the secret American effort to aid the Contras in Nicaragua. Despite Congress's prohibition of such aid, North, who was by now William Casey's "operational man" at the NSC, set up his own private network working out of the White House.[2] He organized a network of private contributors, met with leaders of the Contras, visited their training camps in Costa Rica and El Salvador, and planned the mining of Nicaragua's ports. With the help of several former army officers and intelligence agents, North dealt with private corporations that were run by or tied to General Secord and that opened secret Swiss bank accounts and hired boats and planes to ship arms to the anti-Sandinista rebels. North also conducted several secret intelligence operations relating to the hostages in Lebanon. In his dealings with the Israelis he often appeared tense. North hated small talk; he always spoke to the point. Whenever he entered a room, his eyes scoured the place nervously, as if he were looking for an escape route, should something go wrong. The Israelis testify to his being "a real patriot and an extreme nationalist," who identified utterly with President Reagan's policy in Central America.[3] When he took on a mission he would go all out—not always caring where the line between law and illegality was. In many ways, North was both frightening and awesome. After the exposure of the Iran arms deal, President Reagan called him a national hero. His opponents, however, called him an unbridled adventurer. In his determination to succeed he assumed, in effect, powers that had never been given him. He betrayed people and was betrayed by them,[4] and after the revelations about his part in the Iranian episode, he publicly acknowledged that, in his efforts to obtain the release of the hostages, he lied to the Iranians and even to his closest associates.

North stumbled over Iran partly because of the baggage he brought with him to this complex and sensitive operation. As part of his work for the Contras, North had called on retired general Richard Secord to organize the logistic side of the aid to the Nicraraguan rebels. A former combat pilot of 55, short and with a sharp, piercing glance, Secord had served 30 years in the air force. Former Secretary of State Alexander Haig had been his commander at West Point. A veteran of more than 200 intelligence flights during the Vietnam War, he had been decorated several times. He had gone on several secret missions to Laos, and had participated in convoying UN forces to Zaire. In 1975 Secord had been appointed head of the American air force mission in Iran—which then included more than 1,000 officers and technicians—assigned to train the Iranian air force.

During his three years in Tehran, Secord appears to have been very impressed by the huge profits that various arms salesmen had earned from supplying American weapons to the Shah's army. In Tehran, Secord had made the acquaintance of Albert Hakim, an Iranian Jew of about 50, who had studied for three years in the U.S. Upon returning to Tehran in 1958 Hakim had worked for several years in his father's insurance company, and had afterward worked as a Persian-English interpreter at the Iranian branch of a company that built communication systems in Iran. He then set up a company that provided various types of electronic equipment to the Iranian army and to the Savak. Hakim later set up several financial companies in Switzerland, Panama, and California. After he met Secord, the American embassy in Tehran began to recommend him to various American companies that supplied arms to Iran. Hakim then set up his Stanford Technology Corporation, with its central offices in Vienna, Virginia, and supplied electronic surveillance equipment to the Iranian armed services. This relationship between Secord and Hakim was later to produce a fruitful business partnership between them, and to bring about Hakim's active involvement in the Iran affair.

On the eve of the Shah's downfall, in the summer of 1978, Secord returned to the U.S. In 1981 he was named deputy assistant secretary of defense and headed the division that oversaw military aid to some 40 foreign countries. In this position, Secord worked together with North, who had then begun to serve as a junior officer in the National Security Council, to win congressional approval for a government proposal to sell AWACS planes to Saudi Arabia.

The year 1983, however, brought a sudden end to Secord's military career. While in Laos he had made the acquaintance of two intelligence agents, Theordore Shackley and Thomas Clines. The three of them had become friendly with Edwin Wilson, another intelligence man turned arms salesman (now serving a 52-year sentence for supplying weapons to Muammar Qadhafi). After the conclusion of the peace treaty between Israel and Egypt in March 1979, the U.S. had begun giving Egypt a steady supply of arms and military equipment. Secord, in his position at the Pentagon, was of great help to his friends. Clines set up a shipping company, Egyptian-American Transport & Services Corp. (EATSCO), with an Egyptian partner in 1982, for the purpose of carrying American arms to Egypt. Clines is said to be Secord's best friend and, according to Wilson, Secord was a silent partner in EATSCO. Secord denies this. The company submitted inflated bills to the Pentagon and EATSCO, in 1983, pleaded guilty to illegal billings in shipping charges.[5] Clines and his Egyptian partner paid $3 million in restitution and a fine of $20,000.[6] When Justice Department officials began investigating Secord's alleged involvement in EATSCO, the Pentagon suspended the general from his position. The inquiry failed to prove any financial wrongdoing, and Secord was never charged. He nevertheless decided to leave the Pentagon.[7]

A month later Secord became a partner in the Stanford Technology Corporation headed by Albert Hakim. The two of them set up a subsidiary called the Stanford Technology and International Trade Group, headed by Secord, which tried to obtain construction contracts in Saudi Arabia, Abu Dhabi, Sudan, and Egypt. The efforts were not successful. In May 1984, however, Secord's economic situation took a turn for the better. After the American Congress had forbidden the administration to give official aid to the Contras, Colonel North asked Secord to organize a system of covert aid. Secord and Hakim set up many corporations and opened several secret bank accounts in Switzerland and the Cayman Islands. One of the companies, Lake Resources, registered in Panama, would later become involved in supplying arms to Iran. Secord later hired his friend Thomas Clines to help him in his Central American activities.

North's involvement in the Iranian initiative and, especially, his appointment of Secord, were among the most serious errors of the whole episode. Neither of them knew the important figures in Iran, and North did not understand the complexity of the issue. More importantly, in the management of covert operations, it is important that each operation be kept carefully separate from all others, and that, because of confidentiality, people involved in one secret mission not be part of another.

North, who already managed aid to the Contras and was involved in winning the release of the hostages, now also took on the Iran operation. He enlisted Secord and Hakim to this project as well. Furthermore, he allowed Secord and Hakim to manage the financial side of the arms sales to Iran and the aid to the Contras through the same secret bank accounts. He would later admit publicly in his congressional testimony that he had not properly supervised their use of the money.

Kimche, Schwimmer, and Nimrodi certainly did not realize what they were getting into when McFarlane and Poindexter assigned North to coordinate the Iran operation. None of them doubted the Marine officer's intelligence or reasoning. Only after the episode became public and Congress began its investigation did it become clear that Secord and Hakim had financial motives for joining the Iran project, and that they had hoped to make large profits from it.

Kimche, Nimrodi, and Schwimmer met with Ghorbanifar in London. The latter brought a request for the supply of 600 improved Hawk ("I-Hawk") missiles and large quantities of Phoenix and Sidewinder missiles. He said that Iran desperately needed the Hawks in order to hit high-flying Iraqi and Soviet planes. Kimche immediately made it clear that, because of the American embargo, it would be impossible to give Iran those types of weapons, and certainly not in the amounts requested. He told Ghorbanifar that the U.S. insisted on first receiving all the hostages. Only afterward would it allow Israel to pass on to Iran limited quantities of Hawks. Ghorbanifar declared that the matter could not be handled that way. Iran first wanted the weapons, and after each shipment a hostage would be freed.

The participants began calling Washington, Jerusalem, and Tehran. Ghorbanifar called Deputy Prime Minister Kengarlou and asked his permission to negotiate for I-Hawks only. He also suggested that Israel supply 80 missiles in a single shipment, with five American hostages and two Lebanese Jews, also captives, being released simultaneously. Kimche briefed McFarlane on his conversation with Ghorbanifar. Even if the ideas discussed with the Iranian were not yet firm, they were enough to lead McFarlane to report to Casey, on November 14, that "the Israelis intend to supply arms to certain elements in the Iranian army ready to overthrow their government."[8]

On November 14, North met in Washington with Amiram

Nir, the Israeli Prime Minister's adviser on combatting terrorism, in order to discuss a series of joint covert actions.[9] Among them was an operation to rescue the hostages by force, which North referred to in his notes as T.H. 1. The preparations would cost about $1 million a month for several months. No decision was made. North listed the following problems that still lacked solutions: Who would pay? Where would the money come from? Would the U.S. act alone, or in cooperation with Israel? Or should Israel act on its own, with the funding coming from the U.S.? The two men returned to the subject on November 19, and also discussed an alternative known as T.H. 2. This plan also needed funding, and again no decision was made. It now seems likely that, even at this early stage, North and Nir were thinking of using the profits from the arms sales to Iran to fund the joint covert operations. Officially, the arms sales to Iran were not discussed, but North was already involved in the Iranian initiative and it seems likely that Nir, too, had gotten several hints about it.

During the following days the Hawk deal would come together in long telephone conversations between American and Israeli officials, and between them and the Israeli and Iranian middlemen. On Friday, November 15, Minister of Defense Yitzhak Rabin paid a working visit to Washington. He talked with Secretary of Defense Weinberger about further supplies of American arms to Israel, including the construction of new submarines for the Israeli navy. Rabin also took the opportunity to meet with McFarlane and to speed up the delivery of the 504 new TOW missiles to replace those supplied to Iran in August and September.

In his discussion with the national security adviser, Rabin complained that the U.S. had not yet fulfilled its promise for replenishment, and noted that this would make it difficult for Israel to agree to supply additional quantities of arms to Iran. McFarlane promised to send North to Israel "within two weeks," in order to find a solution to this problem. Rabin told Avraham Ben-Yosef, director of the Israeli military procurement mission in New York, to continue pursuing the matter. Rabin's main concern was the extent to which President Reagan still endorsed the concept of Israel's negotiating arms sales to Iran. The Israeli defense minister also wanted assurances that the Iran initiative was a joint U.S.–Israeli project.[10]

On November 17, Schwimmer informed North that Israel

would agree to send 80 improved Hawk missiles to Iran on condition that the replenishment problem was solved. This operation was to be named "Espresso," and it was scheduled for Friday, November 22. Kimche sent a similar message to McFarlane. The latter, however, still had doubts. He did not hide his fears that Israel and the U.S. were slipping against their will into an arms-for-hostages deal. He was afraid that if this process continued it would be impossible to test Iran's real intentions, and an opportunity for a diplomatic break-through would be lost. Ghorbanifar's unreliability was also a problem. McFarlane realized, however, that at this point it was too late to withdraw from the deal. He accordingly notified the President on November 17, a short time before Air Force 1 set out for the summit meeting in Geneva. Reagan's response was brief: "Cross your fingers and let's hope for the best. Keep me informed."[11] McFarlane also reported to the CIA director. On November 18, in Geneva, he told the secretary of state that Israel was about to ship to Iran 80 Hawk missiles, through Portugal, against the release of the hostages.

Shultz was furious. He told McFarlane that, had he known about it earlier, he would have tried to prevent the deal. The secretary of state expressed his hope that the hostages really would be released, but that he was opposed to an arms-for-hostages deal. Yet he, too, understood that, at this late stage, the horse was already out of the barn.[12]

Although Israel had decided to supply only 80 Hawks, Ghorbanifar pleaded again and again for a larger quantity. He freely admitted that Iran needed large amounts of all kinds of arms in order to continue its war against Iraq. North spoke of this with Schwimmer on November 18, and on the following day with Avraham Ben-Yosef. North was inclined to supply Iran with 600 Hawks. In his meeting with Ben-Yosef, he assured Israel that the U.S. would replenish. Israel stuck with the amount it had set. After the release of the hostages, and if Iran would commit itself unequivocally to refraining from any new acts of terrorism, it would be possible to send 40 more Hawks, 200 Sidewinders, and 1,900 TOWs.[13]

The shipment encountered several logistic problems. Hawk missiles are very long—nearly 18 feet—and it was difficult to find an appropriate freight plane. Schwimmer discovered that there were only three charter companies in the world renting

Boeing 747 cargo planes that opened from the front. Because of the risks involved in flying to Tehran, they all demanded guarantees of $50 million. Schwimmer and Nimrodi were unwilling to make so huge a commitment, and the Israeli government also demurred, because it was not supposed to be officially involved in the shipment. The Ministry of Defense contacted Rabin, who was still in the U.S. On November 17 he telephoned McFarlane in Geneva. The defense minister wanted to be sure that President Reagan had approved the deal, and that it was being carried out jointly by the U.S. and Israel. McFarlane reiterated that the presidential approval of the TOW shipments of August and September was still in force, and that the President knew that Israel was to send 80 Hawks to Iran. As for logistic problems, McFarlane said, North would take care of them, and he would also try to solve the problem of replenishment sales to Israel—not only of the 80 Hawks but also the 504 TOW missiles that Israel had sent to Iran in August and September 1985.[14]

Rabin spoke with North that same evening. The colonel told him that he would be coming to New York the next day to talk to Rabin and his assistants and to solve the problems that had arisen.[15] When he arrived he heard Rabin's description of the difficulties. Rabin told him that Avraham Ben-Yosef was to conclude the arrangements for the replacement missiles. As for the transport of the Hawks, North called Schwimmer and told him that the matter would be taken care of by "Copp" (Secord). Secord left that night for Israel and met the next day with the Ministry of Defense director-general, General (ret.) Menachem (Mendi) Meron, his deputy Chaim Carmon, and Al Schwimmer. Secord proposed that, given the difficulty of hiring a 747, Israel could bring the 80 Hawk missiles to Lisbon on one of its own planes. He would use his good connections in Portugal, he said, to arrange landing rights for the Israeli plane. Secord also promised to ensure that the cargo went on to Iran in three chartered planes that were under neither Israeli nor American ownership. The planes would take off at two-hour intervals. After the first plane took off, "Ashghari" (Ghorbanifar) would tell Kengarlou to instruct the Iranian embassy in Damascus to see to it that the commander of the Revolutionary Guards in Beirut received the five American hostages from Hezbollah, and that he handed them over to the American embassy in Lebanon. The first arms shipment would not land in Tehran until the hostages had been released. "Copp" left on November 20 for Portugal, leaving Schwimmer his telephone numbers in Lisbon. North had asked Schwimmer on November 18 to deposit $1 million in the Lake Resources bank account, number 386–430–22–1 at Crédit Suisse in Geneva, in order to pay for the shipment from Lisbon to Tehran and the transport of the replacement missiles from the U.S. to Israel. Schwimmer did not know that Lake Resources was one of the corporations Secord and Hakim had set up in Panama to funnel money to the Contras. He deposited the money on November 20.

No one in Israel was surprised by the indirect flight path and the choice of Lisbon as a transfer point for the missiles. It has long been known, especially by those with experience in secret missions, that Portugal serves as a major center for arms transfers to all parts of the world. Only afterward did the Israelis discover that Lisbon was an important logistic base for Secord in sending arms and military equipment to the Contras.[16] Hence, obtaining landing rights in Lisbon for an El Al Boeing 747 appeared in Israel as a routine matter for Secord. He was soon to be rudely awakened. On Thursday, November 21, "Copp" told Schwimmer that he had spoken with the Portuguese minister of defense, who told him that his Prime Minister had approved the landing rights, and that the Portuguese Foreign Ministry also knew about it "and is supportive." That same evening Schwimmer called a meeting at his Tel Aviv home to finalize arrangements. It was attended by David Kimche, Yehuda Alboher (Nimrodi's assistant), assistant director-general of the Ministry of Defense Chaim Carmon, and others. During the course of the meeting they had several telephone conversations with North in Washington, with Avraham Ben-Yosef in New York, with Nimrodi and Ghorbanifar in Geneva, and with "Copp" in Lisbon. Ben-Yosef was asked to ensure that the U.S. give Israel the new Hawk missiles as soon as possible, and at a reasonable price. Two Syrian Mig-23 fighter planes had been shot down by the Israelis on November 19, heightening Israel's sensitivity to its need for air defenses. Prime Minister Shimon Peres demanded that the shortfall be made up in the near future. Rabin and Kimche had also called Washington several times on November 21 and asked North to put White House pressure on the Pentagon to expedite the replenishment.

At that same meeting at Schwimmer's house, Yehuda Alboher

heard one of those present whisper to Carmon that the Israeli army would not send the newest improved Hawks, but the older model. The Israeli even expressed his satisfaction that, in place of the outdated missiles, Israel would receive more up-to-date ones. Alboher mentioned this to Schwimmer, and he immediately warned Carmon against betraying Iranian good faith. Schwimmer did not leave it at that. He called the director-general of the Ministry of Defense the next morning. He told Meron that Israel and the U.S. were trying to repair relations with Iran and that, when the plane landed in Tehran, Hezbollah was to release the American hostages. The Iranian order should be filled as agreed.

Iran considered this shipment of I-Hawks extremely important. In order to be sure that the shipment reach its destination without mishaps, Prime Minister Mussavi of Iran sent his deputy, Kengarlou, to Geneva, to be with Nimrodi and Ghorbanifar. This was Nimrodi's first face-to-face meeting with Kengarlou. Short, chubby, and strong-featured, Kengarlou had been a Khomeini loyalist in the bazaar during the Shah's days. His small tailor shop had served as a headquarters for incitement against the monarchy and for the organization of demonstrations and strikes in the commercial sector. He had been arrested frequently by the Savak, but was released each time for lack of evidence. He was a close friend of Ghorbanifar and trusted him completely.

Operation Espresso was now ready to begin. Schwimmer and Nimrodi agreed with North and Secord that the Israeli plane would leave for Lisbon on Friday afteroon, November 22, after business hours. This would make it possible to preserve the secrecy of the operation and prevent it from being prematurely revealed by employees of the airport or of the adjacent Israel Aircraft Industries complex. The representative of the chartered Israeli plane in Lisbon was asked to be in touch with "Copp" should any additional help be necessary.

But on Friday morning Secord called Schwimmer and asked for takeoff to be delayed by a few hours, since he had not yet been able to arrange the landing rights in Lisbon. It was a surprising announcement—one day previously Secord had told Schwimmer that Portugal's Prime Minister had given his personal approval to the plane's landing, and that the foreign and defense ministers were aware of the decision.

It later became clear that the whole matter had been badly

handled. The documents later submitted to the congressional investigatory committees revealed that one of Secord's European business partners (one of the three owners of the arms sales firm Defex-Portugal, Jose Garnel) had called a Portuguese government official on November 16 and offered what the official understood to be a bribe in exchange for expediting a certain shipment involving the U.S., Israel, and Iran. The official rejected the offer.[17] On November 20 Garnel spoke to an official in the Portuguese Foreign Ministry and asked, in the name of "an American General," for right of passage through Lisbon for two planes carrying arms from Israel to Iran. The official told his superior, who contacted the American chargé d'affaires in Lisbon. The American diplomat, who knew nothing of the matter, told the Portuguese official that supplying weapons to Iran ran counter to the policies of the American government and that he knew of no request by an American general.

Caught up in this tangle of events, Secord began a nerve-racking effort to obtain landing rights for the Israeli plane. In coordination with North and together with two of his associates, Secord again applied to the Portuguese government and asked for permission for an Israeli plane carrying "drilling equipment" to Iran to land in Lisbon. The Portuguese, however, demanded written certification that the plane indeed carried drills. Secord could not produce such a document.

Despite the difficulties, North wrote Poindexter on November 20 that the operation was "going as planned," and that Secord deserved a medal for his hard work and his extraordinary efforts on short notice.[18]

By November 22 it was clear that Secord and his helpers had not succeeded in budging the Portuguese from their stand. North asked McFarlane to speak to the Portuguese Prime Minister.[19] McFarlane spoke with the Foreign Minister, but this produced no results. At the request of North, the CIA instructed its chief of station in Lisbon to assist, but to no avail. North had no choice but to notify Schwimmer of the expected delay. Schwimmer immediately notified Nimrodi in Geneva. Ghorbanifar and Kengarlou were in Nimrodi's room at the Noga Hilton, with four armed Iranian guards at the door. Kengarlou was tense. He was worried because, unlike the TOW shipment's interim funding from Adnan Khashoggi, this shipment had been paid for directly by Iran. He had given instructions to allow Ghorbanifar to withdraw $24 million from the National Iranian

Oil Company (NIOC) account and deposit it in Nimrodi's personal account. Any mishap was likely to cost Kengarlou his head.

Now religion intervened. Religious parties in the Israeli government coalition had recently pushed through legislation forbidding El Al to fly on the Jewish Sabbath, from Friday sundown to Saturday night. So on Friday afternoon at 5:00 P. M., Al Schwimmer was informed that, to prevent desecration of the Sabbath, the plane carrying the missiles could not take off for Lisbon until the following night. There seemed to be no way out. The plane had already been loaded, Nimrodi was under pressure—and threats—from Kengarlou, but "Copp," despite North's assurances, had not been able to get the landing rights in Lisbon. To add to the confusion, Secord called from Lisbon and told Schwimmer that the landing permit was expected "any minute" and asked that the plane take off as planned. This guarantee in hand, Schwimmer called the Israeli Prime Minister. Peres spoke to the two chief rabbis of Israel, explained to them that this was a sensitive matter that could save human lives, and asked them to allow the Boeing 747 to take off after the beginning of the Sabbath of Friday evening, and to return on Saturday morning. The chief rabbis gave their consent.

The plane took off at 7:00 P.M., and was scheduled to land in Lisbon after midnight. At 10:00 P.M. North suddenly called and told Schwimmer that Portugal had still not issued the landing permit, and that the plane should be returned to Israel. The 747 had just reached the French coast when it was ordered to turn back. It landed at Ben Gurion Airport in the early morning with only a few drops of fuel left in its tanks. Schwimmer was dumbfounded. He immediately reported to Nimrodi in Geneva and asked him to keep Kengarlou and Ghorbanifar calm.

The shock for Schwimmer and Nimrodi went beyond the mental anguish they had suffered and the unnecessary expenses they had incurred. They suddenly realized that the people the White House had assigned to the project were incompetent. Schwimmer was now worried that the whole affair would be uncovered before it was completed. Now another logistic problem had to be dealt with. The period for which the Israeli plane had been chartered had expired, and it was impossible to extend it for another day. Unsure of what would happen next, Schwimmer also canceled the charters for three planes which were to take the missiles from Lisbon to Tehran. North protested to Kimche, but to no effect.

A marathon of telephone consultations that ended on Saturday morning led to a decision to forget about the Lisbon route and to find a plane that could take the Hawks directly from Israel to Tehran. After Secord's mishandling of the arrangements, Schwimmer asked North himself to find a cargo plane. This, of course, injected no little tension into the relations between North, Secord, and Schwimmer, tension which continued for weeks afterward. Schwimmer also told North to arrange for the plane's free passage over Turkey. North asked for help from the CIA and told Secord to find another plane as quickly as possible. North at one point considered using a plane that Secord's Lake Resources company had chartered from Southern Air Transport for its Contra-support operations.[20] He then had second thoughts and decided to let that plane perform its scheduled run and find something else for Operation Espresso.

With help from Duane Claridge of the CIA, Secord found a Boeing 707 belonging to the Santa Lucia Corporation, registered in a Caribbean island-state, and which was used by the CIA. This quick work again won Secord praise from North.

Secord chartered the plane in Frankfurt, but did not tell Schwimmer about the connection between the plane and the CIA. Secord paid the Santa Lucia Corporation $127,000 for the use of the plane. He removed another $21,983 from the $1 million transferred to the Lake Resources account by Schwimmer and Nimrodi for chartering a private jet and other personal expenses.[21] The plane arrived at Ben Gurion Airport on Saturday morning, November 23, flown by two Germans. It was a small craft, and the missiles were loaded onto it only with difficulty. Nimrodi and Ghorbanifar spoke with the Iranian Prime Minister several times from Geneva, and promised that the Hawks would arrive. Ghorbanifar and Kengarlou were being threatened by Iranian army officers, and Nimrodi was worried about the Revolutionary Guards at the door to his hotel room. It was finally agreed that, since each shipment would include 18 missiles, the American hostages would be released one by one. This was, for all intents and purposes, identical to an "understanding" reached between Ghorbanifar, Israel, and North before the complications arose. Contradicting his report to Poindexter, that the first shipment would not land in Iran until the five hostages had been freed, North had written in his diary on November 20 that the hostages would be released piecemeal. According to this understanding, two hostages would be released after the arrival of the first shipment of 27 Hawks, three more after the second shipment of 27, and a single seriously ill French captive after the third shipment of 26 missiles.[22] North apparently did not dare to tell Poindexter that he had disobeyed his and McFarlane's instructions not to ship weapons to Iran without the prior release of the hostages.[22a]

By noon Saturday the plane was loaded and ready to fly. The flight path was identical to that previously used, and North notified Schwimmer that the CIA had already obtained permission for a refueling stop in Turkey. Kengarlou informed Mussavi of the estimated arrival time, and asked the Prime Minister to notify his liaison in Beirut to arrange the release of one hostage.

Yet one hour before takeoff North called again and said that the landing permit was not for Turkey, but for Cyprus. The Turks said they were willing to permit the plane to land, but only if they were told what exactly the plane was carrying— since it was clear to them that it was not on a pleasure flight. Then they added another condition, that the plane not come from Cyprus. Schwimmer was beside himself. It was the fifth delay, and like the others it involved huge and unnecessary expenses. Since the plane was to refuel in Cyprus, it was now necessary to empty its fuel tanks at Ben Gurion, leaving only the small quantity needed to fly to its new destination. Worse, it was necessary to come up with $8,000 in cash to pay for the fuel in Cyprus. It was 9:00 P.M. and all the banks were closed. Schwimmer ran from one acquaintance to another collecting every dollar he could lay his hands on. Finally, at 1:00 A.M., the necessary sum had been found and the plane took off.

Then, at 2:00 A.M., Schwimmer received an urgent phone call from the plane's owner, who lived in Brussels. He told Schwimmer that the Cypriot authorities had arrested the pilots and detained the plane, and planned to examine its contents in the morning. They claimed that the plane had arrived without a cargo manifest, and that they therefore had to open the boxes. Schwimmer passed on the alarm to North. He warned the colonel that if the plane and its crew were not released immediately, the Cypriots were liable to discover what it really carried and the whole story would be exposed. North again turned to the CIA. Its representative in Nicosia rushed to the airport and, making use of his connections, saw to it that the plane took off at 6:00 A.M. Sunday morning, November 24.

That, however, was not the last of the bungles. When the plane entered Turkish airspace, the Istanbul air control tower asked the pilot for the number of his permit to pass over the country. The pilot made up a number.[23] A short while later the controller told him that there was no permit with that number. The controller and the pilot argued for an hour and a half. Adding to the confusion were contradictory reports on the contents of the plane. The original request for passage stated that it contained oil drilling equipment. The owners of Santa Lucia changed not only the destination from Tabriz to Tehran; they listed the cargo as medical goods. The pilot told the control tower crisply that he was carrying military supplies. He even joked with his navigator: "We should be firing the missiles at Iran rather than flying them into Iran."[24] The contradictory reports forced the pilot to evade the control tower through changes in altitude, location, and route, until he finally succeeded in crossing from Turkish airspace into Iran.

A few hours later, when the plane had landed in Tehran, Schwimmer called North and notified him that the hostages would soon be released. North could barely control his emotions. "God bless you," he said.

But at that moment a real drama was in progress at Tehran airport. A man in civilian clothes, carrying a submachine gun, presented himself as a senior officer in the Pasdaran, the Revolutionary Guards, and ordered the pilot not to reveal to anyone that the plane had come from Israel.[25] Prime Minister Mussavi ordered the boxes of missiles opened before releasing the plane and its crew. Colonel Behesht, an Iranian officer who had spent some time at the American factory where the Hawks were manufactured, and who now commanded Iran's antiaircraft defenses, was shocked to discover that the missiles were out of date and could not hit planes flying at 70,000 feet. Colonel Behesht had an American army manual in hand and he examined the missiles carefully and professionally. There was, however, no room for doubt. The missiles sent from Israel had been manufactured many years ago, and their serial numbers showed them to be even older than missiles the U.S. had supplied to Iran during the Shah's days. Mussavi felt he had been cheated. He called Kengarlou in Geneva. Nimrodi called Schwimmer, who in turn called Chaim Carmon at the Israeli Ministry of Defense. Half an hour later Schwimmer informed Nimrodi that, according to the Ministry, the missiles had been improved by the Israeli air force and that the Iranian officer could find the symbol indicating this on the tails of the missiles. Colonel Behesht checked again. He told Mussavi that the only symbol he had found was an Israeli army insignia that had not been properly erased. Further examination led to the discovery of Stars of David and other Israeli army symbols on nine of the 18 Hawks. Mussavi shouted through the phone at Kengarlou: "You idiot! They tricked you again. We can't depend on you!" Kengarlou was left speechless. Nimrodi took the receiver and spoke with the Prime Minister. Mussavi did not know who was talking to him. He thought Nimrodi was a Persian-speaking American. The Israeli reassured Mussavi that there had obviously been a mistake and that it would be taken care of.

The Ministry of Defense continued to insist that the missiles had been improved by the Israeli air force, but Colonel Behesht was adamant—he found no sign that the missiles had been overhauled. Carmon admitted that the Hawks were from an old production run, but insisted that they had been reworked and were being used by the Israeli army.

Mussavi was furious. He notified Kengarlou that he had ordered the plane delayed, the missiles confiscated, and the crewmen arrested until "the last toman" of the money was returned. He blamed Kengarlou for the fraud. Kengarlou knew what that meant. He fainted, and was rushed to the hospital, where he remained for four days. Ghorbanifar told Mussavi that Kengarlou had fainted, and the Prime Minister responded curtly, "May he go to hell." Ghorbanifar broke down crying and screamed at Nimrodi: "You're thieves, cheats!" Then he began wailing and worrying about the fate of his father and mother in Tehran. On November 25, Ghorbanifar—on the edge of hysteria—called Michael Ledeen in Washington and asked him to give his superiors a message in the name of Prime Minister Mussavi: "We have done everything we promised to do, and you are now cheating us. You must remedy the situation quickly."[26] Nimrodi took up the telephone and spoke once more with Mussavi.

He swore that there had been no intention of cheating Iran, and that if something had gone wrong it was due to "human error." He promised to return the money the next day, and asked the Prime Minister to free the plane and its crew, leaving the missiles in Tehran as a guarantee. Mussavi agreed, but warned Nimrodi: "Don't you even think of leaving Geneva without returning the money."

While this telephone dispute between Tehran and Geneva was in progress, the crewmen of the plane were the "guests" of several Revolutionary Guards in the Tehran Sheraton. They were given a sumptuous meal, including vodka and caviar, and on the assumption that they would return the next day with another shipment of missiles, the pilot bought an expensive Persian carpet and asked the merchant to pack it and prepare it for shipment. Soon after takeoff, however, the director of the Santa Lucia Corporation notified him of a mishap and told him to head for Europe instead of Israel.

As he had promised, Nimrodi went the next day, November 25, to the Israel Discount Bank branch in Geneva in order to withdraw from the Ministry of Defense's account the sum he had deposited for the missiles. He strode to the bank accompanied by Ghorbanifar and three armed Revolutionary Guards. The transfer of the money back and forth caused no few headaches for those involved. The Ministry had earlier agreed with Nimrodi and Schwimmer that the two arms salesmen would pay $140,000 per missile. They sold the missiles to Ghorbanifar for $225,000, and he sold them to Iran at $300,000 each. On November 20, Iran had deposited $24,720,000 in Ghorbanifar's account in Geneva as payment for 80 improved Hawk missiles. On November 25 the Iranian government transferred to Ghorbanifar an additional $20 million toward future purchases. Ghorbanifar on November 20 made two payments to Nimrodi out of this money: one of $18 million and another of $6 million.[27] According to the report the Israeli government submitted to the congressional investigatory committees, the $6 million was intended as a sort of "deposit" for Ghorbanifar. After the deal was completed, Ghorbanifar said that he intended to take $1 million for himself and leave $5 million for paying various Iranian leaders. Prior to this, Nimrodi had, at North's request, deposited $1 million in the Lake Resources account in Geneva to cover the shipment of the Hawks to Iran and the shipment of replenishment missiles from the U.S. to Israel. On November 22 Nimrodi had transferred $11,800,000 to the Ministry of Defense account in Geneva in exchange for the 80 Hawks. Israel meant to use this money to pay for the replacement missiles from America. In a conversation with Avraham Ben-Yosef in New York on November 18, however, North said that the replacements would run between $220,000 and $230,000 per missile. After several additional clarifications North told Ben-Yosef that the U.S. would supply the 80 replacements "at a cost Israel can handle," but the exact price was not set.[28]

Now, with the complications in Tehran over the quality of the 18 missiles from Israel, the Ministry of Defense refunded $8,170,000 to Nimrodi. The difference of $3,030,000 was meant to cover the 18 missiles remaining in Tehran, as well as $510,000 to cover the expense of the aborted deal to the Ministry— such as erasing Israeli army insignia, shipment to the airport, and loading. That same day, November 26, Nimrodi returned $18,600,000 to Ghorbanifar, for the 62 missiles not yet supplied. The rest of the sum, $5,400,000, was returned to Ghorbanifar in February 1986, after the missiles were returned to Israel by Iran. Deducted from this sum was $140,000 for the Ministry of Defense, in payment for a missile the Iranians had shot at an Iraqi plane. According to the Israeli report, Nimrodi's and Schwimmer's expenses were also deducted, a sum of $88,752, and some $700,000 was paid out in bribes to various Iranians.

Operation Espresso caused a serious crisis of trust between Iran, the U.S., and Israel. It also wounded Ghorbanifar's reputation, and delayed the release of the hostages. An immediate Israeli investigation revealed that the Hawks sent to Tehran had, in fact, been improved by the air force. They had been taken from an Israeli army antiaircraft array, and after they were returned from Tehran, in February 1986, they were integrated once more into Israel's air defenses. The misunderstanding grew out of Iran's desire for missiles that would hit planes at high altitudes. Ghorbanifar had told the Iranians that I-Hawks would do this. In fact, however, there are no such Hawk missiles. The Iranian officer who examined the missiles therefore found them to be "out of date" and was convinced that Israel had defrauded Iran. In fact, Iran had received misinformation from

Ghorbanifar, something for which neither Israel nor the U.S. were at fault.

Toward the end of November 1985, it became clear that all the parties involved were nevertheless interested in making another attempt. President Reagan was eager to free the hostages before Christmas, Prime Minister Peres was willing to help, and Iran was anxious to get American weapons. Internal developments in Iran contributed to this anxiety.

On November 23 the Islamic Council of Experts in Tehran chose Ayatollah Husein Ali Montazeri as Khomeini's designated successor. Khomeini approved the decision, and it seemed another step in the institutionalization of the Islamic Revolution. Within a few days, however, it was clear that the decision had renewed the battle of succession. The leaders of the different factions—Speaker Rafsanjani, President Khamenei, and Prime Minister Mussavi in particular—renewed their maneuvering, each one trying to score points that would help him defeat his rivals. The American arms shipments played an important role in this contest for influence. Despite the failure of Operation Espresso, Mussavi asked Kengarlou, Ayatollah Karoubi, and Ghorbanifar to try to renew the American arms shipments.

A serious crisis in its relations with the U.S. added to Israel's desire to help the Americans with Iran. Jonathan J. Pollard, an American Jew who worked in American navy intelligence, was arrested on November 21 at the entrance to the Israeli embassy in Washington and charged with spying for that country. The next day his wife, Anne Henderson, was also arrested after she was discovered in possession of secret documents given to her by her husband. Pollard's immediate Israeli contacts, Yosef Yagur ("consul for scientific affairs") and his secretary, Irit Erb, immediately left Washington for Israel.

The crisis threatened to destroy the hard-earned trust between the intelligence communities of the two countries. Prime Minister Peres apologized for the incident and announced the dissolution of the Bureau for Scientific Relations for which Pollard had worked, and declared that it was not Israeli policy to spy on the U.S. Facing public uproar in America and confusion among its Jewish community, Peres sent minister without portfolio and former ambassador to the U.S. Moshe Arens to speak with Secretary of State George Shultz in an effort to calm things down.

The Pollard case eclipsed the Iranian affair for the time being. Peres pressed Kimche and his staff "to do something" in order to get Pollard out of the American newspaper headlines. Under the conditions then prevailing, nothing could have contributed more to lowering the tension between the two countries than Israeli assistance in freeing the American hostages.

President Reagan had instructed his aides to pursue the Iranian initiative, and on November 27 Poindexter and North drafted a new plan which would help support a pragmatic, army-oriented faction in Tehran.[29] Iran would receive 120 improved Hawk missiles of the latest design, on condition that all the five hostages be released after the first shipment and Iran made an unequivocal commitment to halt its terrorist activities. North spoke with the director-general of the Israeli Ministry of Defense, Menachem Meron, then in Washington, and pleaded with him to agree to the plan, promising swift supply of replacement missiles.[30] Meron could not make any commitment, and told North that his superiors in Israel would have to make the decision.

North decided to send Secord to Israel. Prior to that, however, he had to renew the contacts with the Iranians. After several urgent telephone calls, Secord, Kimche, Schwimmer, and Nimrodi met with Ghorbanifar on November 29 in Paris and discussed ways of reviving the Iranian initiative.[31] Ghorbanifar spoke angrily of the failure of Operation Espresso, and argued that in light of the agony caused Iran, Mussavi had raised his price and was demanding 800 TOW missiles for each of the five hostages. Ghorbanifar also asked for Dragon ground-to-ground missiles, Maverick air-to-surface missiles, improved Hawks, spare parts for Phantom jets, field artillery, and shells. Secord and the Israelis made it clear that Iran could not hope to get these kinds of weapons. In the end they agreed to examine the possibility of supplying only 4,000 TOWs in exchange for the release of the five American hostages.

Secord came to Israel for a day-long visit immediately after the meeting in Paris. In talks with Kimche, Schwimmer, and Air Force Commander General Amos Lapidot, Secord pleaded that they acquiesce to North's request and send Iran more

modern missiles. The Israelis refused. They found Secord's burst
of activity strange, but none of them yet suspected his motives.
In retrospect, it appears that Secord was exploiting the failure
of Operation Espresso to get himself involved in the Iranian
dealings, in place of Schwimmer and Nimrodi. Having served
in Iran, he knew the great potential for arms sales to this
country and wanted to make profits for himself. Despite the
fact that Secord did not trust Ghorbanifar, he adopted the
Iranian's claim that the Hawk deal had been a fraud and told
North that this fiasco caused Ghorbanifar to explode with rage
at what he saw as an example of "Israeli incompetence." Disappointed that no hostages had been freed, McFarlane recommended that the U.S. manage the operation for itself. In a
message to North, McFarlane wrote that he was inclined to
think that this operation should be brought into the NSC and
Mike Ledeen should be taken out of it. North claimed that
"private arms merchants"—Schwimmer and Nimrodi—could
not act in the name of the U.S., especially when the fate of
American hostages hung in the balance.[32] He also argued that
the U.S. could not allow those who were to help free the hostages—the Iranians—to be cheated. McFarlane, however,
thought it would be impossible to distance Nimrodi, Schwimmer, and Kimche from the operation, since they had initiated
it. Poindexter and North also discussed a "change of team."[33]

At the Paris meeting, all the participants had agreed to meet
again in London on December 8. President Reagan, they were
told, was to confer with his advisers about Iran on December
7. No decision could be made until then; the most that could
be done was to prepare the ground for a renewal of the initiative.

Kimche, Schwimmer, and Nimrodi met with Ghorbanifar and
with Ayatollah Karoubi in Geneva on December 4. The Ayatollah
reiterated his deep disappointment at the failure of Operation
Espresso. He claimed that Iran desperately needed the missiles,
not only to defend itself from Iraqi bombardment, but also to
prevent the penetration of Soviet surveillance planes. He related
that there had been cases of Soviet aircraft reaching as far as
40–50 miles into Iran, and no one had been able to shoot
them down. He now understood that the U.S. did not have
missiles effective against planes at high altitudes. But given
Iran's disappointment, and in order to reestablish trust between
the sides, Karoubi demanded the immediate supply of 4,000

TOW missiles in exchange for freeing the five American hostages.

As was his custom, Karoubi brought fresh information on events in Iran. He described the military situation as "hopeless." The leadership was incompetent and could not direct a modern war. Supplies were lacking, and the soldiers could not operate sophisticated equipment. Ghorbanifar said that Iran at times had fewer than 12 fighter planes and 50 tanks in use. Given Iraq's absolute superiority in armor and air power, Iranian arms dealers had been ordered to increase their efforts in Europe and to sign long-term contracts. Iran realized America's limits in supplying arms, and was therefore willing to continue to use Israel as an intermediary.

During this conversation, as in the past, Ghorbanifar proposed working through Karoubi to replace the Iranian leadership. He claimed that Karoubi was close to Prime Minister Mussavi and President Khamenei, and that he had access to sources of intelligence. As the brother of Mehdi Karoubi, deputy speaker of the Majlis and chairman of the *Shahid* fund, he could invite his supporters to visit Saudi Arabia and Kuwait without arousing suspicion. Ghorbanifar explained that in the Middle East it was customary to give "gifts," and that trips to Kuwait and Saudi Arabia would not be considered bribery were they financed through the Shahid fund. What was most important was that the visits not be funded by the CIA. Because of that organization's once close cooperation with the Shah's Savak secret police, none of the clerics who might support Karoubi's effort to replace the government would want his name revealed in Congress or leaked to the press. If Karoubi succeeded, the war would end and a new moderate and pro-Western government would repudiate the use of terrorism and hostage taking.

Ghorbanifar importuned Schwimmer and Nimrodi to respond favorably to Karoubi's offer. He claimed that this was Israel's opportunity to abandon the "corner store method" that had characterized the Hawk missile deal and to begin to behave in a more businesslike way. The very fact that Karoubi had come to Geneva testified to Mussavi's desire to continue the dialogue, he said, and the opportunity should not be missed. Ghorbanifar also reminded them, in a deliberately offhand manner, that since he and the Israelis had begun cooperating, no additional American hostages had been taken, a veiled threat that Iran might lose its influence over Hezbollah and the Islamic

Jihad, who might then resume the kidnappings and possibly even murder the hostages they now had.

This was no idle threat. Ghorbanifar argued that, since the connection between Iran and the Shiite terrorist groups in Lebanon had been proven, it could be said that there were two "generators" supplying power to international terror—Khomeini and Qadhafi. Libya had money, but Qadhafi himself was "an idiot, a madman, and a cheat." Iran, on the other hand, was led by a group of highly motivated fanatics willing to make sacrifices to achieve their goals. This combination of Khomeini's ideology and Qadhafi's money was dangerous and had to be broken. Ghorbanifar proposed neutralizing the Iranian component, which would force the Libyan one to shut down of its own accord. This could be done only by fostering men like Karoubi, and when the time came, when they had widened their power bases, they would take control of the country and liquidate the radical elements.

Schwimmer and Nimrodi returned to Jerusalem and asked Peres to make a "generous gesture" to Iran and supply it with the 4,000 TOWs it was asking for even before U.S. approval. They argued that, should this bring about the release of the American hostages, people in the U.S. would be so overjoyed that no one in the administration would accuse Israel of acting on its own, and President Reagan would order the immediate replenishment of the 4,000 missiles. Peres, supported by Rabin and Shamir, rejected the proposal. The Ministry of Defense said that the U.S. had still not replaced the 504 TOWs sent in August and September, and that 18 Hawks were still stuck in Tehran without any replacements from the U.S. for them either. The tension on the Syrian border made it impossible for Israel to thin out its antiarmor defenses by 4,000 TOW missiles. Another reason for the refusal was Peres's and Rabin's unwillingness to decide on any new move without U.S. approval and before they knew who would be in and who out after the expected reshuffle of the National Security Council. Accordingly, Peres told Nimrodi: "Ya'acov, forget about it. It won't work."

From the vantage point of today, Peres was right. He felt that after nine months of indirect contacts with Iran the time had come for the U.S. and Israel to reevaluate the initiative and the results obtained so far. Precisely because of the Pollard affair, Peres reached the conclusion that Israel could not afford to strain further its relations with the U.S. and that the Iranian initiative should be rethought and new decisions made after consultations with the new team at the White House.

On December 1, 1985, Secord briefed North on his meeting with Kimche and Ghorbanifar. Secord reported that Ghorbanifar suggested a phased exchange of 3,200 TOW missiles for hostages, as follows: Delivery of 600 TOWs and the release of one hostage. Six hours later, 2,000 TOWs would be supplied and three hostages released. The last hostage would be released at $H + 23$ hours and after 600 additional missiles were supplied.[34]

On December 6, the eve of the decisive discussion at the White House, Oliver North set out for London to meet Ghorbanifar and the Israeli team. He stopped off in New York for a conversation with Avraham Ben-Yosef, the head of the Israeli military procurement mission in the U.S., about the supply of the replacement missiles. North had in hand a document he had submitted to Admiral Poindexter on December 4, in which he proposed supplying Iran with 3,300 TOW missiles and 50 improved Hawks. He claimed that this document would be discussed the next day in the White House. In his note to Poindexter, North wrote that he and Kimche had no illusions about the Iranians' character: "They are a primitive, unsophisticated group who are extraordinarily distrustful of . . . the Israelis and the U.S." While acknowledging "a high degree of risk" in continuing the operation, North thought that stopping it now would have even more serious repercussions. He exhorted Poindexter to press on in a way that suggested North thought the U.S. was already subject to Iranian extortion, warning that if the U.S. did not make at least one more try, some or all the hostages would be killed and kidnappings would be renewed.[35] North told Ben-Yosef that the U.S. did not have the money to pay for the 504 missiles already supplied to Iran. Since Ghorbanifar had paid Schwimmer and Nimrodi for them, if Israel wanted 504 replacements from the U.S., it should get the money from the two Israeli arms dealers. North added that in future arms sales to Iran, he intended to divert part of the profits to the Contras.[36] This was the first time that North mentioned this idea to a senior Israeli official. Since, however, there was still no Israeli decision to renew the supply of weapons to Iran, no one in Israel attributed any immediate operative importance to North's announcement. However, what is clear is that the notion to use Iran sales as a vehicle for the Contras was already firmly planted in North's mind.

North left for London immediately after his conversation with Ben-Yosef. Before meeting with Ghorbanifar, he had a long conversation with David Kimche. Kimche tried to focus the discussion on the strategic aspect of the Iranian initiative and not on any specific operative procedure or on tactical considerations connected to the release of the hostages. Kimche was aware, of course, of President Reagan's feelings about the hostages, and had heard from North that the President was "driving everyone crazy" over the subject. Kimche nevertheless thought that the nature of future relations with Iran was much more important.

In contrast to Kimche, North was clearly interested in continuing the Iranian operation in order to free the hostages. He told Kimche that he agreed with the evaluation that continuing contacts with Iran involved certain dangers, but on the other hand, all the parties had come a long way and they could not stop the process without serious consequences. He expressed his fear that the hostages would remain in the hands of their captors, or perhaps even be murdered, and that the U.S. would lose its only forseeable opportunity to gain a foothold in Iran.

In any case, Kimche and North agreed that it was still possible to pursue a joint American-Israeli policy aimed at achieving three goals: aid to Iranian moderates in their effort to win control of the country, the release of the American hostages, and the end of Shiite terror against the U.S.

The tone of the Kimche-North conversation was positive and to the point, and included some discussion of procedures. They spoke, for instance, about communications security, supply routes, and the establishment of a stopover point at which an Iranian representative could examine the cargo before it landed in Iran. They also agreed that after reaching an agreement in principle, Kimche, Schwimmer, and Nimrodi would meet North and Secord to determine funding, rental of planes, flight corridors, and so on, and to arrange free passage and landing rights at the stopover point. If Ghorbanifar, perhaps together with some other Iranian representative, approved the plan, and if appropriate arrangements were made for the release of the five American hostages, Secord would on December 11 establish a "command post" in Europe in order to oversee the execution of the agreement.

Immediately after the meeting with Kimche, North met with Ghorbanifar, Nimrodi, Schwimmer, and Secord.[37] Ghorbanifar again hinted that Iran was losing control over Hezbollah and that the arms shipments should be resumed quickly in order to ensure the release of the prisoners.

That same day Iran made an important move that provoked some optimism about its intentions. The Iranian foreign minister, Ali Akbar Velayati, paid a three-day visit to Saudi Arabia. It was the first such visit by an Iranian foreign minister since Khomeini's revolution. He met with King Fahd and with Saudi foreign minister Saud Al-Faisal. Many observers saw this visit as a signal to the U.S. and to Saudi Arabia that Iran really was abandoning its ambition of exporting its Islamic Revolution to the other countries of the Persian Gulf, and that it meant to end its support of international terrorism.

It was in this atmosphere of expectation that an American-Israeli meeting with Manucher Ghorbanifar was held in Nimrodi's London apartment on December 8, 1985. Robert McFarlane headed the American delegation, which included Oliver North and Richard Secord. On the Israeli side were Kimche, Schwimmer, Nimrodi, Yehuda Alboher, Brigadier General Haggai Regev—the minister of defense's military secretary, and Chaim Carmon.

McFarlane had come to London in a special American plane and stayed at the Hilton. Prior to the large meeting, McFarlane met with Kimche in his room separately. McFarlane told Kimche that he was resigning, and about the discussion the previous day at the White House, led by the President and attended by Weinberger, Shultz, Deputy CIA Director John MacMahon, Donald Regan, and Poindexter. McFarlane told Kimche that Weinberger and Shultz had vehemently opposed arms transfers to Iran. They doubted that there were moderate elements in Iran, and warned against angry reactions from the Europeans and the Arab world at the time when the U.S. was pressing them not to sell arms to Iran. They said that the U.S. had in effect turned into a hostage itself, and that Israel and Iran could blow open the episode whenever it was convenient for them. McFarlane did not agree with them, but he was disturbed by two things. One was that the U.S. still did not talk directly to Iran, but rather through Israel and private Iranian intermediaries. The second was that what had begun as an effort to open a channel of communication had now become more and more of an arms-for-hostages bargain. At the beginning, McFarlane had set himself a trial period of three months. This had passed and he had now come to London to find out what the chances were of freeing the American hostages before Christmas. In parallel, he wished to establish links with the decision makers themselves, if possible with Prime Minister Mussavi. McFarlane believed in the need to bring about a change in Iran's policy. If there were people capable of making this change, they should be encouraged and helped. "After all," he said, "if there are moderate elements in Iran, they will not succeed in making changes by fasts, self-denial, and prayers to Allah. They will need help. But if it becomes clear that Ghorbanifar's people don't have the power to do this, contacts with them should be halted."

Kimche accepted this approach, but advised McFarlane to wait patiently. The Middle East did not work at an American pace. Actions should be carefully thought out. If nothing else, Ghorbanifar and his friends were supplying Israel and the U.S. with good intelligence, and such an intelligence channel should not be destroyed. It might even be that the initiative would bring about some results. Kimche also felt, however, that if there was no progress after an additional attempt, there would be no choice but to end the affair.

The meeting at Nimrodi's house was a disappointment to everyone. It brought together two self-contained worlds, with nothing to bridge between them. Kimche called the three-hour conversation with McFarlane and Ghorbanifar a meeting between a "boy scout and a shrewd horse dealer." McFarlane began with an hour-long monologue. He expressed his regret about the problems with the Hawk shipment, and hoped that everyone had learned something from it. He emphasized the importance that the U.S. attached to its contacts with the so-called "moderates" in Iran, and also noted his anger at the capture of American citizens in Lebanon by pro-Iranian groups. He therefore demanded the release of these hostages before Christmas, and promised that the U.S. would supply it not only with 4,000 TOW missiles, but with whatever it wanted—

modern weapons, sophisticated equipment, reconstruction of tanks, technicians, and instructors. The condition, however, had to be the prior release of the hostages. McFarlane added that, afterward, as part of the effort to repair relations between the two countries, it would be necessary to think about a high-level meeting in Tehran or in some other location. He emphasized that in the past he had supported supplying weapons to Iran on a limited basis, not as a prize for terrorists, but rather as encouragement to those elements opposed to terror who wished to change their country's relations with the U.S. for the better. The hour had now come to find out whether Iran's intentions were pure, and if Ghorbanifar's contacts really had the ability and the power to change things. If they did not want to or could not free the hostages, the U.S. would not be willing to continue supplying Iran arms through them. Those were President Reagan's personal instructions.

Al Schwimmer sat next to David Kimche. When McFarlane was done, Schwimmer whispered to him: "It's dead. The Iranians will never accept that condition."

Ghorbanifar immediately said as much to McFarlane, though out of courtesy said he would try to influence Khomeini's government to moderate its position. He expressed concern for the fate of the hostages should he give Iran McFarlane's message. Over the course of a half an hour Ghorbanifar explained to McFarlane how the Iranians thought and acted. He emphasized that they had been cheated numerous times in the past, and that this made it doubtful whether he could find even one person in Tehran willing to free the hostages without receiving the arms first. He clearly implied that there were those in Iran who sincerely believed that the hostages were the only card they had to play against the U.S., one they would give up only for an appropriate price. Some of those present at the meeting received the impression that Ghorbanifar's main concern was arms, while McFarlane was more interested in a political dialogue.

The London meeting ended in a stalemate. McFarlane returned to Washington the next day, having decided to recommend to the President that the U.S. cut off its contacts with Ghorbanifar. "Bud" was sure that Ghorbanifar was not the right man to use in opening up a channel of communication with Khomeini's successors. The Iranian arms dealer was, he said, the most despicable man he had ever met.[38] He now regretted all the contacts with Iran through Ghorbanifar and Khashoggi.

Kimche, for his part, recommended to Peres that it was time for a moratorium on the Iranian initiative. He told the Prime Minister that there was no common ground between the two sides, and that Israel could do nothing to change this. Should either the U.S. or Iran soften their stands, he said, he would be willing to renew his efforts immediately.

McFarlane met with President Reagan on December 10, 1985, and gave him a personal report on the London meeting. Weinberger, Casey, Poindexter, North, and Donald Regan were also present.[39] McFarlane called Ghorbanifar a "liar and cheat," and expressed doubts about his ability to influence those making the decisions in Iran. Weinberger supported his recommendation to bring the contacts with Ghorbanifar to an end. According to notes later found in Casey's files, the President "mumbled" a few unclear sentences. He said he was sorry that another Christmas would pass with the hostages still in Beirut. He wondered if it might not be best to let Israel continue the contacts on its own, without American intervention, but with a promise to replenish any arms sent to Iran.

No conclusions were reached; those present differed on what they thought the President wanted. Casey and Poindexter received the impression that Reagan wished to see the Iranian initiative continued. The coming days were to confirm this. McFarlane had underestimated the determination of the President and the CIA director to pursue their efforts to free the hostages. He also underestimated North's ambition and Secord's greed. Kimche, Nimrodi, and Schwimmer were equally complacent about the stirrings behind their backs in Washington and Jerusalem. When they took notice, it was too late—and they were no longer in the picture.

CHAPTER 9

North and Nir Enter the Field

McFarlane had been the White House staff's cautionary conscience against an all-out plunge into Iran. With him gone, North assumed greater control over the Iran initiative. His partner on the American side was Secord. He would soon gain a new Israeli partner as well.

The Hawk deal had already highlighted the differences in style and temperament between Schwimmer and North. North and Secord did not appear to understand the Iranian mentality. In contrast to McFarlane, who did not trust Ghorbanifar and called him a "liar and cheat," North, on Ledeen's strong recommendation, seemed to believe that it was still possible to continue working with Ghorbanifar.[1] In order, however, to prevent bungles like the one involving the shipment of the 18 Hawks to Iran (Operation Espresso), North proposed to Poindexter that the U.S. itself oversee the operation, taking responsibility for each step along the way. In a note to Poindexter, North wrote, "We could, with an appropriate covert action finding, commence deliveries ourselves, using Secord as our conduit to control Ghorbanifar and delivery operations."[2] This necessitated the substitution for Kimche, Nimrodi, and Schwimmer—who had started the initiative—of another Israeli who had no experience in the issue and therefore would not be able to question North's decisions. North and Secord were aided by the Prime Minister's adviser on terrorism affairs, Amiram Nir, who had some ideas on how to release the hostages and was soon rewarded by being named by Peres to represent Israel's interests in the Iran initiative.

Like North's appointment by the Americans, Nir's appointment by the Prime Minister did not appear to have been thoroughly considered. Nir, 38 years old, had formerly been a military correspondent for Israeli Television, commanded an armored battalion in the reserves, and been involved in Peres's election campaign in the summer of 1981. He had never studied the Middle East and lacked the background in intelligence that his new assignment required. When he had been appointed adviser on terrorism in 1984, in place of Raphael Eitan (with the same name as but not identical with the Israeli army's Chief of Staff during the war in Lebanon, Eitan had participated in the capture of Adolf Eichmann and had more recently recruited Jonathan Pollard as an Israeli spy in America), many in the intelligence community had asked themselves whether it was appropriate that such a sensitive security position, requiring professionalism and personal experience, be handed out as a political favor to satisfy someone's personal ambitions.

For this reason the chiefs of the intelligence agencies preferred to maintain daily contact on professional matters with Nir's deputy, Brigadier General Gideon Mahanaimi, an army old-timer who had been a highly regarded intelligence officer, with expertise and experience in counterterrorism. Nir, however, was not the type of man to concede the power and prestige of his position without a fight. Despite the low regard the Israeli intelligence community had for his abilities, he had no small measure of success in gaining the favor of foreign, and especially American, intelligence agencies. He had a number of personal qualities that helped him do this: he was a master of persuasion and of personal charm, a man who made a good impression. When the TWA plane was hijacked in Beirut in 1985, Nir was in constant contact with Oliver North and reviewed with him the military or covert options for freeing the plane and its passengers.[3] During the exhausting negotiations with President Assad of Syria and with Nabih Berri of the Lebanese Shiite Amal movement over the fate of the plane and its passengers, Nir was in Washington and in touch continuously with

Admiral Poindexter (then in charge both of counterterrorism and of strategic coordination with Israel).[4] Relations between Nir, Poindexter, and North became even closer with the hijacking of the *Achille Lauro* cruise ship in October 1985.[5] Accurate and quickly supplied information from Israeli intelligence made it possible for the U.S. to force down the Egyptian plane carrying the four hijackers and their commander, Abu El-Abbas. It appears that during the course of this incident Nir heard—for the first time—that "something serious" was developing between the U.S., Israel, and Iran. North later confided to Nir the problems surrounding the failure of the Hawk deal, and expressed the hope that he could carry on with the Iranian initiative without the involvement of the Israeli "troika" that had opened up Iran for him.

Nir appeared to have identical hopes. Involvement in the Iran initiative would not only gain him entry to the White House's power centers and open new possibilities of advancement for him, but would most likely strengthen his credentials within the Israeli intelligence services. It would allow him more room for independent activity. True, Oliver North had more experience than Nir in organizing covert operations, but they were both blunt, stubborn, and extremely ambitious.

The error in naming Nir to coordinate the Iranian initiative, according to Secord, was that "Nir was apparently too inexperienced and thus unqualified for such an extremely sensitive intelligence operation."[6] Nir was easy prey for Manucher Ghorbanifar's evasive tongue, and he was thought to be unable to discern when the Iranians were telling the truth and when they were misleading him. Even more serious was Nir's alleged participation in North's slander campaign against Michael Ledeen, Nimrodi, and Schwimmer, in order to ingratiate himself in the White House. It was also alleged that he had supplied the U.S. with information behind the Mossad's back.[7]

North saw Nir as a useful operative who would perform special tasks without asking too many questions. North himself wrote as much to Poindexter: "Nir is prepared to proceed any way we wish. So far Nir has promptly agreed to every proposal we've made to date, except for the final one of shipping 1,000 TOW missiles w/o promise of replenishment."[8] In retrospect it appears that the North-Nir partnership, bringing together their lack of understanding of Iran and their inability to restrain

Ghorbanifar's imagination, was one of the factors that eventually led to the exposure of the Iranian initiative and to its failure.

Nir's involvement with Iran began in the middle of December 1985. There were at that time rumors that, in an effort to improve his image with the American public, PLO chief Yassir Arafat had decided to help the U.S. obtain the release of the hostages. Nir suggested making a move before Arafat did by freeing 20 or 30 Shiite prisoners from the Al-Khiam Prison in southern Lebanon, from among those who had not been involved in terrorist acts against Israel or the U.S.[9] This, it was hoped, would encourage Iran and Hezbollah to free the American hostages in Beirut.

It would eventually turn out that the rumors about Arafat's expected initiative were without foundation. Hezbollah, on the contrary, was in no hurry to dispense with the hostages. They were, in fact, a sort of insurance policy against Israeli or American attacks on their bases. (Israel had in fact acquiesced to an American request and for several weeks did not attack Hezbollah bases in Lebanon's Bekaa Valley.)

In an effort to get around the problem of the supply of replacements to Israel, especially during a period of tension with Syria that required a high level of readiness, Nir made another proposal. The U.S., as part of the strategic cooperation between both countries, could "preposition" 4,000 substitute TOW missiles in Israel, the same amount Israel was to supply to Iran. In case of emergency, Israel would not have to wait for an airlift from the U.S., as had happened during the Yom Kippur War; there would be immediate access to these prepositioned missiles. Israel would pay for the missiles with part of the profit made from selling the weapons to Iran. It would continue to supply logistical services in transferring arms to Iran and would acknowledge all responsibility should the matter come to light, allowing the U.S. to deny any direct involvement. In such a case, however, Israel would expect the U.S. to announce publicly that it had been aware of the arms shipments and had not opposed them.

Peres and Rabin approved these suggestions and allowed Nir to feel out the U.S. response to them.[10]

At that stage, Peres had not meant to remove Kimche, Schwimmer, and Nimrodi from the Iranian initiative completely. In a conversation with Schwimmer on December 25, 1985, Peres explained that, given McFarlane's resignation and Nir's close ties to Poindexter and North, it was worth bringing Nir onto the Israeli team. Schwimmer had no objections.

Even before Nir set out for the U.S., terrorism once more caught the attention of the world. On December 27, Palestinian terrorists of the Abu Nidal faction sprayed machine-gun fire and threw hand grenades at passengers waiting in line by the El Al counters at the Vienna and Rome airports. Sixteen people were killed and 110 injured. Several of the victims were Americans. El Al security guards and local police opened fire on the attackers, killing four of them and capturing three others wounded. Under interrogation they said that they had planned to capture an El Al plane and blow it up over Tel Aviv. Ibrahim Mahmoud Khaled, the only survivor from among the four attackers in Rome, revealed that Abu Nidal's senior assistant, Rashid El-Hamida, had been in the airport lobby and had given the signal to open fire. The terrorists said they had a base in Syria, and that Abu Nidal was connected with Syrian intelligence. They described their training, their modes of action, and weapons stores they had in different places in Europe. Intensive cooperative work including the security forces of the U.S., Israel, Italy, and Austria also uncovered a Libyan connection.

These attacks were the subject of a large number of consultations between Poindexter, North, and Nir. They exchanged information on Abu Nidal's organization and on the help he received from Libya and other countries. The U.S. knew about 15 training bases that Qadhafi had established in his country for training Palestinian and other terrorists. North waxed enthusiastic as he related what direct measures the Soviet Union had taken in Lebanon. After Shiite terrorists kidnapped three Soviet diplomats in Beirut and murdered one, Soviet agents kidnapped the relatives of the terrorists, killed one of them, and threatened to do the same to the others if the Soviet hostages were not returned immediately.

All these events added urgency to Nir's trip to Washington in January 1986. He spent December 30, 1985, in London, where he met Nimrodi and Ghorbanifar. Having been added to the Israeli team at the request of the Prime Minister, Nir received full cooperation from his colleagues. Nimrodi related all the details of the previous deals with Iran, showed him documents, gave him Khashoggi's phone numbers, and introduced him to Ghorbanifar. Nir was supposed to meet Al Schwimmer in New York before going to Washington to see Poindexter and North. Schwimmer waited in vain, however. On January 4, 1986, at Kennedy Airport on his way back to Israel, Nir called Schwimmer and told him that he had already met with the two Americans, as well as with William Casey. When Schwimmer asked what they had discussed, Nir answered that he would tell him at their next meeting in Jerusalem.

Schwimmer was stunned. He felt himself betrayed. From the start of the Iranian initiative in the spring of 1985, he had cooperated fully with Nimrodi and Kimche in an atmosphere of absolute mutual trust. Suddenly an upstart, a freshman on the team had tricked him. No doubt he could not believe that Nir meant to take charge and ease the rest of the team out of the Iranian initiative. He complained to Peres, and the "troika" decided to sit down with Nir at the earliest opportunity and find out what was going on.

In a meeting with Poindexter in Washington on January 2, 1986, Nir detailed his plan for American prepositioning of TOW missiles in Israel and for the release of Shiite prisoners in southern Lebanon, in exchange for the release of the American hostages.[11] The Americans were far from enthusiastic about the prepositioning plan, and were considering two other possibilities for the supply of replacements—either the sale of new missiles to Israel or, in case of emergency, a U.S. transfer of the necessary weapons to Israel in Galaxy jets within 18 hours of the outbreak of hostilities.

Speaking in the name of Defense Minister Rabin, Nir emphasized that the replacements were a precondition for any further Israeli sales to Iran. He noted that the 504 TOWs Israel had supplied Iran the previous summer had still not been replaced, and that Israel could not allow itself to thin out its antiarmor defenses without assurances that it would receive other missiles, and quickly. This, he said, was a test of American sincerity. North explained that Avraham Ben-Yosef, head of the Israeli military procurement mission in the U.S., could not simply walk into the Pentagon and buy 504 missiles. There was a legal process, including congressional approval, which could take about two months. North also promised that the price tag would be within Israel's means. North asked Nir how much Israel had received from Iran for the missiles. Nir explained that Israel had received from Ghorbanifar payment adequate to purchase only the old TOWs. "Whether this is because Schwimmer pocketed the rest or whether there was a kickback [to Iranian officials in Tehran] neither Nir nor I know," North is quoted as saying in the Tower report.[12] Nir and North agreed that the missiles would be sold to Iran at an inflated price, and that the difference would be used to buy replacements for Israel and to fund joint covert activities, mostly in the area of counterterrorism. This was not a new idea—the two had already discussed it in November. North now presented the idea to Casey, who received it enthusiastically. Casey thought that this would make it possible to set up a "covert operations command" within the National Security Council. This command could function outside the framework of the CIA and without any obligation to report to Congress. In his testimony to Congress, North said that Casey "was interested in the ability to go an existing off-the-shelf, self-sustaining, stand-alone entity that could perform certain activities on behalf of the U.S."[13]

Nir suggested that, in order to test Iran's intentions, Israel would supply it with only 500 TOWs. If the hostages were freed and Iran would undertake not to engage in terror, the remaining 3,500 missiles would be delivered. If the hostages were not freed, the U.S. would not be required to replenish and Israel would have lost 500 TOW missiles.[14] Poindexter, North, and Nir agreed that even if the chances for success were no greater than 25 percent, it was still worth trying.

As might have been expected, Poindexter, North, and Nir devoted much discussion to Ghorbanifar's personality and reliability. They had all concluded he was a liar and that he was motivated by insatiable greed. However, Ghorbanifar was the deepest penetration the U.S. and Israel had achieved into Iran; there was no one else to work with, at least not for the time being. North put it picturesquely: "In this kind of activity, you sometimes have no choice but to work with what you've got. One can't go to Mother Teresa and ask her to go to Tehran on your behalf. You have to deal with who you've got at the time and the good fairy wasn't there."[15]

North told Nir that after his meeting with Ghorbanifar in Geneva, in the middle of December, Michael Ledeen had recommended to the CIA that the contacts be continued, because "Ghorbanifar has good connections in the Iranian leadership

that could help the CIA to gain insight into the Iranian regime."
At Casey's request, Ledeen invited Ghorbanifar for talks during
the second half of December with National Security Council
staff members and American intelligence officers involved with
Iran. The purpose was to clear up the controversy over Ghorbanifar's credibility.[16] Ghorbanifar arrived on December 22, 1985,
again using the Greek passport identifying him as "Nicholas
Keralis," and stayed at the Madison Hotel.[17] Meeting with the
intelligence officers at Ledeen's house, the Iranian revealed
that a three-man Iranian death squad had arrived in Hamburg,
assigned to strike against opponents of the Islamic regime in
Europe. He also claimed to have contacts with Libyan opposition leaders, and offered his help in overthrowing Qadhafi.
His interlocutors were unable to establish whether the information was true, or whether it was intended as a "plant" for the
CIA. The head of the CIA's Iranian desk said that, after hearing
Ghorbanifar out, he was surer than ever that the Iranian arms
merchant was dishonest and untrustworthy. In a memorandum
to President Reagan dated December 23, Casey wrote that "it
is possible that the information given to Ghorbanifar is a deception and meant simply to impress the U.S."[18] The CIA recommended treating Ghorbanifar with suspicion until he took a
polygraph test. This was to be administered in Washington
on January 11. Until then, and since the President in any case
still needed to give final approval to the continuation of the
Iranian initiative, nothing beyond planning was to be done
for the present.

Discussions with Nir were, of course, devoted to counterterrorism in addition to his work on Iran. On January 6, 1986,
President Reagan publicly confirmed that there were indeed
15 terrorist training bases in Libya. Despite European objections
to the imposition of economic sanctions on Qadhafi, Reagan
announced a series of unilateral American economic measures
against Libya, terming Qadhafi a "barbarian."[19] Most of the
discussion of terror centered, however, on the hostages. Nir
and North discussed the military options for rescuing them,
should the Iran initiative fail. A precondition for any such use
of force was the gathering of additional intelligence and the
recruitment of Lebanese who could help out if needed. Israel
made no small effort to discover the whereabouts of the hostages. Hezbollah had been spreading numerous rumors, some

claiming that the hostages had been taken to Iran for interrogation, or that they were distributed among several villages in the Bekaa Valley, or that they were in various houses in the Beirut suburbs. Israel did not succeed in discovering their exact location, but in the end the U.S. was able to determine that they were being held in the neighborhood of Bir Al-Abed, a Shiite district in Southwest Beirut. Israel established contact with elements in the Druze community that would be able to help free the hostages, should the need arise.

Israel's new proposals were the subject of a special meeting of the National Security Council on January 7, 1986. Participating were the President, Vice President Bush, Casey, Poindexter, Secretary of State Shultz, Secretary of Defense Weinberger, and Attorney General Edwin Meese, as well as White House Chief of Staff Donald Regan.[20] As on previous occasions, Reagan's men disagreed over the Iranian initiative's chances of success. Weinberger and Shultz strongly opposed sending American arms to Iran, even if through Israel. Shultz argued that if Israel could supply weapons to Iran, the U.S. could not prevent its European allies from doing the same. He even expressed his suspicion that Israel would, in time, leak the details of the contacts with Iran to the press in order to legitimize its arms sales to Khomeini. The general impression, however, was that the President had decided to continue the Iranian initiative.

On January 7, Nir received the following coded message from North:

1. Joshua [President Reagan] has approved the continuation of the initiative, as we had hoped. 2. Joshua and Samuel [Weinberger] have also agreed on method one [selling replacements to Israel rather than prepositioning]. . . . A. Resupply should be as routine as possible to prevent disclosure on our side, and may take longer than two months. However, Albert says if crisis arises, Joshua promises that we will deliver all required by Galaxie [apparently C5A cargo plane] in less than 18 hours. B. Joshua also wants both your gov't and ours to stay with no comment if operation is disclosed. If these conditions are acceptable to Banana [Israel], th[e]n Oranges [the U.S.] are ready to proceed.[21]

On January 10, Ghorbanifar arrived for his third visit in Washington. As during his previous stays, his movements were followed and his telephone conversations recorded. The day after his arrival he took a polygraph test at CIA headquarters, which lasted about five hours. The machine indicated that he was lying on 13 of the 15 questions asked of him. The only two true answers he gave were his name and his birthplace.[22] In his conversations with American intelligence officers, Ghorbanifar fabricated stories of Iranian terror operations in Europe and tried to misinform them about the existence of a right-wing opposition in Iran. Among other things, he described one of his acquaintances, Hajjotelislam Mohammed Khatemi, as one of the leaders of Islamic Jihad when, in fact, Khatemi was not at all involved in terrorism.

Ghorbanifar was aware of the negative results of the polygraph test, so he tried to repair what was left of his credibility. In long conversations with North and CIA official Charles Allen, at Michael Ledeen's house, Ghorbanifar said that he was frustrated and wounded by the attitude toward him.[23] He repeated his commitment to work for the release of the hostages, for a change in the Libyan government, and for an end to Iranian-Libyan-Syrian terrorism against the U.S. He claimed that, should the U.S. not continue to supply weapons through him, the positions of President Khamenei, Prime Minister Mussavi, and the oil minister, Gholam Reza Agha Zadeh, would weaken. Terrorism against the U.S. was liable to resume. The fact was, he said, that for seven months no additional hostages had been taken in Lebanon. But were Iran to discover that the U.S. was leading it on a wild-goose chase, it would have no reason to hold back Hezbollah. The bugging of Ghorbanifar's telephone conversations revealed that he was indeed in touch with Mussavi, Agha Zadeh, and Kengarlou, as well as with other people in Tehran. Nevertheless, the CIA's opinion remained negative and it once more ordered all its stations to break off contact with the Iranian arms salesman. William Casey himself was not party to this analysis, and he searched for ways to get around it.[24]

North and Nir were in regular contact over the Iranian initiative during Ghorbanifar's two-day stay in Washington. North reported the polygraph results to Nir, as well as the doubts about the Iranian's trustworthiness, and confided his doubts about the continued use of the "Ghorbanifar channel." Nir and North agreed that there was no replacement for Ghorbanifar at that point. Israel and the U.S. had no diplomatic relations with Iran, and both of them had to gain a foothold there. Khomeini was old, and might disappear at any time. Iran could not be allowed to fall under Soviet influence.

There were two points that the U.S. emphasized in its contacts with Israel and its Western allies:

- The Soviet Union was displaying increasing concern over the possibility of an Iranian victory over Iraq. The treaty of friendship signed with Iraq in 1972 required "consultations" between the two countries whenever they were endangered. Despite the most flexible and noncommittal wording, the Soviets realized that an Iraqi defeat would weaken their position in the Arab world and in the Persian Gulf. For this reason the U.S.S.R. continued its regular supply of arms and spare parts to the Iraqi army, and increased its joint intelligence activities. The U.S., Western Europe, and the moderate Arab regimes shared these worries. Unlike the West, however, the Soviets could threaten Iran directly should an Iraqi collapse seem in the offing. Moscow could concentrate troops on Iran's northern border, and so force the Iranian army and the Revolutionary Guards to divide their forces between two fronts. This situation was a rare opportunity for the West. It could on the one hand prevent an Iraqi collapse by supplying French, British, and Egyptian weapons to Baghdad, while neutralizing the Soviet threat by signaling to Iran that it could continue to count on American support.

- The more Iran's involvement in Lebanon increased, the more tensions between Damascus and Tehran did also. President Assad did not want to see a Shiite republic in Baghdad also, and he was beginning to evidence concern over the possibility of an Iranian victory in the Gulf War. Syria wanted a weak Iraq, but not a defeated one. An Iranian victory, aside from stirring up extremist Moslem groups in Syria, was liable to make Lebanon even more unstable and make a clash between Syria and Hezbollah unavoidable. The West had an interest in fostering such feelings in Damascus, and in giving Iran the impression that its alliance with Syria was a shaky one and that Iran might end up isolated internationally. This would force Iran to keep its lines open to Washington.

Israel had no basic disagreement with this approach, and saw no great conflict between its uncompromising war against

Syrian-Iranian-Libyan terrorism and its effort to regain a stake in Iran. In mid-January 1986, the feeling in Washington and Jersualem was that President Reagan's decision in Iran was near.

On January 15 Nir increased the pressure on North for a final answer, both with regard to the Iranian initiative and with regard to the supply replacement missiles. Upon returning from a 36-hour tour of southern Lebanon, Nir argued that the situation in Beirut was deteriorating, and that the Israeli government was likely to retreat from its willingness to maintain contact with Ghorbanifar, since it did not want to have responsibility for the death of the hostages. North reassured Nir that the decision would be made "at any moment."[25]

Nir again pressed for the supply of replacement missiles. He complained to North that he was working in a very hostile environment, and that he did not dare bring up the proposal to send Iran an additional 1,000 TOW missiles until the 504 Israel had already sent were replaced. It turned out that this was not as simple as it sounded. The head of the Israeli military acquisitions mission in the U.S., Avraham Ben-Yosef, had inquired of the Pentagon the price of a regular TOW missile.[26] The question had astonished defense officials. They told him that the U.S. had, of course, a large inventory of the old line of TOW missiles, but why was Israel interested in an outdated model when it had already begun purchasing the improved version? Fearing that the sale to Iran would be uncovered, Ben-Yosef halted his inquiries and suggested that the problem be handled through the White House.

Pricing was also a difficult issue.[27] Israel had been paid the price of the old missiles for the 504 it had sent, but an improved TOW cost $9,500, and one with night-vision equipment cost $15,000. On the other hand, Ghorbanifar had paid $10,000 for each missile, and had taken out of that a $500 handling fee. The difference did not cover the cost of improved missiles. The only option open was for Israel to receive old missiles from the American army's stocks. North assumed that the army would be more than happy to get rid of its spares. Nir again emphasized that the arrangements had to be firm, and expressed fear that some elements in the Israeli government would oppose such a deal. They might leak the matter to the press and that would put an end to the Iran initiative. Was Nir only trying to exert pressure? North did not think so. In a memorandum to Poindexter on January 14, 1986, North wrote: "I believe that Nir himself is both so exhausted and in such jeopardy of losing his job that he may no longer be functional. I do not believe that Nir is lying to us. I do believe that he is sincerely concerned about the outcome. . . . He has promptly agreed to every proposal we have made to date except for the final one of shipping 1,000 TOWs w/o promise of replenishment."[28]

A few hours later, North notified Nir that Reagan's decision was expected "very soon." Weinberger, he warned, would continue to make difficulties. The secretary of defense did not accept Ghorbanifar's estimation, received by the U.S. via Nir, that the Iranian army was in a desperate state. The Pentagon's information indicated the opposite—that Iran still had the initiative in the war. Weinberger in any case did not believe that Iran could bring about the release of the prisoners. Casey, on the other hand, argued that while Ghorbanifar might be dishonest, his channel of communication had proved itself to be genuine. Only if that channel were blocked should the U.S. halt its contacts with him.

The next 24 hours brought, however, a dramatic development that reduced Israel's role in the Iran initiative to the minimum and solved the problem of replacing the missiles. A legal brief submitted to Poindexter determined that the CIA could purchase various quantities of weapons from the Pentagon and supply them secretly to other countries without going through the normal process of congressional approval. In other words, Israel did not need to take the missiles from its own stocks and wait for replacements. The missiles could be sent directly from the U.S.[29] The weapons would be supplied to Iran through the companies Secord and Hakim had set up to funnel aid to the Contras and by way of Israel, in order to camouflage the deal. The U.S. thereby took upon itself the entire responsibility for the Iran initiative, leaving Israel to serve as no more than a liaison with Ghorbanifar and his contacts in Tehran. Israel's main role was to make it possible for the U.S. to deny involvement, should the initiative be uncovered. The administration could argue, as it tried to some months later, that Israel had supplied weapons to Iran "without the knowledge of the United States."[30]

The legal brief was the basis for the presidential finding of

January 17, 1986, that laid out the second stage of the Iran initiative. It was based on a memorandum from Poindexter to the President of the same date. The contents of the memorandum, and the President's approval of it, were not made known to Weinberger and Shultz, and were also withheld from Congress.

PRESIDENTIAL FINDING ON COVERT ACTIVITY IN IRAN

Prime Minister Peres of Israel secretly dispatched his special advisor on terrorism with instructions to propose a plan by which Israel, with limited assistance from the United States, can create conditions to help bring about a more moderate government in Iran. The Israelis are very concerned that Iran's deteriorating position in the war with Iraq, the potential for further radicalization in Iran, and the possibility to enhance Soviet influence in the Gulf all pose significant threats to the security of Israel. They believe it is essential that they act to at least preserve a balance of power in the region.

The Israeli plan is premised on the assumption that moderate elements in Iran can come to power if these factions demonstrate their credibility in defending Iran against Iraq and in deterring Soviet intervention. To achieve the strategic goal of a more moderate Iranian government, the Israelis are prepared to unilaterally commence selling military materiel to Western-oriented Iranian factions. It is their belief that by so doing they can achieve a heretofore unobtainable penetration of the Iranian governing hierarchy. The Israelis are convinced that the Iranians are so desperate for military materiel, expertise and intelligence that the provision of these resources will result in favorable long-term changes in personnel and attitudes within the Iranian government. Further, once the exchange relationship has commenced, a dependency would be established on those who are providing the requisite resources, thus allowing the provider(s) to coercively influence near-term events. Such an outcome is consistent with our policy objectives and would present significant advantages for U.S. national interests. As described by the prime minister's emissary, the only requirement the Israelis have is an assurance that they will be allowed to purchase U.S.

replenishments for the stocks that they sell to Iran. We have researched the legal problems of Israel's selling U.S. manufactured arms to Iran. Because of the requirement in the U.S. law for recipients of U.S. arms to notify the U.S. government of transfers to third countries, I do not recommend that you agree with the specific details of the Israeli plan. However, there is another possibility. Some time ago Attorney General William French Smith determined that under an appropriate finding you could authorize the CIA to sell arms to countries outside of the provisions of the laws and reporting requirements for foreign military sales. The objectives of the Israeli plan could be met if the CIA, using an authorized agent as necessary, purchased arms from the Department of Defense under the Economy Act and then transferred them to Iran directly after receiving appropriate payment from Iran.

The Covert Action finding attached at Tab A provides the latitude for the transactions indicated above to proceed. The Iranians have indicated an immediate requirement for 4,000 basic TOW weapons for use in the launchers they already hold.

The Israeli's [sic] are also sensitive to a strong U.S. desire to free our Beirut hostages and have insisted that the Iranians demonstrate both influence and good intent by an early release of the five Americans. Both sides have agreed that the hostages will be immediately released upon commencement of this action. Prime Minister Peres had his emissary pointedly note that they well understand our position on not making concessions to terrorists. They also point out, however, that terrorist groups, movements, and organizations are significantly easier to influence through governments than they are by direct approach. In that we have been unable to exercise any suasion over Hezbollah during the course of nearly two years of kidnappings, this approach through the government of Iran may well be our only way to achieve the release of the Americans held in Beirut. It must again be noted that since this dialogue with the Iranians began in September, Reverend Weir has been released and there have been no Shia terrorist attacks against American or Israeli persons, property, or interests.

Therefore it is proposed that Israel make the necessary arrangements for the sale of 4,000 TOW weapons to Iran.

Sufficient funds to cover the sale would be transferred to an agent of the CIA. The CIA would then purchase the weapons from the Department of Defense and deliver the weapons to Iran through the agent. If all of the hostages are not released after the first shipment of 1,000 weapons, further transfers would cease. On the other hand, since hostage release is in some respects a by-product of a larger effort to develop ties to potentially moderate forces in Iran, you may wish to redirect such transfers to other groups within the government at a later time.

The Israelis have asked for our urgent response to this proposal so that they can plan accordingly. They note that conditions inside both Iran and Lebanon are highly volatile. The Israelis are cognizant that this entire operation will be terminated if the Iranians abandon their goal of moderating their government or allow further acts of terrorism. You have discussed the general outlines of the Israeli plan with Secretaries Shultz and Weinberger, Attorney General Meese and (CIA) Director Casey. The secretaries do not recommend you proceed with this plan. Attorney General Meese and Director Casey believe the short-term and long-term objectives of the plan warrant the policy risks involved and recommend you approve the attached finding. Because of the extreme sensitivity of this project, it is recommended that you exercise your statutory prerogative to withhold notification of the finding to the congressional oversight committees until such time that you deem it to be appropriate.

RECOMMENDATION: OK [initialed: RR by JP]

PREPARED BY: Oliver North

ATTACHMENT: Appendix A—Presidential Order for Covert Activity 1000, 17 January 1986.

President Reagan's "finding," or order for the execution of the operation, was attached:

I hereby find that the following operation in a foreign country (including all support necessary to such operation) is important to the national security of the United States, and due to its extreme sensitivity and security risks, I determine it is essential to limit prior notice, and direct the director of Central Intelligence to refrain from reporting this finding

to the Congress as provided in Section 501 of the National
Security Act of 1947, as amended, until I otherwise direct.

SCOPE: Iran

DESCRIPTION: Assist selected friendly foreign liasion [sic] services, third countries and third parties which have established
relationships with Iranian elements, groups, and individuals
sympathetic to U.S. government interests and which do not
conduct or support terrorist actions directed against U.S.
persons, property or interests, for the purpose of: (1) establishing a more moderate government in Iran, (2) obtaining
from them significant intelligence not otherwise obtainable,
to determine the current Iranian government's intentions
with respect to its neighbors and with respect to terrorist
acts, and (3) furthering the release of the American hostages
held in Beirut and preventing additional terrorist acts by
these groups. Provide funds, intelligence, counter-intelli-
gence, training, guidance and communicatons [sic] and other
necessary assistance to these elements, groups, individuals,
liason [sic] services and third countries in support of these
activities.

The U.S. government will act to facilitate efforts by third
parties and third countries to establish contact with moderate
elements within and outside the government of Iran by providing these elements with arms, equipment and related
materiel in order to enhance the credibility of these elements
in their effort to achieve a more pro-U.S. government in Iran
by demonstrating their ability to obtain requisite resources
to defend their country against Iraq and intervention by the
Soviet Union. This support will be discontinued if the U.S.
government learns that these elements have abandoned their
goals of moderating their government and approprated [sic]
the materiel for purposes other than that provided by this
finding.

[signed] Ronald Reagan

Another presidential order dealt with terrorism. This, over
FBI objections, allowed American agents to capture terrorists
anywhere in the world and bring them to the U.S. for trial.
The order also permitted action against terrorist bases, sources
of funding, command centers, and supply channels.

The order was initiated by North, after he received legal

backing from Abraham Sofaer, the general counsel of the State Department. Sofaer wrote a brief stating that there was no legal prohibition against kidnapping terrorists and bringing them to trial in the U.S. President Reagan signed the order in light of what had been learned from the interception of the plane containing the *Achille Lauro* terrorists and from the terrorist attacks at the Rome and Vienna airports.

While North was preparing to renew the Iran initiative, the Israeli team was clarifying Amiram Nir's role in the operation. Kimche, Schwimmer, Nimrodi, and Nir met on January 21, 1986, at Nimrodi's house in Savion. Nir showed up for the meeting in army uniform, claiming that he was serving a stint in the reserves. It was apparent at the beginning of the conversation that Nir felt he was talking from a position of strength. President Reagan had already signed the finding allowing the continuation of the Iran intiative, and all the contacts with Washington on this matter had been through him and not through Kimche. Nir told the others about Ghorbanifar's trip to Washington, and claimed that Poindexter had told him that the U.S. preferred maintaining its own contacts with Iran "without Israeli interference." In any case, he claimed, since McFarlane had resigned and Kimche did not know Poindexter and North as well as he, Nir, did, the contacts with the U.S. were now his preserve. Turning to Schwimmer and Nimrodi, he added: "You're private arms dealers, and the U.S. is not interested in maintaining its contacts with Iran through you."

During the course of the conversation Nimrodi left the room to telephone Ghorbanifar in Paris. The two spoke in Persian. Nimrodi called Ghorbanifar a "traitor," and castigated him for not revealing all the details of his Washington trip. Ghorbanifar answered with a whimper that, since the Americans bugged his telephone, he could not speak freely, but promised to call the next day from Frankfurt, where he was to meet with Amiram Nir. Ghorbanifar said that during his trip to Washington he had seen "death staring [him] in the face," and had been convinced that the CIA would not allow him to leave the U.S. alive.

The conversation left Nimrodi dazed. Here was Nir, sitting in his house, pretending he was on reserve duty, and not mentioning that he was going to meet Ghorbanifar the next day in Frankfurt. It was additional proof that Nir had deceived them, pushed them aside, and begun to act on his own in Washington.

Nimrodi reentered the room, saying nothing. He listened as Schwimmer suggested that Nir meet him the next day in the Prime Minister's office in order to inquire together what Nir's actual position on the Israeli team was. Not batting an eyelash, Nir answered: "I'm in the reserves, but if Peres decides he wants to talk with us, I'll come, of course." Nimrodi could not hold himself back any longer. "You're a liar. You know that you're flying to Frankfurt tomorrow to meet Ghorbanifar." Nir fell silent and did not answer.

Nir took off the next day at 6:00 A.M. His meeting with Ghorbanifar was preparatory to the conference with North and Secord scheduled for later in the day at the Churchill Hotel in London. Ghorbanifar called Nimrodi that evening from a pay phone, as he had promised, and related the circumstances of his visit to Washington on January 11. He said that Ledeen had come to Paris specially to escort him to the U.S., and had not allowed him to call Nimrodi and Schwimmer to notify them of the trip. Ghorbanifar added that, prior to the polygraph test, CIA agents had played him tapes of his telephone conversations with Mussavi, Kengarlou, Nimrodi, and Schwimmer. After failing the test, North had told him that the U.S. knew everything about him, but that he was willing to continue working with him on condition that he cut off his contacts with Kimche, Nimrodi, and Schwimmer, as well as with Michael Ledeen, "who has been removed from the initiative because of his failures." North warned Ghorbanifar not to tell Nimrodi and Schwimmer about that conversation.

Ghorbanifar called Nimrodi again on the following day, January 23, and told him that he was scheduled to meet Peres, Poindexter, North, and Secord in London on January 25.

Nimrodi and Schwimmer were once again taken off guard. While they knew that Peres had gone to London to meet with British Prime Minister Margaret Thatcher, they did not know of his plans to meet the Americans and Ghorbanifar. Was the Iranian arms merchant telling the truth, or had Ghorbanifar been misled by Nir? Schwimmer decided to find out. On Saturday morning, January 25, he flew to London and met Peres that afternoon at his hotel. The Prime Minister said he knew nothing about such a meeting. After he saw how angry Schwimmer was, however, he promised to take the matter up with Nir upon his return to Jerusalem.

That inquiry took place on January 29. Kimche, Schwimmer,

and Nimrodi protested against the way Nir was working, and asked Peres whether Nir was meant to assist them, or whether they were no longer running the initiative. Nimrodi lost control of himself and shouted at Nir: "You're an American spy, the Americans own you!" Peres ignored the outburst. He explained that, after President Reagan's January 17 finding to begin direct supply of American arms to Iran, Israel could no longer take an active role in the initiative. Israel was now doing no more than covering for America, he explained. He suggested that, in light of this, the matter be left to the U.S. and Iran. Nimrodi was not convinced, and whispered to Schwimmer as they left the Prime Minister's office: "Peres has screwed you again."

Nimrodi's suspicions, it turns out, were justified, since Nir continued to play a part in the Iran initiative despite Israel's now reduced role in it. On February 2, 1986, Ghorbanifar called Nimrodi from Paris, again from a pay phone, and briefed him on the meeting with North and Nir in London. Ghorbanifar did not tell Nimrodi that the meeting had taken place on January 22; he implied that it had occurred later. He related that Nir had brought Brigadier General Azriel Nevo, the Prime Minister's military adviser, with him. Nevo's picture had appeared that same day in the British newspapers. Nir had spread a newspaper out in front of him and said, "General Nevo represents the Prime Minister." Ghorbanifar also related that Nir told him that "according to orders from high up," Schwimmer, Nimrodi, and Kimche were "out of the picture," and that Ledeen was also no longer part of the initiative. Ghorbanifar added that North warned him, in Nir's presence, that were he to talk with Kimche, Schwimmer, or Nimrodi, "he would get a bullet in the head."

Ghorbanifar repeated North's threat to him in a letter he sent to Nimrodi on February 10:

> I am most sorry for the pain and inconvenience I have caused you. I received your message and my answer is that I have been ordered in the most forceful manner not to contact you in any way. I have not betrayed you, and especially not our dear and beloved friend, Al Schwimmer. Please give him my warmest regards, and the same to dear David [Kimche], whom I consider a great man. In the meantime I am busy

with a most human and holy matter, of which I will tell you later. I will never forget that you are the man who began this project with me.

                              With my best love and regards.
                              Manucher Ghorbanifar

Brigadier General Nevo would later confess to Schwimmer and Nimrodi: "I swear to you that Peres did not know of my participation in that meeting. What happened was that Nir asked me if I was busy that evening. When I said I wasn't, he said: 'Then come with me to a fascinating meeting.' " Nevo claimed that, had he known that Nir planned to use him for his own purposes, he would not have gone.

Either way, it is clear that at the Churchill Hotel meeting of January 22 the foundations were laid for "Operation Recovery"—a complex plan drafted on January 24 by North, and in the framework of which the U.S. was to supply 4,000 TOW missiles to Iran, as well as fresh intelligence on Iraqi army positions around Basra.[31] In exchange, the American hostages would be released and the 18 I-Hawk missiles sent to Tehran the previous November would be returned to Israel. The U.S. was to supply the missiles in four equal shipments. The first of these would be on February 8, simultaneous with the release of 25 Shiites imprisoned in southern Lebanon. The next day, on February 9, all the American hostages would be freed and delivered to the American, British, or Swiss embassies in Beirut. On February 10 would come the second shipment of TOW missiles, and Israel would free another quantity of Shiites. In exchange for this, Hezbollah would free some additional hostages. After Iran had received all the missiles, all the hostages who were citizens of Western European countries would be released, and William Buckley's body would be handed over. Despite opposition by some CIA officials,[32] North informed Ghorbanifar that Secord would be the "logistical coordinator" of the operation. As North later testified, Secord's role was to negotiate prices, set delivery schedules, and make all the necessary arrangements. Secord was an outside entity who had been established as an outside entity many, many months before to support the Nicaraguan resistance.[33] Thus, in agreeing to have the hostages released piecemeal, after each shipment of missiles, North consciously ignored previous instructions to have all the hostages freed before any arms were supplied.

The release of the Shiite prisoners was the subject of a short exchange between the Iranian arms merchant and Nir. According to a transcript of the January 22 conversation, tape-recorded by North, Ghorbanifar asked for the release of 100 Shiites. Nir said that General Antoine Lahad's South Lebanon army had less than 50 prisoners. Ghorbanifar replied that 50 prisoners were "the minimium" to be released, even if it meant detaining additional Shiites in order to release that number.[34]

In order to give a humanitarian air to the release of the Hezbollah men Israel held, and to prevent linkage between this and the release of the hostages, the White House considered involving Cardinal O'Connor, Archbishop of New York in the U.S., in an appeal to the Pope to call publicly on General Lahad to free the Shiite prisoners he held. The idea was, however, rejected.

Providing intelligence on Iraq to Iran aroused much opposition in the CIA, partly because it could help Khomeini pursue his war against Iraqi President Saddam Hussein, but mostly because of the lack of trust in Ghorbanifar. The Iranians demanded an updated aerial map of the deployment of Iraq's forces on the front. American intelligence officials thought that handing over such a map to Iran would be detrimental to the settlement the U.S. hoped to reach in the Persian Gulf.[35] They withdrew their objections, however, under pressure from Poindexter, and the documents the Iranians demanded were given to Ghorbanifar when he met with the CIA's Charles Allen in London on January 26.[36] It later became clear that this intelligence was of limited value and could not affect the situation at the front. Yet the delivery of the information deepened the CIA's involvement in the Iran initiative, in league with Poindexter and North.

In his public testimony to the congressional investigatory committees, North gave a vivid description of the January 22 encounter. North claimed that he had gone to London doubtful as to the Iranian middleman's ability to bring about any real change in his government's position. Ghorbanifar sensed these doubts. He took North into the bathroom in his hotel room and offered him a few "incentives." Testifying before the congressional committee on July 14, 1987, North had the following exchange with Senator Sam Nunn (D., Ga.):

NUNN: Do you recall any of the other incentives?

NORTH: I recall one specifically. Ghorbanifar offered me a million dollars if we could make this prosper.

NUNN: Tell us what you said in response to that.

NORTH: It's out of the question. I told him I could not, would not, accept any financial favors and if those kind of discussions pursued, he would be out of the picture very quickly.[37]

Ghorbanifar then proposed, North claimed, that the U.S. supply Iran with the missiles at an inflated price, and that the profits be diverted to the Contras. North added: "I must confess to you that I thought using the Ayatollah's money to support the Nicaraguan resistance was the right idea and I must confess to you that I advocated that."[38]

But the facts as they are known in Israel do not mesh with North's version. On November 24, 1985, even before North became responsible for the Iran initiative, Schwimmer and Nimrodi had deposited $1 million in the Geneva bank account of Lake Resources in order to cover the costs of transporting the Hawk missiles to Iran. Secord spent close to $150,000 of this money without McFarlane's approval and without Israel's knowledge. The balance remained in the Lake Resources account. Secord himself confirmed in his congressional testimony, on May 7, 1987, that he had asked North at the time what to do with the remaining money. North answered: "Don't worry, the money is ours now and we'll use it for the Contras."[39] When Nir came to Washington on January 2, 1986, he asked North what had happened to the remaining money. North testified to Congress that he had told Nir that the money had gone to the Contras, and added: "Nir did not make any protest, and did not continue to ask for the money." Nir disputes this account, and claims that North told him that the money was earmarked for "other purposes."

Moreover, a recording of the January 22 conversation found in North's files at the NSC indicates that North and Ghorbanifar openly discussed diverting the money to the Contras in the presence of Nir and Secord.[40] In light of all the evidence now available, it appears that North's realization that this money could go to the Contras, together with Secord's and Hakim's interest in making a large profit, were among the decisive factors that led to the continuation of the Iran initiative. Despite his great enthusiasm for the Iranian operation, North believed that using funds from arms sales for the Contras was a "neat idea."[41] Unlike McFarlane, who had viewed the contacts with Iran as an opportunity for reviving strategic cooperation with that country, North thought of the initiative as a simple arms-for-hostages deal, and as a way of making profits that would help accomplish President Reagan's Central American policy.

North's and Nir's incompetence and the ease with which Ghorbanifar misled them could already be felt even at this early stage of Operation Recovery. The Iranian arms merchant told North, for instance, that senior Iranian officials were pressing Khomeini to abdicate and arrange an orderly transfer of power. Ghorbanifar claimed that Khomeini had agreed to step down on February 11, 1986, the seventh anniversary of the Islamic Revolution. Israeli intelligence dismissed this "information," and Ghorbanifar's already low reputation for reliability sunk even lower.

Preparations for Operation Recovery nevertheless continued apace. In conversations with North and Nir, Ghorbanifar promised that, after the arrival of the first shipment of TOWs, there would be a high-level meeting in Europe of Iranian and American officials.[42] The Iranian delegation would be headed by deputy prime minister Mohsen Kengarlou, the personal friend of Ghorbanifar who had already taken part in the arms deal of the previous summer. While Kengarlou had met previously with Nimrodi in Geneva, this would be his first meeting with official representatives of the U.S. and Israel. According to the original plan, the shipment of the missiles to Iran would begin 10 days after payment was deposited in the Crédit Suisse bank in Geneva. Nir would transfer the money to account number 386–430–22–1, belonging to Lake Resources, in the same bank's Eaux Vives branch, and Secord's company would pass on part of that money to the CIA—the price of the missiles as set by the Pentagon. The Pentagon would then transfer the missiles from its armory in Anniston, Alabama, and deliver them to the CIA at the Kelly air force base in Texas. The CIA would transfer the first 1,000 missiles (out of 4,000 negotiated) to Secord, who would arrange their shipment in planes chartered from Southern Air Transport to Amiram Nir in Eilat. The TOWs would then be loaded on an Israeli Boeing 707 from which Israeli identifications markings had been erased. The plane would be flown by an American crew provided by Secord to Bandar Abbas, on the shores of the Persian Gulf. The flight path would be unusually long—over southern Saudi Arabia and Oman. After the cargo was unloaded, the plane would go on to Tehran in order to return the 18 improved Hawk missiles from Operation Espressso to Israel. The Israeli plane was to be chartered by Secord, and he would give the Israeli government a security deposit of $2 million.

The financial arrangements were indeed intricate. The TOW missiles were purchased from the Pentagon by the CIA for a sum of $3.7 million. Secord sold them to Ghorbanifar for $10 million, and Ghorbanifar sold them to Iran for $12 million. Interim funding came from Adnan Khashoggi, who received from Ghorbanifar four checks, each made out for $3 million. This included $1 million in interest and $1 million for "expenses and service charges." In other words, after Secord paid the $3.7 million to the CIA, he would still have another $6.3 million from the deal in the Lake Resources account, which could be passed on to the Contras or used to fund joint counterterrorism activities between the U.S. and Israel, or to pay for the replacements for the 504 TOW missiles Israel had supplied to Iran in August–September 1985. In the end, however, the greater part of this money, as well as of the profits of later sales, remained in Secord's private account.

The Israelis involved noted with surprise the complete freedom of action Secord had in managing Operation Recovery. North, it seemed, could not or did not want to supervise the movement of the money through the 13 different accounts that Secord and Hakim maintained in Switzerland and the Cayman Islands. The result was that Secord and Hakim were extremely liberal in their use of the sums they received. Secord, for instance, bought himself a private Piper Seneca plane and a completely outfitted Porsche sports car, as well as using several thousand dollars for visits to various health spas.[43] In his testimony to the congressional committees, Secord claimed that he had not made any profit from the arms deals because he feared it might hurt his chances for rejoining the military. Hence he had received a monthly salary of $6,000 and expenses.[44] This was later shown to be less than accurate; North said in his testimony that he believed it was the right of Secord and Hakim to make a fair profit for themselves—but that he had left it to them to decide what a fair profit was.

After the Iranian affair was uncovered, the Reagan administration asked the Swiss government to freeze the various Crédit Suisse accounts through which the money from the arms sales to Iran had been funneled to the Contras. In a series of letters to Pascal Gossin, chief counsel in the Swiss Federal Police Department, the American Department of Justice demanded its right under the Treaty of Mutual Assistance in Criminal Matters to gain information about the bank accounts. The Americans were able to identify to whom several of the accounts belonged. Account number 283–838–91–2 belonged to Manucher Ghorbanifar, as did number 370–113–12–1, listed under the pseudonym Abdollah Khak. Account number 311–775–42–1 belonged to Gulf Marketing Consultants; 207–225–92–1 belonged to Dolmy Business Inc. Other corporations identified in the indictment sheet, published by Special Counsel Lawrence Walsh, were: Albon Values Corp., Hyde Park Square Corp., Toyco Inc., Udall Research Corp. (registered in Panama), and Defex S.A.[45]

The Department of Justice also asked for information on the transfer of money from these accounts, and from other accounts controlled by North, Secord, and Hakim, to the Citizens and Southern National Bank in Atlanta, Georgia, account number DDC.001–08096497, which belonged to Southern Air Transport, Inc.

Operation Recovery was scheduled to begin on February 8, 1986, but was delayed until February 13. Nir, North, Secord, and Charles Allen of the CIA went on February 5 to meet Ghorbanifar at the Intercontinental Hotel in Frankfurt, and over dinner they agreed on all the technical arrangements for the new deal.[46] North noted in his personal diary on that date that Ghorbanifar would deposit the money the next day. On February 7, Khashoggi deposited $10 million in the Lake Resources account in Geneva. On February 11 Secord transferred $3.7 million to the CIA account, to be used by the agency to pay the Department of Defense. On February 13 the missiles started out on their long trip to Iran.

Secord arrived in Israel on Friday, February 13, in order to brief the members of the American crew who would fly the Boeing 707 from Israel to Bandar Abbas. The missiles arrived in Israel on two chartered Southern Air Transport planes on February 15 and 16. Five hundred of them were flown the next day to Bandar Abbas. The plane returned on February 18 with 17 improved Hawk missiles sent to Tehran in November 1985. The eighteenth missile had been test-fired by the Iranians and, the Iranians said, had not satisfied them.[47]

An hour after the plane's return from Tehran, Ghorbanifar called from Geneva and notified Secord and Nir that, the U.S. having kept its promise to supply Iran with 500 TOWs, the way was now clear for a meeting of American and Iranian officials in Frankfurt on February 19. After the release of all the hostages, there would be another meeting of officials of the highest level on Kish Island in April, which would deal with the future relations between the two countries. The Iranian delegation to Frankfurt would be headed, he said, by deputy prime minister Mohsen Kengarlou and would include five other Iranians. Ghorbanifar suggested that the meeting take place at the offices of Iran's consul-general in the city. Secord firmly rejected the idea. They agreed instead that the two delegations would first meet at North's room at the Intercontinental Hotel, and then again in Kengarlou's room at the Sheraton Hotel near Frankfurt Airport.

Ghorbanifar promised that the hostages would be released on Saturday, February 21, immediately after the second shipment of 500 TOW missiles was delivered on Friday, February 20, and "if the intelligence is good." This remark should have raised North's and Secord's suspicion, since at no time in the past did the Iranians link the release of the American hostages to the quality of the intelligence they would receive from the CIA. Ghorbanifar's remark suggested that Iran would claim that the intelligence was not good and would refuse to release the hostages. And, indeed, it turned out that the information the CIA supplied gave the Iranians no knowledge they did not already have.

On February 19, North and a senior American intelligence official came from Washington to Frankfurt to meet Kengarlou and his party.[48] Secord and Nir arrived from Tel Aviv. But Kengarlou never showed up. Ghorbanifar tried to make excuses for his friend's absence, claiming that "Prime Minister Mussavi thinks this meeting is of prime importance, so it is certain to take place." North was not convinced, and told Ghorbanifar that he was returning to Washington. Despite North's disappointment, and after several emotional telephone conversations with the Iranian arms merchant, several participants suggested putting Ghorbanifar to another test in order to find out if he could really bring about the promised meeting.

North was persuaded, and on February 25 everyone returned to Frankfurt. North was presented to the Iranians as "William Goode," Secord as "General Adams," and Nir as "Miller." Charles Allen of the CIA and Secord's business partner, Albert (Abe) Hakim, also participated, the latter serving as an interpreter. The use of false names was more than a little ridiculous. Since Ghorbanifar knew North, Secord, and Nir, it was obvious that he had given Kengarlou the actual identities of all the participants.

Hakim's presence was problematic. In all previous meetings with Iranians, Ghorbanifar had interpreted from English to Persian and the reverse. North did not trust Ghorbanifar, however, and suspected that he would not present the American ideas to Kengarlou with precision. For this reason North preferred an interpreter of his own. When the subject was brought up in mid-February the choice fell on Hakim. Ghorbanifar was utterly opposed. He said that Hakim was known to Iranian intelligence as a man who acted against the Islamic Revolution and Iranians would never agree to meet with him. North pretended to agree to drop Hakim. But after Kengarlou's failure to appear on the originally scheduled date, North insisted on bringing Hakim and dismissed the reservations the CIA had about his presence. In order to prevent him from being recognized by Ghobanifar and his fellow countrymen, Hakim wore a wig, put on dark sunglasses, and applied a heavy coat of makeup. He was presented as Ibrahim Ibrahimian, a Persian-speaking Turk.[49]

It was the only time Hakim played the role of interpreter. CIA officials feared that Hakim would make use of what he heard to advance his own business interests. In the future, they recommended, the interpreter should be George Cave, an American intelligence official fluent in several dialects of Persian. Cave had served in Iran and knew the country well.[50] He had been the man responsible for cutting off contact between the CIA and Ghorbanifar in 1984, and had prepared the questions for the recent polygraph examination.

North had prepared carefully for this first meeting of American and Iranian officials in five years. The first gathering, over dinner, lasted until 3:00 A.M.[51] The atmosphere was tense and suspicious, and the Iranians gave simple, ingenuous answers to the American proposals. The Americans soon discovered that despite his title of deputy prime minister, Kengarlou's actual influence in Mussavi's office was marginal. It quickly became apparent that Kengarlou had come to Frankfurt only because Ghorbanifar had lied to both sides. He had promised the Iranians that the Americans would give them Phoenix missiles, Howitzer guns, and thousands of TOW missiles, and had promised the Americans, directly and through Amiram Nir, not only the release of the hostages but also a high-level meeting in Tehran—within two months—with President Khamenei, Prime Minister Mussavi, and Majlis Speaker Hashimi Rafsanjani.

Kengarlou appeared frightened and insecure. He nevertheless emphasized that he had full authority to make commitments in the name of his government without having to consult his superiors. It was necessary, he said, to place Iranian-American relations on a firmer foundation than the one based on arms and hostages. His country was very worried about Soviet activity in the Persian Gulf region and wanted to cooperate with the West, but was still wary of the U.S. Kengarlou made it clear that, after the supply of the next 500 TOWs, "several, but not all, of the hostages" would be released. The rest would be freed after the meeting on Kish Island in April. Iran hoped that the U.S. would complete the shipment of the remaining 3,000 missiles it had promised after that meeting. To prevent the failure of the talks on Kish Island, Kengarlou suggested a preparatory meeting in Europe. He asked that the U.S. demonstrate its goodwill by immediately supplying the remaining 500 TOW missiles for which Iran had already paid. The Iranians received an affirmative response when the two parties met again the next day and were told that the next shipment would come on February 27. Ghorbanifar would receive a commission of $260 per missile.

Both the Americans and the Iranians hinted in Frankfurt that future meetings should be held without the presence of intermediaries. Nir and Ghorbanifar were nervous. It meant pushing Israel out of the initiative and ending Ghorbanifar's personal involvement in arms sales from which he earned a healthy profit. Ghorbanifar suspected that the interest in using Hakim as an interpreter was motivated by the desire to end his role as mediator[52]—and just at a moment, he claimed, when he was in financial straits. Nir did his best to convince the Americans to continue working through Ghorbanifar. Nir told North and Secord that Israel had known Ghorbanifar even before Khomeini's revolution and that, while he was a liar and a cheat, "Israel knows how to handle him."[53] Nir was persuasive, and in the end it was decided to allow Ghorbanifar to serve as middleman through the conclusion of the TOW sale, and then to decide whether or not to continue with the Iran initiative.

The U.S. nevertheless established direct, if limited, contacts with Iran. After Nir returned to Israel, Secord and Hakim met with Kengarlou and Ghorbanifar again on February 27 to coordinate the next shipment of 500 missiles that Israel was to send that same day from Eilat to Bandar Abbas. Secord and Hakim took advantage of a short absence by Ghorbanifar to stuff a Washington telephone number into Kengarlou's pocket. The deputy prime minister could now call them directly, without Ghorbanifar's intervention.

North and Nir waited for the hostages to be released, but nothing happened. It quickly became clear that Kengarlou and Ghorbanifar had lied once more and not carried out their promise. Officials in Washington and Jerusalem noted that, after the shipment of 504 TOW missiles in the summer of 1985, one hostage had been released, but that double the amount of missles and a batch of intelligence documents had not produced any hostages this time around. Nevertheless, Nir and North pressed on.

Preparations now began for the Kish Island talks. The White House designated McFarlane as the leader of the American delegation. In anticipation of these talks, Poindexter conferred on February 27 with Casey and North to define American goals.[54] Casey suggested that the first meeting be used for feeling out the intentions of the other side. Only at the second meeting, he said, should the major issues come up: the Soviet threat to Iran, the situation in Afghanistan, Soviet supplies of weapons to Iraq, and the conclusion of the Gulf War. The emphasis should be on Soviet involvement, so that if the meeting should somehow be made public, it would be possible to explain to moderate Arab states that the talks had dealt only with Soviet interference in the region.

Casey established another guideline as well: no Israelis and no Ghorbanifar on Kish Island. He claimed that the Soviets were constantly listening in to telephone coversations between Washington and Israel, and that Ghorbanifar also made too much use of open telephone lines.

The news of Casey's interest in circumventing Israel made its way to Jerusalem, it seems, and on February 28, Prime Minister Shimon Peres sent a personal letter to President Reagan in which he urged the U.S. to continue its efforts to establish a strategic dialogue with Iran, and promised the continued assistance of Israel in this matter. Casey advised Reagan to thank Peres for his letter and to promise him that the Iranian initiative would continue. He also suggested to Reagan, however, that the high-level meeting with the Iranians should proceed without any Israeli presence.[55] It was the first time that the U.S. stated officially, if not publicly, its desire to free itself of its partnership with Israel in the Iranian issue, a desire that would grow ever stronger in the coming months.

CHAPTER
10

Chocolate Cake
Diplomacy

McFarlane's journey to Tehran in May 1986 was the most serious of the innumerable blunders made during the course of the contacts with Iran. It reflected more sharply than ever the web of contradictions and cross-purposes that characterized the Iranian policy of both the U.S. and Israel. From the time of the first contacts with Iran in the summer of 1985, President Reagan had made use of Israel in an attempt to resolve the contradiction between the secret supply of arms to Khomeini and his public condemnation of Iran as a country sponsoring international terror and, therefore, ineligible to receive American and Western arms. But a direct shipment of 1,000 TOW missiles from the U.S. to Iran, with Israel serving as no more than a transfer point, and McFarlane's visit, underlined the central role the U.S. was playing, making it one of the pawns in the game being played by the groups battling to succeed Khomeini. The American government could now be blackmailed by any of the factions, and they exploited this power to the limit.

People familiar with the Persian court's tradition of intrigue and deception might have warned McFarlane that the presence of a special American plane at Mehrabad Airport and the lodging of a high-level American delegation in the Tehran Hilton could not be kept secret. Both the warring factions in the Iranian government and the Soviet Union together with its Communist allies would be sure to sniff them out. But North, and certainly Nir, were apparently oblivious to this, while Ghorbanifar seemed to be focusing only on the large profits he would make—which is why he was so eager that McFarlane go to Tehran.

In fact, from the beginning of March 1986, the feeling grew among the CIA officials and members of the White House staff that Ghorbanifar had taken them about as far as he could, and that the U.S. would never succeed in achieving a break-through in its relationship with Iran, and obtain release of all the hostages, by working through the Iranian arms merchant. North, for this reason, searched for some other channel of communication with Iran, both in order to find a more trustwor-thy mediator and to dispense with the Israeli chaperone that accompanied him in all his contacts with Iran's new rulers. One of the CIA officials, George Cave, who joined the American team as interpreter, expressed his concern that Israel had such a prominent role in the affair. Another official expressed his doubts that Ghorbanifar could deliver on his promises, and added: "However, our other friend, Nir, will also be present [at a Paris meeting]. We sense strongly that he is unilaterally providing additional arms as an incentive to the Kish Island [meeting]."[1] North, in his congressional testimony, said: "I think that there was a sufficient understanding that he [Nir] knew we needed to have our own sources of intelligence, that [we] couldn't be totally dependent upon Israel. I don't think Israel has any reluctance to understand that we needed to have our own sources inside Iran too."[2] On the other hand, since Ghorba-nifar was the only tie Israel had to the Iran initiative, Nir did his best to make the arms merchant seem more reliable and continued to recommend supplying arms through him.

It is less clear why the U.S. continued to ignore all these alarming signals. When most of the obstacles were cleared away and McFarlane's visit agreed upon, the U.S. did not prop-erly consider the dangers involved. In light of the capture of the hostages at the U.S. embassy in Tehran in November 1979, the U.S. had to take into account the possibility that McFarlane, North, and the rest of the delegation might be taken prisoner. Any one of them would have been a treasure trove of intelligence for the Iranians. McFarlane and North in fact took poison pills with them for just this eventuality.[3] They did not consider, however, that their captors might be aware that they were so equipped and prevent them from killing themselves.

North had assigned the preparations for the trip to Ghorbanifar and in so doing had given him the means with which to blackmail the administration—if the Americans continued to work with him, Ghorbanifar would keep his mouth shut; if they tried to shake him off, he could make the whole affair public. Furthermore, the entire exercise of using falsified passports was ridiculous—both Ghorbanifar and Kengarlou knew some of the members of the delegation and could have revealed them at any moment to the Iranian government. Furthermore, according to Ghorbanifar, Kengarlou was responsible for the kidnapping of William Buckley, the CIA station chief in Beirut. Iran had demonstrated in the past that it would not prevent the holding of American diplomats as hostages. The State Department was unaware of the mission, and hence embassies of friendly governments in Tehran were not alerted. McFarlane and his delegation were, in effect, on their own.

McFarlane would later say that he had felt, on the eve of his trip to Iran, like Henry Kissinger setting off on his secret trip to China.[3a] But Tehran was not Peking, and the Chinese had never kidnapped Americans in order to force the U.S. to sell them arms. An administration official who has known McFarlane is quoted as having said that McFarlane often fashioned himself in Kissinger's mold as a strategic thinker, "even though he was not of the same depth."[4]

It seems fairly clear now that the seeds of the Iran-Contra affair's exposure, in November 1986, were planted during McFarlane's visit to Tehran, and that they sprouted when, after McFarlane's mission failed, North, Secord, and Hakim opened a second channel of communication with Iran through Sadegh Tabatabai, Khomeini's son-in-law, who held the title of "special ambassador" and was sent from time to time on sensitive diplomatic missions. Other participants in this channel or associated with it were Mehdi Bahremani, the eldest son of Majlis Speaker Rafsanjani, and Ahmed Rafsanjani, the Speaker's nephew and a personal friend of Khomeini's son, Ahmed. The link with Rafsanjani's relatives ran through a contact of Albert Hakim, Secord's business partner. The establishment of this channel, without Israel's knowledge and behind Ghorbanifar's back, left the Iranian arms merchant without any good reason to remain silent. In mid-October 1986, he wrote of McFarlane's visit to Tehran in a detailed letter to Ayatollah Ali Montazeri, Khomeini's heir-apparent and Rafsanjani's foe. Exposure and publication were now certain; only the timing remained an unknown.

The preparations for the high-level meeting in Iran began immediately after the Frankfurt meeting in late February 1986. On March 2, 1986, North called Nir and asked him to urge Ghorbanifar to overcome the obstacles to the Kish Island meeting. North told Nir that, in a telephone conversation with Albert Hakim, Kengarlou had reiterated his demand for Phoenix missiles as a condition for this meeting. The Iranians completely ignored the American position on the hostages and demanded more weapons for their release. The direct contact between Hakim and Kengarlou reinforced Ghorbanifar's fears that North and Secord meant to push him out of the initiative. He complained of this to Nir and demanded that he take action. Ghorbanifar also made a direct call to Charles Allen in Washington on March 4, and suggested direct contact between him and the CIA. Nir also became concerned that he would be excluded from further meetings and that Israeli interests would be ignored. Nevertheless, at North's request, Nir contacted Ghorbanifar and urged him to "pull out all stops."[5]

At Nir's intervention, Ghorbanifar, North, Secord, George Cave, and a senior CIA official met in Paris on Saturday, March 8.[6] The Paris meeting opened with a few remarks by Ghorbanifar in which he tried to prove his importance to the affair, and that the supply of arms to Iran would help the U.S. fund the Contras in Nicaragua. He added that the hostage problem would be solved, in the end, only if the U.S. added more incentives. He claimed that Kengarlou's position in Tehran had been damaged after the Frankfurt meeting of February 25. In order to strengthen his own position, Ghorbanifar submitted a list of 240 items, including spare parts for Hawk missiles, 200 Phoenix missiles, and several Harpoon missiles—all in addition to the remaining 3,000 TOW missiles previously agreed upon. He concluded by announcing that Iran did not agree to holding the meeting on Kish Island, and suggested having it, after appropriate preparations, in Tehran.

North was furious at these new demands. He told Ghorbanifar

that he did not understand why Iran needed Phoenix and Harpoon missiles if the launchers it had for them were inoperative, as the U.S. knew full well. North added that the U.S. was still willing to participate in a high-level meeting, on Kish Island or anywhere else, to discuss Afghanistan and Soviet threats to Iran, but it was not willing to give Iran any more arms until the American hostages were freed, before or during the meeting.

Changing the venue of the meeting to Tehran did, however, create a security problem. Kish Island was within the range of the American fleet in the Persian Gulf; in Tehran there was no American military protection. Despite this, North made no objections to the new location.

The Paris meeting was a disappointment to all those who participated. Secord commented that a new channel should be sought because Ghorbanifar's channel was "obviously flawed." Cave made a similar comment: "The Israelis, particularly Nir, insisted on Ghorbanifar. I was at the other end, insisting he couldn't be trusted."[7] Poindexter was also angry that Iran dared make new demands. After being briefed by North, Poindexter made known his concern that the U.S.'s positions were not being presented to the decision makers in Tehran. He further charged that Ghorbanifar's only interest was in making the highest possible profits for himself. He said that he was fed up with the Iranian affair and wanted to cut it off entirely. "Forget it, it wasn't going anywhere," Poindexter said.[8] Nir again pleaded with North to leave the Ghorbanifar channel open. He claimed that Ghorbanifar controlled Kengarlou, and that it would be unwise to cut him out of the process. McFarlane, who had received a report on the Paris meeting, was also very worried. He asked North angrily: "Who the hell reports to us about the preparations for the Kish Island meeting—Nir or Ghorbanifar?"[9]

But the Iranian initiative did not end, nor was contact cut off with Ghorbanifar. President Reagan's concern about the fate of the hostages was so great that it overcame all other considerations. There was also overwhelming pressure from the families of the hostages. An American attempt to get the help of Syria and Algeria led nowhere, and the Iranians repeated their demands for the release of 17 Shiites arrested in Kuwait, charged with the bombing of the American and French embassies there. As for Ghorbanifar, everyone worried that circumventing him would encourage him to go public with the entire story.

On March 13 Ghorbanifar went to Tehran, returning to Paris four days later. Despite the original objections, the U.S. agreed to examine the possibility of supplying spare parts for Hawk missiles to Iran. In a conversation with Nir, Ghorbanifar said that he had talked to Majlis Speaker Hashimi Rafsanjani, Prime Minister Mir Hussein Mussavi, and to Ahmed Khomeini, the Ayatollah's son. He related that Khomeini the elder was "very sick" and the Mussavi had uncovered "Soviet penetration" of his office. Mussavi had said, Ghorbanifar reported, that despite the difficulties, the high-level meeting would take place "in the near future." Nir's impression was that Ghorbanifar was losing his credibility in Tehran, and he urged North to back him up by cooperating with him. Nir told North that Ghorbanifar had run into financial difficulties, and had complained that Albert Hakim had twice tried to convince Mohsen Kengarlou to communicate with the U.S. directly, and that there was no need for Ghorbanifar to be involved. Partly to reassure him, North invited Ghorbanifar to Washington.[10]

In the period between March 24 and April 2, 1986, Nir remained in constant contact with both North and Ghorbanifar. Nir tried, in his talks with North, to find out how much of the profits from the Hawk missile spare parts deal would be set aside for the purchase of the 504 replacement TOW missiles Israel had supplied Iran in the summer of 1985.[11] On April 2 Nir met with Ghorbanifar in London and discussed the various financial aspects of the new deal. The next day Ghorbanifar arrived in Washington on the Concorde, and his talks with North, Cave, and a CIA official, conducted that same evening at a small hotel in Herndon, Virginia, lasted until dawn.[12] Ghorbanifar called Tehran several times during the course of this conversation, clarifying various points with Kengarlou. The talks were recorded. Ghorbanifar claimed that Khomeini planned to publish an Islamic legal ruling (*fatwah*) prohibiting hostage taking. He said that McFarlane's visit could take place on April 19, and that McFarlane would meet Speaker Rafsanjani, who was himself overseeing the arrangements for the visit. McFarlane would also meet President Khamenei and Prime Minister Mussavi. It was agreed that the American delegation would be lodged in a spacious mansion and that it would have an independent communications system. North insisted that McFarlane meet with Rafsanjani first, and that the hostages then be freed, prior to delivery of the arms. North promised that the weapons would arrive in Bandar Abbas eight hours after the hostages were freed. Ghorbanifar, for his part, demanded that the Americans bring "samples" of the spare parts with them, and insisted on receiving other items as well, such as two radar systems and several mobile batteries of improved Hawk missiles.

Ghorbanifar and North agreed that the subjects to be discussed in Tehran would include aid to the Afghan rebels and Iran's willingness to give the rebels 200 TOW missiles out of every 1,000 the U.S. supplied. The U.S. also wanted to discuss the assistance Iran gave to the Sandinista regime in Nicaragua. North claimed that, in 1985 alone, Iran had supplied the Sandinistas with oil and arms worth some $100 million.

Ghorbanifar made sure to establish what his commission would be. He claimed that he had already paid out $300,000 in bribes to various Iranian officials, and that he should be reimbursed. The ever-generous North did not check Ghorbanifar's accounts, telling him that he could add any sum he thought he was entitled to.[13]

On April 7 Nir reported to North on his contacts with Kengarlou and Ghorbanifar. The Israeli claimed that Kengarlou did not trust Ghorbanifar, and that he trusted the U.S. even less. As for the sale of the spare parts, Nir told North that the "merchant"—Ghorbanifar—wanted $1.5 million for himself. He concluded by warning against any thought of leaving him, as Israel's representative, out of the process and out of the delegation to Tehran.

According to the schedule worked out at the beginning of April, Ghorbanifar was, on April 7, to transfer $15 million to an "appropriate account" in a Swiss bank (the Lake Resources account).[14] Out of this sum, $2 million would be used for buying TOW missiles to replace the original 504 missiles sold by Israel to Iran prior to the release of Reverend Benjamin Weir in September 1985. Lake Resources would pay the CIA $3.65 million for the spare parts for the Hawk missiles, and the rest would finance activities of the Contras and joint U.S.–Israeli covert activities.

Yet Iran again failed to keep to the timetable. Given its refusal to pay for the arms in advance, it was necessary to find interim funding, and urgently. In addition, as a result of internal disagreement in Tehran, there were now doubts about Iran's willingness to release the hostages before the promised weapons were received. All this made some Americans wonder whether Kengarlou and Ghorbanifar really could get the prisoners released.

The contradictions in the administration's Iran policy were receiving public expression as early as April 1986. Proof of Libya's involvement in international terror came out of a series of attacks in Europe, and in particular the bombing of a West Berlin nightclub frequented by American soldiers. On President Reagan's orders, the American air force bombed targets in Tripoli and Bengazi on April 15. By this act President Reagan proved his determination to use force to prevent attacks on American citizens and property. The military operation was directed by Admiral Poindexter, but the moving spirit behind it was Oliver North. Making use of detailed information about terrorist bases in Libya and up-to-date intelligence on Qadhafi's movements, the American planes hit the Libyan leader's house. Qadhafi was unharmed but one of his daughters was killed. In revenge, Hezbollah killed Peter Kilburn, one of its American hostages, on April 17. Two British hostages were also murdered, in response to the British government's decision to allow the American bombers to take off from bases on its territory.

America's forceful response underlined the administration's declared policy of using force against countries abetting terror. While the operation did not run completely smoothly, it achieved its goals, and Libya's active role in international terror shrank considerably.

Even after the success of the bombing, the U.S. continued to try to bring Qadhafi down. On North's orders, Albert Hakim on April 28, 1986, purchased the Danish ship Erria for covert operations,[15] to serve as a floating radio station for broadcasting anti-Qadhafi propaganda off the Libyan coast. Hakim bought the boat with money from one of his secret accounts in Geneva. He bought it for $312,000 through Dolmy Business, Inc., of Panama. It was remodeled to hold communications and broadcasting equipment, but in the end the propaganda project never got off the ground and the boat was assigned to other covert operations before it was resold.[16] (The *Erria* had been used in the past and continued to be used to carry arms to the Contras. On at least one occasion, on October 13, 1986, the ship was also involved in shipping Soviet-made Israeli arms from Haifa to the Contras, but after the revelation of the Iran-Contra affair, the *Erria* returned to Eilat and unloaded the weapons.[17])

The administration did not stop at that. After the bombing of Libya, Ghorbanifar notified Nir that he could establish contact with El-Waldi Hamadeh, "head of the Libyan internal security and a possible successor to Qadhafi."[18] Nir passed the information on to North. The proposal to set up a meeting with Hamadeh came just as the administration had received information of Iranian intentions to carry out terrorist attacks against American targets and of Qadhafi's interest in "buying" the American hostages from Hezbollah. These were understandably the cause of much concern in Washington. On May 13, 1986, and on Poindexter's orders, North asked Amiram Nir and Secord to meet Ghorbanifar in London to warn him that the renewal of terrorist activities by Iran was inconsistent with its interest in purchasing American arms,[19] and to hear more about the Libyan connection.

On May 15, 1986, after meeting with Ghorbanifar, Nir sent North—via Secord's secure line—additional details. He reported that his files revealed that Hamadeh was indeed chief of the Libyan security services, an adviser to Qadhafi on international terror, and a man with a wide range of contacts with terrorist organizations abroad. His position made him an expert on the terrorist bases in his country as well. Hamadeh was willing to meet North in Europe or elsewhere on seven days' notice, and was willing to commit himself to three things: halting Libyan terrorist actions against the U.S., formulating a timetable for the evacuation of terrorist bases from Libya, and the gradual transfer of Libyan foreign trade from the Communist bloc to the west. Ghorbanifar claimed that Hamadeh considered himself Qadhafi's heir. He also said that Hamadeh knew of the U.S.'s efforts to overthrow Qadhafi with the help of Libyan exiles in Europe. This would never be successful, he said.[20]

According to North, Nir passed along a request together with his report. In a memorandum to Poindexter dated May 15, North wrote that Nir had asked that his involvement in the Libyan contacts remain absolutely secret, for his own protection. "As you know," North wrote, "Nir is operating without the Mossad back-up, and has considerable concern about the CIA becoming more knowledgeable about his activities. Based on what Ghorbanifar has told us, Nir has reason to be concerned."[21] It is unclear exactly what would give Nir cause to worry, unless the information passed to North was classified and Nir was not authorized by the Mossad to release it. Despite North's message, no disciplinary action was taken against Nir. His actions were not a breach of the law.

North told this to Casey personally, and they agreed to continue preparations for a possible meeting with Hamadeh in Europe at the beginning of June, after the trip to Tehran. In order to protect Nir, however, they agreed to make the arrangements with Ghorbanifar directly and not through Nir. In the end, nothing came of the contacts with Hamadeh. The CIA looked through its files and discovered that, while Hamadeh was indeed a Libyan officer, he was very far from being the number two man in the country, as Ghorbanifar had claimed. The administration did not believe that it could overthrow the Libyan government with Hamadeh's help. Given the doubtful reliability of Ghorbanifar, Washington decided to abandon any Libyan initiative for the time being.

North's active involvement in the bombing of Libya led to his identification by Palestinian terrorist groups. The FBI told North in late April that Abu Bahr, spokesman for the Abu Nidal faction, had targeted him for assassination.[22] A State Department summary stated that the Abu Nidal group, which numbered 500 members, had killed 181 persons and wounded 200 others in two years. North asked the White House Chief of Staff to have a security system installed at his house, but he was told that he was not eligible. The Secret Service also refused to provide him with a bodyguard or to protect his family. The terrorist threats against him came at the height of the preparations for McFarlane's visit to Tehran. North told Secord of the threats; Secord, after consulting with Hakim, agreed to pay for the installation of a security fence around North's house at a cost of $13,900. "I did probably the grossest misjudgement that I have made in my life," North would later admit in his testimony to the congressional investigatory committees.[23]

This was the opportunity for the U.S. and Israel to end the

Iran initiative. In doing so, the two countries would have underlined their principles and their determination to fight international terror. But North and Nir were oblivious to Ghorbanifar's attempts to mislead them and ignored Iran's failure to keep any of its promises. They continued to chase after the "meeting at a senior level" as if this would solve all America's and Israel's problems.

On April 14 Ghorbanifar called Charles Allen of the CIA and told him that Iran had gone back on its agreement to free all the hostages either before or immediately after the arrival of the American delegation. The hostages would be freed one by one; in addition, there were new demands for other weapons. Poindexter reacted sharply.[24] In a note to North before the latter's planned April 18 trip to Frankfurt to meet Kengarlou, Ghorbanifar, and Nir, Poindexter stated that he had no objections to the visit to Frankfurt, but that North must make it clear to Kengarlou that the only acceptable order of events was the high-level meeting, the release of the hostages, with the Hawk spare parts coming last.

The Frankfurt meeting never took place. Ghorbanifar claimed that Kengarlou could not get out of Tehran. The other channels from Iran revealed, however, that Kengarlou and Ghorbanifar were not confident of their ability to gain the release of the American hostages. After a conversation with Nir on April 21, Secord notified North that "Adam [Nir] is quite pessimistic about second Iranian official [Kengarlou]–Ghorbanifar cabal, and knows time is nearly over."[25]

The contacts with Ghorbanifar nevertheless continued. Toward the end of April he announced to North that the internal situation in Lebanon was deteriorating, and that Libya had resumed its efforts to "buy" the hostages. Kengarlou's conclusion, as told to North, was that it was necessary to act quickly because time was running out in Beirut. Despite this alarm, and America's readiness in principle to participate in the meeting in Tehran, Ghorbanifar ran into trouble in the Iranian capital in his efforts to raise the money necessary to fund the purchase of the spare parts for the Hawk missiles. In early May Ghorbanifar again turned to Khashoggi for interim funding. This time, however, the Saudi millionaire said he could not put up the money himself. He and Ghorbanifar turned to Tiny Rowlands, a British businessman, arms merchant, and casino king, head of the giant Lonrho chain of stores.[26] In order to convince Rowlands that the arms deal with Iran was an official one, and that the Israeli and American governments were behind it, Khashoggi and Ghorbanifar took Amiram Nir with them to meet Rowlands. Here again Nir's lack of experience stood out: he apparently did not understand that, by participating in the meeting bringing a stranger into the secret of the Iran initiative, he was making it harder for the U.S. to deny having contacts with Iran. Nir told the British businessman that the matter was a huge transaction in which Iran would be supplied with large quantities of wheat, arms, and spare parts. Khashoggi showed Rowlands the receipts he had on the large transfers of money in Switzerland, and tried to convince him that putting up the necessary money would be profitable for him. Nir and Khashoggi told him that several businessmen were already taking part in the deal. They also told him that "in the American administration only four people know about it, and Secretary of State Shultz is not one of them."

Tiny Rowlands was so surprised by the story that he asked to confirm it with his Israeli friend, David Kimche. "If you want my opinion, don't touch it with a ten-foot pole," was Kimche's advice. Rowlands also went for confirmation to the U.S. embassy in London.[27] This led to Charles Price, the American ambassador in London, reporting to the State Department about the meeting Khashoggi, Nir, and Ghorbanifar had held with the British millionaire.

Shultz happened to be in Tokyo at the time, along with Reagan and Poindexter, for the summit meeting of the leaders of the industrialized nations. The secretary of state was astonished. Could it be that the White House was once again dealing with Iran behind his back, just when the U.S. was trying to ensure the support of its allies in its battle against international terrorism? Shultz spoke to Poindexter, in Tokyo, on May 4.[28] He told the national security adviser that he refused to be involved with people like Khashoggi and Ghorbanifar. Poindexter answered that "there was only a smidgen of truth" in the report, that "it's not our deal," and that Nir was pursuing an independent effort without any direct American involvement. Poindexter asked Ambassador Price to tell Rowlands not to get involved.

In a cable to North, Poindexter asked: "What the hell was Nir doing with Ghorbanifar and Khashoggi? You just can't trust those SOB's." North answered: "You're right—in this game we can't trust anyone. I've told Nir to steer clear and to stay off the skyline on this issue."[29]

But Khashoggi did not give up. Working through another wealthy Arab, he was able to get the necessary money from two Canadian businessmen, Ernst Miller and Donald Fraser, who were his partners in several business ventures in the U.S.[30] With the interim funding arranged, Nir and Ghorbanifar remained in London to meet on May 6 with North and Cave. The meeting took place at the Churchill Hotel and was meant to focus on the financial aspects of the spare parts deal. Because of Ambassador Price's telegram to Shultz, as well as the meeting with Tiny Rowlands, North came to London on a passport identifying him as "Goode," and he avoided all contact with the American embassy.

The conversation was a harsh one. North told Ghorbanifar that the matter of the high-level meeting had been going on for too long, and that if the arrangements were not made within the week, the U.S. would withdraw its agreement to participate. Ghorbanifar said that interim funding was no longer a problem, and that the delays in completing the arrangements for the American delegation's arrival were connected to disagreement over how the hostages should be freed in relation to the supply of the weapons. Ghorbanifar consulted with Kengarlou by telephone several times during the course of the meeting. The deputy prime minister repeated his promise that McFarlane would meet in Tehran with Khamenei, Mussavi, and Rafsanjani, and perhaps also with Khomeini's son.[31] Ghorbanifar suggested including Ayatollah Faresi as well. Faresi had run against the Islamic republic's first (and later deposed) President, Bani-Sadr, and was considered a leader of the rightists in Tehran who had good connections with the commercial interests concentrated in the bazaar. Kengarlou insisted, however, that McFarlane bring all the spare parts with him. George Cave then got on the line. He explained to Kengarlou that, simply from a technical point of view, there was no way to load the 240 Hawk missile components Iran wanted onto McFarlane's plane. With North's agreement and as a token of good faith, Cave suggested that the plane carry a small number of the parts on a single pallet. After the first meeting and the release of the hostages, a special plane would arrive with the rest. Iran demanded, however, that at least half of the parts come on McFarlane's plane. The final agreement was that the U.S. would make its best effort to cram as many parts onto McFarlane's plane as possible. After their delivery, an Iranian delegation would go to Beirut to receive the hostages. Immediately thereafter, an additional plane carrying the rest of the spare parts would arrive. Nir, who attended this meeting, would later confirm the contents of the agreement.[32]

The American position had again slipped. It was clear to both sides that this problem was not yet solved, and would cause complications when McFarlane arrived in Tehran. In order to prevent any last-minute mishaps, Nir and Ghorbanifar suggested a preparatory trip to Tehran. The idea had come up before, but when North spoke of it with Poindexter and Casey, the CIA director became frightened. He saw the tortured figure of William Buckley before him, as well as those of his cruel tormentors who had wrung more than 400 pages of confessions from him about the CIA's activities in the Middle East.[33] Charles Allen and Albert Hakim, who had heard the idea from Ghorbanifar during the February 25 meeting in Frankfurt, both thought that a preparatory trip would be madness. They argued that, in light of Iran's maneuvering, it was necessary to consider the possibility that North, as coordinator of the fight against international terror, would be too much of a temptation for the Iranians for them to allow him to leave Tehran. After the damage the CIA had suffered as a result of Buckley's capture, the U.S. could not permit itself any further such damage. Poindexter dismissed the idea at once.[34]

Poindexter argued that if there was a more senior person with the advance group, there would be less risk to the whole group. Poindexter thought that the Iranians would not dare to harm a group headed by a senior American representative. This view was echoed by Casey, who said: "This advance trip is so hidden, we are going to use non–U.S. government assets throughout, European or M.E. airlines, no U.S. air registration air flights. You might never be heard from again. The Government might disavow the whole thing."[35]

And so, despite the fact that North, Cave, Secord, and Nir recommended an advance trip, the idea was again rejected by Poindexter and Casey.

Despite the absence of a clear solution to the question of the amount of arms to be supplied in exchange for the release of the hostages, North reported to Poindexter that all the problems had been resolved. The preparations went into high gear. On May 14, Khashoggi deposited $10 million in the Lake Resources account at Crédit Suisse Bank in Geneva. Two days later he deposited an additional $5 million. In exchange he received from Ghorbanifar postdated checks in the sum of $18 million (including $3 million in service charges and interest). From the sum Khashoggi deposited, Secord transferred $6.5 million to the CIA account, with $8.5 million remaining in his own.[36]

It was at this point that Secord and Hakim decided to give "something of value" to North as a token of appreciation for his assistance to their private business. In light of the danger involved in the trip to Iran, Hakim suggested depositing $500,000 in a Swiss bank account under the name of North's wife, to pay the educational expenses of North's children. Secord thought that half a million dollars was too much, and decided that $200,000 was sufficient. The bank account was set up on May 20, 1986.[37] Hakim's attorney made an appointment with Mrs. Betsy North in Philadelphia and asked for personal details about her and her children. Hakim also included North as a beneficiary in his $2 million will.

In an indictment released by special prosecutor Lawrence E. Walsh, Secord and Hakim were accused of giving "things of value" to North, to encourage him to remain on the staff of the NSC, where he could make sure that Secord and Hakim "would continue to receive opportunities for substantial revenues and profits in connection with lucrative activities referred to them by North."

As part of the conspiracy, the indictment said, Willard I. Zucker, an American lawyer who worked formerly for the Internal Revenue Service and who is now directing a Swiss financial services company, Compagnie de Services Fiduciares S.A., traveled to Philadelphia and met with Elizabeth North, the colonel's wife, in order to make the necessary arrangements.

In testimony before Congress, Hakim acknowledged that the meeting was held at his suggestion and that Zucker told Mrs. North that her husband had an "anonymous admirer" who wished to help out with the university and educational expenses of the children.[38]

Later, North would give Congress his version. He said, "In the course of the discussion [about the trip to Tehran], Hakim said to me, 'If you don't come back, I will do something for your family.' By that point in time, I had come to know that Hakim was a wealthy man in his own right. When he suggested that my wife meet his lawyer in Philadelphia, I agreed that my wife should do so. The purpose, as I understood it, was that my wife would be in touch with the person who would, if I didn't return, do something for my family. My wife went to the very brief meeting. There was no money mentioned, no account mentioned, no amount mentioned, no will mentioned, no arrangement. The meeting focused on how many children I had, their ages, and a general description of my family. [It was] a brief meeting in the offices of Touche Ross, a respectable firm in Philadelphia. I then went and, thank God, returned safely from Iran. After that, there was no more contact with the lawyer. No money was ever transferred to my possession, control, account or that of my wife, or that of my children."[39]

The CIA now raised the question of Amiram Nir's participation in the American delegation. Given Casey's recommendation that "the next meeting with the Iranians should take place without the Israelis,"[40] the head of the Middle East division in the agency notified North of his objections to the inclusion of Nir. He believed that, were Nir's Israeli nationality to be discovered, it would lead to a crisis of confidence between the U.S. and Iran—and even worse, the Iranians might hold Nir hostage. This would create a moral problem for the American members of the delegation. They would have to decide whether to return to the U.S. and leave Nir behind—knowing that the Iranians were liable to torture him to death, or whether to remain in Tehran until Nir was released, extending their stay considerably. Nir enlisted the Israeli Prime Minister on his side. Peres consulted with Shamir and Rabin, the foreign and defense ministers. Nir passed on the message to North: Israel was ready to take the risk. The final decision was made by McFarlane, who agreed to include Nir in the delegation.[41]

This was a grave error, particularly in light of Ghorbanifar's presence in Tehran. Might he not betray Israel, as he had betrayed others, in order to improve his credibility with the Iranian government? It is easy to guess how much damage to Israel's intelligence system could be done in such a case. Iran would also win a valuable propaganda asset if it could tell the Arab world and Palestinian organizations that it held Nir. In fact, when the U.S. opened its second channel of communication with Iran, Rafsanjani's nephew revealed to North that Nir's presence in McFarlane's delegation had been known in Tehran. They played along, calling Nir by his code name "Miller"—to avoid creating a crisis with the U.S. at that time.

Neither was there any diplomatic reason for taking Nir along. In the atmosphere of suspicion between the U.S. and Iran, there was no chance that matters of interest to Israel would come up during the talks—not even the possibility of releasing Israeli soldiers captured or missing in action in Lebanon. Nir's presence did nothing more than strengthen the arguments of those who would later accuse Israel of dragging the U.S. into its Iranian adventure, and of preventing the U.S. from shaking off Ghorbanifar.

North's and Nir's inexperience was apparent also in the preparations for the visit. The trip was to begin on May 25, 1986, during the holy month of Ramadan, when Moslems—including, of course, all the Iranian officials they were to meet—fast from sunup to sunset.

The CIA prepared an intelligence file that included information about the Soviet buildup on its borders with Iran and Afghanistan.[42] This was given to Ghorbanifar by North and Secord in London on May 22. Immediately after receiving the material, Ghorbanifar flew to Tehran to complete the arrangements for the arrival of the American delegation. The CIA also prepared the radio equipment the Americans would need, assigning them satellite frequencies and two radio operators who would manage the contacts with the White House, via a command station to be set up by Secord in Israel.

Ghorbanifar would soon tell Nir and Charles Allen that McFarlane would receive a "very warm welcome" in Tehran, that the meetings with Rafsanjani, Khamenei, and Mussavi were "guaranteed," and, more important, that the American hostages would already be in Tehran when McFarlane arrived there.

McFarlane and Poindexter consulted with Casey and decided that the members of the delegation would be McFarlane, North, Howard Teicher (chief of the political-military department of the National Security Council), George Cave, and the two radio operators. Nir would join them in Israel. On Friday, May 23,

504 TOW missiles were flown to Israel to replace those previously sent to Iran, together with Hawk spare parts for Iran.[43] The total shipment weighed 45 tons. The equipment was brought to Israel in two chartered planes belonging to Southern Air Transport that took off from the Kelly air force base in San Antonio, Texas. One pallet would be loaded on an Israeli Boeing 707 from which all identifying markings had been removed, to be flown together with the delegation to Tehran by an American crew handpicked by Secord. An additional Israeli plane, also manned by Americans, containing the 12 pallets with the remaining spare parts, would be ready to take off for Tehran as soon as word of the release of the hostages was received. To preserve the highest level of secrecy, the takeoff and landing times of the planes were scheduled in such a way that the two crews did not meet. The crews knew nothing of their cargo, and received their flight instructions (from Eilat south over Saudi Arabia, looping north over the Gulf of Oman to Iran) only after arriving in Israel.

(The cargo of 504 TOW missiles sent to Israel caused consternation in the Israeli army. Examination of the equipment revealed that the missile batteries and the launching apparatus were damaged. Some of the missiles fell off the launching pads before being fired, releasing explosive materials that endangered the soldiers using them. On orders from the minister of defense, Yitzhak Rabin, the missiles remained in their boxes. Israel received replacements only five months later.)

On Friday afternoon, May 23, the American delegation arrived in Israel. The weekend was used by McFarlane and his associates to rest and to receive last-minute instructions about details connected with the release of the hostages. Since they all had their doubts about Ghorbanifar's ability to get the hostages from Beirut to Tehran, they suggested that the hostages—Father Lawrence Martin Jenco, Terry Anderson, David Jacobsen, and Thomas Sutherland—be brought to one of the few Western embassies remaining in the Lebanese capital, or to the hospital of the American University of Beirut. If, however, Hezbollah proved to be unwilling to take such a risk, the Americans would offer to have the hostages taken to the Lebanese army's military hospital, situated on the dividing line between the Moslem and Christian parts of Beirut.

Despite the careful planning and the thought given to every

detail, it seems that North was not, in fact, really confident that the hostages would be freed. Just before the Tehran mission began, North enlisted Secord's help in an effort to release the hostages. North called the Texan millionaire Ross Perot, and asked him for $1 million in cash as a ransom for the hostages.[44]

It was not surprising that North turned to Perot again. The Texan had provided money for purposes that the American government could not achieve officially since 1969. In that year he had been asked by President Nixon to put up ransom money for American prisoners of war in Vietnam. In 1979 he ransomed two of his employees who had been imprisoned in Tehran. When a mob of Iranian students overran the American embassy in Tehran in November 1979, taking 52 Americans hostage, the Carter administration asked his opinion of several rescue plans (none of which were used in the end).

In May 1985 —despite President Reagan's and Secretary of State Shultz's past statements that the American government would not negotate with terrorists or pay them ransom—Perot had received an urgent phone call from North requesting $200,000 in cash as ransom for William Buckley. Perot did not hesitate to hand over the $200,000, but nothing came of it. The mediator in the 1985 deal, a Canadian of Arab descent, went to Beirut and returned with a newspaper emblazoned with what he claimed was Buckley's signature. This was handed over to Buckley's secretary for identification, and was also examined in CIA laboratories. Both concluded that the signature was forged.[45] The Canadian middleman had, in the meantime, run off with the money.

Now, in May 1986, North went back to Perot. In light of past experience, Perot sent one of his own men to Cyprus, depositing the sum requested in a local bank in his agent's name. According to North's plan, once the hostages were freed, they would be taken by the ship Erria, that Hakim and Secord had bought, to Cyprus. But the plan collapsed: The contacts in Beirut demanded the money before releasing the hostages. This demand was rejected.[46] The man waited in Cyprus for seven days, and when no one came to get the money from him, he went home.

A similar disappointment awaited McFarlane in Tehran. The trip to Iran was meant to demonstrate the desire of the U.S.

to open a new era in its relations with the Khomeini regime, and reestablish its influence in this important country. American policy in the Gulf had blown this way and that ever since the Iran-Iraq War broke out in September 1980. At one time it overlooked the supply of military equipment to Iran by its allies in order to prevent the collapse of that country; yet, beginning 1984, when Khomeini seemed to have the upper hand, the U.S. switched sides and came to the rescue of Saddam Hussein by supplying Iraq with adequate intelligence. McFarlane's mission was intended to express a certain change in emphasis, if not in the fundamentals, in American policy. The U.S. was still interested in a draw in the Persian Gulf, one without victors and losers, but one which would nevertheless point to Iran's advantage over Iraq. In order to institutionalize an extended dialogue with Iran without resort to Israeli mediation and private arms traders, McFarlane was authorized to suggest the establishment of a permanent CIA station in Tehran (two officers). This would allow direct contacts with Washington without Israel's mediation.[47]

But McFarlane's trip was interpreted entirely differently by the Iranian leadership, at least as reflected in a series of interviews in the local and foreign press in which Speaker Rafsanjani declared that McFarlane's visit proved that "the U.S. is unable to defeat the Islamic Revolution,"[48] and that American leaders "are now coming to Iran on their knees." Khomeini only grew more stubborn, preventing any productive exchange between the two countries.

The Americans were well prepared for a friendly reception when they took off on Saturday night, May 25, and landed in the military section of Mehrabad Airport early the following morning. They had with them six burnished, handmade walnut-wood cases, each containing a Colt pistol, presents for the members of the Iranian delegation. North exited the plane carrying a large chocolate cake he had purchased in Tel Aviv, meant by him as a symbol of a new, sweet beginning to American-Iranian relations.[49]

No one was there to meet them. McFarlane had expected to see Rafsanjani at the airport. Ghorbanifar had, after all, been in Tehran for three days already, and the Americans had gone over the timetable with him several times. Two hours later, Ghorbanifar and Kengarlou finally showed up. The two apologized and claimed that the plane had landed early, even though a glance at the papers they had with them would have shown that it had landed at the agreed-upon time. (Of course, the fasting Iranians could not share the chocolate cake with the Americans. The cake was finally disposed of by the Iranian guards at the hotel, who broke their fast with it that evening.)[50]

Ghorbanifar arranged their passage through passport control, presenting the airport authorities with Irish passports for all the members of the delegation. McFarlane would later claim that he had traveled to Tehran on his diplomatic passport. He could not have known that Ghorbanifar had made photocopies of all his Irish passports. McFarlane's was made out in the name of Sean Devlin; Cave's identified him as "O'Neill." As they waited for the formal arrangements to be completed, the Iranian air force gave them a show. Four Phantom jets took off from the airport, and a few minutes later another quartet landed; other planes and helicopters circled overhead all the while. "It looks like they want to impress us and keep us from thinking that their military situation is as serious as we think," McFarlane sardonically noted to members of the delegation.

After a long wait, the delegation set out for Independence Hotel (formerly the Hilton), and took over the entire sixth floor, which was kept safe for them by dozens of Revolutionary Guards. One of the two radio operators remained on the plane at the airport, both to stand watch there and to maintain continuous contact between McFarlane at the hotel and Secord in Tel Aviv.

McFarlane had not, of course, expected a grand public welcome, but he had been sure he would receive a warm reception that would underline the importance of his arrival.[51] Instead, he found himself dealing with rough and insulting treatment. He noted his frustration in his first coded cable to Poindexter: "Try to picture what it would be like if, after a nuclear attack, a surviving tailor became Vice-President, a recent grad student became Secretary of State, and a bookie became the interlocutor for all discourse with foreign countries. While the principals are a cut above this level of qualification, the incompetence of the Iranian government to do business requires a rethinking on our part of why there have been so many frustrating failure[s] to deliver on their part."[52]

The first of the promises to be broken was that involving

the accommodations. In prior negotiations, as noted, it had been agreed that the delegation would be housed in a spacious estate far from prying eyes, in order to ensure the secrecy of the meeting. Ghorbanifar explained the change in plans as the result of the Ramadan fast—it would be impossible to get fresh food to a private residence, while at the hotel this was not a problem.

Ghorbanifar continued to make generous promises: "Matters are progressing in the right direction, don't worry, the hostages will be freed very soon, expect some surprises," and so on, but McFarlane lost confidence in his promises.[53]

The American and Iranian delegations finally met at 5:00 that evening, and it quickly became clear that Ghorbanifar had again made a fool of the Americans. In order to get McFarlane and North to Tehran, he had misrepresented the significance of things said to him, lied to both sides, and completely distorted the framework of the negotiations. McFarlane, who had in the past been received by heads of state and government ministers around the world and who wielded great power, found himself facing Kengarlou and a few minor officials, who were frightened, confused, and helpless. The subjects that McFarlane wished to raise were of no interest to them, and they in any case lacked the power to make any decisions. So, after the normal formalities, and after hearing McFarlane's official message—that the U.S. accepted the Islamic Revolution as a fact, would not try to overthrow it, and was ready to put its relations with Iran on a new footing—the Iranian officials turned the conversation to what they considered its real purpose. Why hadn't the Americans brought more Hawk missile parts? Why were the parts they had brought old and not in their original packaging? Didn't that indicate a lack of good faith on the part of the Americans and raise even more suspicions about American intentions?

It seemed that even before the Americans had left the airport, Revolutionary Guards had unloaded the plane and made known their disappointment at the small quantity of equipment they had found. McFarlane argued that Iran had not kept its promises and had not released the American hostages. He added that he had cabinet rank and that he should be meeting with decision makers and not with minor officials. Kengarlou insisted that there had been no promises that McFarlane would meet with a government minister. McFarlane then exited and left the talks to North.

It was clear that Ghorbanifar was at fault, having deceived North about the commitments he had received from the Iranians. In any case, the Iranian leadership, after an internal debate, the next day upgraded the delegation, but it still did not include anyone of cabinet rank—McFarlane would meet no ministers during his entire four-day stay in Tehran. The reconstituted Iranian team now included the chairman of the Majlis's Foreign Affairs Committee, Mohammed Ali Hadi Najafabadi, who was close to Speaker Rafsanjani and had Prime Minister Mussavi's support as well; Ali Mohammed Bisharati, senior deputy to the foreign minister; Deputy Foreign Minister Hossein Sheikh El-Islam Zadeh, who served as a sort of "governor-general" of the Shiite terrorist groups in Lebanon; and the head of the political department in the Foreign Ministry, Mohammed Lavassani.

The Americans soon learned that, in addition to President Khamenei, Speaker Rafsanjani, and Prime Minister Mussavi, two ministers had also been party to the secret of McFarlane's arrival: Minister of the Interior Moghtashemi and Minister for Intelligence Affairs Hajjotelislam Mohammed Reishari. Also involved, although not as deeply, were Ahmed Khomeini, the Ayatollah's son; the deputy commander of the Revolutionary Guards, Sham Khani, who was in charge of the protection of the Americans and their plane; and Sadegh Tabatabaï, Khomeini's son-in-law and one of Rafsanjani's closest advisers. Rafsanjani would eventually include his son and his three cousins, all of whom did business in Germany, in which they had made large profits thanks to their connections in Tehran. These relatives of the Speaker did not meet with the Americans in Tehran, but one of them would later become a link in the "second channel" of communication between the White House and the Iranian regime.

But why did none of Iran's three most powerful officials (other than Khomeini himself)—Khamenei, Mussavi, and Rafsanjani—agree to meet with McFarlane? The members of the Iranian delegation were frank. They said that the leadership appreciated the importance of the dialogue with the U.S., but were acting on the basis of the experience of a previous meeting between an American national security adviser and an Iranian Prime

Minister. In the autumn of 1979, Zbigniew Brzezinski, President Jimmy Carter's national security adviser, had met with Iranian Prime Minister Mehdi Bazargan in Algiers. Bazargan had been dismissed two days later. Rafsanjani, Mussavi, and Khamenei now realized the need for cooperation with the U.S. in several areas, but their more immediate problem was how to remain in the good graces of a <u>fanatic religious establishment that they did not completely control.</u>

During the course of the lengthy, exhausting talks, there were some interesting and useful exchanges in which the two sides clarified their positions on a large number of issues.[54] In conversations with Najafabadi, for instance, McFarlane impressed on him that, while the U.S. accepted Khomeini's regime and would not act against it, it also expected Iran to commit itself to respect the sovereignty, independence, and territorial integrity of its neighbors, and refrain from efforts to export its Islamic Revolution to them. McFarlane explained the principles of U.S. policy in the Middle East, emphasizing the Soviet Union's ambitions in the Persian Gulf region. He said that the Soviet Union would never allow Iran to win the war, because an Iraqi defeat would damage Moscow's credibility in the Arab world. The Soviets would therefore supply Iraq with all her military needs, and if that did not suffice, they would not hesitate to build up forces on the Iranian border in order to force Tehran to divide its forces between two fronts. Howard Teicher told the Iranians that the Soviets had some 26 divisions near the Iranian border, and that the Soviet army regularly rehearsed its plans for an invasion of Iran. Soviet units even crossed the Pakistani border occasionally, he said, in order to help underground movements there; Soviet agents also operated in Iran. The U.S. was interested in balancing this Soviet activity by aiding Iran, but since Khomeini seemed to the U.S. to be interested in carrying his revolution onward to the Persian Gulf states, the U.S. could not supply him with large amounts of weapons.

With the goal of reestablishing trust and improving relations between the two countries, McFarlane made three proposals: that Iran moderate the tone of its propaganda against its pro-Western Arab neighbors and against the U.S.; that within the next two weeks, after the release of the hostages, there be another meeting, in Tehran, Europe, or even in the U.S., in which the entire spectrum of relations between the two countries could be discussed; and that they install a reliable communications network that the Soviets could not listen in on. This would make it possible to maintain direct contact between the U.S. and Iran without the involvement of other parties.

The Iranians, for their part, also succeeded in making their intentions clear. They boasted that Khomeini's revolution was more important than the French or Bolshevik revolutions. Iran, they said, did not want to identify itself with either East or West, and wanted to have proper relations with both camps. In their relations with the U.S.S.R., the Iranians also continually emphasized the need for patience and for the reestablishment of mutual trust. For example, when Leonid Brezhnev died in 1982, Iran had sent an official delegation to his funeral. The religious establishment had been furious. Khomeini took the lesson to heart. When Chernenko died in 1985, Iran sent no representative, they noted.

Iran was aware of the Soviet threat, they insisted. They needled the Soviets just as they did the Americans. For example, a strong powerful religious awakening was underway in the U.S.S.R.'s Central Asian republics; the Koran was being widely and illegally disseminated, with Iran's encouragement. Iran's assistance to the Afghan rebels was also a thorn in the Soviets' side. Iran had training camps for the rebels on its territory, and supplied them with weapons and other equipment. The Russians were constantly complaining that Soviet soldiers were being killed by Iranian weapons. When North asked if the supply of TOW missiles to the Afghan rebels would improve their ability to face Soviet tanks, the Iranians answered that they were willing to set aside 200 out of every 1,000 TOWs that the U.S. supplied for the Afghans. But the real problem for the Afghan rebels, they said, was not tanks but gas bombs and napalm. Many of them had died from burns and poison gas. They needed medical help urgently. Despite their heavy losses, they were still fighting; their fortifications were decorated with pictures of Khomeini. This frightened the Soviets and was the reason for their pressure on Iran. The Iranians concluded this section of the talks with a folk proverb: "It's not easy to sleep next to an elephant you've wounded."

The single largest issue remained the hostages. The Iranians again tried to extort more from McFarlane than had been agreed to previously. Erroneously assuming that McFarlane would not want to return to Washington empty-handed, the Iranians tried to exhaust him with sterile debate. Their strategy guided by another folk proverb, "patience brings victory," the Iranians dragged out the talks, engaged the Americans in long disputations over minor points, and made unreasonable demands. Only after McFarlane told them explicitly that he was leaving Tehran did they suddenly feel themselves under pressure. Then they began speeding up the talks, proposing the immediate release of two hostages, and pleading with the Americans to remain in Tehran in order to discuss the release of the other two hostages and the supply of additional military equipment to Iran. McFarlane stood immovable and rejected the compromise. "I'm sorry, it's too late. Release them all, or none of them," he declared. His opponents, unfortunately, were not used to that kind of negotiating, and in the end McFarlane would return to Washington and the hostages remain in Beirut.

McFarlane's heroic posture was unproductive because he had no experience with Iranian bargaining. In the tradition of the bazaar, Iranian diplomats ask a high opening price and agree in the end to something much lower. McFarlane was furious when the Iranians presented him at first with Kengarlou and a handful of powerless minor officials. Yet this was done on purpose in order to demonstrate their contempt for him and to put him on the defensive. They pursued their strategy with the reconstruction of their negotiating team the next day at a higher level, still without including any of the country's top decision makers among them. When McFarlane demanded to meet cabinet members, both Kengarlou and Najafabadi, chairman of the Foreign Affairs Committee of the Majlis, answered that such a thing had never been promised, and that all Iran had offered was a preparatory meeting between North and Ghorbanifar. Najafabadi was "startled" when McFarlane said that Ghorbanifar had promised meetings with Rafsanjani, Khamenei, and Mussavi. Najafabadi's conclusion was that "Ghorbanifar lied to both parties."

The Iranians had a clear and consistent message for the Americans during the entire four days of talks: They wanted a dialogue with the U.S., were ready for negotiations on the rehabilitation of the relations between the two countries, and were interested in receiving arms and technical help from the Americans—but the progress had to be slow and cautious. There were too many painful memories from the past for it to be otherwise, they said. The U.S.'s sheltering of the Shah had poisoned the atmosphere between them and the American efforts to undermine the Islamic Revolution had deepened the distrust. They quoted Khomeini: Iran, he had said, was willing to have relations with every country in the world other than Israel and South Africa. They noted, however, that they would have to prepare public opinion for the renewal of ties with the U.S. The presence of the American delegation was a step in the right direction. Yet before Iran could make its "humanitarian gesture" and press its allies in Lebanon to free the hostages, it was necessary to increase the trust between the two countries gradually. This could be done only by supplying the rest of the Hawk missile parts that had been promised, and by a willingness to supply Iran with additional weapons. Najafabadi, for example, mentioned a long-term agreement of $2.5 billion.

At one point the Iranians also brought up the subject of the price they would pay for the weapons supplied them. They claimed that the U.S. had overcharged them. Ghorbanifar had told them that the weapons cost $24.5 million, but the original American price lists had revealed that the price was much lower. The Americans refused to enter this trap, however. The pricing issue and Iran's refusal to pay the amounts agreed upon would cause many difficulties in the coming weeks, and was one of the factors that, in the end, led to the revelation of the Iran affair.

However, despite these "declarations of intent," negotiations continued. On Tuesday, May 27, the Iranians presented the Americans with Hezbollah's conditions for freeing the hostages. The talks began at 10:00 A.M. and went on nonstop until 2:00 A.M. the following morning. The conditions were: Israeli withdrawal from the Golan Heights, Israel's evacuation of its security zone in south Lebanon, the dissolution of the Israel-supported South Lebanon army and the extradition of General Antoiné Lahad to East Beirut, the release of the 17 El-Da'awa prisoners in Kuwait, and payment for the cost of feeding the American hostages during their imprisonment in Lebanon. When they noticed the astonishment on the faces of the Americans, the Iranians quickly calmed them: "Don't worry, we know these conditions are exaggerated. We don't expect the U.S. to pay

Hezbollah for the costs they incurred in maintaining the hostages. We'll cover that. But we expect the U.S. to make it up to us elsewhere, by supplying the arms and military equipment that we requested."

At North's recommendation, McFarlane met Najafabadi for a private conversation that lasted three hours. He made it clear to him that the conditions could not serve even as a basis for negotiation. If, that night, all four hostages were not released in Beirut, the American delegation would return to Washington, he said.

This set off a mad race with the clock. Late at night the two delegations met again. The Iranians claimed to have news: they had succeeded in persuading Hezbollah to withdraw all its demands with the exception of the release of the 17 El-Da'awa prisoners in Kuwait. McFarlane, for his part, said that he could not make any commitment on that issue, and that the U.S. could not force another sovereign government's hands. At 11:00 P.M., McFarlane had another face-to-face meeting with the head of the Iranian delegation. He set the deadline for the release of the hostages at 4:00 A.M. Najafabadi appeared to be surprised to hear that Kengarlou and Ghorbanifar had promised to release the hostages before receiving all the Hawk missile spare parts. Deputy Prime Minister Kengarlou asked for an extension until 6:00 A.M. McFarlane was willing, but in order to prove he was serious he told Najafabadi to see to the refueling of the "American" plane so that it would be ready to take off.

In the early morning hours of May 28, as McFarlane grabbed a short nap, North, Nir, and the Iranians reached an agreement. Two hostages would be released immediately, and the remaining two would be freed after the supply of the remaining Hawk components. In accordance with the agreement, which was translated into Persian by Cave and Ghorbanifar, the Israeli plane with the rest of the spare parts was ordered to take off for Tehran. If, however, the remaining two hostages were not released by 4:00 A.M., the plane would not land in Tehran and would return immediately to Israel. North seemed to think this was a great achievement, and he woke up McFarlane to tell him about it. McFarlane was furious at the deviation from his instructions, and despite the fact that the plane had already been in the air for some hours, he called Secord on a secret channel and ordered it back to Tel Aviv.

This was yet another illustration of the different conceptions of the whole Iran initiative held by North and Nir on the one hand and by McFarlane on the other. Ghorbanifar would later testify that North and Nir were "in panic" at McFarlane's attitude,[55] and wanted to leave Tehran with something to show for themselves. McFarlane, however, stood fast on principle. He reasoned that the U.S. could not allow itself to be blackmailed by a country like Iran, and believed that the prestige of the U.S. was in the balance. Had he given in to Iranian blackmail, he would have laid the basis for further kidnappings, which in fact took place. He understood that the hostages were cards for Khomeini's regime to play, and that the Iranian leaders would do all they could to make sure they always had a few such cards in hand. He wanted to make it clear that there was a limit beyond which it was impossible to take advantage of President Reagan's concern for the hostages, and he reiterated to the Iranians that, without the release of all the hostages, the rest of the equipment they wanted would not arrive. Both Kengarlou and Najafabadi tried their best to delay the departure of the American delegation. They had received their extension until 6:00 A.M., but that hour arrived and no progress had been made. McFarlane ordered the Americans to leave the hotel and set out for the airport. Najafabadi pleaded with McFarlane to agree to the release of two hostages. McFarlane was insistent: "We kept our part of the agreement, and you haven't."

At 8:00 A.M. Kengarlou appeared at the airport and announced that "as a gesture of good faith" Hezbollah had agreed to release two prisoners immediately. He asked the Americans to delay their departure by six hours, to allow additional negotiations that would lead to the release of the rest of the hostages and the supply of the spare parts. McFarlane did not give in. He told Kengarlou to tell his superiors that Iran had, for the fourth time, failed to live up to its commitments, and that it would be a long time before it would be possible to restore trust between the two sides.

At 8:55 A.M., North and Nir almost in tears,[56] the plane took off from Tehran, landing in Israel a few hours later. McFarlane's mission was a complete failure; the continued captivity of the hostages was an open wound. The only positive achievement in Tehran was the agreement to continue secret contacts between the two countries via a reliable communications system. Upon returning to Washington, McFarlane on May 29, 1986, reported to President Reagan and Vice President Bush about the Tehran mission. He suggested ending the Iran initiative and cutting off all contacts with Ghorbanifar.[57] He also recommended taking one of the two covert operations—Iran or the Contras—away from North. But, as had happened after his meeting with Ghorbanifar in London on December 8, 1985, McFarlane was thwarted by North's determination, Nir's attachment to his Iranian game, and the greed of Ghorbanifar and Secord. Despite the failure of the Tehran mission, North continued to coordinate both operations, and Nir continued to be the link between the U.S. and Ghorbanifar.

The mission's failure gave rise once again to thoughts of rescuing the hostages by force. At Poindexter's request, CIA chief William Casey intensified intelligence-gathering efforts in Lebanon, trying to find out where exactly the hostages were being held. According to information from various sources, they were in the El-Salum neighborhood of Beirut. Poindexter accordingly wrote to North: "I'm beginning to think seriously about a rescue effort. Is there any way we can get a spy into Hayy El-Salum area? In time maybe we could probably move covertly some people into Yarze as well."[58] (Yarze is a Christian suburb in East Beirut, not far from the presidential mansion in Ba'abda.)

North reported back to Poindexter on June 3. "Dick [Secord] has been working with Nir on this. They developed Druze contacts. Dick now has three men in Beirut and a 40-man Druze force working for us. Dick rates the chances of success no greater than 30 percent, but that's better than nothing."[59]

Nothing came of this, however, because neither the U.S. nor Israel succeeded in pinpointing where the hostages were. At one point the CIA made use of an agent named Mundhir El-Qassar, who had some links with Abu El-Abbas of *Achille Lauro* fame. But despite the large amount of money he received, El-Qassar was not able to produce any information of real value that would justify the risk of a military operation.

All these failures should have demanded clear decisions

about the Iran initiative. Nevertheless, it continued. In the coming weeks, a strange interdependence had developed between the parties: President Reagan wanted the hostages; Israel wanted a link to Tehran; Iran wanted weapons, while Ghorbanifar and Kengarlou wanted to make money. Like in a Greek tragedy, all the actors continued to play until the tragic end.

Exposure

The two Iranian messengers who arrived in Beirut from Damascus on October 27, 1986, made their way through the narrow alleys of the Shiite neighborhood of Museitbeh, very close to the "Green Line" separating the Christian and Moslem parts of the Lebanese capital, arriving finally at the modest building housing the staff of the *El-Shira'a* newspaper. They spent more than three hours telling Hassan Sabra, the 44-year-old editor of the little-read weekly, all they knew about Robert McFarlane's visit to Tehran. The two had been sent by Mehdi Hashemi, a relative and supporter of Ayatollah Ali Montazeri, Khomeini's heir-apparent. They left no doubt with their Lebanese comrade that their purpose was to frustrate Majlis Speaker Rafsanjani's hopes of rehabilitating relations with the United States, and to prevent the release of the American hostages kidnapped by Hezbollah in Beirut.

Their story was sensational, but even Sabra, a sharp newspaperman, could not grasp its potential explosiveness. He understood the revelation to be part of Montazeri's and Rafsanjani's battle for power in Iran. Since the Speaker controlled all government institutions, Montazeri had little chance of exposing the scandal in the Tehran newspapers.

This was not Montazeri's first attempt to publicize the infor-

mation he had received from Ghorbanifar's detailed letter about
the contacts between Tehran and Washington. Although Ghorbanifar denies that he had sent such a letter to Montazeri,
two former U.S. officials confirmed that the Reagan administration obtained a copy of it in late October. Ghorbanifar would
only say: "People betray me, I betray them. People are honest,
I give everything. If not, I cut their throat."[1] At the beginning
of October, several hundred leaflets had been distributed in
the streets of Tehran, condemning "leaders who have had contacts with the U.S. and who have negotiated with American
representatives." At that time Revolutionary Guards in Tehran
had also kidnapped Iyad Mahmoud, a Syrian diplomat who in
1982 had played an active role in the release of the American
hostage David Dodge, and who was thus aware of the contacts
between Iran, Hezbollah, and the U.S. Montazeri's faction hoped
this would frustrate Rafsanjani's efforts to achieve a break-
through in relations with the U.S. Mahmoud was released some
hours later, after Rafsanjani personally intervened.

The leaflets had not made much of an impression on the
public. They were judiciously worded and did not name names,
neither of the Iranians in contact with the U.S. nor of McFarlane.
The leaflet was put out by Mehdi and Hadi Hashemi, the members of the Revolutionary Guard command responsible for exporting the Islamic Revolution to Moslem countries around
the globe. Hadi Hashemi was Montazeri's son-in-law, and his
arrest in late October 1986, along with that of his brother,
was immediately interpreted as part of the succession struggle
in Tehran, an attempt to reduce the influence of Khomeini's
designated heir. This impression was strengthened when the
minister for intelligence affairs, Hajjotelislam Reishari, ordered
the arrest in Isfahan—considered Montazeri's power base—of
several hundred local activists and Revolutionary Guard commanders on charges of cooperating with the Hashemi brothers.
Among those detained were Mehdi Hashemi's son, Ahmed,
and two members of the Majlis, Eydi Mohammed Mirzai and
Mohammed Jaafar Sadgianifar. In a letter to Khomeini broadcast
on Tehran Radio,[2] Reishari accused Mehdi Hashemi of having
worked for the Savak under the Shah, and charged that the
two brothers had "committed murder, kidnapping, and illegal
arrests—both before and after the revolution—and that they
had held illegal guns and military equipment, had fabricated

documents, and initiated covert activities meant to create disturbances and divide the people."

In his response, also broadcast on the radio, Khomeini emphasized that the suspicions against Mehdi Hashemi were "justified," and that they were strengthened by the "poisonous atmosphere created by anti-revolutionary elements linked to this group, who aspire to divert the Islamic republic from the path of the Islamic Revolution." Khomeini granted Reishari "full authority" to continue the interrogation of those arrested and "of those still to be˙ arrested," in order to protect the country's security and "defend Islam."[3] Thus, without mentioning Montazeri's name, Khomeini suddenly threw him off balance. Montazeri seemed unable to defend his associates, raising questions about whether he would really succeed Khomeini. The confusion was increased by Mehdi Hashemi's detailed confession to all the charges against him. He asked Montazeri to forgive him for his sins, acknowledged having betrayed the trust of the heir-apparent, and called upon his followers to fall in behind "Khomeini's line."[4] On September 28, 1987, Mehdi Hashemi was executed.

Reishari was among those who had been in on the secret of McFarlane's visit to Tehran. After having been responsible for the elimination of the followers of Ayatollah Shariat Madari and of the former foreign minister, Sadek Qotbzadeh, in 1983 he liquidated the major activists of the Tudeh, the Iranian Communist party. His determined campaign against Mehdi and Hadi Hashemi immediately gave rise to suspicions that he intended to destroy Montazeri's entire following. For his part, Montazeri remained secluded at home and a split developed within the religious establishment. His loyalists and the supporters of the Hashemi brothers distributed leaflets in Tehran accusing Rafsanjani's men of "a plot to destroy the revolution."

They did not leave it at that. They decided to expose McFarlane's visit to Tehran, with the help of their Lebanese supporter, Hassan Sabra. The leaders of the Islamic Revolution had taken note of Sabra immediately after Khomeini ended his exile in Iraq and left for France. Sabra became part of Khomeini's entourage and, upon Khomeini's return to Tehran in February 1979, he lived for a time in Montazeri's house in Qom and became friendly with his son, Mohammed Montazeri, and with Mehdi Hashemi. When Montazeri was chosen to be Khomeini's successor, Sabra played up the story in his newspaper. He continued to cover the power struggles in the religious establishment and at the top of the Iranian regime. So, when the two Iranian messengers came to him and gave him the stunning details of McFarlane's visit to Tehran, as well as of the arrest of the Hashemi brothers, he saw the publication of the story as the payment of a debt of honor to Montazeri—without realizing at all the effect it would have in Washington. In fact, Sabra hesitated to publish the story, not wanting to get caught up in an internal Iranian dispute. The issue of El-Shira'a that he had put out the week that the two envoys came to see him had run an article criticizing the way Iran was conducting the Gulf War; and an anonymous phone caller had threatened Sabra's life. Therefore the Lebanese journalist expressed his doubts to his two guests about provoking further antagonism. They suggested that he come with them to Tehran in order to hear the story from Revolutionary Guard commanders who had seen McFarlane's plane with their own eyes at Mehrabad Airport, and from others who had guarded the American party at the Independence Hotel in the Iranian capital.

His wife and colleagues feared for his life, but Sabra went ahead and published the news of McFarlane's visit on one of the inside pages of the newspaper on November 2, 1986.

Signs, both political and financial, of the storm about to hit Washington in November had already been apparent immediately after McFarlane returned from Tehran. The failure of the mission left the latest arms deal dangerously dangling. While the Iranians had taken one pallet of parts from McFarlane's plane, they refused to pay Ghorbanifar until they received the rest of the parts.[5] Ghorbanifar had received his interim funding from Khashoggi for a period of one month, and any delay in repaying it would mean incurring interest payments of $1.5 million a month. The U.S. was willing to supply the rest of the parts, but only if the hostages were released. Israel, while not involved in the financing of the deal, was worried. Its leaders feared that cutting off contact with Ghorbanifar would mean the end of the Iran initiative and immeasurable damage to Israel's prestige in the U.S. because of the failure of the initiative in which Israel was involved.

On June 6, Ghorbanifar called Nir and asked him to arrange

an additional meeting with North.[6] The Iranian arms merchant claimed that the failure of the McFarlane mission was the result of internal disagreements in Iran and of McFarlane's obstinacy in rejecting the offer to free two hostages in exchange for the Hawk spare parts. Nir made it clear to Ghorbanifar that without the release of the hostages there would probably not be any more talks between the two sides. On June 13, Kengarlou spoke with "Sam O'Neill" (Cave) on the telephone, confirming that Iran controlled Hezbollah and would see to the release of two hostages in exchange for the rest of the spare parts.[7] Two additional hostages would be freed after America supplied radar systems for the Hawk missiles. Kengarlou claimed that such an exchange could have been made while McFarlane was in "Dubai" (Tehran), but that it was still not too late. Cave repeated McFarlane's position—release of the hostages had to come before the weapons were supplied. In any case, in order to prevent further misunderstandings, Cave suggested meeting in Germany in order to try to solve the problem. Afterward, there could be another meeting in "Dubai."

The day after this conversation Kengarlou notified Ghorbanifar that he was prepared to come to a meeting with North and Nir in Germany, but the Americans would have to supply Iran first with the rest of the spare parts and the two radar systems. "If we receive all the equipment, we will release all the hostages. If the Americans supply only half the amount, we will release only half of the hostages," Kengarlou said.[8]

During the second half of June the Iranians again raised an additional problem—the price of the spare parts. In a conversation with Ghorbanifar on June 30, Kengarlou claimed that the U.S. was asking a price six times higher than their actual worth. Ghorbanifar protested, claiming that Kengarlou was bringing up the price only in order to divert attention from his mishandling of the release of the hostages. Ghorbanifar claimed that his profit margin was "no more than 40 percent."[9]

In actual fact, the price question did not come as a surprise. It came up first while McFarlane was in the Iranian capital. As noted, Ghorbanifar had purchased the spare parts from the U.S. for $15 million, and he paid Khashoggi an additional $3 million in interest and service charges. He asked the Iranians, however, for $24.5 million. While they were in Tehran, Ghorbanifar whispered to Cave that "should the Iranians raise the issue

of the price, please tell them that $24.5 million is all right."
When North and Cave asked Nir about this, he answered, "Don't
worry, the price is OK. There were a lot of overhead costs in
this deal."[10]

Now, when the Iranians raised the price issue again, Ghorbanifar proposed an "incentive" to Kengarlou. The U.S. would
add a small gift to the remaining spare parts—ten generators
for operating Hawk missile radar systems—and would even
send American technicians to care for them. The U.S. rejected
the proposal, and on President Reagan's instructions it was
decided to cut off contact with the Iranians until the hostages
were released.

On June 24, Nir informed North that Kengarlou was willing
to make a gesture and release a single hostage. Nothing actually
happened, however. On the contrary, in conversations with
Ghorbanifar, Kengarlou again brought up the price. Neither
North nor Nir, however, was willing to start renegotiating this
part of the deal with Ghorbanifar.

In the face of Ghorbanifar's increasing difficulties as a result
of Khashoggi's pressure to get his interim funding back, Nir
looked for ways to make some sort of progress on the hostage
issue. Toward the Fourth of July and its attendant centenary
celebrations of the Statue of Liberty, Nir came up with an
original idea. On June 30, he proposed that Ghorbanifar telephone Kengarlou and ask him for Iran to make a gesture by
releasing the Reverend Martin Jenco, so that he might take
part in the celebrations. Ghorbanifar notified Nir the next day
that Iran was willing to make such a gesture. But in a conversation with Cave, Kengarlou continued to insist that the U.S.
would have to lower the price of the spare parts and radar
systems. When they spoke, also on June 30, Cave informed
Kengarlou that "the president of our company" (Reagan) had
been insulted by the way McFarlane had been treated in "Dubai," and by the renewed haggling over prices, and had ordered
cutting off all contacts. Cave added that "Goode" (North) and
he were in trouble, since they were the ones who had recommended continuing the contacts with Iran.[11]

To everyone's surprise, and despite the fact that the price
and hostage problems had not been solved, Nir informed North
on July 2 that Ghorbanifar had promised that one hostage
would be released the next day. Nir, however, expressed doubts

as to whether the Iranians would effect the release. North was so overcome by the news that he forgot the disappointments of the past and immediately sent a debriefing team to Wiesbaden, West Germany. Reality, unfortunately, again slapped him in the face when nothing happened.

Poindexter reprimanded North severely for the false alarm. He claimed that, on the basis of Nir's expectations and Ghorbanifar's promises, he had informed the President, the State Department, and other government offices of the impending release of the hostage. Now he was in a delicate position and his credibility was liable to be damaged. North was also frustrated, and after the reprimand he cut off contact with Nir and refused to speak to him on the telephone for three weeks.[12]

The ongoing contacts on Iran between Israel and the U.S. during this period were carried out through Charles Allen, a CIA official.[13] Nir was hurt badly by this "punishment" but made no response. On the contrary, he redoubled his efforts and urged Ghorbanifar to act with more determination in Tehran. Nir told him that Iran had "missed a great opportunity" in not freeing even one hostage. In a letter to Kengarlou written on July 8,[14] copies of which were sent to Nir and North, Ghorbanifar repeated his arguments. He claimed that Iran was exaggerating the importance of the hostages. In America several thousand people are killed each year in automobile accidents alone. What were four hostages worth as against these thousands of dead Americans? In his letter to Kengarlou, Ghorbanifar claimed that, as a gesture in response to the release of the Reverend Benjamin Weir in September 1985, the U.S. had condemned Iraq for the use of poison gas bombs, and had called the Mujahidin Khalk movement headed by Masoud Rajavi a "terrorist organization." The U.S. had also supplied Iran with up-to-date intelligence on the Iraqi army and, during McFarlane's visit, had given Iran information on Soviet activity in Afghanistan and on Soviet intentions with regard to Iran. In light of this history, if the hostage issue was not solved soon, President Reagan would cut off contacts with Iran "once and for all."

Ghorbanifar spoke with Kengarlou several times in Tehran, and Nir himself went to Europe and, with the approval of Peres and Rabin, proposed supplying the Iranians with a small quantity of Israeli-made weapons as an incentive to free the hostages.

Finally, on July 21, Iran decided to make a "humanitarian

gesture" and free a single hostage. On July 23, Nir informed Charles Allen that the candidate for release was the Reverend Lawrence Martin Jenco, but asked him not to notify North, "so as not to create exaggerated expectations."

Nir was at that time in London, and together with Ghorbanifar he tried to confirm that Kengarlou would indeed keep his promise this time. On July 24, Jenco was separated from the other hostages and taken to one of the villages near Lake Kar'oun in Lebanon's Bekaa Valley. On July 26 he was handed over to Lebanese authorities, who transferred him to a Syrian army outpost in the valley. From there he was immediately sent on to Damascus, where he was handed over to the American ambassador. A few hours later Jenco was in Wiesbaden. He gave the debriefing team the little information he had on his captors and his fellow hostages, and gave them a video cassette of David Jacobsen pleading for the U.S. to work for his release. On July 29, Jenco met North in Wiesbaden, West Germany, and thanked him for his efforts to free the hostages.

Israel saw Jenco's release as a great achievement for itself, but in the U.S. there were doubts about the price Ghorbanifar had promised. In order to clarify this, North left on July 27 for Frankfurt to meet with Ghorbanifar, Nir, Cave, and Secord. Nir and Ghorbanifar came from London, while Cave came from Geneva.[15] This meeting was, in effect, the end of the "boycott" North had imposed on Nir. Ghorbanifar described in detail the promises he had given to the Iranians. He related that he and Nir had invited Kengarlou to join the talks in Frankfurt, but the deputy prime minister had not been able to come. He added that he had suggested the sequential release of the hostages in exchange for the Hawk spare parts and the two radar systems. As for the price of the spare parts, Ghorbanifar said that he had told Kengarlou that, if it could be proven that the U.S. had demanded $10 million more than the real value of the items, then he, Ghorbanifar, would see that the U.S. repaid Iran by sending free 1,000 TOW missiles. He would also see to it that the U.S. supplied Iran with another 2,000 TOWs, as well as 200 Sidewinder missiles at cost. All this, of course, was on condition that Iran give Ghorbanifar his fair cut.

In a series of telephone calls from Tehran, Kengarlou said that revealing his part in the release of Father Jenco would put him in an uncomfortable position.[16] To save his skin, he had promised Prime Minister Mussavi that the U.S. would supply Iran with the rest of the spare parts. He feared for his life should this not be done. In order to impress this on those listening to him, Kengarlou asked to be promised, should his life be endangered, political asylum in the U.S. He also asked that a secret Swiss bank account be opened in his name. North gave him these promises, but he was also given to understand that the U.S. had videotapes and photographs from their previous meetings in Tehran, and that if he betrayed them, the U.S. would not hesitate to make them public. Despite these veiled threats, the general tenor of the conversation was that the Americans were now willing to reverse their previous positions and were ready to resume arms deliveries to Iran, even before the release of all hostages.[17]

This was in direct opposition to declared U.S. policy, and to the instructions McFarlane and Poindexter had given. North nevertheless pressed his superiors for such an arrangement, and he coupled this pressure with a warning. In a memorandum to Poindexter on July 29, North cautioned: "It is entirely possible that if nothing is received, the Iranian official [Kengarlou] will be killed by his opponents in Tehran, Ghorbanifar will be killed by his creditors . . . and one hostage will probably be killed in order to demonstrate displeasure."[18]

Vice President George Bush was in Israel on the same day that North composed his note. Bush met with Prime Minister Peres, as well as with Foreign Minister Shamir and Defense Minister Rabin. After a preliminary conversation with Israel's Chief of Staff, Major General Moshe Levy, and his deputy, General Amnon Shahak, he went by helicopter to an air force base in the south of Israel and watched combat and paratrooper maneuvers. The next day, in the early morning, he had a 30-minute conversation in his suite at the King David Hotel in Jerusalem with Amiram Nir. The meeting was kept secret, and was approved only after Bush talked by telephone with North.[19] North wanted Nir to brief the vice president so that Bush could help him get Reagan's approval of Ghorbanifar's conditions for sequential release of the hostages. Peres too had an interest in this briefing—since the inception of the Iran initiative, Bush had had some reservations about the importance of Israel's role in it. Peres believed that a careful explanation, against the background of the work Israel had put into achieving Jenco's freedom, would help change the vice president's mind. Israel had staked its reputation on the Kengarlou-Ghorbanifar channel and saw in it the only hope to recover its missing soldiers. Nir was, apparently, not persuasive, because even after the briefing, Bush continued to voice reservations. A three-page summary of the meeting prepared by Bush's aide, Craig Fuller, indicates that Nir advised Bush to abandon the "all or nothing" strategy the U.S. was pursuing and adopt one of obtaining the sequential release of the hostages, as Iran had always insisted. Nir explained to the vice president that, as long as they had bargaining chips, the Iranians would try to squeeze as many concessions as they could from the U.S. and Israel. Under the present circumstances, there was no choice but to continue the negotiations. The Iran initiative, he said, was being conducted on two layers—the tactical, aimed at freeing the hostages; and the strategic, aimed at establishing better relations with Khomeini's successors.

Nir's briefing was saturated with self-praise and exaggerations about Israel's role in the Iran initiative.[20] After telling Bush that the first stage of the initiative—that involving Kimche, Schwimmer, and Nimrodi—"had not worked well," he attributed the continuation of the effort to himself. He noted that "in November and December there were additional talks. In January we thought we had a better approach, and Poindexter agreed." He added that, "we activated the channel, we gave a front to the operation, we provided a physical base, and we provided aircraft. We did all this to make sure the U.S. would not be involved in logistical aspects." Nir admitted that McFarlane's visit had ended without results and had been very frustrating, but said that this was because "it had not been properly prepared." He explained that the Iranians had assumed from the start that the U.S. was not interested in building better strategic cooperation, and thought U.S. concern was focused mainly on the hostages. For this reason they tried to extort further concessions at every opportunity. "If the Iranians thought that we are really interested in strategic links, they would have not bothered too much with the price right now," Nir argued.

In telling the vice president about the efforts to free Jenco, Nir revealed that Israel had intercepted communications between Tehran and Hezbollah in Beirut about the impending release of the hostage. Nir concluded by analyzing the options available to the U.S. and Israel, and while he may not have recommended any specific plan of action, he expressed preference for the "sequential release" of the hostages. He justified this position by arguing that the U.S. and Israel in any case had two or three years to wait before there would be any change in the Iranian leadership. Until then, he argued, "we have no real choice but to proceed."

Nir's presentation contradicted the official Israeli version of events issued a few months later. When the initiative was uncovered, Israel claimed to have attempted to establish contact with moderate elements in Iran who might succeed Khomeini, and to have acted at America's behest, rather than having led the U.S. into the Iranian morass. Nir told Bush, however, that Israel had set up the communications channel with Iran and had paved the way for the arms deals. As for Khomeini's successors, Nir told the vice president that "we are dealing with the most radical elements, because they can deliver. In the meantime, we have established additional contacts and we've had some success. Now we expect further success, because other groups, when they discover that we are talking with the radicals, will feel it is less risky for them to make contact with us."

North enlisted the help of the CIA director as well. In a memorandum to Poindexter on July 26, 1986, Casey wrote: Ghorbanifar is an uncontrollable factor, but appears to respond generally to Nir's direction." The Ghorbanifar-Kengarlou connection had proved itself twice, leading to the release of Weir and Jenco, Casey noted. He recommended allowing Nir to continue to work for the release of the hostages, "because Peres and Rabin have put their reputations on the Ghorbanifar-Kengarlou connection, and because the link with Iran serves, in the end, Israel's interests and might make it possible to release their captured soldiers as well." Casey concluded by saying that "Although I am not pleased by the sequential releases of the hostages, I am convinced that this may be the only way to proceed." Casey also warned the President that, were the rest of the arms not supplied to Iran, Hezbollah might murder one of the hostages.[21]

Poindexter now agreed that there was no choice but to continue the arms deals with Iran, and he accepted in principle the sequential release of the hostages. Thus, he recommended to President Reagan on July 30 that the rest of the Hawk missile spare parts, in Israel since May, be sent to Iran.[22] They arrived in Bandar Abbas on August 4, and like previous shipments, they were sent in an Israeli Boeing 707 without identifying markings, manned by an American crew supplied by Secord. By prior arrangement with Israeli and American officials, and with Kengarlou, the plane flew from Tel Aviv to the Red Sea, turning east between Socotra and South Yemen, flying over Shar-Bahar, and then to Bandar Abbas. The plane was refueled without charge by the Iranians and returned the next day to Israel. It was the last time Israel would be directly involved in all stages of an arms shipment to Iran. The next shipment, in October, would be carried out by North and Secord using the "second channel" of communication, set up without Ghorbanifar's knowledge. Israel would learn of it only shortly before it was activated.

Even though the spare parts had been supplied in exchange for but a single hostage, Kengarlou continued to haggle about the price, and demanded the supply of 1,000 TOW missiles at no cost, as Ghorbanifar had promised. He claimed that 63 items from the August 4 shipment were defective, and that 177 other components did not match the order Iran had placed. At North's request, Cave notified Kengarlou that Ghorbanifar's promises did not obligate the United States.[23] Cave also brought up the matter of payment. On July 24, just prior to the most recent shipment, Iran had given Ghorbanifar a $4 million down payment, paying an additional $4 million after the shipment was received.[24] Ghorbanifar, however, owed Khashoggi $18 million, leaving him $10 million in the red. Cave explained to Kengarlou that if Iran did not give Ghorbanifar the rest of his money, the U.S. would stop all arms shipments to Iran. If the people who had supplied the interim funding for the transaction were not repaid by Ghorbanifar, they were liable to go public with all they knew, he warned.

In order to resolve this dispute and discuss further steps, North, Nir, and Cave met with Ghorbanifar in London on August 8. This was the last time the Israeli adviser and the Iranian arms merchant met with North and Cave before the press began publishing the details of the initiative.[25] From then on North would meet only with the men involved in the "second channel." At the London meeting, North worked out a plan for additional arms shipments in exchange for the sequential release of the hostages and the return of Buckley's body. Ghorbanifar related "in Rafsanjani's name," that releasing all the hostages together would immediately arouse suspicion that Iran and the U.S. had been negotiating a deal together. Even though North made his plan conditional on the approval of his superiors, he had in essence conceded the point to the Iranians.

A few days later, Nir notified North that his impression was that Ghorbanifar was losing credibility with the Iranian government. Nir suggested strengthening Ghorbanifar's hand by supplying through him the two Hawk radar systems that Iran wanted. Nir proposed that Iran receive an "incentive"—1,000 TOW missiles and a small amount of Israeli arms and military equipment. In exchange, Iran would obtain the release of the remaining three hostages, would return Buckley's body, and would lay the foundations for an additional meeting at a senior level in "Tango" (Tehran). Iran, however, was not interested in Israeli weapons, so Ghorbanifar suggested an additional 1,000 TOWs instead. As for the top-level meeting in Tehran, no one really believed it would take place in the near future.[26]

While Ghorbanifar and Nir were making a tremendous effort to continue the contacts with Iran through them, North, with Poindexter's approval, was already working on the "second channel." On June 27, in the offices of Senator Jesse Helms of North Carolina, North met with an Iranian exile related to important figures in Tehran.[27] By the end of the meeting North was persuaded to pursue this track instead of the Ghorbanifar-Kengarlou channel, inaugurated by Schwimmer and Nimrodi and continued by Nir. North gave responsibility for the new line of communication to Secord and Hakim. Officially, it was meant to open a new channel in Iran's government. But it appears that North hoped that this would be an efficient way of using the profits from the arms sales from Iran to fund Contra activities—avoiding Israel's participation and without having to share the profits with Ghorbanifar and Kengarlou. The advantages for Secord and Hakim were obvious—establishing contact with various elements in revolutionary Iran would help them gain a foothold in this important country, giving them an opportunity to profit not only from arms sales, but also from the various contracts that would result from the future need to rebuild the war-damaged country. Hakim estimated the trade market between the U.S. and Iran to be worth $15 billion.[28]

The diplomatic importance of the "second channel" was even more significant. It would relegate Israel to a minor role in the links with Iran. But Israel, it turned out, would make do with its reduced role and would continue to serve as a transfer point between Iran and the U.S.

The various congressional committees that had investigated the Iran-Contra affair did not reveal how many persons were involved in the opening of the "second channel," nor did they reveal their real identities. Both the *Tower Commission Report* and the *Iran-Contra Report* mentioned the "Relative" as being the key man in the second channel. He was contacted through an Iranian expatriate, the "First Contact," who in return for a promise to receive a "good commission" turned to a fellow Iranian businessman, the "Second Contact," with direct connection to the Iran government.

The *Tower Commission Report* described the Relative as a "very sharp, well-educated young man, who speaks no English and a well-known favorite of Majlis Speaker, Rafsanjani."[29] The *Iran-Contra Report* added that the Relative had distinguished himself in the ranks of the Iranian Revolutionary Guards in the war with Iraq, and that his relationship to a "leading Iranian official had been verified."[30]

Speakers at an extraordinary session of the "Islamic Student Congress," held in Tehran on November 14–16, 1986, named Sadegh Tabatabai, "one of the closest advisors of Khomeini," as the man who orchestrated the negotiations with the United States.[31] Tabatabai is Khomeini's son-in-law. He divided his time between Iran, Britain, and Germany. He had once been friendly with Ali Amini, a former Prime Minister under the Shah and now an exile in Paris. Tabatabai now had the title "special emissary," and was sent on different kinds of missions by the government of Iran. In December 1987 he would mediate between Iran and France and bring the "Embassy War" between the two countries to an end. Tabatabai was also among the few senior Iranian officials who knew of McFarlane's visit to Tehran, even though he had not taken part in the negotiations.

Another person mentioned in connection with the second channel is Mahmoud Rafsanjani, the Speaker's brother and a former ambassador to Damascus, who was later to be included in the delegation that visited Washington in late September 1986.[32]

Another of Rafsanjani's brothers who was mentioned in this connection was Mohsen Rafsanjani, who was involved in an effort to buy in Madrid TOW missiles at a cost of $13,000 each, for a total amount of $16 million.[33]

Finally, in late December 1986, yet another of Rafsanjani's relatives was mentioned, Mehdi Bahremani, the eldest son of the Iranian Speaker. A report in the *Observer* (London) (December 21, 1986) claimed that on November 15, 1986, shortly after the exposure of the sales of the American arms to Iran, Mehdi Bahremani left his Brussels apartment and went to Toronto, after he had allegedly pocketed $6 million for his role in this affair. The Canadian government, however, announced on December 22, 1986, that it could not trace Bahremani's legal entry into Canada.[34]

These were, then, some of the persons who, together, were reportedly involved in the opening of the new channel to Iran. No single individual constituted the "second channel," as the term was used in the *Iran-Contra Report*. The channel was opened early July, after a meeting in London between Albert Hakim and an Iranian expatriate (the First Contact) whom he had employed in the past. At least twice in 1983, Hakim brought his name to the attention of the CIA, but nothing came of these contacts in the end.[35]

On North's orders, Hakim invited the Iranian agent to Washington, where he could be evaluated and where his credibility could be checked. The First Contact arrived on July 9 and, during his two days in the American capital, he underwent a polygraph test and had lengthy talks with Hakim and Cave. The talks focused on supplying arms and medicine to Iran. The First Contact made a positive impression and North decided to continue contacts with him. The agent asked for "appropriate compensation" for his help in establishing contact with "reliable people in Tehran." After receiving promises for such remuneration, Hakim told the agent that he would pursue the trade avenue, irrespective of whether the U.S. government used the channel.[36] One proposal that later bore fruit was for some medical supplies to be sold at cost.

With the promise of a payoff, the First Contact turned to a fellow Iranian businessman (the "Second Contact") with direct connections to the Iranian government. They quickly found another avenue into Iran. On July 25, Cave and Hakim met in Frankfurt with Tabatabai and the Second Contact. North identified the Second Contact as "a relation of a powerful Iranian official."[37] In a note to Poindexter, North described Tabatabai as "well connected to Rafsanjani and several of the so-called 'pragmatists.' " The purpose of the meeting was to determine Tabatabai's real access and willingness to act as an interlocutor.[38] Tabatabai said that Iran was indeed interested in renewing its relations with the U.S., but preferred to do so only after the end of the Gulf War. He expressed his willingness to serve as a link with Rafsanjani and to work for the release of the hostages in order to build a new bridge to the U.S.[39] Cave and Hakim were most impressed by Tabatabai's personality, and recommended maintaining regular contact with him. A quick CIA check confirmed that Tabatabai was indeed Khomeini's son-in-law, and that he was very close to Rafsanjani.

North decided to pursue this avenue. After a series of contacts between Hakim and the Iranian agents (in London on August 7 and in Madrid on August 10), it was agreed that a meeting with the second channel would take place in Brussels on August 25. After three conversations totaling eight hours,[40] Secord and Hakim had formed an excellent opinion of the Relative and of the quality of his connections with the Iranian establishment. The Relative was introduced to Secord by the First Contact and the Second Contact, who was identified as "a former Iranian navy officer—20 years—and alleged London businessman now—definitely an important agent for [the] Rafsanjani group and possibly 'Savana' [the Iranian Secret Service]."[41] The talks covered many subjects, including the war with Iraq, Soviet involvement in Afghanistan, Communist subversion in Tehran, and American policy in the Persian Gulf region. As for arms, the Relative said that his country had many needs: spare parts for tanks, antiaircraft and antitank weapons, spare parts for helicopters, and intelligence on the Iraqi army. He confirmed that he knew of McFarlane's visit to Tehran, and was aware of Israel's role in the contacts with his country and that "Miller" (Nir) in McFarlane's group was an Israeli. He termed Ghorbanifar and Kengarlou "greedy swindlers." He nevertheless promised not to subvert their efforts to free the hostages. He also said he would speak to Rafsanjani on the subject and that, upon returning to Brussels 10 days hence, he would tell them what had happened. Secord's conclusion was that he and Hakim had opened up a new "and probably much better" channel into Iran.

Despite Secord's recommendation and his own impression that the Relative was preferable to Ghorbanifar, North decided not to rush things. He attempted to operate both channels simultaneously. Nir maintained regular contact with Ghorbanifar while Secord and Hakim did the same with the second channel. So long as the Relative's ability to free hostages remained unproven, North did not want to shut out Ghorbanifar completely. He was told by Hakim's Iranian expatriate agent that even if the Relative turned out not to be as close to Rafsanjani as he claimed, he could still be an important source of intelligence on Iran and its leaders.[42]

The establishment of the second channel caused complications and confusion among all those involved in the Iran initiative. Despite his promise on August 25 that he would not subvert the efforts of Ghorbanifar and Kengarlou, on the 27th the Relative notified Secord and Hakim that an Iranian arms salesman in Madrid was trying to sell Iran TOW missiles at $13,000 per missile. He suspected that this deal was ultimately traceable to Ghorbanifar and Khashoggi, and he feared that this would sabotage his efforts in Tehran. The Relative said that he was trying to arrange a high-level meeting between American officials and Rafsanjani, and that as of now he should be considered the principal channel of communication with Iran. During the first stage of the contacts, and before the visit of the U.S. officials to Tehran, Mahmoud Rafsanjani, the Speaker's brother and formerly Iran's ambassador in Damascus, would be included in the Iranian delegation. The Relative claimed that Mohsen Rafiq-Doust, commander of the Revolutionary Guards, was aware of what was going on and was following its development.

Whether the Relative had presented the matter to Secord, or whether it was Secord who presented this to North, one thing was clear: Poindexter and North would have to decide quickly whether to continue to work with Ghorbanifar, or to go with the second channel. This was especially important given the pressures from Nir and from the CIA to carry out the agreements reached with Ghorbanifar in London at the beginning of August. While Secord and Hakim were meeting the Relative in Brussels, Nir had called North and urged him to speed up the preparations for a second mission to Tehran. The arrangements were to be made by Kengarlou. The condition was the renewal of arms supplies to Iran.

With the end of August came an additional complication. Ghorbanifar notified Nir that the U.S. was trying to establish a second line of communication with Tehran behind his back. Kengarlou also hinted to the U.S. that he knew about the contacts with the Relative. In a telephone conversation with Cave, Kengarlou said that his "boss" (Mussavi) favored the idea of a meeting between the Relative and American officials.[43] The second channel was no longer a secret.

Ghorbanifar and Kengarlou most likely felt cheated. Ghorbanifar had an immediate financial problem. In conversations with CIA people, he had in the past claimed that his profit margin on the arms deals was 40 percent. When the details of the various transactions were analyzed, however, it became clear that in some cases his profit had been as much as 200 percent. Testifying before the congressional committee, North said: "Although we had certainly run the charges up, Ghorbanifar had almost doubled it on top of that.[44] The Iranian authorities discovered this and stopped paying him. Ghorbanifar had asked Iran for $24.5 million, of which he had received less than a third. He still owed Khashoggi $10 million. The problem was an explosive one and demanded a quick solution. CIA officer Charles Allen, who was in regular personal contact with Ghorbanifar, warned North that dropping the Iranian arms merchant could lead to the exposure of the whole initiative. He estimated that closing of the "Ghorbanifar channel" without running the risk of exposure would require paying the Iranian $4 million.[45]

The inauguration of the second channel created another problem: the moratorium on kidnappings in Beirut, which had lasted for 14 months, came to an end. On September 9, an Islamic Jihad unit commanded by Imad Mughaniyeh (who had been involved in the hijacking of the TWA airliner in June 1985) kidnapped an American educator, Frank Reed. Mughaniyeh's brother was among the 17 Shiite terrorists of the El-Da'awa organization imprisoned in Kuwait, and whose release Kengarlou had demanded as a condition for the release of the American hostages. Three days later, Joseph Ciccipio, an accountant, was kidnapped from the American University campus, and on October 21 another American, the writer Edward Tracy, was kidnapped. At least in one case Kengarlou's hand was apparent. Kengarlou, it was clear, had ordered the resumption of the kidnappings as a way of pressuring the U.S. to renew the arms shipments through him.

The shift to the second channel led to the conclusion of the first commercial deal between Secord-Hakim and the Iranian intermediary (the First Contact). In early September, a shipment of medical supplies that Hakim and the First Contact had discussed in July was sent to Iran. Sources in Tehran said the shipment went to the air force. The Iranian intermediary was identified as Farzin Azimi, while the Iranian logistics officer, Djavid Nya, was responsible for the arrangements in Tehran.[46] The shipment was made in a Boeing 707 belonging to Ferhad Azimi, an Iranian-American living in Kansas City, Missouri. The plane was chartered from a company managed by Farzin Azimi, Ferhad's brother.

It was against this background that Amiram Nir came to Washington on September 10 to meet with Poindexter and North. Nir arrived a week before Shimon Peres was to pay his last state visit to the White House before turning over the prime ministership to Yitzhak Shamir, under the terms of the coalition agreement signed between Israel's two major parties in 1984. Because of the complexity of the Iran problem, as well as the new complications, Peres and Shamir agreed that Nir would, in the meantime, stay on as the Prime Minister's adviser on terrorism. Before Peres's arrival Nir also met with William Casey and with the Reverend Martin Jenco. He asked to meet again with Vice President George Bush, but his request was turned down.

In his conversation with Nir, Poindexter said he was happy that Nir would be staying on in his job after the rotation in Prime Ministers. By prior arrangement with North, Poindexter told him about the links established with the second channel through Secord and Hakim. He emphasized that the Relative was connected with Rafsanjani and he knew that "Miller" of the McFarlane delegation was Nir.[47] Nir worried out loud that "changing horses" would mean the abandonment of efforts to free the Israeli soldiers kidnapped in Lebanon. Nir emphasized that Peres very much wanted to conclude his term in office with the release of the kidnapped soldiers, and that he was aware that the kidnapping of Frank Reed now complicated the situation. In accordance with Peres's instructions, Nir emphasized two points: from the inception of the Iran initiative, for over a year, Israel had never acted on its own, but rather always in tandem with the U.S.; and that Israel hoped that the work to free the hostages would continue to be a joint effort, and that the U.S. would include the release of the Israeli soldiers among its demands.

Poindexter said that these two points were acceptable to him. He met two days later with Israel's minister of defense, Yitzhak Rabin. Rabin categorically rejected a proposal to supply Israeli weapons to the Contras, but after much pleading from Poindexter and North he agreed to give the U.S. a small quantity of Soviet rifles captured in Lebanon, for transfer to South America. The rifles were to be sent from Haifa aboard the *Erria*, the ship that Secord and Hakim had bought for various covert operations. The U.S. government was to transfer these arms to the Contras via a South American country. So as not to run afoul of the Arab boycott, along the way the name of the ship was altered to read *Ria*. On October 13, the ship had loaded a crate containing eight tons of Eastern Bloc Arms.

Before sailing to the U.S., the ship was ordered to go to Fujairah in the Gulf of Oman. The second channel had promised North two Soviet T-72 tanks, but after the *Erria* waited six weeks in the Gulf, the plan failed to materialize. On December 9, the *Erria's* captain opened the Israeli crate. He found only 600 well-used AK-47 assault rifles and 15 cases of ammunition—valued at approximately $100,000—a cargo not worth transporting to Central America. After the public exposure of the Iran-Contra affair, the *Erria* sailed from the Gulf of Oman to Eilat and unloaded the weapons it had received in Haifa.[48]

On September 15, Shimon Peres met President Reagan at the White House. Nir met once again with Poindexter shortly before this, for ten minutes, and told him what subjects were likely to come up in the conversation between the two leaders. The emphasis would be on the peace process between Israel and its Arab neighbors. Peres was frustrated at the lack of progress in this sphere, and he would tell Reagan that he intended to continue to advance the cause of peace in his new position, as foreign minister. Reagan thanked Peres for his help in establishing contact with Tehran. He noted that, without Israel's cooperation, Weir and Jenco would not have been freed.[49]

Schwimmer had accompanied Peres to Washington and asked to meet with Poindexter, but the meeting never took place. He was told that Poindexter was ill. It would seem that Poindexter did not want to reintegrate Schwimmer into the arms deals with Iran, especially after the establishment of the second channel. Peres, however, received promises from Poindexter and North, through Nir, that the Iran initiative would continue, "with Israel's full cooperation."[50]

But a few days later it was clear that there was a wide gap between words and deeds. While the Israeli Prime Minister was in Washington, North was busy organizing a visit for the Relative and his associates, without Nir's participation. After they had opened the second channel, it was clear that Secord and Hakim would not let this new initiative—and the financial opportunities involved—slip out of their hands. They did all they could to distance Israel from the furture dealings with Iran.

The Relative and the two Iranian expatriates who had introduced him to Secord and Hakim spent from September 19 to September 21, 1986, in Washington, having been flown in from Istanbul on a special plane chartered by Secord. The meeting was videotaped, and all the conversations were recorded. By prior arrangement with the immigration authorities, the three visitors did not go through the normal passport control procedures, and from the minute they entered the country they were under FBI surveillance. The meeting on the first day was held in the Old Executive Office Building and was attended by North, Secord, Hakim, and Cave. The Iranians related that their trip to Washington had been approved in a consultation between Rafsanjani, Mussavi, and Khamenei, and that the foreign minister, Ali Akbar Velayati, and the minister responsible for the Revolutionary Guards, Mohsen Rafiq-Doust, had taken part in some of the discussions of the matter.

The Iranians emphasized that the purpose of their trip to Washington was to raise the level of the contacts between the two countries, and that in addition to arms and hostages they wanted to find out how they might be assisted by the U.S. in rehabilitating Iran's 2 million war homeless, and in repairing the oil business and the economy of their country.

They suggested setting up a joint committee of eight members, four from each country, that would meet in Lisbon or Istanbul and would deal with subjects of strategic importance to the two countries. At some later time it might be possible to talk about stationing a CIA liaison team in Tehran.

The conversations also covered the Soviet threat and ways of ending the war with Iraq, as well as possibilities for giving more assistance to the Afghan rebels. The Relative demanded that North end America's support of Iraq, and asked the U.S. to put pressure on its allies in the Persian Gulf to end their support of Saddam Hussein. North rejected this demand utterly. Much time, of course, was spent discussing the hostages. North emphasized that, from the point of view of the U.S., the strategic link was very important, but the hostage issue was a barrier to the future development of relations between the two countries. The Iranians answered that their government opposed taking hostages, and that Khomeini would soon issue an Islamic legal ruling (*fatwah*) on this matter. Iran, however, had a problem: 17 members of the El-Da'awa organization were still in prison in Kuwait. These terrorists had been caught after an attack on the American and French embassies in Kuwait, and after sabotaging the offices of the local airline and the country's oil facilities. Six people were killed and eight others wounded in these attacks. Hezbollah insisted on the release of these prisoners, but Kuwait, with U.S. support, was not giving in to pressure. Khomeini's relative now wanted the U.S. to use its influence in Kuwait to free these Shiite prisoners. North rejected this demand as well. As for Khomeini's legal ruling, North recalled that Ghorbanifar had also promised something similar in April 1986, but that Khomeini had never come out publicly against hostage taking in Lebanon.

The Iranians submitted a very long list of arms and military equipment they wanted, and demanded intelligence on Iraq. Their list included offensive weapons as well, among them 500 Howitzer guns. North told them that the U.S. could not fulfill this request, the President having approved the supply of defensive weapons only.

In order to eliminate any possibility of the renewal of the contacts between the U.S. and Ghorbanifar, the Relative confirmed that Frank Reed had been kidnapped in Beirut on Kengarlou's orders. He added that one of Kengarlou's associates was suspected of working for the KGB. The U.S. would have to cut off contact with Kengarlou, he said, so as to keep its secrets from being leaked to the Soviet Union. Finally, the Relative claimed that Buckley had not died from his tortures but from a heart attack. This conflicted, however, with the information that the CIA had.

During the course of the discussion, the Iranian agent who had put the U.S. in touch with Tabatabai and Rafsanjani's nephew left the room for a short "consultation" with Albert Hakim: He asked for assurances that he would be paid. Hakim returned to the room with him and, in the presence of North and the other Iranians, he said that if these contacts were successful, he, Hakim, would not forget that all the Iranians who had come to Washington would deserve "appropriate financial compensation."

At the end of the discussion those present agreed to meet again in Europe in order to examine the possibility of releasing some of the hostages. Before that meeting took place, however, the Iranians wanted "proof" of America's serious intentions. North told them that, in its Persian-language programs, the voice of America would broadcast for three days running praise of Iran for not allowing a Pan American airliner hijacked in Pakistan to land in Tehran. North had another "prize" for them, too—late on Saturday night, September 20, North took his guests on a tour of the White House, including among other things the Oval Office and the Roosevelt Room.[51] North told them that Reagan was willing to put great effort into ending the war with Iraq, and he pointed to the Bible on the President's desk as proof that the American president was a "God-fearing man." The next day at 11:00 A.M. the talks were concluded and the three guests left on their chartered plane for Istanbul, from where they continued on a regular civilian flight to Tehran.

Nir's worries about North's silence began growing. Ghorbanifar and Kengarlou also called North, Secord, Cave, and Charles Allen, sometimes several times a day, asking why they were not being allowed to continue their efforts to free the hostages in exchange for further American arms shipments. North made it clear to Nir, and through him to Ghorbanifar, that the new kidnappings had forced the U.S. to cut off any new arms shipments until Frank Reed and Joseph Ciccipio were freed. North hinted that, at least in one case, the U.S. had proof that Kengarlou had ordered the kidnapping.[52]

At the beginning of October, after the Voice of America had broadcast the agreed-upon text about Iran's positive response to the Pakistani hijacking, the second channel called Secord and suggested that the next meeting be held on Monday, October 6, in Frankfurt. He also deposited $7 million in the Lake Resources account in Geneva as a down payment for the next arms deal.[53] He told Secord that he had just come back from Tehran and Beirut, and that he would bring "good news" to Frankfurt. The Relative said that Rafsanjani intended to give him a Koran for President Reagan, as proof that the coming meeting had his blessing.

With Poindexter's agreement, North decided not to invite Nir to this meeting. This decision conflicted with the promise given two weeks previously to the Israeli Prime Minister. North justified this by saying that the Relative "really disliked" Israelis, but that should there be a high-level meeting Nir would be included, as he had been in McFarlane's delegation to Iran. North drew up a detailed plan, approved by Poindexter, to make sure that Nir would not be able to come to the meeting even if he wanted to. It was a delicate operation, since the U.S. wanted to continue to use Israel as a stopping-off point for arms shipments to Iran. Keeping Nir away had to be done in such a way that he and his superiors would continue to believe that the initiative was a joint one.

The diversion of Nir began with a letter that North sent with Secord to Israel on October 5.[54] The letter, from President Reagan to Shimon Peres, contained several compliments on Nir's work. Secord was told to tell Nir that the U.S. remained faithful to its promise to see the Iran initiative as a "joint project," and that the U.S. would in the future continue to consult with Israel about the next steps to be taken. Secord updated Nir on two matters: the new difficulties with the "Ghorbanifar channel," and the contacts with the "second channel."

The problems with Ghorbanifar were financial, but also had to do with the kidnapping of additional Americans. Secord told Nir that he had proposed to Kengarlou, a meeting in Europe on October 9, but that he had still not received an answer. In any case, so long as this meeting did not take place, and so long as Frank Reed and Joseph Ciccipio were not released, there was no point in talking about additional arms shipments through Ghorbanifar. (There was, of course, no intention of meeting Kengarlou on October 9. Secord had made up the story as a diversion.[55])

The second channel, he said, was developing, and until the decision was made to have more official contacts between Iran and the U.S., he, Secord, would remain the American liaison.On North's instructions, Secord told Nir of the planned meeting of North and the Relative in Frankfurt at the very last minute and, as expected, Nir could not make the meeting, even though he wanted to very much.

The Relative came to the Frankfurt meeting with two of his associates, as well as with a senior intelligence officer from the Revolutionary Guards who had participated in the talks with McFarlane in Tehran. North called this officer the "Engine" since he had been the prime mover in the talks in Tehran, where all the other Iranians had deferred to him and acted in accordance with his instructions. Sending the Engine to Frankfurt was meant to convince the U.S. that the talks had the approval of the Iranian leadership, and that all agreements reached with the second channel and the Engine would be honored.

The Frankfurt talks were restricted to the usual subject—arms for hostages—but by the time they were concluded North, Secord, and Hakim had seriously deviated from the principles of America's foreign policy.[56] In their enthusiasm for obtaining the release of the hostages at any price, North and his colleagues promised the Relative that the U.S. would "look the other way" if Kuwait decided to free the 17 imprisoned members of El-Da'awa, and that the U.S. would not oppose a solution to the Gulf War that included the removal of Iraq's President, Saddam Hussein, as Iran demanded. The Israeli POWs were not brought up at all, even though Israel was again to serve as a logistical base for the American arms shipments to Tehran.

In his testimony to the congressional investigatory committees, North later openly admitted that, in his effort to release the hostages, he deliberately lied to the Iranian delegation. North said: "I lied everytime I met the Iranians."[57]

At the end of the Frankfurt meeting, and despite the fact that the Relative had not brought the promised Koran with him, North gave his Iranian counterpart a Bible in a decorated leather binding, with a dedication from President Reagan to Speaker Rafsanjani, inscribed on October 3. The passage inscribed is from Galatians 3:8 and it reads: "And the Scripture, foreseeing that God would justify the Gentiles by faith, preached the gospel beforehand to Abraham, saying, 'All the nations shall be blessed in you.'"

President Reagan would later tell the Tower Commission that he made the inscription to show the recipient that he was "getting through."[58] After the Iran initiative had been exposed in the press, Rafsanjani would wave this Bible over his head in front of an Iranian crowd as proof of the secret contacts with the U.S. during the previous 18 months. North accompanied the presentation of the Bible with a story he made up: Reagan, he said, had spent the weekend in prayer for guidance on whether to authorize North to tell the Iranians that we accepted the Islamic Revolution as an established fact. God, North said, told him that it was.[59]

Since North had to return to Washington on October 8, while Secord had to go to Brussels, the continuation of the talks was left to Hakim.[60] This decision is hard to explain. Hakim was an arms dealer and had no official position in the U.S. government. Hakim nevertheless, after exhausting negotiations, reached an agreement with the Engine and the Relative on nine points, providing for the release of a single hostage in exchange for an additional shipment of 500 TOW missiles. The weapons would be supplied before the hostage was freed, and another shipment would follow. The "Hakim agreement" included several more retreats from the previous U.S. position. Hakim no longer insisted on the return of Buckley's body, no timetable was set for the release of the rest of the hostages, and the price of the TOW missiles was reduced considerably. North would later testify that "Nir was very upset when he learned that the price would be significantly lower this time than it had been in previous transactions. Nir thought that, if the U.S. would charge the old price, it would be possible to use the difference to compensate Ghorbanifar, Khashoggi, and his other financiers.[61]

The switch to the second channel left Ghorbanifar no choice but to demand the money Iran owed him. At the beginning of October Roy Furmark, an American businessman and a sometime partner of Khashoggi, met with his old friend William Casey.[62] The two had been introduced by the American industralist John Shaheen, a former naval officer who had served with Casey during World War II in American intelligence in Europe. After the war, Shaheen built an oil empire. Furmark had joined his company in 1966 and had been gradually promoted from accountant to vice president. Casey sometimes consulted with Shaheen on legal issues.

"Bill," Furmark said, "I need your help." Furmark spent 30 minutes recounting Khashoggi's financial difficulties, the result of his interim funding of the arms deal to the tune of $15 million. Khashoggi had himself received the money from two Canadian investors. Furmark warned Casey that, if Khashoggi did not get his money back, the Canadians would sue him, exposing the whole affair.

At the same time, Charles Allen was telling his superiors in the CIA that Ghorbanifar was extremely frustrated about the lack of a solution to his financial problems, and that as a result there was an "operational risk" involved in the continuation of the Iran initiative.[63] Allen added that Ghorbanifar had told him that he knew that the price of missiles had been intentionally inflated in order to skim off the profits for the Contras, for the Afghan rebels, and for other projects he did not know of. There was now a real possibility that Ghorbanifar would go public with everything he knew and accuse the U.S. of failing to meet its obligations to him.

Despite all this, the U.S. did not recognize the storm warnings and continued with plans to carry out the first arms deal through the second channel. North, Secord, and Nir met in Geneva on October 22 to plan the shipment of another 500 TOW missiles to Iran. The three of them agreed that the shipment would once again go in an Israeli plane with a two-man American crew, and would consist of the 500 replacement TOWs Israel had received from the U.S. in February 1986—and which Israel had decided did not fit its army's needs. Israel would in turn receive 500 other missiles from the U.S. early in November.

The two American crewmen arrived in Israel on October 27, and the next day the missiles left for Tehran. Contrary to the principles that the U.S. and Israel had originally established, stipulating that the arms were to be used to foster moderate elements in Iran, this shipment, like that of February 1986, was handed over to the Revolutionary Guards and not to the regular army.[64]

According to the agreement with the Relative, Iran was to see to the release of one or more hostages within four days of receiving the missiles. In preparation for this release, Secord, Cave, and Hakim met on October 29 in Mainz, West Germany, with the Relative and the Engine. At the meeting, Khomeini's relative reported some worrying developments in the relations between his country and the U.S. He revealed to North that Montazeri's loyalists, led by Mehdi Hashemi, had distributed "millions of leaflets" telling of McFarlane's trip to Tehran, and that the news had also been printed in a small newsletter published by Hezbollah in Baalbek.[65] The Relative thought that this publication would hasten the exposure of the entire affair. These developments had almost prevented the Engine from leaving Tehran. The Relative's conclusion was that the nine-point plan he had agreed upon with Hakim should be expedited. More immediately he demanded, "in Rafsanjani's name," several American technicians who could fix the Phoenix missiles Iran had, as well as the supply of 22 helicopters and cameras for the Iranian air force's Phantom jets. North pressed for the immediate release of all the American hostages (a development likely to boost the Republican party's fortunes in the upcoming congressional elections). The Iranians, however, evaded making any commitment. They said that they could not guarantee the release of more than one hostage, but they were willing to supply the U.S. with information about where the other hostages were being kept so that the U.S. could free them by force. The Relative again brought up the question of the 17 El-Da'awa prisoners in Kuwait and asked what the U.S.'s position was on Iran's demand to overthrow President Saddam Hussein.

The major surprise came, however, when the Relative gave North the names of the four Iranian representatives who were to participate in the "joint committee" with the U.S. One was none other than Mohsen Kengarlou, and another was Ali Najafa-badi, chairman of the Majlis's Foreign Affairs Committee, who had participated in the talks with McFarlane in Tehran.

North was shocked. He had opened the second channel in order to get rid of Ghorbanifar and Kengarlou, and here was Tabatabai proposing the latter's reinstatement as an intermediary between the two countries. Noting North's surprise, the

Relative explained that Rafsanjani really wanted to improve relations with the U.S., but that guarding his flank required including President Khamenei and Prime Minister Mussavi in the contacts. Kengarlou and Najafabadi were their representatives, with himself representing Rafsanjani. That way, should the initiative be exposed, none of the three leaders could use it against his two other fellows. At the end of the Mainz meeting the Relative presented North with an expensive Persian carpet worth $8,000, but North refused the gift.

In accordance with the Relative's promise, North and Secord left on October 29 for East Beirut in order to make preparations for the release of the American hostages and for the receipt of the T-72 tank long ago promised to the U.S. Expectations were high, but in the end only David Jacobsen was freed. North asked Poindexter to delay the official announcement of the release, hoping to receive another hostage or at least information about where they were being held. Neither information nor additional hostages were forthcoming.

During the days that followed North's main concern was no longer the fate of the hostages but rather how to prevent an avalanche in the White House. The day Jacobsen was released was the day *El-Shira'a* published its report of McFarlane's visit to Tehran, shaking the foundations of the American administration. Poindexter and North continued to believe Tabatabai and to hold fast to their illusion that additional hostages would be freed.

Jacobsen's release was secured after 500 TOW missiles were sent from Israel to Tehran on October 30, through the agency of new Iranian middlemen of the second channel. North and Secord had arrived in East Beirut immediately after the missiles were sent to oversee the efforts to free the hostages. They had hoped that an additional hostage would also be freed, but to no avail.

The news item in the small Lebanese paper about McFarlane's visit to Tehran was picked up by the news agencies but was drowned in the flood of reports about Jacobsen's release and the U.S. elections. Journalists who asked the State Department for comment received categorical denials. Shultz's denial was, in fact, sincere, since he knew nothing of the visit. On November 4, however, all doubt as to the accuracy of the report was swept aside. In a speech to several thousand people who had gathered outside the Majlis building, Rafsanjani confirmed that McFarlane had been in Tehran, adding that the U.S. had lately been investing great effort in improving its relations with Iran. He revealed that the decision to publicize the visit had been made by the Iranian leadership on November 3, the next day being the anniversary of the capture of the American hostages in Iran.

Rafsanjani's tale was quite entertaining and was meant more to exonerate the role he and his colleagues had played in the affair than to accurately recount the story of the visit. He related that "McFarlane and four other Americans came to Tehran disguised as crew members in a plane that brought arms and spare parts from Europe. The five of them were taken to a hotel, where they were held until being expelled from the country five days later. McFarlane had a Bible signed by President Reagan and several gifts. We held a hurried meeting and notified Khomeini of the arrival of the delegation. Imam Khomeini instructed us not to talk with the Americans and not to accept their presents. The Americans also brought a cake, which they mean to symbolize the turning over of a new leaf in U.S.–Iran relations. But the security boys were hungry and ate the cake. McFarlane was furious when he saw that his gesture had been rejected completely."[66]

This story, however, included Rafsanjani's conditions for an agreement. He said that "the U.S. and France must prove that they are not at war with us, and that they do not intend to lead us on. The U.S. does not need to embargo our property, nor France our money. The just demands of the oppressed Moslems in Lebanon [the Shiites] must also be met. The prisoners in Israel, France, Kuwait, and elsewhere must be freed. If those conditions are met, Iran will make its views clear to its friends in Lebanon. They, of course, are free to act as they wish, but if they listen to us, the hostages will be freed."[67] The Iranian chargé d'affaires in London clarified Rafsanjani's statement, announcing that the "embargoed property" in the U.S., which had belonged to the Shah, was worth $3.5 billion, and that the U.S. had so far been unwilling to hand it over to Iran without a court order.

Rafsanjani's ambiguous words were contrasted by the straightforward statement of Prime Minister Mussavi. "There is no possibility of negotiations between us and the United

States. Because of its crimes against the Islamic Revolution, the relations between us and the Americans are like those between the wolf and the lamb," he said.[68]

President Khamenei argued that, "if the U.S. had wanted to demonstrate its goodwill, instead of sending McFarlane to Tehran it would have released the frozen Iranian assets and sent Iran arms worth hundreds of millions of dollars, paid for in full, purchased during the Shah's reign." He added that "as long as the current American policy toward the Arabs, Moslems, and Palestinians continues, and as long as America continues to give the Zionist regime in Israel its unqualified support, there can be no reconciliation between us and the U.S."[69]

Faced with myriad questions from reporters, the White House at first did its best to keep its responses on the McFarlane visit to a minimum and hold back the storm. Reagan even publicly disparaged *El-Shira'a*, calling it "a Beirut rag."[70] This did not last long, given the contradictory reports coming from various sources and the flood of revelations in the American press. Casey, Poindexter, McFarlane, and North tried to protect the President, saying that the arms sent to Iran were Israeli shipments delivered to Khomeini in 1985 without Reagan's approval. Such statements were contradicted by McFarlane's subsequent admission that in a memorandum to Reagan prepared for a presidential press conference on November 19, North had written that the U.S. had approved the shipments to Iran. A day later, however, the same members of the National Security Council staff decided to write a new version and distort the facts. This document said that Reagan had been very angry about the Israeli shipments "made without his knowledge."[71]

Israel preserved maximum restraint for several weeks, refraining from making any official statement that might have put the administration in an awkward position. Even when the American press printed articles claiming that Israel had dragged the U.S. into the Iran initiative and taken advantage of it for her own purposes, Israel remained silent, serving as a "shock absorber" for the Reagan administration. But in the second half of November it was already clear what Israel's limits of patience were. On November 23, North notified Nir that he had been questioned by Attorney General Edwin Meese about the diversion of part of the profits from the arms deals with Iran to the Contras. North told Nir that he had informed Meese that "Israel had initiated" the diversion of money to the Contras, and he asked that Israel accept responsibility for this. Nir rejected the request, but North ignored this and did not revise his testimony.[72]

This was not surprising. Exactly two weeks previously, North and Secord had met Nir in Geneva and had told him that they had decided to close the Lake Resources account at Crédit Suisse because the money from Iran and the money meant for the Contras had gotten mixed up there. It appeared that North and Secord were trying to take advantage of Nir's inexperience to shift the responsibility for illegal activities to Israel. Nir told them that Ghorbanifar had always claimed that the prices of the arms to Iran had been purposely inflated in order to provide money for the Contras. Nevertheless, on November 25, Meese announced at a press conference in Washington that the profits from the arms deals with Iran had been diverted to the Nicaraguan rebels "at the initiative of and with the knowledge of" the Israeli government. Israel immediately took the offensive to defend its image in Congress and in American public opinion. Shimon Peres telephoned Meese and announced that Israel was about to publish a denial. After a late-night consultation among Shamir, Peres, and Rabin, an official statement was issued on November 25 in Jerusalem:

> The government of Israel confirms that it helped transfer defensive weapons and spare parts from the U.S. to Iran, at the request of the United States Government. Payment for this equipment was transferred directly by an Iranian representative to a Swiss bank, in accordance with the instructions of American representatives, without the money going through Israel.
>
>   The government of Israel was surprised by the report that part of this money was transferred to the Contras. This has nothing to do with Israel, and the government of Israel had no knowledge of this. It should be understood that Israel was not and will not be willing to serve as a pipeline for such transfers.[73]

Suspecting that officials in Washington were trying to draw fire away from Reagan by deflecting criticism from him to Israel, the Israelis informed the White House that they were willing to cover for Casey, Poindexter, and North "up to a certain point," but not to be scapegoats for the blunders of members of the White House staff. On January 12, 1987, the White House tried to reassure Prime Minister Yitzhak Shamir. The American ambassador to Israel, Thomas Pickering, told Shamir in Jerusalem that "the U.S. is not trying to hide behind Israel or pin responsibility for the Iranian initiative on it." Pickering added that the various investigations going on in the U.S. were meant to uncover the facts and not to turn Israel into a scapegoat for decisions made in Washington.[74]

The public storm quickened; North was fired and President Reagan accepted Admiral Poindexter's resignation "with regret." Several House and Senate committees began to conduct investigations on November 25, 1986, the day of Attorney General Meese's press conference revealing the diversion of Iranian arms profits to the Contras. In response to public pressure, President Reagan appointed a panel headed by former senator John Tower to investigate the functioning of the National Security Council. The Foreign Affairs and Defense Committee of the Israeli Knesset, chaired by Abba Eban, investigated the Israeli side of the scandal, while the Israeli government appointed General (Res.) Raphael Vardi to prepare a report for submission to the American Congress.

Finally, Select Committees of the Senate and the House of Representatives were appointed in January 1987 to conduct an even more thorough investigation. At the end of 41 days of questioning spread over three months, during which 29 witnesses testified for 250 hours (and after the publication of 1,059 documents from among the 250,000 examined), the Senate committee's chairman, Senator Daniel K. Inouye, summed up the findings: "We heard a chilling story, a story of fraud, hypocrisy, and violations of the law."

The Iran initiative had come to an end.

Notes

CHAPTER 1. THE ABORTED ANTI-KHOMEINI COUP

1. *New York Times*, April 1, 1986.

1a. *New York Times*, November 22, 1986.

2. Ibid. also *Ma'ariv* (Tel Aviv), November 23, 1986.

3. "Panorama," BBC, February 1, 1982.

4. Ibid.

5. *Ma'ariv* (Tel Aviv), November 23, 1986.

6. The account of this meeting and all others, unless otherwise specified, is based on interviews with participants or their aides and on government documents not yet officially declassified.

7. Interview with Khashoggi, *Haolam Hazeh* (Tel Aviv), April 15, 1987.

8. Khashoggi's and Ghorbanifar's own accounts as related later to Israeli participants.

9. Ibid.

10. Ibid.

10a. U.S. Congress, committees investigating the Iran-Contra affair, report (henceforth *Iran-Contra Report*), 1987, p. 171.

11. Interview with one of the participants.

12. Ibid.

13. Ibid.

14. Ibid.

15. *Iran-Contra Report*, chap. 9, p. 164.

16. Ariel Sharon's article, *Ma'ariv* (Tel Aviv), November 23, 1986.

17. Ibid.

CHAPTER 2. CONSTRUCTING THE IRANIAN TRIANGLE

1. Interview with Caroz.

2. *Washington Post*, August 16, 1987.

3. Interview with envoy.

4. Interview with Ezri.

5. Samuel Segev, "Hameshulash Hairani," *Ma'ariv* (Tel Aviv), 1981, p. 98.

6. Ibid.

7. Ibid., p. 99.

8. Ibid.

9. Interview with Ezri.

10. *Davar Newspaper* (Tel Aviv), August 8, 1980.

11. Ibid.

11a. The account of this meeting and all others, unless otherwise specified, is based on interviews with participants or their aides and on government documents not yet officially declassified.

12. Interview with Nimrodi.

13. Interview with Gazit.

14. Ibid.

15. The account of this meeting is based on an interview with Z. Dinstein, who was then a senior official in the Israeli Ministry of Finance.

16. Ibid.

17. Ibid.

18. Interview with Ezri.

19. *Newsweek*, December 30, 1979.

20. *Ettela'at* (Tehran), May 2 and 14, 1979.

21. *Yechiot Ah'ronot* (Tel Aviv), January 30, 1987.

22. Interview with Nimrodi.

23. Radio Tehran, July 23, 1960.

24. Segev, "Hameshulash Hairani," p. 103.

25. Ibid.

26. *New York Times*, March 16, 1961.

27. Mansur Rafizadeh, *Witness* (New York: Morrow, 1987), p. 114.

28. *Al-Nahar* (Beirut), August 22, 1970.

29. Interview with Ezri.

30. Interview with Nimrodi.

31. Ma'ariv (Tel Aviv), December 5, 1961.

32. Interview with Nimrodi.

33. Segev, "Hameshulash Hairani," p. 106.

34. Ibid., p. 109.

35. Letter from Doriel to Rabin, May 10, 1964.

CHAPTER 3. THE EGYPTIAN CONNECTION

1. Radio Tehran, January 21 and 22, 1965.

2. The account of this meeting and all others, unless otherwise specified, is based on interviews with participants or their aides and on government documents not yet officially declassified.

3. Ma'ariv (Tel Aviv), June 6, 1966.

4. Interview with Ezri.

5. Ibid.

6. Interview with Nimrodi.

7. Ibid.

8. Ibid.

9. Ibid.

10. Jeune Afrique (Paris), July 7, 1971.

11. On March 7, 1969, the Washington Post published an article stating that Iranian paratroopers and pilots had trained in Israel. The British Daily Telegraph (London), in its issue of August 24, 1970, wrote that "Israeli pilots served as instructors in the Iranian air force, and Iranian officers have been seen in the streets of Tel Aviv." On July 1, 1969, the Iraqi newspaper Al-Jumhouriya announced that Israel and Iran had signed a military cooperation agreement, and that 19 Israeli officers had arrived in Tehran on June 26 to serve as instructors in the Iranian army.

12. Interview with President Sadat, September 1980.

13. The account of this conversation is based on an interview with Ezri.

14. Interview with a former Israeli diplomat in Washington.

15. Ibid.

CHAPTER 4. THE SHAH AT THE CENTER

1. Interview with Lubrani.

2. The account of this meeting and all others described in this chapter are based on interviews with participants or their aides and on government documents not yet declassified, unless otherwise noted.

3. Ma'ariv (Tel Aviv), August 23, 1975.

4. Interview with Lubrani.

5. Interview with an aide to one of the participants.

6. Ibid.

7. *New York Times*, April 1, 1986.

8. Interview with an aide to one of the participants.

9. Interview with Lubrani.

10. Interview with an aide to one of the participants.

11. CIA documents captured by Iranian students at the American embassy in Tehran.

12. Interview with General Segev.

13. Ibid.

CHAPTER 5. KHOMEINI TAKES CHARGE

1. Samuel Segev, "Hameshulash Hairani," *Ma'ariv* (Tel Aviv), 1981, p. 68.

2. Ibid., p. 69.

3. Ibid., p. 247.

4. Ibid., p. 240.

5. Mansur Rafizadeh, *Witness* (New York: Morrow, 1987), p. 347.

6. Yosef Obmert, *Iranian-Syrian Relationships: Between Islam and Realpolitik* (Tel Aviv: Dayan Center, Tel Aviv University, January 1988), p. 19.

7. Ibid.

8. Ibid., p. 20.

9. On Iran's economic support to Hezbollah see testimony by Ambassador Paul Bremmer before House Appropriations Subcommittee on April 13, 1988.

10. *Iran-Contra Report*, p. 160.

11. Rafizadeh, *Witness*, p. 352.

11a. *Iran-Contra Report*, pp. 252 and 265.

12. *Iran-Contra Report*, p. 164.

13. *Tower Commission Report*, New York Times edition, p. 105. (All citations of this report are to the New York Times edition.)

14. Ibid., pp. 106–107; also *Iran-Contra Report*, p. 164.

15. *Iran-Contra Report*, p. 164.

16. Ibid.

17. *Tower Commission Report*, p. 122.

18. Interview with Khashoggi, *El-Watan El-Arabi* (Paris), January 16, 1987.

19. *Iran-Contra Report*, p. 165.

20. *Tower Commission Report*, p. 111.

21. *Iran-Contra Report*, p. 165.

22. *Tower Commission Report*, p. 111.

23. Ibid.

24. *Iran-Contra Report*, p. 171.

25. Ibid.

26. *Sunday Times* (London), April 24, 1988.

27. *New York Times*, October 26, 1984.

28. *Iran-Contra Report*, p. 160.

CHAPTER 6. AN AYATOLLAH IN HAMBURG

1. As related by one of the participants to his foreign contacts.

2. *Iran-Contra Report*, p. 164.

3. McFarlane's testimony, May 11, 1987, as reported by *Ha'aretz* (Tel Aviv), May 12, 1987.

4. McFarlane's testimony, *Jerusalem Post*, May 12, 1987.

5. *Iran-Contra Report*, p. 38.

6. McFarlane's testimony, *Jerusalem Post*, May 12, 1987.

7. *Iran-Contra Report*, p. 38.

8. McFarlane's testimony, as reported by *Yediot Ah'ronot* (Tel Aviv), May 12, 1987.

9. *Iran-Contra Report*, p. 165.

10. Excerpts here and on the following pages are taken from the Hebrew translation of the transcript.

11. The account of this meeting and all others, unless otherwise specified, is based on interviews with participants or their aides and on government papers not yet officially declassified.

12. *Iran-Contra Report*, p. 166.

13. Shultz testimony, ibid., remark p. 172.

14. McFarlane testimony, ibid., p. 167.

15. *Ma'ariv* (Tel Aviv), January 30, 1987.

16. *Iran-Contra Report*, p. 167.

CHAPTER 7. OPERATION CAPPUCCINO

1. *Iran-Contra Report*, p. 167.

2. McFarlane's testimony, *International Herald Tribune* (Paris), May 15, 1987.

3. The account of this meeting and all others, unless otherwise specified, is based on interviews with the participants or their aides and on government records not yet officially declassified.

4. *Iran-Contra Report*, p. 167.

5. Ibid.

6. Ibid.

7. *New York Times*, July 27, 1987.

8. *Iran-Contra Report*, p. 168.

9. *International Herald Tribune*, November 14, 1986.

10. Ibid., January 12, 1987.

11. "Kol Israel," BBC, September 15, 1985.

12. *Ma'ariv* (Tel Aviv), December 5, 1986.

13. Dispatch of Reuters news agency from Rome, May 11, 1988.

14. *Taking the Stand: The Testimony of Lieutenant Colonel Oliver North* (New York: Pocket Books, 1987), p. 300.

15. Ibid., p. 508.

16. *Iran-Contra Report*, p. 169.

17. Letters from Ghorbanifar to Nimrodi, October 31, 1985.

18. Ibid.

19. *Iran-Contra Report*, p. 175.

CHAPTER 8. OPERATION ESPRESSO

1. *International Herald Tribune* (Paris), May 8, 1987.

2. Ibid., January 22, 1987, and May 12, 1987.

3. The account of this statement and all other statements or meetings in this chapter, unless otherwise specified, is based on interviews with Israeli participants or their aides and on government papers not yet officially declassified.

4. *New York Times*, June 7, 1987, and *Washington Post*, June 7, 1987.

5. *Newsweek*, May 11, 1987, p. 20.

6. Ibid.

7. Ibid.

8. *Iran-Contra Report*, p. 176.

9. Ibid., p. 175.

10. Ibid., p. 176.

11. Ibid.

12. Ibid., p. 178.

13. Ibid., p. 177.

14. Ibid.

15. Ibid.

16. *International Herald Tribune*, January 12 and January 19, 1987.

17. *Iran-Contra Report*, p. 180.

18. Ibid.

19. Ibid.

20. *International Herald Tribune*, January 12, 1987.

21. *Iran-Contra Report*, p. 190.

22. Ibid., p. 177.

22a. Ibid.

23. Ibid., p. 184.

24. Ibid., p. 191.

25. Ibid., p. 185.

26. Ibid., p. 187.

27. Ibid.

28. Ibid.

29. *Tower Commission Report*, New York Times edition, p. 165. (All citations of this report are to the New York Times edition.)

30. Ibid., p. 166.

31. *Iran-Contra Report*, p. 193.

32. *Tower Commission Report*, p. 531, note 23.

33. *Iran-Contra Report*, p. 193.

34. Ibid.

35. Ibid., p. 194.

36. Ibid., p. 270.

37. Ibid., p. 197.

38. Ibid., p. 199.

39. Ibid., p. 200.

CHAPTER 9. NORTH AND NIR ENTER THE FIELD

1. *Iran-Contra Report*, p. 200.

2. *Tower Commission Report*, New York Times edition, p. 196. (All citations of this report are to the New York Times edition.)

3. *Taking the Stand: The Testimony of Lieutenant Colonel Oliver North* (New York: Pocket Books, 1987), p. 298.

4. *Ma'ariv* (Tel Aviv), January 30, 1987.

5. *Taking the Stand*, pp. 300, 310.

6. Secord's testimony, May 7, 1987, as reported in the *Jerusalem Post*, May 8, 1987.

7. The *Tower Commission Report* quotes a note North wrote to Poindexter: "Ami Nir suspects that there is probably a secret business agreement among Schwimmer, Ledeen, and Gorba, that is being conducted without the knowledge of any of the three respective governments" (p. 237). Elsewhere in the same report North is quoted as saying: "Nir says he has information that Mike [Ledeen] has a financial relationship with Gorba, Nimrodi, and

perhaps with Schwimmer" (p. 254). North also stated that Nir told him that Ledeen had received a "service fee" of $50 for the TOW missiles supplied to Iran. North claimed that Nir supplied him with secret intelligence about Libya without the knowledge of the Mossad, and asked North to cover for him and not identify him as the source of the information. However, here, too, there is no proof that Nir violated any Israeli law. It is not known whether Nir actually made these remarks or North simply attributed them to him.

Later, however, North repeated his allegation in testimony before the congressional committee. He said: "Ledeen assured me that he had not made money on the 1985 transactions. I have no reason to believe that what the Iranians told me, or that what one of the Israelis told me is necessarily true. I do not want it noted by the Committee record, that I have accused Ledeen of making money. When he told me he didn't, I believed him" (*Taking the Stand*, p. 318).

8. *Tower Commission Report*, p. 236.

9. *Ma'ariv* (Tel Aviv), January 30, 1987.

10. The account of this meeting as well as all other meetings mentioned in this chapter, unless otherwise specified, is based on interviews with participants or their aides and on government papers not yet officially declassified.

11. *Iran-Contra Report*, p. 201.

12. *Tower Commission Report*, p. 235.

13. *Taking the Stand*, p. 443.

14. *Iran-Contra Report*, p. 201.

15. *Taking the Stand*, p. 307.

16. *Tower Commission Report*, p. 205.

17. *Iran-Contra Report*, p. 200.

18. *Tower Commission Report*, p. 206.

19. *Ma'ariv* (Tel Aviv), January 7, 1986.

20. *Iran-Contra Report*, p. 203.

21. Ibid., p. 204.

22. Ibid., p. 205.

23. Ibid.

24. Ibid.

25. *Tower Commission Report*, pp. 233–235.

26. Ibid., p. 235.

27. Ibid., also *Iran-Contra Report*, pp. 204, 207.

28. *Tower Commission Report*, p. 236.

29. *Iran-Contra Report*, p. 208.

30. Ibid., pp. 298–299.

31. Ibid., p. 215.

32. Ibid., p. 213.

33. Ibid., p. 217.

34. Ibid., p. 216.

35. *Tower Commission Report*, p. 239.

36. Ibid., p. 240.

37. *Taking the Stand*, p. 703.

38. *Iran-Contra Report*, p. 216.

39. *New York Times*, May 7, 1987.

40. *Iran-Contra Report*, pp. 216, 271.

41. Ibid., p. 271.

42. Ibid., p. 218.

43. Hakim testimony, *International Herald Tribune*, June 6, 1987.

44. Secord testimony, *New York Times*, May 7, 1987.

45. Indictment sheet, p. 14.

46. *Tower Commission Report*, p. 245.

47. *Iran-Contra Report*, p. 218.

48. Ibid.

49. Ibid.

50. Ibid., p. 219.

51. *Tower Commission Report*, p. 251.

52. Ibid.

53. Ibid., p. 252.

54. *Iran-Contra Report*, p. 219.

55. *Tower Commission Report*, p. 258.

CHAPTER 10. CHOCOLATE CAKE DIPLOMACY

1. *Iran-Contra Report*, p. 222.

2. *Taking the Stand: The Testimony of Lieutenant Colonel Oliver North* (New York: Pocket Books, 1987), pp. 310–311.

3. Ibid., p. 195; *Washington Post*, May 14, 1987.

3a. *Washington Post*, November 14, 1986.

4. *International Herald Tribune* (Paris), February 12, 1987.

5. *Iran-Contra Report*, p. 222.

6. Ibid., p. 223.

7. Ibid.

8. *Tower Commission Report*, New York Times edition, p. 260. (All citations of this report are to the New York Times edition.)

9. Ibid., p. 262.

10. Ibid., p. 538; also the account of this meeting and all others, unless otherwise specified, is based on interviews with participants or their aides and on government papers not yet officially declassified.

11. *Iran-Contra Report*, p. 224.

12. Ibid.

13. Ibid.

14. *Tower Commission Report*, p. 266.

15. *Iran-Contra Report*, p. 368.

16. Ibid., p. 369.

17. Ibid.

18. *Tower Commission Report*, p. 285.

19. Ibid., p. 284.

20. Ibid., p. 285.

21. Ibid., p. 286.

22. *Taking the Stand*, p. 181.

23. Ibid., p. 185.

24. *Iran-Contra Report*, p. 227.

25. Ibid. The author has concluded from other sources that the "second Iranian official" must have been Kengarlou. Kengarlou is not named on this page of the *Iran-Contra Report*.

26. Ibid., p. 228.

27. Ibid., p. 229; also see note 10.

28. Ibid.

29. Ibid.; also *Tower Commission Report*, p. 282.

30. *International Herald Tribune* (Paris), December 13, 1986.

31. *Iran-Contra Report*, p. 230.

32. Ibid.

33. *Taking the Stand*, p. 194.

34. *Iran-Contra Report*, p. 225.

35. Ibid.

36. Ibid.

37. Hakim testimony, *International Herald Tribune* (Paris), June 6, 1987.

38. *New York Times*, March 17, 1988.

39. *Taking the Stand*, p. 195.

40. *Tower Commission Report*, p. 257.

41. Ibid., p. 296; also *Iran-Contra Report*, p. 237.

42. *Tower Commission Report*, pp. 291, 293.

43. Ibid., p. 289.

44. *Iran-Contra Report*, p. 365.

45. Ibid., p. 363.

46. Ibid., p. 365.

47. *Tower Commission Report*, p. 292.

48. *Observer* (London), May 10, 1987.

49. *Iran-Contra Report*, p. 237.

50. *Le Monde* (Paris), November 6, 1986.

51. *Iran-Contra Report*, p. 238.

52. Ibid.

53. Ibid.; also *Tower Commission Report*, p. 298.

54. Details on these discussions, unless otherwise specified, are reported extensively in *Tower Commission Report*, pp. 296–335; also *Iran-Contra Report*, pp. 238–242.

55. *Tower Commission Report*, p. 336.

56. Ghorbanifar testimony, *Tower Commission Report*, p. 336.

57. *Tower Commission Report*, p. 350.

58. Ibid., p. 351.

59. Ibid., p. 352.

CHAPTER 11. EXPOSURE

1. *International Herald Tribune* (Paris), June 24, 1987.

2. Radio Tehran, October 27, 1986.

3. Ibid.

4. Ibid., December 9, 1986.

5. *Iran-Contra Report*, p. 245.

6. The account of this meeting and all others, unless otherwise specified, is based on interviews with participants or their aides and on government papers not yet officially declassified.

7. *Tower Commission Report*, New York Times edition, p. 353. (All citations of this report are to the New York Times edition.) Kengarlou is not named in the report. The author has concluded from other sources that he was the Iranian official referred to.

8. Ibid., p. 354. See remarks about Kengarlou in note 7.

9. *Iran-Contra Report*, p. 18.

10. *Tower Commission Report*, p. 540.

11. Ibid., p. 358.

12. *Iran-Contra Report*, p. 246.

13. Ibid., p. 264.

14. Ibid., p. 246; also *Tower Commission Report*, p. 359.

15. *Iran-Contra Report*, p. 246.

16. *Tower Commission Report*, p. 380.

17. Ibid., p. 383.

18. Ibid., p. 382. The author has concluded from other sources that the "Iranian official" was Kengarlou. Kengarlou is not named on this page of the report.

19. Ibid., p. 384.

20. Ibid.

21. Ibid., p. 376.

22. Ibid., p. 384.

23. Ibid., p. 382.

24. Ibid., pp. 375, 539.

25. *Iran-Contra Report*, p. 248.

26. *Tower Commission Report*, pp. 395–396.

27. Ibid., p. 541.

28. *Iran-Contra Report*, p. 249.

29. *Tower Commission Report*, p. 392.

30. *Iran-Contra Report*, p. 249.

31. *Le Monde* (Paris), November 21, 1986.

32. *Tower Commission Report*, p. 401.

33. Ibid., p. 402.

34. A despatch of AFP, quoted in *Le Monde* (Paris), December 24, 1986.

35. *Iran-Contra Report*, p. 249.

36. Ibid.

37. *Tower Commission Report*, p. 372.

38. Ibid.

39. Ibid., p. 543.

40. Ibid., p. 392.

41. Ibid.

42. Ibid., p. 543.

43. *Iran-Contra Report*, p. 250.

44. "The Story of Oliver North," *U.S. News and World Report*, special issue, undated, p. 92.

45. *Tower Commission Report*, p. 400.

46. *Le Monde* (Paris), November 21, 1986.

47. *Tower Commission Report*, pp. 402, 403; also *Iran-Contra Report*, p. 251; also Israeli government papers not yet officially declassified.

48. *Iran-Contra Report*, p. 369.

49. *Tower Commission Report*, p. 405.

50. Israeli government papers not yet officially declassified.

51. *Taking the Stand: The Testimony of Lieutenant Colonel Oliver North* (New York: Pocket Books, 1987), p. 397.

52. *Tower Commission Report*, pp. 420–421.

53. Ibid., p. 414.

54. Ibid., pp. 420–424.

55. Ibid.

56. *Iran-Contra Report*, p. 395.

57. *Taking the Stand*, p. 325.

58. *Tower Commission Report*, p. 544.

59. *Iran-Contra Report*, p. 255.

60. Ibid., p. 256.

61. Ibid., p. 258.

62. Ibid., p. 274.

63. Ibid.

64. Ibid., p. 259.

65. Ibid.

66. *Le Monde* (Paris), November 6, 1986.

67. Ibid.

68. *International Herald Tribune* (Paris), November 6, 1986.

69. Ibid., November 15–16, 1986.

70. Reagan interview with *Time*, quoted in *International Herald Tribune* (Paris), December 11, 1986.

71. *Iran-Contra Report*, p. 285.

72. Ibid., p. 313.

73. *Ma'ariv* (Tel Aviv), November 16, 1986.

74. *International Herald Tribune* (Paris), January 14, 1987.

Select Bibliography

REPORTS OF CONGRESSIONAL COMMITTEES

Taking the Stand: The Testimony of Lieutenant Colonel Oliver North. With an Introduction by Daniel Schorr. New York: Pocket Books, 1987.

Tower Commission Report. Introduction by R. W. Apple, Jr. New York: Times Books/Bantam Books, 1987.

U.S. Congress. Joint Committee. *The Iran-Contra Affair. Report of the Congressional Committees Investigating the Iran-Contra Affair.* 100th Cong., 1st sess. 1987.

U.S. Congress. Senate. Select Committee on Intelligence. *Report on Preliminary Inquiry on Secret Military Assistance to Iran and the Nicaraguan Opposition.* 100th Cong., 1st sess. 1987.

BOOKS

Abdulghani, Jasim M. *Iraq and Iran: The Years of Crisis.* Baltimore: Johns Hopkins University Press, 1984.

Alexander, Yona, and Nanes, Allan, eds. *The U.S. and Iran: A Documentary History.* Austin, Tex.: Aletheia Books, University Publications of America, Inc., 1980.

Bakhash, Shaul. *The Reign of the Ayatollahs: Iran and the Islamic Revolution.* New York: Basic Books, 1984.

Bradley, E. Paul. *Recent U.S. Policy in the Persian Gulf.* Grantham, N.H.: Thompson-Rutter, 1982.

Fischer, Michael M. J. *Iran: From Religious Dispute to Revolution.* Cambridge: Harvard University Press, 1980.

Forbis, William H. *The Fall of the Peacock Throne.* New York: Harper & Row, 1980.

Grummon, Stephen R. *The Iran-Iraq War: Islam Embattled.* The Washington Papers, no. 92. New York: Praeger, 1982.

Heikal, Mohammad. *Autumn of Fury: The Assassination of Sadat.* New York: Random House, 1983.

Hiro, Dilip. *Iran Under the Ayatollahs.* London: Routledge & Kegan Paul, 1985.

Kazemi, Farhad. *Poverty and Revolution in Iran.* New York: New York University Press, 1980.

Keddi, Nikki R. *Roots of Revolution: An Interpretative History of Modern Iran.* New Haven: Yale University Press, 1981.

Rafizadeh, Mansur. *Witness: From the Shah to Secret Arms Deal.* New York: Morrow, 1987.

Ramazani, Rouhollah K. *The United States and Iran: The Patterns of Influence.* New York: Praeger, 1982.

Rosen, Barry M., ed. *Iran Since the Revolution.* New York: Brooklyn College Press, 1985.

Rubin, Barry. *Paved with Good Intentions.* New York: Oxford University Press, 1980.

Sick, Gary. *All Fall Down.* New York: Random House, 1985.

Sullivan, William H. *Mission to Iran.* New York: W. W. Norton & Co., 1981.

HEBREW

Menashri, David. *Iran Bemahpecha.* Moshe Dayan Center, Tel Aviv University, 1987.

Segev, Samuel. "Hameshulash Ha'irani." *Ma'ariv* (Tel Aviv), 1981.

———. *Sadat-Haderech Lashalom.* Tel Aviv: Massada, 1978.

Index